WHEATON PUBLIC LIBRARY

3 5143 00812758 8

MW00442076

940.544 WEE

JAN   2011   Stacks

Weekley, Harold D., 1921-

The last of the combat B-17
drivers   WITHDRAWN

WHEATON PUBLIC LIBRARY
225 N. CROSS
WHEATON, IL 60187
(630) 668-1374

The Last of the
Combat B-17 Drivers

by
Col. Harold D. Weekley, USAF (Ret.)
and
James B. Zazas

Copyright © 2007 James B. Zazas, All Rights Reserved

Published in U.S.A. by
Flying Fortress International, LLC
PO Box 1450
Carthage, NC 28327-1450

Printed in U.S.A. by
BookMasters, Inc.
30 Amberwood Parkway
PO Box 388
Ashland, OH   44805

Distributed in the United States by
AtlasBooks, a division of BookMasters, Inc.
30 Amberwood Parkway
PO Box 388
Ashland, OH   44805
1-800-247-6553
www.atlasbooks.com

With the exception of quoting brief passages for the purposes of review,
no part or portion of this publication may be reproduced or stored mechanically
or electronically without prior permission from the Publisher.

The information in this book is true and complete to the best of the authors'
knowledge. All narratives, text and data are made without any guarantee on
the part of the authors or publisher. Both the authors and the publisher disclaim
any liability incurred in connection with the use of the data or specific details
presented within this book.

First Printing: June 2007
Second Printing: December 2007
Third Printing: September 2008
Fourth Printing: March 2009

Softback: ISBN 978-0-9785980-0-6
Hardback: ISBN 978-0-9785980-1-3

Library of Congress Catalog No. 2006926673

Printed in the United States of America

Table of Contents

7548

Dedication

... Their wings of silver
touched the passing clouds,
made soft white trails across the
azure blue. But not for them
this life we share on Earth ...
they sacrificed that gift for
me and you.
—Nuthampstead Memorial

The *Sally B* (AAF 44-85784), a Vega-built B-17G based at Duxford Airfield, Cambridge, England, makes a "fly over" of 398th Memorial at Nuthampstead, England on the day this memorial was dedicated, September 23, 1982. The memorial was dedicated "to the everlasting memory of the air crews and support units who served so gallantly at AAF Station 131, Nuthampstead, Hertfordshire, England, 1944 - 1945."

(Photo by Ralph J. Ambrose)

Foreword

Who would have believed that a World War II combat pilot would still be flying the legendary Flying Fortress at the age of eighty? Well, believe it. Colonel Harold D. "Hal" Weekley, USAF (Ret) has done just that.

His book, *The Last of the Combat B-17 Drivers* brings to life his remarkable career in aviation, from his first flying lessons in a two-cylinder Aeronca C-3, through his Army Air Forces flight training, his B-17 combat experiences including being shot down and evading capture, his subsequent flying assignments as an Air Force Reserve officer, through his 23 years flying the Experimental Aircraft Association's (EAA) B-17 "Aluminum Overcast."

One thing that Hal does very well in this book is to explain in some detail what happened inside a B-17 during combat. Most readers of aviation combat books want to know "how it really was," and Hal does a fine job of filling that need. He goes into great detail about the planning and execution of various types of missions flown by his group and describes some of the losses due to the deadly flak and the almost obscene weather in which they operated.

I found the story of his evasion and escape after being shot down in France extremely interesting. Hal was lucky to some extent in that he was spotted by some young French boys who helped him to a church where he could be hidden, but he was smart enough to trust the right people. He spent a good deal of time with some very courageous French citizens. He actually ate at a table with German soldiers.

As the end of the war approached, Hal bicycled through France toward the advancing Allied troops. During his travel he passed many retreating German soldiers. Hal carefully memorized the terrain and the location of the enemy troop concentrations. When he met a group of British soldiers he was able to pass on this information to their commanders and actually led the intelligence officer, at the commander's request, back into enemy territory to point out some of the troop locations.

One feature of the book that is not often included in war memoirs is Hal's follow-up on what happened to his crewmembers after the war. I found this particularly rewarding. It was quite interesting to learn how their lives changed in the years following the war. Despite their varied careers, the bond that was formed while flying combat missions together was never broken.

The last sections of the book are dedicated to the varied and productive remainder of Hal's Air Force career and of his flying the EAA B-17 in air shows and tours from 1979 through 2001. He describes the many touching reunions with B-17 veterans, widows and children of crewmen that were lost in the war.

All in all, this is an excellent and well written book, which should be of interest to aviation buffs and to all patriotic Americans. I recommend it highly.

Col. Donald S. Lopez
USAF (Ret.)
Washington, D.C.
December 2006

Donald S. Lopez is senior advisor emeritus at the Smithsonian Institution's National Air and Space Museum, having served as deputy director and chair of the Aeronautics Department. He is a talented author and has written a total of six books.

Preface

Commentary by Harold D. Weekley

Family histories are recorded in many different ways: passed by word of mouth, written in a diary or a family Bible, recorded on a cassette tape or on video tape. Sometimes, these narratives are written in a book for posterity. Regardless of how these family histories are preserved, all are meant for another generation to learn from and enjoy.

Although I often entertained the possibility of writing a book about my wartime experiences, I never looked seriously into such an ambitious endeavor. Now, as my grandchildren come of age, I am asked, "What did you do in the big war Granddad?"

From this innocent question, I knew it was time to record my wartime experiences for my family. I wanted to provide them with something tangible, not only of my experiences as a World War II B-17 pilot, but also something that would reflect the deep respect I have for the citizens of France.

Moreover, I wanted my family to know how brave the French were and how they love their country every bit as much as we love ours. I wanted them to know and understand that the French went to great lengths to save and protect, not only myself, but many

downed Allied fliers during the Second World War, often at great personal risk.

To that end, I recorded a series of cassette tapes beginning in the late 1980s. Initially, I thought these tapes, and any transcriptions, would be sufficient as they were intended for my family only. A few years later, I entertained thoughts of molding these tapes into a book.

Over time, and working with various authors and organizations, including the late Jeffery Ethell and the Experimental Aircraft Association (EAA), I began my quest. But no sooner had I started than I was stymied as each author or organization contacted could not devote the resources necessary to collaborate on this ambitious endeavor.

Then, during the summer of 1997, I approached Jim Zazas, a friend, an author and a fellow "warbird" pilot, to explore the possibility of assisting me in writing my book. He liked my ideas and we shared similar thoughts. In turn, he offered suggestions on how best to proceed. Soon, we were turning my tape recorded narratives into a written manuscript, then into an abundantly illustrated book.

Outside of recording something for my family, there is another equally rewarding reason why I initiated this book.

I became a team pilot/crewmember on a B-17 with Dr. William E. Harrison of Tulsa, Oklahoma after he purchased this airplane in Alabama in 1978. His intention was to fly it around the world. Unfortunately, this ambitious project was soon abandoned when he discovered the proper fuel would not be available at the selected sites. In 1981, he and his partners donated this proud airplane to the Experimental Aircraft Association in Oshkosh, Wisconsin, with the stipulation it would be maintained in an airworthy status.

The B-17's new owners lavished much care on their prized airplane. Fortunately, Dr. Harrison, other pilots and I continued to fly this proud airplane until I retired flying the EAA's B-17G *Aluminum Overcast* on July 27, 2001.

Here is where the name of this book, *The Last of the Combat B-17 Drivers*, originated. I am the last "First Pilot" or command rated B-17 pilot from World War II to fly a B-17 as Pilot-in-Command into the current millennia.

Between 1980 and 1989, the EAA's B-17 toured the United States, mostly on a limited basis to various requested air shows and EAA chapters. This World War II bomber drew a tremendous following. At the time, the aircraft was painted in a scheme not identified with any particular bomb group or squadron. This small oversight was soon changed.

In 1989, the 398th Bomb Group (H) Memorial Association approached the EAA and offered to pay the expense of repainting the aircraft in the colors of the 601st Bomb Squadron of the 398th Bomb Group. The 398th BG Association Board of Directors presented six possible paint scheme options, each with its own unique historical perspective. In the end, they selected the markings of the airplane in which I was shot down in

France. Obviously, I was very honored and pleased by their selection.

Resplendent in its new colors, the EAA B-17 began to tour the United States, again on a limited basis. In 1994, the EAA initiated a positive tour schedule throughout the United States for nine months of the year. During this period, my enthusiasm to write a book peaked.

Everywhere we stopped, we were met by aviation buffs, curious sightseers, old crewmembers, wartime survivors and the children and grandchildren of living or deceased B-17 crewmembers. I soon discovered many had a strong bond with the B-17 as they asked me questions by the hour.

Invariably, at the end of many of these discussions, one of the comments would be "Why don't you write a book about your experiences? I would like to know the whole story."

Dear friends, here is the whole story. I hope you enjoy reading it as much as Jim Zazas and I had writing it.

Col. Harold D. "Hal" Weekley

Col. Harold D. Weekley
USAF (Ret.)
Mableton, Georgia
December 2006

Commentary by James B. Zazas

The Boeing B-17 Flying Fortress, and its wartime companion, the Consolidated B-24 Liberator, delivered the brunt of the Allied daylight aerial bombing campaign in World War II. Both bombers proved effective and the brave young men who flew, crewed and maintained these bombers developed a close kinship with these aircraft.

The B-17 developed a sort of Hollywood glamour. It became the darling of bomber enthusiasts worldwide. Most newsreel films of the day featured the B-17 proportionately more often than the B-24. Admittedly, the B-17 had Clark Gable as a combat crewmember; the B-24 had Jimmy Stewart. Comments from both camps, some serious and some joking, were tossed back and forth. Each camp claimed their airplane was better. Active interest in the B-17 and the B-24 and their exemplary history remains very strong to this day.

But whether the crewmember flew in a B-17 or a B-24, survival was questionable. The cardboard thick, 24ST aluminum shell afforded little protection from the elements and enemy action. Though enemy action extracted a terrible toll, so did the rigors and dangers of flying in a non-pressurized, unheated environment at altitudes often exceeding 30,000 feet. Amazingly, frostbite accounted for more combat casualties than did enemy action!

Statistically, no job was more dangerous in the United States armed forces during World War II than in a heavy bomber over Europe. The chances of a crewmember completing a twenty-five or thirty-five mission tour were less than fifty percent. Statistically speaking, a crewmember was flying on borrowed time after his tenth mission.

Working and flying from wartime England was a most beautiful, almost romantic experience. But this idyllic environment was tempered by the harsh realities of a world at war. Weary aircrews faced a daily aerial hell that left few opportunities to enjoy England at its best.

Hal Weekley's time in combat was fraught with many dangers, the most probable being wounded or killed in action. Simply, the Eighth Air Force's losses were appalling. Dozens of planes and sometimes hundreds of airmen were either killed, wounded or went missing in action every day in the hostile skies over Fortress Europe. Everyday!

Many folks reading this book may not fully understand and appreciate the ultimate sacrifices made by thousands of young men and women involved in World War II. Moreover, many of these same folks may not recognize the total commitment our great nation and its determined citizens made during this worldwide conflict to win this horrible war. Little wonder many writers relate to this hardy generation as America's "Greatest Generation."

To this end, Hal and I sought to present a small segment of the Eighth Air Force's celebrated participation in World War II as accurately as we could. Hal Weekley's individual combat missions are highlighted, but so are many of the other 398th Bomb Group's combat missions flown during Hal's mid-1944 tour in England. The pertinent, often chilling details of each mission are described and include the numbers of Eighth Air Force heavy bombers and fighters dispatched or flown on a particular mission, the number of airplanes lost, and the number of crewmembers killed, wounded and missing in action.

Throughout this work, Hal Weekley relates his experience of flying one of Boeing Airplane Company's most beloved four-engine airplanes, the B-17 Flying Fortress. He takes the reader on an exciting ride from his earliest interest in aviation through his stateside wartime primary and advanced flight training to his combat missions and the Eighth Air Force's daylight bombing campaign over wartime Europe. He describes in detail his eventual shootdown over France and his subsequent evasion and escape. He concludes with a heartfelt reunion with the surviving relatives of the courageous folks in France who sheltered a young Hal Weekley from German troops more than sixty years earlier.

Finally, Hal Weekley shares his love of Billie, his wife, freely and unabashedly. The reader learns quickly her contributions to his life are significant and every bit as important as any of Hal Weekley's training or wartime experiences. One of many of Billie's original "V-Mail" letters sent to Hal during his time in England is reproduced in this book in its original size and form.

Hal Weekley's idea for this book began many years ago. In 1997, Hal challenged me to work with him to write this book. He provided the heart of the story and overall facts; I added the background material and pertinent details to highlight certain events and passages.

Over time, countless e-mails, letters and edited copies of the manuscript flew back and forth between Mableton, Georgia and Carthage, North Carolina, each adding pieces to the jigsaw puzzle of personal history that combined to become Hal's wartime memoirs. Together, we created a worthwhile book that we are very proud to publish together.

I turned to many sources to uncover the numerous details used to highlight Hal's fascinating war and post-war experiences. The Acknowledgements that follow and the Bibliography at the end reflect only a small part of the overall research effort required to bring Hal's incredible story to book form. What is not shown are the many people whose untiring enthusiasm, encouragement and support proved so very important and essential. To all of these wonderful folks, I offer a most heartfelt "Thank you!"

Many exciting details came to light during the course of my research that allowed Hal to rekindle many memories. New friendships formed for me and strengthened for Hal. We aimed to separate historical facts from popular fiction and present all information in an appealing, interesting to read format. We trust we have succeeded in our goal.

Hal Weekley's story is but one of a great many personal narratives from World War II. His detailed chronicle offers a candid insight to various wartime events that took place during hostilities in Europe. His first-hand accounts describe events that occurred in the fog of war not published anywhere else.

This is Hal Weekley's story.

Take off and enjoy!

James B. Zazas
Carthage, North Carolina
December 2006

Acknowledgments

First of all, I, Harold D. Weekley, would like to thank those dearest to my heart, without whom this book would not have been written. There are my good friends in France, whose personal sacrifices at a most difficult time during our human history allowed me to live and be free to share a most fulfilling life with my wife and family.

There are my two sons, William and H. Gary, and other members of my family whose simple question, "What did you do in the war?" gave me the initial reason to write this book.

Most importantly, Billie, my good wife, shared in this effort as much or more than anyone did. She shared with me many hours of proofreading and improving the manuscript; always available to offer a well-thought suggestion or fact I may have missed.

Jim is indebted to his family, including Barbara Zazas, Robert Zazas (deceased), Eric and Anny Edelson, Joe and Ellen Cole, Clara Webb and the late Della Tinsley.

Writing a book is an ambitious endeavor that involves many good people and resources. No one person or organization can provide, or is even capable of providing all the facts and figures needed in this undertaking. Many people and organizations came forward to help in this endeavor and all deserve to be recognized.

We are indebted to the surviving crewmembers of the *Bronx Bomber II* and their families. Bob Unger added several anecdotes and clarified certain events pertaining to our crew. Claudia Bock (daughter of Louis Buchsbaum), Tony Delbart, and Gary and Randy Skarda all provided important information about their fathers' lives during and after the war. Likewise, Pearl E. Stombaugh, widow of "Pops" Stombaugh, and Norma Leonard, widow of Gene Leonard, provided photographs and post-war descriptions of their late husbands.

LaDean Seago, our gallant transcriber, struggled through unfamiliar terms and phrases to turn four audiotapes into a readable, printed format which formed the basis for this book.

Dan Hagedorn, Dana Bell and others at the National Air and Space Museum Archives/ Library in Washington, D.C. offered invaluable assistance where more details could be found and included within this work.

Likewise, the fine staff at the National Archives and Records Administration II in College Park, Maryland provided invaluable assistance. Their untiring efforts produced many of the original wartime photographs and a substantial portion of the 398th Bomb Group Mission Reports and specific details of this Group's impressive combat record.

A special thank you goes to the late Lt. Col. Willis Frazier, USAF, the 398th Bomb Group Memorial Association historian and former 601st Bomb Squadron Operations Officer, who came forward to offer his knowledgeable input and candid insight into the overall story. He provided much information about specific combat missions, many in which he was involved directly. Additionally, he provided many of the 398th Bomb Group and Eighth Air Force facts and figures.

Additionally, the 398th Bomb Group Memorial Association provided many photographs and documentation. Dave Jordan, Wally Blackwell and Geoff Rice deserve special mention for granting the authors permission to use the many 398th Bomb Group Memorial Association's photographs used within this book.

Furthermore, we wish to thank Maj. General Charles D. Metcalf, USAF (Ret.), Terry Aitken, Wesley Henry and many others at the National Museum of the United States Air Force in Dayton, Ohio who made available this museum's vast collections of archived material and wartime photographs.

The Mighty Eighth Air Force Heritage Museum's Library and Archives in Savannah, Ga. proved an invaluable source of information. Rusty Bloxom, the museum's Chief Historian, and Laura Shuman and Shasta Ireland answered many queries untiringly and enthusiastically.

Casey Smith, Assistant Archivist at the San Diego Aerospace Museum Library / Archives, deserves a special nod of appreciation, as well. He pointed the way to obscure references and articles rarely found in any other collections.

Likewise, we would like to thank Dr. Duane Reed and the staff of the United States Air Force Academy Library. They made available original Army Air Force photographs and documents not found in other libraries and collections.

Similarly, we would like to thank Mrs. Lynn Gamma, Col. John Miller and the good folks at the Air Force Historical Research Agency at Maxwell AFB, Alabama. Col. Miller and his team of researchers proved very helpful in providing microfilmed 398th Bomb Group records and supporting data.

Noted aviation historians Allan G. Blue, Peter M. Bowers (deceased), Wallace Forman (deceased) and Roger A. Freeman (deceased) graciously contributed their time, much-needed information and, in many cases, valuable photographs. Each gentleman shared his own unique perspective and knowledge of Eighth Air Force operations and of the Allied bombing campaign over World War II Europe.

Special recognition is very much due Dr. William Harrison, Paul and Tom Poberezny, and many other folks associated with the Experimental Aircraft Association's B-17 program, all who gave us the impetus to keep moving forward on this project. Additionally, special thanks are due the EAA's enthusiastic staff and membership who have contributed countless hours to keep sport aviation alive and well for others to enjoy and appreciate. To this end, their tireless efforts to keep their B-17G Flying Fortress, *Aluminum Overcast*, airworthy and flying commands distinguished attention.

Similarly, Susan Lurvey at the Experimental Aircraft Association Library / Archives contributed her time to help expand the authors' knowledge of the Boeing B-17 and of European combat operations.

The Carolinas Aviation Museum's Dolph Overton Aviation Library provided many of the Pryor Field, Alabama photographs.

Many of the Steubenville photographs came from the book, *Stebuenville Sesquicentennial, 1797 – 1947, Veterans Homecoming*, provided courtesy of the Jefferson County Historical Association and Mr. Charles Green, this association's curator.

The Hendricks Field, Florida and Sebring, Florida background information and photographs came courtesy of A.W. "Spizz" Pollard. Moreover, his two books, *Hendricks Field…a look back* and *Sebring Men Who Gave*

All, provided invaluable background information on both locations.

The Dalhart Army Air Field, Texas photographs are courtesy or the XIT Museum in Dalhart, Texas and its curator, Mr. Nick Olsen.

No book ever comes to reality without the help of a great publishing staff. To this end, special recognition is due the fine staff at BookMasters, Inc. of Mansfield, Ohio. Cathy Purdy, Kristen Butler, Mike Dever, Tim Snider, Lee Ann Weber and so many others worked tirelessly to bring this work to reality.

The bibliography listed at the end of this work, only touches the many private individuals, research records, books and periodicals used to verify certain events and actions of fifty-plus years ago. All of these information sources jogged countless memories, many forgotten long ago.

Many flight training and crewmember duty details for this book were gleaned from various official Army Air Forces publications. Additionally, the late Roger Freeman's many excellent books about the U. S. Army Air Forces, and the Eighth Air Force in particular, yielded a tremendous amount of detailed information. Wesley Frank Craven's and James Lea Cate's incomparable historical series, *The Army Air Forces in World War II* (Chicago: The University of Chicago Press, 1951), revealed wartime details that we had not known previously.

Many details of *Operation COBRA* came from the multi-volume series, *United States Army in World War II.* The primary reference was *The European Theater of Operations: Breakout and Pursuit* by Martin Blumenson.

The authors are indebted to *Stars and Stripes* magazine, especially Jenifer N. Stepp, Assistant to the Chief Operating Officer, and to Charlene Neuwiller, *Stars and Stripes* Library Researcher, for their assistance finding and granting approval to use the reprint Ernie Pyle article. This article came from Pyle's immensely popular "Straight From the Front" series in Stars and Stripes and appeared originally on August 11, 1944, European-Pacific issue. Permission to use this article was granted by *Stars and Stripes* and is copyright 1944 and 2006.

Similarly, the authors are indebted to Robin Mitchell, a noted B-17 historian, for allowing us to use his comprehensive historical narrative describing the history of the B-17G *Aluminum Overcast.* Many facts about this particular, historic airplane are revealed for the first time in this book.

A great many individuals provided important valuable input and support with this book, including Curtiss Aldrich, Jon Wm. Aldrich (deceased), Ralph J. Ambrose, Taryn Applegate, Andy Austin, Lou Baffaro (deceased), Wayne and Carolyn Boggs, John Booker, Ray Bottom, Jr., Ed and Connie Bowlin, Dan Bowlin, Don Brooks, Bob and Carol Brown, Donna M. Bushman, Christine M. Capps, Dave and Aileen Chase, Gene and Dorothy Chase, Carl Clark (deceased), Maudie Clark, Rob and Caroline-Lindgren Collings, Jack and Golda Cox, Gloria Dalton, George Daubner, Bob Davis, Barbara Dymek, Sean Elliott, Dick Ervin (deceased), Joan Ervin, Cheryl Essex, Jeff Ethell (deceased), Bill Fischer, Ray Fowler, Don Gaddo, Scott and Kyle Guyette, Charles E. Harris, E. E. "Buck" Hilbert, Mary Hilbert (deceased), Dick and Jeannie Hill, Mary Howell, Evonne Iliopulos, Verne Jobst, John C. Kelly, Michelle Kunes, Daryl Lenz (deceased), Therese Litscher, Dick Lewis, Lisa Lynch, Ben Marion, JoAnna Marmon, Kent Misegades, Peter Moll, Barbara Monti, Roscoe and Ginny Morton, Maggie Musemeche, Wanda Nagel, Larry New, Chuck Parnell, Dr. Robert W. Patterson, Chris and Terri Percey, Norm and Loretta Petersen, Bonnie Poberezny, Paul and Audry Poberezny, Tom and Sharon Poberezny, Geoff Robison, Ed and Ginger Schneider, Joe Schumacher, E. C. "Clay" Smith (deceased), Nicole Smith, Don Taylor, Robert L. Taylor, Fred Telling, Walt Troyer, Betty Vaughn, John Underwood, Kermit Weeks, Stephanie Wells, Col. Roy Whitton, USAF (Ret.), John and Paula Wolfe, Wanda Zuege and many others.

Likewise, many thanks are due Kim and Tony Gilley, Janet Stowe, Lisa Smith, Jamie Carroll, Jennifer Cagle, Kelly Bryson at the LK Copy Center in Southern Pines, North Carolina and The Village Printers in nearby Pinehurst. They went through reams of paper to prepare the many draft copies necessary to write and proofread this book.

Kim Gilley deserves special recognition for her tireless efforts to scan the many photographs contained within this book and for the herculean task of bringing this story to life.

Many thanks are also due the good folks at Staples. Micky Konold, Connie Moore, Beverly Buschhardt, Bev McLaughlin and Pat Caron made countless copies of drafts and manuscripts.

The authors are indebted to Ann Engeli-Behnke for her tireless efforts proofreading the manuscript. Her many valuable corrections and constructive comments made this book as readable as it is.

Cherie McClung and Lisa P. Jackson deserve special recognition, also, as noteworthy proofreaders.

There are no doubt other contributors we have forgotten to acknowledge. To those few whose names we have neglected to mention, please know your generous contributions to this book are just as accepted and appreciated as any name or organization mentioned above.

Thank you all!

"What is our life but a succession of preludes to that un-known song whose first solemn note is sounded by death?"
Alphonse de Lamartine (1790–1869), *Meditations Poetigues* [1820]. Sermon 2

Prelude

I looked up at my feet. My black flight boots presented a curiously ominous contrast to the reassuring tranquility of the blue sky overhead, a cheerful comfort that seemed only one step away. Everything was surprisingly calm. Except the noisy, rapid flapping of the olive drab flight suit around my legs, there was no other sound to tell me I was falling. I was in a head-down position with my back facing towards the earth. France was still some fifteen thousand feet below me and closing rapidly.

I looked to my right and saw the English Channel. Just beyond its shimmering waters was England, my wartime home with its creature comforts and freedom. I would have preferred getting closer to the Channel, perhaps even ditch my doomed airplane on its cold surface but, alas, that option was forfeited only moments earlier as my flak-damaged and flaming B-17 began to break-up around me. A successful ditching would have been impossible considering the grave condition of my Flying Fortress.

God knows how many times I trained for this eventuality. My rigorous stateside and in-theater training became reflexive. Now, it saved my life. Though my crew and I trained hard to survive in combat, we knew our chances of getting shot down - or killed - over war-torn Europe were greater than returning home alive after our prescribed tour.

I looked around me, to my left and to my right, for eight white parachutes signaling my crew had bailed-out successfully. I know the others got out. They had to! We were a crew, a team. Unfortunately, I did not see any chutes; we had bailed out over a large area and everyone was scattered.

The earth rose rapidly and I pulled my ripcord. Not knowing what enemy activity existed below me, I delayed opening my parachute until I thought I was between three and four thousand feet above the ground. I was rewarded with a firm tug and a gentle swinging beneath a full canopy. A few short minutes later, I landed hard in an open field, muttering a terse expletive as I rolled to the ground.

I had just fallen four miles. In the short span of fifteen minutes, I went from being a highly-trained, combat B-17 pilot flying the best four-engine bomber ever built to another World War II airman shot down over an unfriendly territory who had to use all his wits and skills to avoid capture and stay alive.

As I gathered my parachute, two boys, about eleven or twelve years old, appeared from some nearby woods and helped me roll-up my parachute. They showed no surprise seeing me, and I felt they presented no harm to me. I asked them where the enemy was located. They pointed in one direction. I moved quickly in the opposite direction as fast as my feet could take me.

The boys signaled they would take care of the parachute and pointed to a church steeple. They indicated I should be there after dark. We parted company, never to meet again. I knew it was best to get into hiding and remain hidden until after dark.

It was 1:45 p.m. on a sunny Sunday afternoon. The date was August 13, 1944. I was on my twentieth B-17 combat mission. I had just survived being shot down. Now I was alive, hiding somewhere in the Normandy region of France, not far from the bustling, German-occupied coastal port city of Le Havre. I had just bombed my target, a railroad bridge, near Le Manoir, France. I knew a lot of folks saw my plane shot down and I knew many of them were looking for me now.

Before moving any further, I remained in hiding, and assessed my current situation. Many thoughts crossed my mind: the status of my crew, the nature of the enemy forces that surrounded me and, yes, how the War Department would notify my family of my current status.

Foremost, I was still a combat pilot, but I had my most important mission ahead of me. I had to survive to get home to my family in Steubenville, Ohio and to my darling wife, Billie.

CHAPTER 1

From Boy to Man to Future Combat Pilot

> *"Not a having and a resting, but a growing and a becoming is character of perfection as culture conceives it."*
> George John Whyte-Melville (1821–1878),
> *Culture and Anarchy* [1869]

e not born; they are with heady dreams of to soar with the eagles. ghters to be their swift hers prefer something . Sometimes, circum- :h they follow on their quest to the clouds.

More than six decades ago, I dreamed of becoming a fighter pilot. I dreamed of pitting newly learned flying skills against a powerful foe in a world wracked by war. As it came to be, I landed the First Pilot's seat in the best of all heavy bombers ever built, the Boeing B-17 Flying Fortress.

Prior to its introduction in 1935, the sky never saw any-

thing like the B-17 and nothing in the sky will ever compare to this remarkable combat airplane. Of the many thousands of B-17s built during World War II, only a few survive today. These remaining airframes remind us of the heroic sacrifices countless young boys and men made so that we may enjoy our freedom and peace today.

The B-17 was powerful, capable, rugged, forgiving and, yes, fun to fly. This bomber was beloved by pilots and crewmembers alike. More times than not, this "Queen of the Skies" brought her crews home safely with damage that would have downed any other airplane.

I may not have flown a fighter in the greatest global

The Boeing B-17 "Flying Fortress" proved to be one of the premier bomber aircraft of World War II. Here, a Boeing-built B-17G banks gracefully over Puget Sound near Seattle, Washington. (Peter M. Bowers)

1

conflict ever fought, but I did fly the greatest heavy bomber of the period, the Boeing B-17 Flying Fortress.

As I scan the roster of the fortunate few pilots privileged to fly a B-17 today, I realize I am the last of the 20th century combat World War II B-17 First Pilot or pilot-in-command rated pilots to fly the B-17 Flying Fortress as a pilot-in-command in the 21st century. I am fortunate, indeed.

I couldn't have done any of it without my wife Billie at my side. She is my strength and my dearest friend. Billie, along with my children, William and Harold Gary, and my grandchildren, Brandi Nicole, Timothy Dean, and Shannon Taylor, are the center point of my life and it has been a good one. We expect the years ahead to be equally exciting and rewarding.

This is my story.

I was born in Carrollton, Ohio, on July 17, 1921, the first child of Okey and Clara Johnson Weekley, in the front bedroom of my maternal grandmother's house. My sister, Maxine, was born on September 29, 1923. Two years later, my brother, Ralph, joined our growing family in 1925. He was a chubby and very cute child, but he died at the age of two from pneumonia. Though I have very few memories of Ralph, Maxine cherished Ralph. She carries fond memories of him and cherishes her older brother, me! It does not get any better than that! (See Endnotes, Chapter 1)

My sister and I lived with Grandmother Johnson, our maternal grandparent, at her Carrollton, Ohio home for considerable periods of time when I was very young. My Grandfather Johnson died before I was born. One of my earliest memories of Grandmother Johnson is her cranking the wood-paneled Victrola and how this machine's sweet music filled the house. Later, she became the first member of our family to get electricity in her home.

My mother and father came from large families, six children in each. My mother was an attractive woman and despite a tight

budget, she managed to keep herself looking good. Mom was a great cook and she gave my sister and me everything she could – love and lots of warm memories. Growing up, I had a great love for my mother, as I am sure most young boys do. This love continued well into my later years until she passed away shortly after I made Colonel in the United States Air Force in 1970. Mom was charming with everyone she met and very outgoing, but she could be a stubborn woman when she wanted. I am sure I got my stubbornness from her.

My father, known as "Oke" to the local folks, was a very outgoing man and he possessed a tremendous charisma with the local ladies. Though his hair turned white when he was quite young, my father was always handsome and the local ladies loved him! He was very particular about his appearance and dress, always taking great effort to look his best. Moreover, my father had a fantastic memory and he could remember people's names, events and places with no problem. In addition, he loved sports, particularly baseball and bowling, and relished any opportunity to play billiards.

Unfortunately, my father and I were never close as father and son. We never enjoyed that special father-son bond. His work and many activities kept a distance between us. I withdrew from him as I felt he did not treat my mother in word or deed as she deserved to be treated. Though my father and I were not close, I discovered in later years I inherited many of his more positive traits and characteristics, especially athletics and a keen memory for details.

Both parents were employed in the pottery business, which during the 1920s and early 1930s was a fairly good sized industry in eastern and southeastern Ohio. The pottery business where my parents worked was just across the railroad tracks from my grandmother's home where I was born. This type of work required long hours and rewarded its workers with meager wages. My father was the "batter-out" and my mother was a pottery decorator. The "batter out" took a handful of soft clay and placed it on a fairly large, circular block of hard clay. He would beat it squarely and evenly until it was flattened, then place it on a mold. After the clay was molded and dried, my mother would decorate the pottery with glaze before it was fired in the kiln.

My parents always sought a better life, but their difficult quest was overshadowed by their abiding desire to remain close to their family roots and the pottery business they knew. We moved often before I was ten years old and generally lived in poor, but clean neighborhoods. We lived in several Ohio towns near Carrollton, including Alliance, Bedford, Toronto, East Liverpool, Scio and Steubenville. On a couple occasions, our family moves took us across the Ohio River into nearby Chester and New Cumberland, West Virginia. Most of these moves occurred before the start of the Great Depression in 1929. I was always making new friends and enjoyed an almost carefree childhood.

Between the first and sixth grade, I didn't have any assigned chores and generally did what my mother told me to do. Summers were great and I enjoyed playing baseball and swimming in a creek about three miles from Carrollton. Building forts and playing cowboys and Indians was great fun. Winter was snowball fights and sledding. One winter, some playmates and I took a ladder and put a sled on each end. We blocked off one of Toronto's streets, with kids acting as "guards," loaded-up the ladder and rode this contraption downhill, crossed the frozen Ohio River and to ended up on the river's opposite bank.

But events beyond our control soon shaped my life and I grew-up fast.

I lived in Scio, Ohio at the start of the Great Depression. My life then was particularly tough and food was scarce. My family generally ate what the family next door gave us. I remember vividly the night we had my pet rabbit for dinner. I was too upset to eat any of the rabbit, but not the rest of my family. Hunger dictated our lives.

When I was nine or ten, we moved to New Cumberland, West Virginia, another pottery town on the banks of the Ohio River. When I wasn't in school or trying to earn some extra money, I spent a lot of my free time at the pottery watching my Dad and my uncle make various pieces of pottery. My dad worked for my uncle, Frank, who was the "jigger man," or the top man in the process. The "jigger man" took the molded clay, placed it on a potter's wheel and trimmed away the excess before giving it to a "mold runner" who, in turn, placed the item on a conveyor belt that took it through the kiln.

I spent a lot of time at the pottery studios where my folks worked, mostly to pass the day. I learned early that little details are important in any enterprise and contribute much to the overall success of any endeavor. I remember sitting alongside another man at the pottery shop who used to whittle a set of working pliers from a solid piece of wood, which in my mind was quite a feat. This happy fellow could identify all of the tugboats by their whistles. They whistled to the lockmaster to open the locks in the flood control dams and they whistled other signals, too. I never could understand why they called them tugboats because they pushed the barges, not pulled them.

Barges were usually tied together two abreast, sometimes three, totaling as many as fifteen or sixteen rows. The whole arrangement was called a tow. These tows carried their goods up and down the Ohio River. Heavy with coal, they traveled up the river to steel plants and powerhouses in and near Pittsburgh, Pennsylvania, Wheeling, West Virginia and Steubenville, Ohio. Going down river, their massive loads were generally steel and closed containers.

Pittsburgh's, Wheeling's and Steubenville's mighty steel mills were not far; thus, most barges carried the raw materials necessary to support these large mills or the resulting steel products for a growing nation. No one then could have foreseen that within a decade these same steel mills would produce a lion's share of the enormous quantities of steel needed to vanquish a host of enemies bent on conquering the world.

When I was nine or ten, I gambled for the first time. I was impressionable and eager to learn new ways to earn a few dollars. I discovered playing the numbers was the big thing in town. One day Dad gave me two nickels and told me to play two numbers. I played 555 and another number. The other one hit! It paid about $22, which was about how much a day laborer made in the mills and the pottery shops in a week. Unfortunately, I didn't see any of these winnings as my father collected the money, but the singular thrill of winning money left an indelible impression on me. Moreover, I was proud I could make this small contribution to my family.

Not long afterwards, we moved to Chester, West Virginia, not far from New Cumberland. My parents worked for the TS&T Pottery Company in nearby Newell. My life improved considerably as I received two fancy Christmas presents, a small orange and a convertible toy car that had battery-powered headlights. I played with that toy car under my bed for hours.

After a comparatively short stay in Chester, we moved once again, this time to Toronto, Ohio, just across and down the Ohio River from Chester. Dad still worked in Newell, so he had to cross the river on a small ferry. He drove a 1931 Ford Model A that he had purchased for $35. My mother left the pottery business and found work in a small bakery. We lived upstairs over the bakery which was next door to Manypenny's.

Manypenny's was a small dry goods store owned and operated by Mr. Manypenny. I always loved that name for a store.

Dad often played baseball in his free time in nearby Bloomfield, Ohio. He played ball with a guy named Clark Gable, the same Clark Gable who later became the internationally famous movie star. In an incredible series of coincidences, Gable went into the military during World War II, was assigned as a combat photographer and took a photo-

Steubeville, Ohio as seen from the air. Market Street, the city's main thoroughfare, is the street running from the hill at the foot of this photograph to the Market Street Bridge. Other prominent landmarks are the Steubenville High School at the upper left and the Wheeling Steel Corporation at the upper right.

(Jefferson County Historical Association)

graph of me dropping bombs from my B-17 bomber in combat!

I was still a pre-teen, about ten or eleven years old, when I beat-up my first bully. Some of the larger neighborhood kids liked to push me around for no apparent reason other than to show who was stronger. I got tired of being pushed around by these immature kids and I fought back. That kid never bothered me again.

I learned to swim about the same time. A bunch of us kids just went down and jumped in the Ohio River and started swimming without any formal instruction. Maybe it was a macho attitude or plain stupidity, but it worked and we taught ourselves how to swim. Our frequent trips to the river were tempered by the sobering knowledge that several kids from the area had drowned in the river over the years. Fortunately, that did not happen in my peer group.

The Ohio River was terribly polluted in those days, but I didn't know it at the time and really didn't care. The only fish that could live in the river were carp, and very few people except the poorest of the poor ate them.

During my early teenage years, I lived in Toronto, Ohio and any fond memories were short-lived. Not long after this move, my parents separated and divorced. Maxine and I stayed with my mother and, shortly thereafter, we moved to Steubenville, a modest industrial town of 40,000 people located on the banks of the Ohio River, about thirty miles west of Pittsburgh, Pennsylvania.

In the mid to late 1930s, Steubenville was a dynamic town and offered a variety of entertainment escapes for the men and women who labored so hard during the week. Saturday night was an important night for most folks. Many went downtown for several hours to visit friends, listen to one of the local stage bands play the latest dance tunes or just go to a movie. For two bits (twenty-five cents), one could see Hollywood's favorite actors and actresses on a big movie screen in any one of the town's five theaters and escape, for a couple hours at least, life's drab-

ness and despair. The town's fancier theaters were the Paramount, the Capital and the Grand.

Across from the Paramount Theater was the Paramount Restaurant. For five cents, a patron could buy the greatest hot dog on a steamed bun he had ever eaten. At one time, either on a bet or a dare, I ate ten hot dogs and two hamburgers, all for sixty cents. That's when soda pop, chewing gum, a Milky Way, a Hershey chocolate bar or other candy bars were five cents apiece. Cigarettes were a penny a piece. People greeted each other by name and passed the time talking about their families, the weather and even grumbled about prices.

Steubenville's other two movie theaters were the Olympic and the Rex, where I once participated in an amateur program playing the Hawaiian guitar and singing "Red Sails in the Sunset." The Rex was next door to the Rex Cigar Store. The front of this cigar store had the usual selection of cigars and magazines, but the back of the store had a gambling casino. One of the operators at the dice table was Dino Crochetti. Admiring audiences knew him later as Dean Martin.

Market Street is the heart of Steubenville's business district. This photograph, taken in the mid-1940s, shows some of the retail stores that have made Steubenville the shopping center of eastern Ohio.

(Jefferson County Historical Association)

Steubenville was also known as "Little Chicago." This energetic town had its rough and tough side. The town's gambling and "red light district" was on Water Street which was along the river. One street up was High Street where most of the working girls lived. Next was 3rd Street where the courthouse stood with a bronze statue of Edwin M. Stanton, Abraham Lincoln's Secretary of War, standing proudly in front. The next street up from 3rd Street was 4th, which was Steubenville's main street. The intersection of 4th Street and Market marked the center of town.

Shortly after my family moved to Steubenville, my mother married a man named Harry A. Littlecott, whom she had met in Toronto, Ohio. Harry, also divorced, worked in a nearby steel mill as a time study consultant. At the time, I was thirteen and was in the 7th grade at the Stanton Elementary School, named after Edwin M. Stanton, President Lincoln's Secretary of War. Many of the schools I attended were named after notable Civil War heroes or government officials.

Not long afterwards our family made another move, but only to the south side of town near the large Steubenville Plant of the Wheeling Steel Corporation, which in 1934 was starting to become active enough to provide a few well-paying jobs. Despite the large number of pottery businesses in the area, Steubenville's economy was oriented primarily towards coal mining and steel production. The sky was full of smoke and soot by day and bright with flame from the furnaces at night.

Steubenville was often "smelly" and quite noisy. The town's peculiar odors and noises were associated with the steel mill and their effects were entirely dependent on the prevailing winds. If the winds blew towards town, the stench was pretty bad, but we got used to it. The frequent loud noises from the mill became an accepted part of day-to-day living as well. Between the steel mill, the river tugboats, the nearby railroads and the many trucks hauling coal, there was more than

An aerial view of the Steubenville Plant of the Wheeling Steel Corporation, looking north towards Steubenville in the top left of the picture.
(Jefferson County Historical Association)

enough sound to go around. Like a lot of things in my young life, I got used to this myriad of odors and noises and accepted all as a function of where I lived.

Years later, after returning from World War II, I could navigate an aircraft simply by the color and volume of smoke from the various mills along the Ohio River. I always knew where I was.

Most of the coal sent to the coke furnaces and steel mills strung along the Ohio River came from strip mines in the Ohio, Pennsylvania and West Virginia area. Huge, ugly gashes in the hilly landscape marked where enormous cranes and shovels stripped away tons of earth to reveal and extract the needed coal. Row after row of these deep gashes filled with water inviting a leisurely swim, but all were much too dangerous to enjoy.

Some of the coal was not stripped from these surface mines but came from a deep shaft mine in Steubenville. The shaft started at the base of a hill in town called Market Street Hill and extended well underneath the town. This mine was called High Shaft Mine and it added to the kaleidoscope of sights and sounds of my teenage years.

The Pennsylvania Railroad passed through the heart of Steubenville, about a six blocks from the Ohio River, and ran a course parallel to it. This railroad operated between New York and Washington on the east and Cincinnati and St. Louis in the west. The trains pulled into the station and yards between Market and North Streets. The railroad's large concrete and steel bridge crossed the river at the north side of town. I remember hearing those coal-laden trains pass through town many times each day.

School was not very challenging for me. My grades were average, even during the four years I attended Grant Junior High School and Wells High School. I was a weight lifter and I tried out for football, but had some sort of confrontation with the coach at the first training session, so I joined the school band and played the snare drums. My mother always said Mr. Austin Kuhns, the school's band director, was responsible for me finishing high school. I played snare drum for him for the four years I attended high school. Our popular band was called the Big Red Band and it was one of the best in the Mideastern and Mid-western United States. We traveled a lot and we won a sizable number of medals in numerous competitions. Best of all, lots of girls came to our gigs!

Several times a year, a steamboat would tie-up on the Ohio River at Market Street and

During his teenage years, Hal Weekley enjoyed riding his Harley-Davidson motorcycle around Steubenville, Ohio. Hal worked at the Stony Hollow Inn briefly as a soda jerk and bartender while he attended high school.   (Harold D. Weekley)

take passengers for daylight and evening excursions. The boat was equipped with a bar and a dance floor, which made for a fine evening.

Each year, my high school contracted with the boat-company to take the senior class up the river to Rock Springs Park in Chester, West Virginia, which was our theme park of the period. This senior trip was a thing of beauty and something to remember. One of the most memorable experiences was listening to the boat's steam calliope when it was in dock. Those beautiful sounds, echoing between the hills was unforgettable. As we progressed up the river, cars would stop and everyone would wave to all of us on the boat. What a thrill it was!

I noticed girls very early in high school and everything went downhill from there. I purchased a rebuilt 1936 Harley-Davidson motorcycle during my high school freshman year, which became my primary pleasure. More often than not, I had a girl riding with me.

Growing-up, I tended to be a kid who did not have big aspirations to do anything except fly. The sky beckoned to me at a young age. My first interest in airplanes came when I was a young boy visiting my grandmother in Carrollton, Ohio and saw a Pitcarin Autogiro fly

Grant Junior High School. The building was dedicated in December 1927.   (Jefferson County Historical Association)

overhead when I was eight years old. I was enthralled.

When I lived in Bedford, Ohio, my parents took me to a local air show. I was fascinated by the incredible aerial displays. Unfortunately, one of the participants was killed when his parachute did not open. Though I witnessed my first air show casualty, it didn't sway me from the thrill of the day and only kindled my desire to fly, a desire that grew stronger every year.

There weren't many airfields in that part of the state. As such, there wasn't much aviation activity, but I was not deterred. I visited what small airfields I could locate and used any available transportation to get to them. In addition, I visited some of the enterprising aircraft builders that were building wings and fuselages in garages and basements. Enthused by everything I saw, I realized I had the opportunity to learn more about the internal workings of aircraft.

During my early teenage years, I worked for Postal Telegraph, a competitor of Western Union, and delivered telegrams on my bicycle. The working girls in Steubenville's "red light district" charged $1.00 for their services. I used to see many of these girls on a regular basis, but not as a customer. Most of my telegram deliveries went to those girls.

When I wasn't delivering telegrams, swimming or watching a show, I'd ride my bicycle to the western edge of town to a large hill. From atop this hill, I'd watch an All American Airways Stinson Reliant airplane

The idyllic Ohio River scene shows a tow pushing its load along the river with the Half Moon Farm in the background. This farm later became the Half Moon Airport where Hal Weekley learned to fly. (Jefferson County Historical Association)

make the daily mail pickup. This large single-engine airplane, with its distinctive gull-shaped wing, would trail a hook on a line and would swoop down and fly between two poles. A loop of rope was strung between these poles, which in turn was tied to the mail sack going outbound. Just before the trailing hook snared the looped rope, the crew tossed out the incoming mail sack. In the next instant, the hook snared the looped rope and the outbound mail sack was on its way. I found this operation very exciting and it fueled my desire to become a pilot.

I wanted to learn how to fly. I dreamed of flying. It took me some time before I was able to save enough money to do any actual flying. Around 1937, I became a newspaper boy, selling the Steubenville Herald Star to earn extra money. I sold newspapers on one of the corners of 4th and Market in Steubenville. Other equally enterprising young men occupied the other three corners. I spent the money I earned learning how to fly. Every afternoon, rain or shine, heat or cold, I purchased the Herald Star at two cents a copy and then sold it for three cents a copy. Starting with a minimum of thirty papers for a minimum of five days a week, my profit for the week was $1.50.

My first day on the job was the day gangster Pretty Boy Floyd was shot in nearby East Liverpool, Ohio. I sold a lot of newspapers that day.

On Saturday or Sunday, depending on the weather, I tried to fly. No airports were near where I lived on the Steubenville side of the Ohio River, so I had to walk four miles to Hollidays Cove, West Virginia on the other side of the river to a little airfield called Half Moon Airport. This rural airport boasted a 2700-foot long, sod runway and one hangar.

Hal Weekley's first flying lessons were in the chummy Aeronca C-3. It cost him $6.00 per hour to rent the airplane, instructor included.   (James B. Zazas)

My initial dual flight training was in an Aeronca C-3, a chummy side-by-side seating, high-wing airplane powered by a two-cylinder, 36-hp engine. It cost $6.00/hour to rent, with the instructor included. Taking my $1.50 weekly profit from selling newspapers, I was able to get fifteen minutes of dual flight instruction, which generally consisted of one take-off, a few turns and one landing at the airport. Upon completing each lesson, I walked another four miles back home, only to sell papers again the next Monday. My retention at the time wasn't the greatest and I imagine it would have taken me many years of operating in that manner to obtain any degree of flight proficiency.

My school days passed quickly and in June of 1940, I graduated from Steubenville's Wells High School. After graduation, I got a job at the Brandt Motor Company, the primary Buick dealer in this area. I worked in the front of the facility, which then was a high quality service station. My co-worker was a redheaded young fellow named Jim Brownlee who was the same age as me.

Jim and I became good friends and we shared many secrets and ambitions. We talked often about what each of us had done in high school. More often than not, our conversations centered on the girls we had dated, where we went with them and what we had done. We learned much about love and life during those heady days.

Each of us believed our lives were already mapped-out. Jim's ambition was to have a nice car and become a good auto mechanic. My ambition was to become a good military pilot, marry a nice lady and raise a family.

One day, a shiny new Buick drove into the car dealership for service. The driver was Georgia Brandt, the very attractive wife of Dean Brandt, one of the owners of the dealership. Seated beside her was a most beautiful young lady, Wilma Jeanne Wigginton, known to everyone as Billie. Shortly after Mrs. Brandt and Billie departed, my mind focused on Billie and I commented, almost impulsively to Jim, "I'm going to marry that lady!"

As events came to be, I did just that.

Billie graduated from Wells High School in Steubenville in 1939. How I spent four years in high school without noticing her, I'll never know. I have always contended she was then and still is today the prettiest lady to come from the Steubenville area.

At first, our courtship progressed slowly, perhaps too slowly for my liking. My family was quite poor whereas Billie's family was fairly well to do. Despite the differences in our respective financial positions, no one in her family ever made me feel uncomfortable.

Billie went to beauty school and later worked in the Horne's Department Store's beauty salon in Pittsburgh, Pennsylvania. At the time, my only transportation was my rebuilt 1936 Harley-Davidson motorcycle, not exactly a suitable means of traveling back and forth on the hilly, winding roads between Steubenville and Pittsburgh to see Billie. Fortunately, she came home on weekends by train or bus, so we were able to spend some time together. Roller-skating was one of our favorite activities, as was going to the movies. We spent a lot of time together at her parents' home.

Hal Weekley was an avid motorcycle enthusiast and enjoyed riding his new, 1940 Harley-Davidson motorcycle. What a ride!

(Harold D. Weekley)

Our romance grew slowly. Local radios played the Big Band music of Jimmy Dorsey, Glenn Miller and other famous bands. We enjoyed listening to the music together. The beat was lively and entertaining, adding much to our growing love. But it was Billie's soft, soothing voice that was the real music in my ears.

Events half a globe away soon captured my attention and, for that matter, the world's. Jim and I were working together on December 7, 1941, when we heard on the radio that the Japanese had attacked Pearl Harbor. Stunned by the events, neither of us could understand how a "Mickey Mouse nation" like Japan could be stupid enough to jump on a country with the resources of the United States. It took a couple of years before the Japanese came to a similar conclusion.

The constant stream of reports of "Peace in our time" and the daily news reports of war in far away lands carried little meaning for us before Pearl Harbor was bombed. Now, as war came knocking on our back door, Jim and I realized the spreading global conflict would soon engulf us as well.

Not long after Pearl Harbor was bombed, I left my automobile service job. School and my job at the Brandt Motor Company seemed of distant importance. I wanted to do something for my country and do something that would get me into aviation. To this end, I landed a Civil Service job at the Fairfield Air Depot in Fairfield, Ohio where I worked as a junior aircraft engine mechanic. Soon afterwards, this air depot became Patterson Field and, later still, Patterson Air Force Base. Today, this base is a major part of the large U.S. Air Force complex known as Wright-Patterson Air Force Base.

I received considerable schooling and became qualified to work on a large variety of aircraft. My first aircraft was a Bell P-39 that had suffered a wheels-up landing at Patterson Field. At the time of this mishap, the base's runways were grass-covered, thus the overall damage to the P-39 was minimal. In the afternoons and evenings, I frequently observed single-engine Army P-39 and P-40 fighters, and twin-engine A-20 Havoc attack bombers flying around the Fairfield area undergoing test flights, practicing aerobatics and other maneuvers. All of this aerial activity heightened my strong desire to fly.

I wanted to fly as far back as I can remember. Now, as war clouds grew darker on the horizon, I knew I had to make some difficult choices – where I wanted to go in life and what I wanted to do.

Having Billie in my life was my first choice. Flying in the United States Army Air Forces was my second choice.

"A coward turns away, but a brave man's choice is danger."

Euripides (c. 485–406 BC),
Iphigenia in Tauris [c. 412 BC]

CHAPTER 2

The Pace to Combat Flying Quickens

By mid-1942, the United States was engaged fully in the war in Europe and in the Pacific. An unfathomable amount of men and material was needed to execute this war on many fronts. With each news broadcast, my dreams to fly a swift fighter grew stronger and more fervent. I took stock of my life's direction and realized immediately I wanted to be a pilot in the United States Army Air Forces.

Eagerly wanting to fly and fight against the enemies of the United States, I contacted the Aviation Cadet Board at Patterson Field where I was working and applied for Aviation Cadet training in the United States Army Air Forces. I was given a physical and a written examination, and shortly thereafter was accepted into the program. Concurrently, the Aviation Cadet Board advised me to return to Steubenville, inform the local draft board of my acceptance in the Aviation Cadet Corps, and wait until I was called. I was frustrated, as I wanted to fly and fight NOW, but I dutifully followed my orders.

The draft board, however, did not wait for the Aviation Cadet Board to act. They saw I was interested in serving my country, so they drafted me. My draft notice was dated July 10, 1942, with instructions to report on July 23, 1942. I was 21 years old. Though I didn't

fully appreciate it then, I soon learned I was but one very small, incremental part of the United States' massive, national manpower mobilization effort. Many millions of men would be drafted. Women too, would enter the military.

After the Pearl Harbor attack, the United States Army Air Forces, or simply USAAF, alone projected a goal of more than two million officers and enlisted men by August 1942. Bringing this many men into the comparatively technical field of flying and maintaining aircraft required special skills and aptitudes. Recognizing the problems with enlistees possessing little technical background and experience and the intelligence necessary for technical training, the USAAF initiated steps to ensure it recruited men who had previous aviation experience and interest. By mid-1942, the USAAF gained, over the other services' objections, all the men who had one month or more of experience in aircraft operations, weather forecasting and observing, aircraft manufacturing, aircraft maintenance and/or many other aviation-related fields. Because of my aviation maintenance experience, I fell into this category.

The other military services complained bitterly about these changes and manpower drain, and were able to overrule the USAAF policy. However, any recruiting or draft advantages the other services enjoyed were brief and the Army Air Forces gained virtually the best of the recruits coming into the military during World War II.

Shortly after reporting for duty, I was transported to Fort Hayes in Columbus, Ohio for induction into the armed forces. There, I received the normal issue of clothing, immunizations, indoctrinations and more testing. Upon completion of this testing, I was transferred to Fort Benjamin Harrison in Indianapolis, Indiana for classification. A few days later, I was part of a small group of enlistees shipped via train to Camp Forrest near Tullahoma, Tennessee, not far from Nashville, and assigned to the 305th Combat Engineers of the 80th Division, known then as the Blue Ridge Division.

Camp Forrest occupied a very large chunk of real estate. Arriving at this expansive base, I had the acute feeling I was a very small cog in a very large undertaking. These initial impressions only increased as my military life expanded.

I dutifully reported to the base theater for orientation. The Regimental Commander came forward to greet the assembled group and, in turn, asked where each individual was from and what his previous occupation had been. When I told him I had been a junior aircraft engine mechanic, the commander was surprised and responded "How in the world did you get here?"

I replied, "I have no idea, Sir." As it came to pass, I was the only one in the entire group selected for the combat engineers.

Shortly before I arrived at Camp Forrest, I advised the Aviation Cadet Board commander at Patterson Field that I had been drafted. The Board commander merely told me to proceed on with things as they were and I was to contact the Aviation Cadet Board as soon as I received a permanent assignment, but I was impatient. As soon as I settled in the barracks at the 305th Combat Engi-

neers, 80th Division, I immediately wrote a letter to the Major who commanded the Aviation Cadet Board.

I was summoned to my commander's office at Camp Forrest less than fifteen minutes after I deposited that letter at the company headquarters building. I met a First Lieutenant who was very interested in learning why one of his new privates was corresponding with a Major. He listened intently while I explained to him the circumstances. He thought over the situation and allowed the letter to be forwarded. He advised me, however, that my transfer from that particular unit of the 80th Division was practically impossible because the military leadership was just beginning to form that division and they had no intention of letting anyone go.

For the next few months, I heard no word from the Aviation Cadet Board. Meanwhile, I continued my work with the combat engineers. I learned a great deal and enjoyed many interesting experiences.

Harold Weekley's initial military assignment in mid-1942 was with the 305th Combat Engineers, 80th Division based at Camp Forrest, Tullahoma, Tennessee. Here, Private Weekley stands in front of the barracks of the 305th Engineers. (Harold D. Weekley)

By the very nature of our military training, we worked ourselves into excellent physical condition. We did calisthenics every day and would go on twenty-five, sometimes thirty-five mile hikes with little or no discomfort. We were in top physical form.

Despite our excellent physical conditioning, we found it odd that we "young people" were always lagging behind a physically fit, somewhat weathered-complexion looking individual from Oklahoma. Evidently, he had been out in the wind, rain and weather all of his life because his skin looked like leather. We could not tell his age from his looks, but we considered him to be an "old man," though in reality he was probably in his mid-thirties. His physical stamina inspired a lot of us to continue forward when we were tired or exhausted. We got quite a thrill trying to keep up with that "old man."

Most of the men in my particular division came from neighboring states. Though many enlistees came from Tennessee, most others came from Kentucky, West Virginia and Ohio. As such, this diverse group had a wide range of personal qualities and intelligence and many interesting stories to share.

I remember one interesting story involving a young fellow from Tennessee. He was standing guard duty when he was approached by the Officer of the Day. The fine lad, dutifully performing his assigned duty, ordered this officer to halt, come forward and be recognized. The guard recognized the officer and acknowledged this recognition. In turn, the Officer of the Day discussed several of the Orders of the Day with the private on guard before proceeding on his way.

He moved only ten or fifteen feet before the guard, again, told him to halt. The officer turned around, looked at him with an admonishing glance and said, "Young man, you've already halted me, already recognized me, we've discussed your responsibilities and I'm proceeding to the next post. Now why did you ask me to halt again?"

The young guard, convinced he was doing his duties properly, said, "Well, sir, I've been instructed to yell halt three times and then fire. You're on your second halt now."

I believe this young man received some additional training shortly thereafter.

Another interesting story involved my unit, the 305th Combat Engineers. I was doing some amateur boxing on a very limited scale and was a light-heavyweight boxer on the 305th boxing team. Most every evening, I walked about three blocks to a gymnasium to work out. I worked out with three other soldiers from Texas, all three being of considerable size. The largest boxed in the heavyweight division. I was in the light-heavyweight division.

My best friend at Camp Forrest was Dexter Clenng, a big, strapping boy from Texas. One night, we were at the gym working out when another friend of Dexter's, also from Texas, informed us he did not have a sparing partner and asked me to spar with him. Being somewhat bigger than me, I declined immediately saying I didn't want to take any chances with someone his size.

After some considerable discussion, he assured me he would go lightly on me and I agreed to spar with him. After several minutes of sparing, I confronted an opening that I could not pass up: I planted a very strong fist into my big friend's midriff with a loud "Whoomp!"

Almost immediately, everything in the gym became very quiet. All we could hear was a muffled grunt and the expelling of air. I looked into my opponent's eyes and saw the look of utter amazement. Immediately, I tore off my gloves, turned and ran. He chased me all the way back to the barracks. Fortunately, by the time I got back to the barracks, he had calmed down somewhat and did not use me as his punching bag as I feared he would.

Our days at Camp Forrest began at 0530 hours. We'd roll from our beds and assemble for Roll Call with one of the officers calling out the names and checking them off their list. Afterwards, we'd march to the large mess hall for a filling breakfast, which usually consisted of creamed chipped beef on toast, or SOS - Shit-On-a-Shingle - as we affectionately called this meal.

Dining was a segregated affair, not only of race, but of rank. Officers sat together in one part of the mess hall and all the privates sat in another. Very rarely were these invisible lines crossed, if ever. Segregation was a significant part of the military structure in those days.

Breakfast was followed by close order drill. After drill practice, we'd go into the field to learn how to build bridges or how to destroy them with explosives. We learned how to handle land mines and how to use them against the enemy. We ate our meals at field kitchens whenever we trained in the field. We learned quickly how to carefully clean our eating utensils; otherwise we'd end up with a bad case of the "GI's," or diarrhea.

On most Sundays, we had a good dinner at noon and a lighter meal in the evening. Sunday evening meals usually consisted of baloney and cheese or, as we crudely called it, "Horse Cock and Chokeass."

On frequent occasions, I was assigned guard duty or KP (Kitchen Police) duty, not so much for any infraction or disobedience, but more as the usual rotation of assigned duties. Once, however, I made the mistake of complaining to a lieutenant that I was always last for pay roll, last for any passes and last for anything that was good. The lieutenant pondered my complaint and told me he would consider my request. He then stated he would assign KP duty, guard duty and latrine cleaning duty to individuals whose names began at the end of the alphabet. Since my last name begins with a "W," I found myself doing more than my share of KP, guard and latrine cleaning duties. That was the last time I offered any complaint or suggestion at Camp Forrest.

I spent some time working in the camp's Motor Pool. Due to my previous mechanical experience gleaned from working at the

With rifle in hand, Private Harold Weekley stands at attention in front of the Company Headquarters of the U.S. Army's 305th Combat Engineers, 80th Division, at Camp Forrest, Tullahoma, Tennessee. Dexter Clenng, Hal's best friend during this training phase, stands in the background. (Harold D. Weekley)

Brandt Motor Company in Steubenville, I was placed in charge of a command car.

Once, I really screwed-up and got some thick, dirty oil on this prized vehicle's olive drab finish. I was unable to clean it up completely and this gleaming car had to be repainted.

I remember the Sergeant in charge of the Motor Pool once told one of the instructors to get his shoes shined. The instructor replied he could not get his shoes to shine with all the oil on them. The sergeant asked the instructor if he would stand guard duty for a week if he could get them to shine. The instructor agreed. The next day, the Sergeant presented the stunned instructor his shoes shined to a high luster. As agreed, the instructor stood guard duty for a week without any complaint.

Camp Forrest had large parade ground at the base's center and we paraded on these expansive grounds every Saturday. I played the drums for the cadence. These parades were a stark contrast and a welcome relief to the rough and tough, sometimes grueling hikes we had in the nearby hills.

The military made every effort to keep morale high. The service sought to produce a good soldier with sound mind and body, and it made every effort to keep us happy. We didn't receive any passes until we had been there for a month. Correspondence with loved ones back home was encouraged. I missed Billie very much and I wrote to her at every opportunity.

We kept in touch almost exclusively by mail during my time at Camp Forrest. The few telephones available were always busy and were very crowded. Billie wrote to me at least three times a week and was always a better correspondent than I was. From time to time, I received a welcomed letter from my mother and sister. Mail Call was held in the evening and was always one of the better experiences of the day, especially after long day of basic training, calisthenics and other activities devised to mold us into future soldiers. Mail Call was held in front of the Company Commander's office and was conducted by the company clerk.

In September 1942, I received a set of orders to report to the Aviation Cadet Classification Center in Nashville, Tennessee. Seven people endorsed my orders, including Mr. Henry L. Stimson, the Secretary of War. Obviously, I was very proud and very happy because I knew I was going to finally learn to fly. I had looked forward to this opportunity for so many years. (See Endnotes, Chapter 2).

My transfer to the U.S. Army Air Forces (USAAF) began on a somewhat arduous note. I started by taking the train from Tullahoma, Tennessee to nearby Nashville.

Upon reaching Nashville, I climbed aboard a "six-by" truck and joined other incoming military personal for a bumpy ride to the classification center. Recalling all of the stories I had heard about the glamour of the U.S. Army Air Forces accorded its pilots, I assumed a limousine would pick me up, so obviously, I was very disappointed by the "six-by" truck. We traveled to what I figured would be a very special complex reserved for the elite of the USAAF. I was in for a tremendous surprise.

As we proceeded down the road, we passed two-story tarpaper barracks that were surrounded by a barbed wire fence. Clothing, presumably laundered, hung on lines in various parts of the barracks and on the barbed wire fence. I turned to one of my fellow riders and remarked, "I'm sure glad we aren't going to be in that area." I had no sooner finished my comment than our truck turned into the compound. We had arrived at our new home.

Those tarpaper barracks each housed about thirty-five to forty men. By coincidence or design, my barracks housed people from the USAAF or other units within the U.S. Army. All of us came from a wide variety of locations throughout the country and the world, including a young man from Panama who later became a good friend.

Our compound was named Berry Hill Gardens. We were close to Berry Field, which was then the Nashville Municipal Airport. Today, the airport carries the identifier BNA with the "B" representing Berry Field.

Berry Hill Gardens was an Aviation Cadet Classification Center. Using a series of mental and aptitude tests, the Army Air Forces determined whether an individual would be an airplane pilot, a glider pilot, a navigator, or a bombardier. The majority of the people working within this organization, with the exception of the commanders, were aviation cadets who had "washed-out" of flight training, including the clerk who handed-out the mail at our daily Mail Calls. Obviously, they weren't thrilled about their duties or their responsibilities, but they fulfilled them without complaint or squabble.

We spent our time in the classification center undergoing a comprehensive battery of qualification tests, physicals and indoctrinations. Where one group of officers poked and prodded us, another group tested and lectured us. Professionals prepared the many psychological and psychomotor tests. From these tests, the Army Air Forces determined if I, as well as all the other cadets going through the same battery of tests, had the aptitude to fly one of Uncle Sam's airplanes or serve in some other flying capacity.

The medical examinations took two days, as did the aptitude testing. All results were checked and rechecked. All of us were measured against the high standards the United States Army Air Forces sought in their recruits. Quite often, the USAAF handed out booklets describing the many tests we would take, including the purpose and function of each test.

The various tests were tough, especially the medical tests, but I knew I could make it. Outside of my normal childhood colds and flu, I believed I had nothing that would keep me from the cockpit of a swift fighter.

In addition, everyone had to undergo a psychiatric examination, or in official Army Air Forces terminology, the "Aptitude Rating for Military Aeronautics." All of us were cautioned that our psychological examination would have great bearing on selection for the type of training we sought or were assigned. My psychiatric examination proved to be an interesting experience.

The doctor had a particular question he asked everyone, which I presume was meant to gauge its shock value. He asked, "How long has it been since you masturbated?"

"I'm not sure, what time is it?" I responded.

"You'll be good cannon fodder," he stated. "We'll make you a pilot."

I spent eighteen days at the classification center and learned quickly one does not volunteer for anything. There were days when things would be slow for my particular group and requests for volunteers soon followed for truck drivers, carpenters, and people with varying skills. The overall plan was probably to keep people busy but, sometimes, this strategy bordered on the ridiculous.

For example, we had sizable wood pile located in our compound. Every day that pile of wood had to be moved someplace else. I realize people had to be kept busy, but I believe our superiors could have used us a little more productively.

The classification process soon ended and I was classified as a pilot, much to my immense joy and relief. Shortly afterwards, several of us who were classified as pilots were transferred to Maxwell Field in Montgomery, Alabama for Cadet Preflight Training or in official USAAF terms, "Preflight School." Maxwell was one of four such preflight schools in the country with the other three located in Texas and California. The prescribed course of military instruction, supervised athletics and academics lasted nine weeks. I attended Cadet Preflight Training from November 1942 through January of 1943.

As my train pulled into the station at Maxwell, I observed many young cadets, all looking very trim and impressive in their military outfits. Each uniformed cadet wore white gloves and a saber. A wave of intrepidation swept through me and I knew then and there I was in trouble. These cadets were very dedicated to their work. They were the "Upperclassmen" and therefore carried the military respect demanded of their position. I realized quickly who was in charge of this particular operation. Commands of "No talking!" "Stay in line!" "Close it up!" "Dress right!" Dress left!" soon filled our days. An upperclassman was always nearby ready to issue a command.

Moreover, unlike the sometimes courteous training experience I had at Camp Forrest, hazing was an integral part of my early, Cadet Preflight Training at Maxwell. Talking was not allowed for any neophyte underclassman and all answers were a simple, "Yes, Sir," "No, Sir," and "No excuse, Sir!" Hazing of lower classmen by the upperclassmen was considered an integral part of our training.

Months later, the commonly accepted practice of hazing at preflight schools came under considerable public attack. Though defended within certain military circles, hazing and its inherent class system was abolished by the Army Air Forces Flying Training Command in May 1943.

One of my first stops at Maxwell Field was to the Quartermaster supply to receive my new uniform. Now, I began to look like a future Army Air Forces aviator. Shortly afterwards, the other cadets and I were provided containers to ship home any civilian clothing. More examinations and immunization shots followed. We trainees lined up, stepped forward one by one and had shots administered in each arm.

Almost immediately, we learned what was to take place in the Cadet Preflight portion of our flight training and this ten-week training program proved educational and very nerve-wracking. The daily routine began at 0530 hours and ended about 1730 hours. My fellow cadets and I absorbed a tremendous amount of academic material and learned the limits of our endurance, and the responsibilities and duties of being an officer. We were in classrooms for approximately six hours a day, calisthenics at least one hour and officer candidate training at least one to two hours. More than half of the allotted academic curriculum was devoted to close order drill, ceremonies and inspections. The balance covered military courtesies and customs, small arms familiarization, Morse Code, aircraft recognition and other military-related subjects.

All Army Air Forces preflight schools followed West Point's Honor Code and discipline. We marched in formation between classes. Everywhere else, we ran. And, if we weren't running, we would be singing the popular Army ballads of the day. We studied the Army's *Articles of War* again and again and again. It took incredible personal discipline to stay awake while reading it or having it read to us.

Our instructors were very dedicated and put the fear of God into our hearts. They taught us lessons we would retain for the rest of our lives. I learned the motto "Lead, follow or get the hell out of the way!" I liked that motto then and still enjoy it today!

We lived in permanent quarters at the base. There were six men to a room. Sleep came quickly after a hard day of mental and physical exertion.

The mess hall was nearby and the meals served were quite good, though not fancy. Here, I learned how to eat a "square meal." As underclassmen, we had to sit ramrod straight on the outermost four inches of our chairs. Our eyes were riveted straight ahead. We could not speak unless spoken to by a cadet officer, or only if we requested something to be passed to us. Each sentence would start with a "Sir" and end with a "Sir," such as "Sir, please pass the butter, sir."

The water glass had to be at the one o'clock position, touching the plate, and the bread plate was at the eleven o'clock position touching the plate. We ate by raising our spoon vertically from our plate to a point immediately in front of our mouth, then horizontally to our mouth. The return of the utensil was to reverse the procedure. This procedure was very time-consuming and tended to keep us a little on the lean side.

Even when we became upperclassmen, four weeks into Cadet Preflight Training, the manners and courtesies we learned carried over, albeit in a more relaxed atmosphere. After we became upperclassmen, we were allowed to go into nearby Montgomery, Alabama for the weekend. The local civic groups very kindly held social dances for us. On occasion, we were invited to someone's home for dinner and to meet their daughter.

We had a rigorous exercise program that constantly improved our bodies and stamina. Besides having to run around the perimeter of Maxwell Field, we had to run an obstacle course that was called "The Burma Road" once a week. This grueling course tested our physical condition and was very instrumental in separating the men from the boys. I am absolutely certain that vanity and a macho attitude were largely responsible for many of us finishing the course.

Violations of any rule during Cadet Preflight Training, either real or perceived, resulted in the walking of "tours." A tour consists of marching a given route, with a rifle, for a period of fifty minutes to one hour. Tours were walked during a cadet's off-duty time.

I do not recall the specific infractions, but I accumulated a number of tours that had to be taken care of during the Christmas holiday. Thus, on Christmas Eve of 1942, I did my duty and walked my tours. The time passed quickly as I listened to Bing Crosby sing "White Christmas" on our community record player.

My desire to fly remained very strong during my time at Cadet Preflight

Training. So was my love for a very special woman back home.

After I joined the United States Armed Forces in July 1942, my courtship of Billie Jeanne Wigginton consisted entirely of letters except for a short leave from Camp Forrest to return home when her father passed away. Now, I sought a more tangible, meaningful relationship. I purchased a diamond ring, very small, to send to my sweetheart. I wanted dearly to indicate my love to her and my longing desire to make her my wife.

In late January1943, I completed Cadet Preflight Training at Maxwell Field. My next stop was Decatur, Alabama where I was selected to report to Primary Flight School.

"Learning is not attained by chance, it must be sought for with ardor and attended to with diligence."
Abigail Adams (1744–1818), *Letter to John Quincy Adams [May 8, 1780]*

CHAPTER 3

Earning the Silver Wings

The prospective Army Air Forces pilot followed a carefully crafted and somewhat lengthy journey from aviation cadet to fully qualified pilot. Three distinct and separate flight training stages – primary, basic and advanced – defined the required ground and flight training. Each stage lasted about two months. The aviation cadet came one step closer to earning his coveted silver wings and an Army Air Forces commission with the successful completion of each phase of specialized instruction. With few exceptions, all Army Air Forces pilots followed these three prescribed instructional stages.

During Primary Flying Training, the aviation cadet generally flew a small aircraft of low horsepower and learned contact or visual flying, simple aerobatics

The main entrance at the Southern Aviation Training School at Decatur, Alabama during World War II.   (Carolinas Aviation Museum)

and basic navigation. Flight instructors placed great emphasis on approaches and landings, proficiency in aerobatics and basic navigation skills.

The Basic Flying Training phase exposed the cadet to a heavier, more complex airplane while he learned and honed important cross-county navigation, instrument, night and formation flying skills. Smoothness and repetition developed proficiency. The instructors' job was to make military pilots out of the Primary Flying Training graduates.

During Advanced Flying Training, the aviation cadet flew a trainer with flying characteristics similar to the one he would fly in combat. Instrument flying, navigation, aerobatics, formation and high altitude flight were practiced and mastered.

Pryor Field hummed with activity. The Quadrangle held the classrooms and administration building. Not far away were the airfield's hangars and the Stearman biplanes cadets flew during this training phase. (Gloria Dalton)

Throughout this last training phase, the cadet refined his flying skills and reactions necessary for combat.

During each phase, the cadet could fail or "wash-out" for any number of reasons, including failing a mandatory checkride or experiencing uncontrollable airsickness. Almost one-third of the aviation cadets that entered the USAAF pilot training pipeline failed or in pilot training parlance, "washed-out." Most were reassigned to navigator, bombardier or other schools as determined by the Army Air Forces.

Upon successful completion of Advanced Flying Training, the cadet received his commission and coveted silver wings. Afterwards, he began training in his assigned type of combat aircraft, or as a member of an aircrew in a combat unit.

The entire process from Primary Flying Training to fully qualified combat pilot took a full year, or more. Even though some flight training in the primary, basic and advanced courses were shortened due to the needs of the war, a pilot was not ready for combat assignment until a year or more after he started flight training.

In late January 1943, I reported to the 65th AAFF Training Detachment operated by the Southern Aviation Training School in Decatur, Alabama for Primary Flying Training, a ten-week course. This civilian-operated, contract pilot school was a part of the Army Air Forces' Southeastern Flying Training Command, and was located about twenty-five miles west of Huntsville, Alabama, three miles north of Decatur and the wide Tennessee River, and about ten miles south of Athens, Alabama on U.S. Highway 31. Both Decatur and the Tennessee River proved to be handy landmarks for any cadet pilot lost on a local or cross-country flight.

This school formed the basis of Southern Airways, which became an airline and, later, was absorbed by North Central Airlines. Later still, North Central Airlines became a part of Northwest Airlines.

The only military personnel on the field were the check pilots, the commander, and a couple of Southern Aviation Training School officers. Civilians comprised the rest of the ground and flight school instructor cadre. Their job was to teach Primary Flying Training cadets the basics of flying – and of staying alive.

Few qualified military and academic instructors were available when the U.S. Army Air Forces developed its preflight program. In July 1941, authority was granted to hire civilian instructors, but their status in the military training programs presented numerous problems with military authorities. Though these civilian instructors were authorized to wear military style uniforms, the military did not go out of its way to make these civilians feel at home in the USAAF schools. In addition, early in the war, the respective selective service boards drafted many of these instructors which, in turn, created an acute shortage of qualified instructors until enough military instructors could be trained.

To retain these civilian instructors and their teaching experience, the USAAF gave direct commissions on many occasions. Instructors under thirty-five years old were allowed to enlist, attend an Officers Candidate School, then return to their original preflight training position upon completion of this school. Those few instructors ineligible for a commission remained as enlisted men. In addition, the USAAF retained a small number of civilian instructors.

The flying field was originally a 640 acre tract of land known as the "Oakland Place"

The Stearman PT-17 was a rugged, two-place pilot trainer. Standing tall on a narrow landing gear, the Stearman sported a fabric-covered fuselage, a pair of fabric-covered wings and was powered by reliable, 220 hp Continental R-670 radial engine. If the JN-4 "Jenny" was the primary pilot training airplane of World War I, then the Stearman was the primary pilot training airplane of World War II. The PT-17 in overall silver finish was standardized for Army Air Forces training in early 1942. The red center "meatball" was deleted in May 1942.

(Peter M. Bowers)

and was surrounded by cotton fields. In April 1941, the Army Air Corps (the Army Air Forces did not yet exist) contracted Frank Hulse to build and operate the Primary Flying Training school. Hulse was president of two other similar schools, one located in Tuscaloosa, Alabama and the other in Camden, South Carolina. Hulse later founded Southern Airways, which first used a surplus Army DC-3 to fly between Memphis, Tennessee; Atlanta, Georgia and Birmingham, Alabama.

Airfield construction at Decatur started in July 1941 with the stipulation the four hangars, two barracks and brick veneer administration building be ready by October 1st. There was no paved runway, only a sod strip. Known initially as Athens-Decatur Field, the airfield was renamed Pryor Field several years later to honor Schuyler Harris Pryor who died in a mid-air crash in 1944.

The first class of fifty-one student flying cadets arrived and started training on October 7th while workmen were still on the job putting finishing touches on the school. The crowded flight line hummed, always busy with instructors, students and linemen sending their young charges into the air. Pryor Field's first class of cadets graduated on December 11, 1941.

The primary training airplane at Decatur was the PT-17 Stearman, a rugged, all-silver painted biplane with upper and lower wings and front and rear open cockpits. Standing tall on a narrow landing gear, the Stearman sported a powerful, 220 hp Continental R-670 radial engine.

Classroom, calathentics and flight training occupied the bulk of the flying cadets' time at the Southern Aviation Training School.

(Carolinas Aviation Museum)

The Stearman was an ideal pilot training airplane. Light and responsive on the controls, it could easily do aerobatics and had a great reputation as a fun airplane. Though almost every cadet and instructor considered the Stearman biplane a joy to fly, it was prone to ground-looping due to its narrow landing gear and high center of gravity and could be an absolutely wicked beast for any neophyte pilot to land in any appreciable crosswind. Many cadets referred to the PT-17 Stearman as the "Washing Machine," an unusual nickname gained from "washing out" so many cadets from flight training.

The PT-17 was definitely a throwback to an earlier era of wire-braced and fabric-covered biplanes. As the Curtiss JN-4 "Jenny" was the primary pilot training airplane of World War I, the PT-17 Stearman was the primary pilot training airplane for World War II.

Upon reporting for duty, we were issued cloth A-9 or fleece-lined B-6 leather flying helmets, A-2 leather flight jackets, and a pair of AN-6530 flying goggles. Standing tall and all decked-out, we looked like pilots, but we knew we all had a very long way to go before earning the coveted silver wings.

We soon learned a new tradition: until we soloed, we had to wear our goggles around our necks and under our chins. Once we soloed, we could wear our goggles on the forehead as all the "hot pilots" did. Thus, with a quick glance, we could tell who had soloed. Obviously, we all sought to become one of the "hot pilots."

I was enthralled to be at Decatur. I was one step closer to becoming a United States Army Air Forces pilot.

The training day started at 0530 hours with breakfast served at 0630 hours. Class started promptly at 0730 hours. One week we would have class in the morning and fly in the afternoon. The next week, we would rotate classroom training and flight training. The day ended at 1800 hours with a retreat ceremony and the rest of the evening was spent studying.

I worked hard to be an exceptional student. I asked a lot of questions in class, and as a result many of the students later queried me with their own questions. I obliged for some of them; others I told curtly to "kiss my ass!" to the guys who thought I asked too many questions in class.

If we weren't flying or spending time in the classroom, we were exercising, receiving instruction in the Link trainer, or shooting rifles and pistols on the firing range.

All of this activity created a healthy appetite. Meals were always great and well prepared. The dining hall was clean and quite attractive. We sat in groups of eight students to a table with no instructors in our area.

Mail Call was always welcome. Mail was distributed by administrative personnel and placed in individual mail boxes. Billie wrote to me about three times a week, my mother at least once a week. Though she had only a sixth grade education, my mother had the most beautiful handwriting I have ever seen. Maxine, my younger sister, wrote me about once every two weeks. I relished reading any mail I received, especially from Billie.

My first flight, an orientation flight, came on February 2, 1943, and my second flight occurred eight days later. Quite often, the winter months in northern Alabama did not offer the best flying weather, especially for a beginning student.

The Link Trainer Room at Pryor Field housed the Link Trainers. These early flight simulators were an important part of a cadet's flying curriculum.

(Carolinas Aviation Museum)

Before any student went aloft, one or more of the instructors would gather his students around a chalk-board drawing of the local area and brief the them on important landmarks. (Carolinas Aviation Museum)

There were some periods we did not fly for a full week. Retention of what was learned suffered greatly.

Much to its credit, the Southern Aviation Training School developed a safety map to be used for emergency landings. This map gave a detailed view of the school's flying practice area and was keyed with guide letters. Its ingenious design allowed any instructor or student to determine his position quickly in the event of a forced landing or crack up. Thus, emergency equipment from the home school could be dispatched to the scene quickly.

Four cadets were assigned to each instructor. My instructor was a young man named James P. Owens from Youngstown, Ohio. We never used his full name and addressed him simply as "Mr. Owens". He was a very capable gentleman and he did a fine job instructing. Much to my surprise, I learned years

later that Mr. Owens was only eight days older than I and that he was the youngest instructor in the Southeastern Training Command. (See Endnotes, Chapter 3)

James P. Owens was Hal Weekley's primary instructor at Pryor Field.
(Carolinas Aviation Museum)

Each lesson lasted about thirty to forty minutes. When one student returned, another student quickly filled the empty seat in the Stearman. Invariably, they'd ask the student who had just returned what was covered, what he did, and what was expected.

We honed our flying skills with each lesson and learned quickly the three most important elements of Army Air Forces flying: "The right way, the wrong way and the Army way." We learned to maintain correct altitude, to maintain airspeed, and to keep the needle and ball centered, except during aerobatics. These last three points gave all us the necessary foundation for future instrument flight training.

Mr. Owens was a good instructor. He did not exhibit the poor attitude and quality of instruction like many of the other instructors. Many of the instructors could handle the aircraft, but they were often rude and their instructing capabilities were very limited.

I remember an instructor who had his students seated at a table next to us. At the conclusion of the first day's orientation flights, he asked if anyone had any questions. At that time, none of them knew enough to ask questions. The cadets replied, "No, Sir!" to which he commented haughtily, "Well, I guess you know it all."

Later, I heard one of his students comment, "I'm going to ask a question tomorrow. That way he's not going to pull that same stunt on me again".

At the conclusion of the next day's training, the instructor asked if there were any questions. The young student queried, "Sir, could you explain torque to us?"

The egotistical instructor looked intently at his young charges and merely commented, "Hell, everybody knows all about torque."

The Decatur airfield was nothing more than a rolling meadow with high and low spots, but this pastoral layout did provide its share of challenges for any student landing or taking off. If one flared for a landing on one of the high spots, he would overshoot and drop into one of the low spots with quite a thump. On the other hand, if he attempted to land in one of the low spots, he was sure to hit one of the high places and end up bouncing into the air. I was very lucky that I never dragged a wingtip, but I did scare a couple of the instructors.

Under Mr. Owens patient tutelage, I quickly mastered loops, rolls and snap rolls. I learned, also, how to land the Stearman in the most brisk of crosswinds. I gained confidence with every flight and I knew my opportunity

The relationship between an instructor and his students was most important. The instructor's main responsibility was to teach his young charges, "The right way, the wrong way and the Army way!"
(Carolinas Aviation Museum)

Cadets check out parachutes in the ready room.   (Carolinas Aviation Museum)

Cadets receive a final briefing from their instructor before making a flight.   (Carolinas Aviation Museum)

A group of Southern Aviation Training School student pilots gather on the airfield in front the control tower (left) and under an awning (below) to share flying stories and wait to fly once more. Note they are wearing their goggles on top of their flight helmets, signifying they had soloed.

(Carolinas Aviation Museum)

to solo was rapidly approaching.

My first solo came on March 2, 1943, exactly one month after my orientation flight. I was both confident and exuberant. There are few words that describe my thrill during my seventeen-minute flight! I soloed after a total of 10:28 hours of instruction. Now, I could wear my flying goggles on my forehead and join the elite group of "hot pilots."

I was extremely proud the day I soloed. I

Checking the paperwork before any flight was an important part of a cadet's daily flying routine.
(Carolinas Aviation Museum)

realized I had the potential to become a military pilot and become a contributor to my country's successful prosecution of the war.

Billie came to town the day I soloed. I was thrilled to see her and give her the news of my successful flight. We went to one of the nicest restaurants in Decatur to celebrate. It was a double thrill for me to see her and to tell her that I had soloed that same afternoon, even if it was only for seventeen minutes.

Other than in the evenings, I had very little opportunity to see Billie. Worse, she had to spend several days in town by herself.

That was the situation until I decided to leave the airfield the same way many of the other guys used to go into town. There was a hole underneath the perimeter fence north of my relatively comfortable barracks. I decided since Billie had come so far and since I wanted to spend more time with her, I should take advantage of that hole in the fence.

Most people got through this hole without any difficulty, but the night I went to town to see Billie, I got caught when I came back through the hole in the fence by a civilian guard standing there with an Army Colt .45-cal. automatic in hand. This incident

Hungry cadets gather to enjoy one of the day's three delicious and filling meals.
(Carolinas Aviation Museum)

The formal Graduation ceremony above was followed by a well-deserved Graduation dance.

(Carolinas Aviation Museum)

nearly washed me out of the program.

To resolve this infraction, I was put up for a check ride to see if I was pilot material. Thankfully, my instructor got me to the point where the evaluating check pilot didn't feel I should be washed out. He did feel, however, I should be disciplined, so I spent quite some time walking tours.

Other students in my class were not as fortunate. Exactly one-half of my class (Cadet Class 43-G) washed-out of Primary Flying Training for various reasons. Some cadets couldn't handle the aerobatics, whereas others couldn't defeat their airsickness. Most made flying mistakes serious enough to "wash-out."

I did have my own scares a few times and once came uncomfortably close to "washing-out" during a solo flight. I was approaching the airfield from the south at about the point where I crossed the Tennessee River, I encountered a tremendous downdraft and dropping several hundred feet really scared the hell out of me! I wanted to land as-soon-as-possible and I flew into the traffic pattern and entered the downwind leg completely ignoring the other aircraft in the landing pat-tern. In my haste, I cut in front of another air-plane that had a check pilot on board.

After landing, the irate check pilot met me at my airplane and we had a "prayer meeting." He put me up for a checkride, which I flew with the offended check pilot. Fortunately, I flew this ride exceptionally well. The check pilot commented I did too good a job to be washed-out, thought I had learned my lesson and told me I should continue in the program.

After completing 60:01 hours in the PT-17, I finished Primary Flying Training on March 28, 1943.

My graduating class from Decatur consisted of seven student officers, several First and Second Lieutenants, one Warrant Officer and one hundred and one Cadets. The first man to graduate was Charles D. Albury from

Miami, Florida. He and I went through flight training together from primary through advanced. Later, he learned to fly B-17s at Columbus, Ohio. I trained with Donald C. Snyder of Wooster, Ohio, who drove Billie and me to and from Florida during a later assignment. Another fellow cadet and great friend was James A. Poston of Columbus, Ohio. He gained much recognition later in life when, as a Lieutenant Colonel, he won the Ricks Trophy for a record speed flight from Ontario, California to Detroit, Michigan in a Republic F-84F fighter jet at a speed of 545.505 miles-per-hour in the corrected time of 2 hours, 57 minutes and 14 seconds. Joseph G. Sullivan was another roommate and a fellow graduate. He was a little guy, always full of life and fun, and was always great to be around. All of these friends added many wonderful memories.

Shortly after graduation, I bid my friends goodbye and good luck and left Decatur, Alabama for Basic Flying Training at Green-

wood Army Air Field near Greenwood, Mississippi in pursuit of the coveted, USAAF silver wings. In early April 1943, I left Decatur's familiar and comfortable single story brick buildings for Greenwood Army Air Field's standard-issue, one-story wood structures with roofs made of tar and paper. Moreover, Army Air Forces instructors would train me, replacing civilian-attired instructors.

Greenwood Army Air Field was located about six miles east of Greenwood, Mississippi, with the Mississippi River no more than sixty miles to the west. Countless acres of brown farmland and white-topped cotton fields surrounded Greenwood. To the north, west and south, this rich farmland was flat as far as the eye could see. Yet, the earth rose sharply several miles east of the airfield. When I arrived, the days were becoming quite warm as an early spring took hold of the area.

As a whole, I found the changes in the liv-

The Vultee BT-13A and B-15 were an ideal pilot training airplanes and featured a more powerful engine and a full instrument panel. Due to the BTs propensity to shake and rattle in flight, especially during stalls and spins, pilots nicknamed them the "Vultee Vibrator." Formally painted blue and yellow, all Army Air Forces primary and basic trainers were painted in silver to conform to AAF regulations that went into effect in early 1942.   (Peter M. Bowers)

Except for minor power plant changes, the Vultee BT-13A and BT-15 were virtually identical airplanes. The BT-13A was powered by a Pratt & Whitney R-985-AN-1 engine, whereas the BT-15 was powered by a Wright R-975-11 engine. Both engines were 450 hp. (San Diego Aerospace Museum)

ing accommodations quite depressing, though not totally unexpected. We always had advance information from cadets who had washed-out and from other word-of-mouth sources. Nothing changed when I arrived. The accommodations were depressingly bad and they remained that way after I left.

The training airplanes during this Basic Flying Training phase were the Vultee BT-13A "Valiant" and the Vultee BT-15, the latter possessing the same airframe as the BT-13A, but with a different radial engine. Both airplanes had a 450 horsepower radial engine on the nose, which was more than twice the power of the PT-17 Stearman. The pilot managed this tremendous power with a two-position propeller, a flatter pitch for takeoff and another pitch for more efficient cruise flight. Due to the Vultee's propensity

to shake and rattle appreciably in flight, pilots nicknamed the BT-13 trainers the "Vultee Vibrator".

Despite this term of endearment, the airplane possessed one characteristic that all of the students appreciated; the BT-13/15 had a wider landing gear than the PT-17 Stearman. Thus, takeoffs and landings were much easier, essentially making ground loops a worry of the past.

There were, as well, many more differences. The "Vultee Vibrator" possessed a pair of sliding canopies, which provided for an enclosed cockpit. The nostalgic days of training with silk scarves, leather helmets and flying goggles were replaced with rubber-cupped earphones and a handheld microphone.

The "Vultee Vibrator" also featured a full instrument panel. The vast array of instruments allowed the students to improve their instrument flying skills and techniques. Unlike the Stearman where a big sky surrounded the student with the wind in his face and the pressure on his bottom to tell him which way was up or down, the BT-13 and BT-15 had an almost dizzying array of instruments to convey the same information. In time, I would master these flight instruments.

Before I ever sat in a "Vultee Vibrator," I had to face my biggest hurdle, the instructors.

While marching down the flight line for our first orientation, a couple of loud-mouthed officers shouted warnings to us about our future in the program. We soon learned the loudest, most obnoxious individual in this group was one of our instructors.

The BT-13A and BT-15 instrument panel presented the novice pilot cadet an almost dizzying array of instruments.

(San Diego Aerospace Museum)

Later, we discovered he had been one of the poorest students in his pilot training class and that he had been assigned to be an instructor. A large, overbearing guy, he hailed from Boston and did a lot of drinking at night. In the morning, he would get a Coca-Cola and throw the empty bottle against a wall. Afterwards, we would go fly. Many instructors thought they were gods and rather than work with a student to keep him flying, they made every effort to "wash-out" a cadet trying to do his best for his country. This obnoxious instructor was new to the organization and exhibited a loathsome attitude towards his students.

For some reason, the USAAF sent their best pilots to combat and often sent their worst to become flight instructors. The British and Canadian armed forces, on the other hand, had the sterling reputation of retaining their better graduates for instructor positions. I always thought this method was better for the student.

When I met Lt. Siegfield, one of my instructors, for the first time, he told me and the seven other eager cadets at my table he could only fly six students and he would have to wash out two cadets immediately. He also told us that even though we heard the BT trainer was a killer airplane, he was going to prove to us that it wasn't. In reality, we had never heard anything about the BT trainers being "killers."

With distinctive bravado, Lt. Siegfield was anxious to prove the "Vultee Vibrator" was a safe airplane. He stated he was going to give one of us a ten-turn spin on the first flight and then asked for volunteers. I didn't think I was up for this guy's first demonstration, especially after what I learned about volunteering while I was at the classification center at Nashville. As such, I held back.

Cadet Martin Sefca, who had come to us after a tour of duty with the U.S. Army in Panama, volunteered to go first. I thought Sefca would get a ten-turn spin and that I might survive after all. After about an hour, Sefca and our esteemed instructor returned. I asked Sefca if he got a ten-turn spin and he said no. Now, it was my turn to fly. I had no option, as I had indicated earlier that I would take the second flight, so off we went.

After a short demonstration of some basic maneuvers, Lt. Siegfield said he was going to show me his famous ten-turn spin. Upon entering the spin, I learned quickly why the BT was nicknamed the "Vultee Vibrator." The airplane shook badly. It shook so badly that I thought the engine was going to fall off.

As we continued in our rotations, I started to ease in a little opposite rudder in an attempt to get the aircraft out of the spin. I should have known better. Without hesitation, Lt. Siegfield immediately gave me a lecture on who had control of the aircraft and that I was to stay off the controls!

Upon recovery, he flew the BT to about ten to fifteen feet off the ground and proceeded to fly along some fence lines. After this demonstration, we returned to base. He picked up another student and went aloft once more. I had a hair-raising story to tell my classmates.

Cadet Harold Weekley, right, talks with a fellow student before beginning another training flight in the "Vultee Vibrator" at Greenwood Army Air Field, Mississippi in March 1943. (Harold D. Weekley)

The training program at Greenwood Army Air Field was an advanced continuation of my earlier training program at Decatur. In the classroom, my fellow cadets and I continued to study Army Air Forces' policy and regulations, aircraft recognition, power plant and systems, physics, meteorology and navigation. We learned how to take radio code at eight words per minute. Outside the classroom we drilled, ran and exercised every day.

Both the Vultee BT-13A and the BT-15 carried a lot of fuel and were capable of some long cross-country flights, so a very strong emphasis was placed on navigation. All cadets learned to use the sectional charts, the aviator's road map, and plot their own cross-country flights with an E6-B computer, a circular slide rule-type device used to plan our flights and update our progress en route. We mastered fuel consumption computations and the effects of wind on range.

Similarly, a strong emphasis was placed on instrument flight training. I honed these skills in ground school, in the Link trainer and during actual in-flight practice before I attempted any cross-country instrument flight.

The most important lesson we learned from instrument flight training was not to trust our senses but, instead, to rely on the airplane's flight instruments to tell up from down. To do otherwise could result in pilot disorientation followed by aircraft structural failure. We learned that early in the war, more pilots were lost to vertigo than to enemy action.

Formation flying was an important part of the syllabus so, as training progressed, instrument and formation training received considerable emphasis.

We also received intensive night flying instruction. This instruction, coupled with our instrument training, proved invaluable. On several occasions while flying in the hazy, moonless skies above west central Mississippi, there was no discernable horizon. The bright stars often blended with the lights on the ground. The artificial horizon and the other instruments located on the center of the BT's wide panel kept us from harm's way.

Later in this training phase, after we had

Cadet Harold Weekley prepares for another training flight in the "Vultee Vibrator" at Greenwood Army Air Field, Mississippi in March 1943.
(Harold D. Weekley)

me discussing their morning 'buddy flight." One said to the other, "That was sure a nice job you did buzzing that little town to the north with the big water tower."

The other cadet hesitated for a moment and replied, "Man, I thought you were flying. It wasn't me!"

Other stories abounded. I heard of a cadet who returned to base with pine tree residue in the left wing landing gear and light. He was still swearing he was never below 5,000 feet as he was being escorted out the front gate. Another time, a cadet went down to buzz a river boat on the Mississippi River. He forgot he had the propeller in the low pitch, high RPM position. When he advanced the throttle to full open it caused the propeller tips to go supersonic. In turn, he blew out the windows on the boat's wheel house.

Both incidents were cause for much discussion back at base.

While I was still in Basic Flying Training, my fellow cadets and I were given a sheet of paper on which we could indicate our preference as to the kind of aircraft we would like to fly in combat. Dreams of being a fighter pilot remained dear to my heart and I selected the Lockheed P-38 as my first choice. The Douglas A-20 bomber and the North American B-25 bomber followed, in that order. I wanted to fly something in combat in which I could show a little aggression and individuality. I most certainly did not want anything larger such as a four-engine bomber.

received a reasonable amount of time flying with and without an instructor, we were allowed to fly with another cadet in the airplane. Called "buddy flights," we would practice instrument flying from the back seat while the cadet in the front seat cleared us from other aircraft and kept us in the flying practice area. This concept was great and could be productive if used properly, but the temptation to vary from the intended curriculum was too great and we engaged in some very low altitude flying, or "buzzing," of open towns and fields, something virtually every enthusiastic fledgling pilot enjoyed doing.

One day, after the morning flight periods, we were all standing in the chow line for lunch when I overheard two cadets in front of

After completing 71:48 hours in the Vultee BTs, I left Greenwood, Mississippi for Blytheville Army Air Field in Blytheville, Arkansas for Advanced Flying Training. I left Greenwood on May 27th, 1943 and was to report in Blytheville in the first week of June. It seemed I was always assigned to report to a new school at the beginning of the month and then transferred to the next school near the end of the following month. Each school I attended was approximately two months long.

Advanced Flying Training was my last training stage before I could receive a Second Lieutenant's commission and the coveted silver wings of a United States Army Air Forces pilot. This last school would determine if I would go to flying the fighters I dreamed of or the large, multi-engine bombers I dreaded.

Blytheville was located in the far northestern corner of Arkansas and was about eighty miles north of Memphis, Tennessee. The Missouri state line was less than ten miles north and the mighty Mississippi River was less than ten miles to the east. The landscape, rich with cotton fields, was flat as far as the eye could see.

The base was activated in July 1942, as an advanced flying school in the Southeastern Training Command's pilot training program. It carried this function until the end of World War II. After the war, the base was used to process military personnel being discharged. Closed in late 1945, it was reactivated in 1955 as Blytheville Air Force Base, home to the 461st Bombardment Wing flying B-47s and, later, B-52s. The base was renamed Eaker Air Force Base in 1988 in honor of General Ira C. Eaker, an air pioneer and the first commander of the Eighth Air Force in World War II. The base closed in 1992, and the facilities were turned over to local civilian control.

Training at Blytheville Army Air Field was conducted in the North American AT-6, the Curtiss-Wright AT-9 and Beech AT-10, the first being a single-engine, all-metal monoplane whereas the last two were multi-engine trainers. The AT-6 was used to train cadets in air-to-ground gunnery, whereas the AT-9 trained pilots for action in my beloved P-38. In addition, the AT-9 and AT-10 were used to train cadets for heavier, multi-engine equipment, which I did not want to fly.

Despite my best efforts to the contrary, but still according to normal military procedure and protocol, I was assigned to train in the AT-9 and AT-10. Disappointed with this assignment, I went immediately to the squadron commander of the AT-6 squadron and asked to transfer to his group. After giving the matter some thought, he granted my request.

When my AT-9/AT-10 commander heard of this change, he came to me and told me I would either be in his squadron or I would be eliminated from flight training altogether. Thus, the decision was made for me; I went into multi-engine training.

The flight instructors at Blytheville were all Army Air Forces rated pilots, and were more proficient and professional than the instructors I had at Greenwood. I was grateful for this change. Though I do not recall his name, my instructor at Blytheville was a particularly fine pilot and I enjoyed flying with him.

We flew AT-9s manufactured by the Curtiss-Wright Aircraft Company in St. Louis, Missouri. The AT-9 was a low-wing, two-place, multi-engine trainer powered by a pair of Lycoming R-680-9, 295 hp radial engines set close together. The centerlines of these engines were only eleven feet apart and it seemed the propeller arcs overlapped! Each engine turned a two-position, Hamilton-Standard metal propeller. The main landing gear was retractable, whereas the tail wheel was not. This plane was difficult to fly on one engine. The plane's exceptionally high wing loading produced an approach speed of 120-mph and a touchdown around 110-mph, which made it a handful to fly properly in a stiff crosswind. Worse, the AT-9 was prone to ground-looping.

The AT-9 carried the moniker "Jeep"

The Curtiss-Wright AT-9 "Jeep" was an ideal transitional aircraft to train Army Air Forces aviation cadets for heavier, multi-engine equipment.
(James B. Zazas)

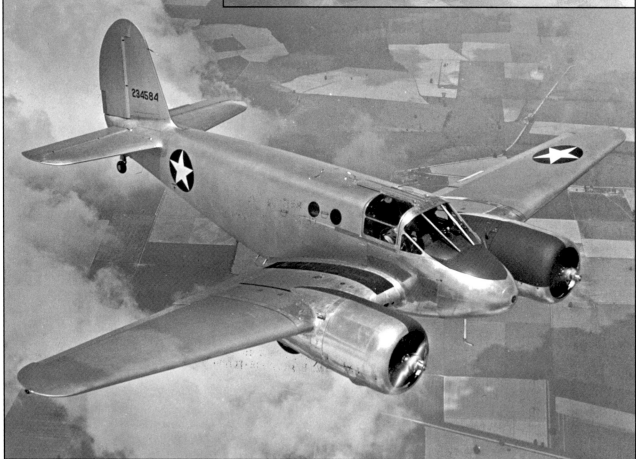

The Beech AT-10 "Wichita" was used to train future U.S. Army Air Forces pilots in multi-engine formation flying, advanced instrument procedures and night formation flying. Unlike the Curtiss-Wright AT-9's all-metal construction, the Beech AT-10 was made of wood and plywood covered with fabric, except for the pilots' compartment, which was an all-metal construction. A pair of 295 hp Lycoming R-680-9 radial engines provided the power.
(Peter M. Bowers)

("Fledgling" according to other sources) and was a noisy airplane to fly. Virtually no noise dampening was provided anywhere in its all-metal construction. Large windows provided ample visibility and allowed cockpit temperatures to build to punishing levels in the summertime. In the semi-standard of the period, the flight instruments were positioned on the left side of the instrument panel and the duplicate engine instruments were mounted on the right.

A pair of "Tell-tale" indicator lights was located on the panel's upper right, a forerunner to the annunciator panel used on more modern aircraft. The "Tell-tale" unit was designed to indicate what was right and what was wrong with the aircraft while in flight. If all was well, the panel was blank. If anything was wrong with the aircraft's configuration, engine oil temperature, pressures or cockpit procedures, the panel would light-up. Keeping these lights blank bedeviled a lot of flying cadets and instructors.

The Beech Aircraft Company of Wichita, Kansas and the Globe Aircraft Corporation of Dallas, Texas produced the AT-10, nicknamed the "Wichita". It was procured originally to be a navigator trainer, but was soon pressed into service as an advanced, two-place multi-engine trainer. At first glance, the AT-10 looked somewhat similar to the better-known Beech AT-7 or AT-11 "Twin Beech,"

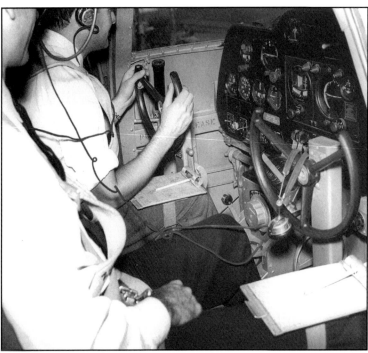

The Curtiss-Wright AT-9 honed a pilot's multi-engine and instrument skills and prepared him to fly more complex multi-engine airplanes such as the Boeing B-17.

(National Museum of the United States Air Force)

but possessed a single fin and rudder. A pair of 295 hp Lycoming R-680-9 radial engines provided the power.

Unlike the stout, all-metal construction of the Curtiss-Wright AT-9 or its Beech cousins, the AT-10 was made of wood and fabric except for the pilot's compartment, which was an all-metal construction. Beech foresaw a possible shortage in metal and wanted to sub-contract production as much as possible. Beech Aircraft Company turned to furniture manufacturers to fabricate various AT-10 parts.

The sole purpose of the Curtiss-Wright AT-9 and the Beech AT-10 were to train multi-engine pilots as fast as possible then push them into operational combat units. I mastered my multi-engine and instrument flying skills in the AT-9 "Jeep" and the AT-10 "Wichita," for which both airplanes allowed me to do a fine job.

As could be expected in a multi-engine flight-training program, we spent a lot of time studying engine-out procedures and their accompanying drag and corrective trim techniques, advanced instrument procedures and formation flying. The formation flying was fun and relatively easy, but the instrument training caused sleepless nights for many trainees. In fact, many cadets washed-out of Advanced Flying Training during the instrument flight training phase.

Three Curtiss-Wright AT-9 "Jeep" trainers fly in formation over the Blytheville, Arkansas countryside. The sporty, all-metal AT-9 was powered by a pair of Lycoming R-680-9, 295 hp radial engines and proved to be an excellent multi-engine training airplane. (Peter M. Bowers)

The instrument training was divided into two parts. The first part was learning how to fly and navigate the radio ranges, or radio range navigation. The second part involved how to recover to a straight and level flight from an unusual attitude by reference to only the flight instruments. I spent a lot of time in the Link Trainer learning and perfecting my instrument scan and flying skills before I applied them in flight.

Radio range navigation presented its own set of unique skills to learn. The radio range was engineered so that four radio beams were transmitted at ninety degrees to each other, generally one beam to the north or northerly direction and the others in relation to that beam. Each adjacent leg of the range transmitted a slightly different signal, and the signals of adjacent legs would overlap slightly, thus, forming the range legs or beams.

On one side of the beam, the signal would be an "A" signal or a dit-dahh tone. The other side of the beam would have an "N" signal, or a dahh-dit tone. When these signals meshed exactly, there would be only a steady tone. When we flew over the transmitting station, there would be only silence; thus referred to as the "cone of silence."

Putting it all together, I learned how to determine in which quadrant I was flying, how to intersect the beam, and how to determine if I was flying towards or away from the transmitter. I determined the latter by turning the radio down to where I could just barely hear the Morse Code identifier, then listen closely if the signal strength got louder or softer; thus, closer or further away respectively.

During training approaches, I was required to fly the beam to 500 feet or so and be reasonably lined-up with the runway, all the while flying the plane under a hood designed to restrict my forward visibility. When I thought I was at the prescribed place on the approach, I'd turn the controls over to the instructor and say, "You've got it!" The instructor would allow me to remove the hood and see where I placed the airplane on the instrument approach. It was always a good feeling to see the runway ahead or slightly to one side or the other. A gentle side-slip of the airplane and we were on the runway.

Flying on instruments was not particularly difficult, but it required a lot of study, hard work and practice to be proficient enough to meet the Army Air Forces' demanding standards.

After we mastered instruments, we started formation flying training. Formation flying was quite fun as now I had two engines to control. I could maintain close position by gently twisting my wrist on the two throttles rather than having to constantly move the ailerons and rudder as I did in the BTs at Greenwood. The key to smooth formation flying was smooth power and control inputs and anticipation. I learned how to make the required inputs before they were actually needed.

Night formation flying was a new and challenging experience for me. Each airplane had lights positioned on the wingtips and tail. In clear weather, it was relatively easy to maintain position, but on cloudy or hazy nights, which were more of the norm for this time of the year, keeping those lights in proper position proved quite challenging. It was easy to become disoriented and confused.

My training at Blytheville proved invalu-

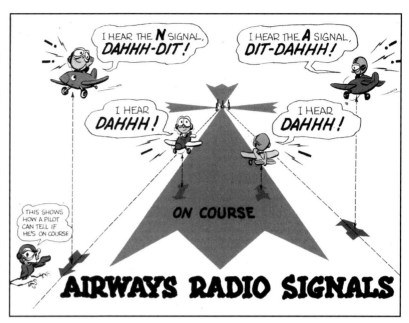

able and I had relatively few problems in the program, but I did have a memorable problem in each airplane.

On my second flight with a fellow cadet serving as my co-pilot in the AT-10, I had a landing gear malfunction and had to land gear-up. Everything was fine until I was on final approach when I heard the control tower advise the crash crew that the disabled aircraft was about to touch down. Only then did I become a little concerned. We landed successfully with no adverse affects. However, given the AT-10's all-wood construction, had it caught fire, it would have been spectacular.

The all-metal AT-9 caused me some concern on my next to last flight in Advanced Flying Training. I was on a night cross-country flight when I had an engine failure over Memphis on the last leg of the mission. I could have landed in Memphis, but I wanted to get back to base as my mother had come down for my graduation, so I flew back to base on one engine. My mother was always a great worrier and I didn't want to frighten her by arriving late. She worried when I got my first bicycle, my first motorcycle and my first automobile, so I knew she wouldn't be thrilled about me having an emergency in an airplane at night. I got back to my base with no further problems and confided my experience to a very relieved mother.

Many of my fellow cadets and I perfected our low-altitude "buzzing" skills while flying at Blytheville. The terrain in this part of Arkansas is very flat and ideal for agriculture. Many of us took great pleasure in buzzing the cotton fields, particularly in the AT-9. During June and July, the cotton was rather high and we would fly along the tops of the cotton plants literally knocking off their tops with the propellers. The cotton pickers in the field would see us bearing down on them and would dive to the ground for safety. By the time we completed our first pass and

This nighttime photograph shows the AT-9 "Jeep's" functional lines to a good advantage. (Peter M. Bowers)

turned to come back for a second pass, the whole group of cotton pickers were running down the rows to get as far away from the buzzing aircraft as they possibly could.

I'm reminded of a stunt that a Navy Cadet from the nearby Naval Air Station Memphis pulled during that period. He had a girlfriend in Arkansas close to the Mississippi River and would visit with her every opportunity. The Navy Cadet would fly over, land on top of the levee and meet with his girlfriend. One day, he was so taken with the thought of seeing the young lady that he failed to extend his landing gear and he slid to a dusty halt on top of the levee.

Being a very bright young man, he came up with one of the best cover-ups I have ever heard and he survived his embarrassment with no loss of dignity. He immediately got on the radio and contacted Navy Memphis to tell them the story that he was at a certain altitude in that particular area and that he had suffered an engine failure. He advised them that he had a levee in sight and it looked like a pretty good landing spot. Navy Memphis advised him to go ahead and proceed with a

wheels-up landing on the levee, which he had already completed very nicely, unbeknownst to them. This cadet advised Navy Memphis that he had landed on the levee with minimum damage and that he would stand by on the radio to receive further instructions.

Though the U.S. Navy may not have thought so, I thought this cadet deserved a "well done" award.

Shortly before graduation, I flew to Greenwood, Mississippi to try and convince the next class of graduating cadets to select multi-engine training as their next assignment. My visit proved successful and the USAAF gained many new multi-engine pilot recruits as a result.

My Army Air Forces training class, Cadet Class 43-G, graduated from Blytheville Army Air Field on July 28, 1943, six months after starting the flight school program. I graduated in the top ten of my class of 149 cadets. The graduation was a short, formal affair. Each graduate received his pair of Silver Wings and certificate of commission as a Second Lieutenant in the United States Army

Air Forces. The presentation of wings was alphabetical and the visitors were asked to hold their applause until the last certificate was presented.

Being last, I received all the applause. Billie was unable to attend my graduation, but my mother was in attendance and she was very proud. I thought it was wonderful my mother could attend considering the distance and difficulties involved in traveling from Steubenville, Ohio to Blytheville, Arkansas. Receiving my USAAF pilot rating was perhaps the greatest thrill of my life next to becoming a husband and a father.

I fulfilled my dreams, sort of. Although I was not destined to fly a swift fighter, I received my coveted Silver Wings and the gleaming gold bars of an U.S. Army Air Forces officer. My mother, Billie and I were all very proud of my accomplishment!

My pilot logbook was growing. My total flying time was 273:31 hours with an additional 33 hours in the Link Trainer. More entries quickly followed.

Second Lieutenant Harold D. Weekley beams proudly after receiving his pilot's wings and his commission in the United States Army Air Forces on July 28, 1943. (Harold D. Weekley)

"Leadership and learning are indispensable to each other."
John Fitzgerald Kennedy (1917–1963), *Remarks*
prepared for delivery at the Trade Mart in Dallas
[November 22, 1963]

CHAPTER 4

Meeting and Mastering the B-17

The day after graduation, my mother and I returned to Steubenville, Ohio for some much deserved rest and time at home. I had to report to Hendricks Field near Sebring, Highlands County, in south-central Florida on August 4, 1943, for flight training in the Boeing B-17 Flying Fortress; therefore, I had only seven days to get my mother home, visit with my family and Billie, and get to Florida. This really wasn't a lot of time considering the state of transportation in 1943. My only options to get to base were train, bus, or catching a ride.

Fortunately, Lt. Donald Snyder of Wooster, Ohio, one of my B-17 classmates and an earlier Greenwood classmate, and his new bride were driving to Sebring. They agreed to pick me up at home and let me ride with them to Florida.

In the meantime, I talked Billie into taking a vacation and going to Florida with us. On August 1st, Billie, Don, his new wife and I started our long drive south. To minimize our travel time, we drove straight through to Florida, all in the days before the interstate highways, which at that time was quite a feat.

On the way, I tried to talk Billie into marrying me, but she was afraid we would argue a lot and didn't like that prospect. It was a long trip, on questionable roads in an old car with gasoline ration stamps, so I had time on my side. The time factor allowed me the opportunity to present my case over and over again. In the end, she

Billie Wigginton and Harold Weekley pose for a photograph shortly after Hal received his pilot's wings and a commission in the United States Army Air Forces.　(Harold D. Weekley)

agreed to be my wife.

We arrived in Sebring on August 3rd in the middle of the night. Fortunately, we found a hotel with two vacancies, one for Don and his bride, and one for Billie and me. This was during an era when you didn't sleep with a girl or woman for three years before you decided to get married. So what would be the sleeping arrangements?

Of course, I told Billie to take the bed and I would sleep in the overstuffed chair. She didn't think this was a good idea since we had all been sitting in the car for two days. She came up with a better way to solve the problem; we both could sleep on the bed. She would be under the blankets and I would sleep on top. Her plan worked great.

The next morning Billie and I were supposed to meet Don and his bride at a small coffee shop they had spotted when we arrived the night before. On our way to meet our friends, Billie and I walked past the county courthouse and thought we should stop in and inquire about getting a marriage license. After receiving the necessary papers, the clerk

Newlyweds, Billie and Harold Weekley pose together near their apartment in Sebring, Florida in August 1943. Hal was going through his initial B-17 training at nearby Hendricks Field during this time.　(Harold D. Weekley)

asked who was going to marry us. Billie and I looked at each other with blank expressions and replied we didn't know. Perhaps amused by the young couple standing before her, the clerk informed us that the judge was available and that he would be happy to do the honor. By the time we met our friends for breakfast, Billie and I were already husband and wife.

I couldn't have been happier. Here I was a young man from a poor family getting ready to fly one of the largest aircraft in the world, and having just married the most beautiful girl I have ever seen. She still is!

After breakfast, Don and I reported to Hendricks Field for the beginning of another new flying experience. We had no sooner arrived and checked the first day's training schedule than we learned our initial lessons included Ditching. I didn't know this lesson meant airplane ditching, so I made some wisecrack to the effect that if I was going to have anything to do with ditches, then the instructors could think again. I definitely had egg on my face over this gaffe.

When the day's lessons were over, the Lieutenant who gave us our orientation advised us that we were all restricted to base. I was dumbstruck! I told the Lieutenant that I had just gotten married that morning and that I did not relish being restricted to base on my wedding night. The Lieutenant looked at me with a somewhat quizzical expression, thought about my emphatic statement for a moment, then out of the kindness of his heart told me I could return to Sebring to celebrate. I am sure I heard him chuckle after we exchanged salutes.

Our training days were too busy to notice that a very important B-17 had visited the base. The famous *Memphis Belle*, commanded by Lt. Col. Robert Morgan, stopped by on the weekend of August 6 - 8, 1943. Col. Morgan and crew - the first to complete twenty-five missions over Europe - talked to an excited gathering of officers, students, and enlisted men and women. This visit was one of the first stops made by this bomber and crew during their nationwide Savings Bond Tour. Years later, Col. Bob Morgan and I would meet several times and in less formal settings.

Meanwhile, Billie kept herself busy and took on the assignment of finding the newest couple in Sebring, Florida a place to live. Billie's task was all the more difficult because housing on base was very limited, if not impossible to find.

In each new class, there were always a large number of newly married couples, all of them looking for places to live. Sebring was a relatively small town, and never had a great number of places in which newly married couples could start their lives together. Sebring's local folk recognized this acute housing shortage and responded graciously. Many townsfolk opened their homes to accommodate the growing military presence. Still, housing remained in very short supply.

Billie didn't have much luck finding a place that first day, so we spent our wedding night in the Sebring Hotel, in the middle of town. (See Endnotes, Chapter 4)

By the third day, Billie found a cute little three-room apartment on the ground floor in the front of the Grey Top Inn. This beautifully-framed inn, with its three buildings connected by an open porch, was almost halfway between the Sebring Hotel and beautiful Lake Hamilton.

The inn was situated on the left side of West Center Street, which ran downhill from Sebring's center to the City Pier on the lake. The pier had two small buildings nearby, one on each of a wide concrete driveway. Approaching the lake, there was a large grassy area, a band shell, two separate dressing areas for boys and girls, a concession stand that faced the pier and a wood diving board at the end of the pier. The small building on the right was the USO club, a social haven for soldiers, sailors and airmen, regardless of rank or branch of service. The clean, sand-bottom lake made for very good diving and swimming.

I was very proud of Billie and thought she

had done very well, indeed!

Sebring itself was a very beautiful little town and remains so today. Sebring's fine climate and almost cosmopolitan atmosphere combined to lure tourists from all over the United States then and continues to do so today. Golf, tennis, baseball, fishing, hunting and many other activities added to the long list of recreational activities. At the time Billie and I lived there, the major source of income in that part of Florida was citrus growing, farming, cattle ranching and tourism. Overall, Billie and I found Sebring to be a very friendly town and a great place to live.

Sebring's streets were clean and the good folks who operated the shops along the palm tree-lined streets welcomed the growing military presence. In fact, it was the Sebring and Highland County officials who convinced the Army Air Forces in late 1940 and early 1941 to build an air base near their fine town. Actual base construction started in mid-1941.

Fruit trees abounded in the area. Orange and grapefruit trees were plentiful. We had a grapefruit tree behind our apartment. I used to go out into the back yard, climb the tree and eat fresh grapefruit. Billie could easily find me by walking out in the back yard and

The USO building on Sebring's Municipal Pier was a popular recreation location for service members.

(A.W. "Spizz" Pollard)

locating the tree where the peelings were falling to the ground.

Billie and I came from homes that were very clean and well kept. As such, we both had quite a surprise waiting for us when we encountered some of the insects native to this area in Florida. Our biggest bug problem occurred when we would buy a couple of pastries, either for a snack or for breakfast the following day, and these giant bugs insisted on getting into our sweets. The locals called them "water bugs." They were cockroaches to us.

Billie came up with a brilliant idea; she placed our sweets in a dish and, in turn, put this dish on a brick in the bathtub and surrounded it with water. Despite their moniker, these "water bugs" didn't care to go swimming to get to their food. This simple solution also proved effective against ants.

My B-17 training at Hendricks Field proved to be a most interesting and tremendously rewarding assignment. I was flying the best four-engine bomber that ever graced the skies. I may have some argument from the B-24 or the B-29 camps, but I never flew the B-24 or the B-29, so I can only comment accurately on the "Queen of the Skies," the B-17. It was not a P-38, the plane I sought to fly during my earlier flight training, but I did enjoy flying this aircraft tremendously!

Compared to the Curtiss-Wright AT-9 or Beech AT-10, the Boeing B-17 was BIG! The most advanced version, the B-17G model, had a wingspan of 103 feet, 9 inches, a length of 74 feet, 4 inches and a height of 19 feet, 2 inches. Four, Wright R-1820-97 Cyclone engines rated at 1200 horsepower apiece were mounted on the airplane's massive wings. When equipped for combat, at least thirteen .50-cal. machine-guns abounded on this "Flying Fortress."

The name "Flying Fortress" came from Richard L. Williams, a *Seattle Times* newspaper reporter who was present at the Boeing bomber's factory rollout several years earlier. He wrote in his article that the prototype

The Boeing B-17 was powered by four, Wright R-1820-97 Cyclone engines rated at 1200 horsepower apiece. Many engines were produced by The Studebaker Corporation, Aviation Division, in South Bend, Indiana under subcontract to Wright Aircraft Corporation. This photograph shows a Wright Aircraft Corporation R-1820-97 engine data plate.
(Curtiss Aldrich)

bomber, the Boeing Model 299, was a "Flying Fortress," a moniker that stuck and has endeared itself in the hearts of bomber crews and airplane enthusiasts worldwide. I am sure he had no idea then how prophetic his description would turn out to be.

The B-17 was a 10-man weapon. The ten crew positions were pilot, copilot, navigator, bombardier, flight engineer/top turret gunner, radio operator, right and left waist gunners, belly/ball turret gunner and tail gunner. Each position played a very important role in the overall successful operation of this aerial bomber.

The training materials I received clearly defined the specific duties and responsibilities of each position, but it would be several months before I integrated these defined duties with other crewmembers at a Combat Crew Training School. At Hendricks Field, I concentrated my efforts on mastering the B-17 and learning to fly as "First Pilot" in this bomber.

My job description was well defined. As the First Pilot, or simply pilot, I was the airplane's commander, responsible for the safety and efficiency of my crew. Through my leadership and command, I had to bring individuals of varied backgrounds and training

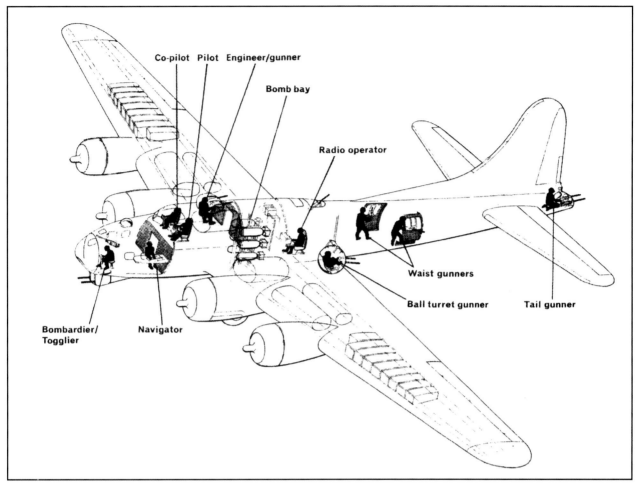

The B-17 was a nine or ten-man weapon. This drawing shows the crew positions usually manned during a combat mission.

together and have them perform as a team. I had to gain and maintain the crew's respect, confidence and trust, as this crew literally placed their lives in my hands. I learned quickly that I was not only checking-out in a superior weapons system, but I was being trained to be an aircraft commander, charged with all the duties and responsibilities of the efficient operation of my combat crew and airplane.

When many of us saw the B-17 for the first time, we thought a ladder was needed to gain entrance into this Flying Fortress; its nose sat so high off the ground. We learned quickly there were at least two preferred ways to enter the B-17. One could enter through a door provided on the right side of the fuselage, just aft of the right waist gunner posi-

tion. Or, one could enter through a small hatch/door located just aft of the navigator/bombardier station and just under the cockpit. Whereas the first entrance allowed the crewmember the ability to simply step-up and walk aboard the B-17, the latter required a bit more finesse as the crewmember had to literally climb aboard. He'd grasp the outside edge of the door's opening, palms facing him, then swing his legs up and over his head and into the cabin, all followed with a brisk pull to get the rest of the body inside. This task was quite simple while wearing a light-weight summer flight suit, but was more difficult when wearing bulky combat flying gear.

I was wordless the first time I sat in a B-17 cockpit! The view from the pilot's seat in the

The B-17 cockpit was a busy array of instruments, switches. throttles, mixture controls, propeller rpm controls and other controls. The prospective B-17 pilot had to quickly master every switch, knob and lever in the B-17's cockpit and memorize the aircraft's many procedures.

(Peter M. Bowers)

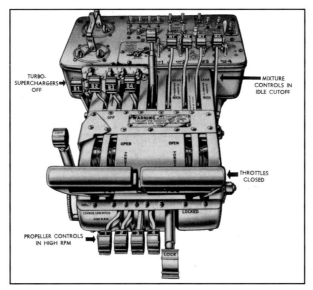

(B-17 Pilot Training Manual for the Flying Fortress)

B-17 was impressive. It was like looking down from a second story window above the flight line. In training, I adapted quickly to the new skills and techniques to determine how high one was off the runway during landing.

The cockpit was a virtual jungle of levers, switches and controls. There were almost four of everything! Four throttles, four mixture controls, four propeller rpm controls and four ignition switches, to name a few, not to mention the many switches for radios, lights, fuel transfer and other controls. We had to master this vast array quickly and memorize the location of every switch, knob and lever in the cockpit.

To test our knowledge, we had to perform a cockpit check, blindfolded. We had to sit in the cockpit, eyes blindfolded, and put our hands on every switch and every instrument and every control in the cockpit without hesitation when instructed. Simple in theory, the task proved somewhat difficult for those unfortunate students not intimately familiar with the cockpit and the precise location of every switch, lever and knob.

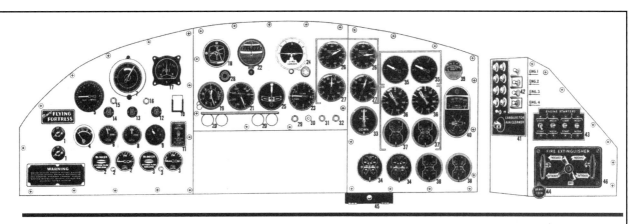

1. Fluorescent light switches
2. Pilot's oxygen flow indicator, warning light and pressure gage
3. Copilot's oxygen flow indicator, warning light and pressure gage
4. Voltmeter (AC)
5. Radio compass
6. Emergency oil pressure gage (Not on G)
7. Flux gate compass
8. Hydraulic oil pressure gage
9. Suction gage
10. Altimeter correction card
11. Airspeed alternate source switch
12. Vacuum warning light
13. Main system hydraulic oil warning light
14. Emergency system hydraulic oil warning light (Not on G)
15. Bomb door position light (Not on G)
16. Bomb release light
17. Pilot's directional indicator
18. Pilot's localizer indicator
19. Altimeter
20. Propeller feathering switches
21. Airspeed indicator
22. Directional gyro
23. Rate-of-climb indicator
24. Flight indicator
25. Turn-and-bank indicator
26. Manifold pressure gages
27. Tachometers
28. Marker beacon light
29. Globe test button
30. Bomber call light
31. Landing gear warning light
32. Tailwheel lock light
33. Flap position indicator
34. Cylinder-head temperature gages
35. Fuel pressure gages
36. Oil pressure gages
37. Oil temperature gages
38. Carburetor air temperature gages
39. Free air temperature gage
40. Fuel quantity gage
41. Carburetor air filter switch
42. Oil dilution switches
43. Starting switches
44. Parking brake control
45. Spare fuse box
46. Engine fire extinguisher controls (on some airplanes)

THIS IS A TYPICAL B-17 INSTRUMENT PANEL.
DETAILS WILL VARY IN DIFFERENT MODELS.

APPROVED B-17F and G CHECKLIST
REVISED 3-1-44

PILOT'S DUTIES IN RED
COPILOT'S DUTIES IN BLACK

BEFORE STARTING
1. Pilot's Preflight—COMPLETE
2. Form 1A—CHECKED
3. Controls and Seats—CHECKED
4. Fuel Transfer Valves & Switch—OFF
5. Intercoolers—Cold
6. Gyros—UNCAGED
7. Fuel Shut-off Switches—OPEN
8. Gear Switch—NEUTRAL
9. Cowl Flaps—Open Right—OPEN LEFT—Locked
10. Turbos—OFF
11. Idle cut-off—CHECKED
12. Throttles—CLOSED
13. High RPM—CHECKED
14. Autopilot—OFF
15. De-icers and Anti-icers, Wing and Prop—OFF
16. Cabin Heat—OFF
17. Generators—OFF

STARTING ENGINES
1. Fire Guard and Call Clear—LEFT Right
2. Master Switch—ON
3. Battery switches and inverters—ON & CHECKED
4. Parking Brakes—Hydraulic Check—On—CHECKED
5. Booster Pumps—Pressure—ON & CHECKED
6. Carburetor Filters—Open
7. Fuel Quantity—Gallons per tank
8. Start Engines: both magnetos on after one revolution
9. Flight Indicator & Vacuum Pressures CHECKED
10. Radio—On
11. Check Instruments—CHECKED
12. Crew Report
13. Radio Call & Altimeter—SET

ENGINE RUN-UP
1. Brakes—Locked
2. Trim Tabs—SET
3. Exercise Turbos and Props
4. Check Generators—CHECKED & OFF
5. Run up Engines

BEFORE TAKEOFF
1. Tailwheel—Locked
2. Gyro—Set
3. Generators—ON

AFTER TAKEOFF
1. Wheel—PILOT'S SIGNAL
2. Power Reduction
3. Cowl Flaps
4. Wheel Check—OK right—OK LEFT

BEFORE LANDING
1. Radio Call, Altimeter—SET
2. Crew Positions—OK
3. Autopilot—OFF
4. Booster Pumps—On
5. Mixture Controls—AUTO-RICH
6. Intercooler—Set
7. Carburetor Filters—Open
8. Wing De-icers—Off
9. Landing Gear
   a. Visual—Down Right—DOWN LEFT Tailwheel Down, Antenna in, Ball Turret Checked
   b. Light—OK
   c. Switch Off—Neutral
10. Hydraulic Pressure—OK Valve closed
11. RPM 2100—Set
12. Turbos—Set
13. Flaps ⅓—½ Down

FINAL APPROACH
14. Flaps—PILOT'S SIGNAL
15. RPM 2200—PILOT'S SIGNAL

AFTER LANDING
1. Hydraulic Pressure—OK
2. Cowl Flaps—Open and Locked
3. Turbos—Off
4. Booster Pumps—Off
5. Wing Flaps—Up
6. Tailwheel—Unlocked
7. Generators—OFF

END OF MISSION
1. Engines—Cut
2. Radio—On ramp
3. Switches—OFF
4. Chocks
5. Controls—LOCKED
6. Form 1

GO-AROUND
1. High RPM & Power—High RPM
2. Wing Flaps—Coming Up
3. Power reduction
4. Wheel Check—OK Right—OK LEFT

RUNNING TAKEOFF
1. Wing Flaps—Coming Up
2. Power
3. Wheel Check—OK Right—OK LEFT

SUBSEQUENT TAKEOFF
1. Trim Tabs—SET
2. Wing Flaps—UP
3. Cowl Flaps—Open Right—OPEN LEFT
4. High RPM—CHECKED
5. Fuel—Gals per tank
6. Booster Pumps—ON
7. Turbos—SET
8. Flight Controls—UNLOCKED
9. Radio Call

SUBSEQUENT LANDING
1. Landing Gear
   a. Visual—Down Right—DOWN LEFT Tailwheel Down, Ball Turret Checked
   b. Light—ON
2. Hydraulic Pressure—OK
3. RPM 2100—Set
4. Turbo Controls—Set
5. Wing Flaps ⅓—½ Down
6. Radio Call

FINAL APPROACH
7. Flaps—PILOT'S SIGNAL
8. RPM 2200—PILOT'S SIGNAL

FEATHERING
1. Throttle Back
2. Feather
3. Mixture and Fuel Booster—Off
4. Turbo Off
5. Prop Low RPM
6. Ignition Off
7. Generator Off
8. Fuel Valve Off

UNFEATHERING
1. Fuel Valve On
2. Ignition On
3. Prop Low RPM
4. Throttle Cracked
5. Supercharger Off
6. Unfeather
7. Mixture Auto-Rich
8. Warm up Engine
9. Generator On

SEQUENCE OF POWER CHANGES

INCREASING POWER
1. Mixture Controls
2. Propellers
3. Throttles
4. Superchargers

DECREASING POWER
1. Superchargers
2. Throttles
3. Propellers
4. Mixture Controls

Checklist usage and discipline during this period was governed by the old philosophy of memorization. As a future B-17 pilot, one of 2nd Lt. Harold Weekely's first assignments was to memorize all the checklists. The B-17F and G checklist reproduced above was very similar to one of the many checklists Hal Weekely memorized in training and later used in combat.

(B-17 Pilot Training Manual for the Flying Fortress)

Checklist usage and discipline during this period was governed by the old philosophy of memorization. As a future B-17 pilot, one of my first assignments was to memorize all the checklists entirely. I was never particularly good at memorizing checklists. Fortunately, Billie was there and made the task so much easier, almost enjoyable. Because it was August and September in Florida, a very beautiful time of the year, we would sit in a small park in the center of town. We'd sit there in the evening and go over the checklists over and over again and again.

The comical part came when Billie was able to put away the checklist. She had memorized everything on the checklists long before me, even though she had no idea what she had memorized. Billie was very helpful getting me through that part of my rigorous training.

To tell the truth, Billie helped me get through all phases of my training. She challenged me when needed, she checked my work when asked and she offered the comforting words a guy loves to hear at the end of a long day at the office, so to speak. I was thrilled to have her near me.

Hendricks Field was a great place to learn how to fly the B-17. This air field was located in the middle of Florida and was named in memory of 1st Lt. Laird Woodruff Hendricks of Ocala, Florida, who died on TDY in London on July 28, 1941. The base's remote location assured continuos instruction without disturbing the nearby town of Sebring. Regardless, the constant sight of B-17s in the air and the drone of dozens of Wright engines became an accepted part of the Sebring residents' lives.

Hendricks Field was a big, relatively new base built on 9200 acres of land leased to the U.S. government at $1.00 per year for ninety-nine years. Built in late 1941 through early 1942, a full-fledged air base arose from the broad and flat, Palmetto-covered prairie about seven miles southeast of Sebring. The many lakes and ponds that dotted this area posed no obstacle for the Army Air Forces engineers and contractors. Four concrete runways, each 5,000 feet long and 150 feet wide, were laid out. Railroads and roads were built to serve the base in its remote location. Five large warehouses were built to house all the materials, supplies and equipment necessary to support such a large undertaking. The Chapel, post office, hospital, hangars, mess halls, barracks and many other facilities were quickly added.

Combat crew training started in March 1942 with the arrival of twenty-five students. Several students were from the Royal Air Force. The native animals of the area - herons, cranes, quail, deer and rabbits - adapted or gave way to the mighty drone of the B-17 Flying Fortress' four Wright radial engines. The first B-17 arrived at Hendricks Field on January 29, 1942 and the first Combat Crew Training School in the United States called Hendricks Field home.

Most of the B-17s used at Hendricks Field were war-weary B-17E and F model airplanes, though a few came directly from the Boeing factory. With rare exception, all sported a battle-tested camouflage combination of green and brown. Dark oil stains streaked behind the engines above and below the wing. Lighter streaks flowed aft of the wing air vents. Each aircraft was identified with large white, block numbers painted on the bomber's nose and massive fin.

For the combat birds, these numbers often obscured a plane's colorful nose art, a combat tradition of a crew naming and painting their airplane. Many bombers had cartoon figures on the nose, others had pin-up girls. Virtually all of the old combat birds had some sort of faded endearing name affixed to them. If these planes could speak of their combat experiences, I am sure they would tell volumes.

The ever-escalating needs of World War II often tapped the base's resources beyond the limit. There was a shortage of instructors (as more were assigned to combat), planes and equipment, and there were barely enough

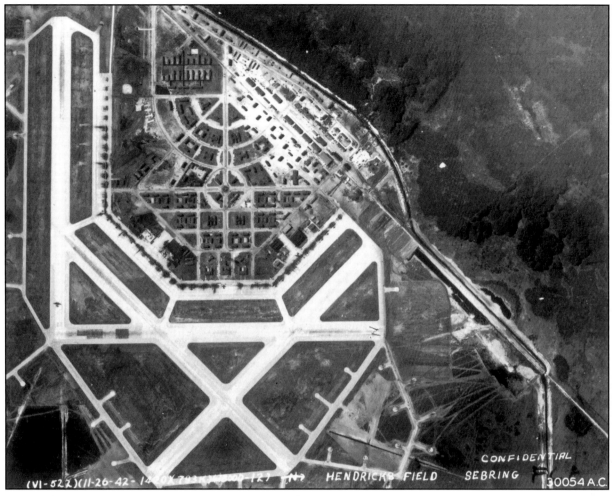

Hendricks Field was a great place to learn how to fly the B-17. Located in the middle of Florida, the base's remote location assured continuous instruction without greatly disturbing the nearby town of Sebring. B-17s, lined-up in a single file wingtip-to-wingtip, can be seen parked on the ramp area. (A.W. "Spizz" Pollard)

facilities to accommodate the ever growing student load. Likewise, many of the early crews never fully completed their combat crew training, as they were needed desperately for combat assignments.

The material needs of the war meant very few personnel had their own automobiles on base. Walking was the primary means of transportation. A scheduled bus service operated to and from town. There were many motorcycles at Hendricks Field. Civilian and military personnel rode them because they were economical, especially at a time when gasoline was rationed. I didn't have one, but it brought back fond memories of the motorcycle I owned when I lived in Steubenville.

In late 1942, the Hendricks Field training curriculum changed from a Combat Crew Training School to a B-17 pilot transition school or in official Army Air Forces parlance, "Army Air Forces Pilot School (Specialized Four-engine)." At one point in the base's history, there were one hundred and twenty-one B-17s in use for pilot transition training.

My B-17 pilot transition school was a ten-week course. I accumulated 105 hours in the B-17, fifteen hours in the Link trainer and countless hours of ground instruction. We studied meteorology, aircraft systems, performance, radio procedures, and so much more. We also learned the intricacies of the secret Norden bombsight, a precision instrument that allowed for extremely accurate bomb drops. Finally, we learned the respon-

Training B-17s based at Hendricks Field were identified with large white, block numbers painted on the bomber's nose and massive fin. (A.W. "Spizz" Pollard)

sibilities of the other crewmembers including the navigator, bombardier, radio operator, flight engineer and the gunners. Everybody aboard the B-17 had a very important role to play to make the airplane a credible and efficient fighting machine. Learning to integrate and optimize the use of these various positions would come at another school in the not-so-distant future. If I wasn't flying, my head was buried in the books.

The B-17 was and is a dream to fly. Any pilot who has ever flown the B-17 will certainly agree it was and remains one of their favorite airplanes. With its large wing, responsive controls and four reliable Wright engines, the B-17 handled more like a docile, single-engine Piper J-3 Cub than a rugged heavy bomber.

The wide landing gear improved takeoff and landing performance, but the elevated nose impaired forward visibility. Thus, it was mandatory to use a ground guide while taxiing around a congested ramp. Without the ground guide, I had to slowly weave left and right to improve my forward visibility and to ensure the taxi path ahead of me was clear.

The B-17 possessed few vices, except on a strong crosswind landing where the pilot really earned his rating keeping the plane on the runway centerline. I remember seeing

some students land short of the runway, bounce high scattering dust and grass everywhere, but recover to make a decent landing. In flight and, later, in combat, I learned to appreciate the B-17's inherently rugged construction, a stout design that brought many crewmembers home with damage that would have downed any other aircraft.

For these and many other reasons, the B-17 carried the endearing moniker, "Queen of the Skies."

The flying syllabus included forty hours of instrument work, five hours of formation flying and twenty-five hours of navigation. Training missions in the well-used B-17Es and Fs based at Hendricks Field usually lasted four to five hours with each student giving his seat to another student after about a half-hour's flying time. During formation training, I'd rotate my time on the controls with another student every fifteen minutes or so.

The B-17 was a big airplane in its day and required a lot of muscle to fly. Unlike the large, modern airplanes of today which have hydraulically boosted controls to assist the pilot, all inputs in the B-17 are a direct cable control. As such, flying the B-17 over long periods was very fatiguing, especially while fighting propeller wash and wake turbulence during formation flying.

Mastering and perfecting formation flying was an important part of a B-17 pilots' training. (Peter M. Bowers)

I learned how to fly the types of formations we would use in combat, such as the "Combat Box" or the "Stepped-Down V."

These formations moved in unison and were staggered and layered, both horizontally and vertically, in a manner that allowed the simultaneous release of bombs without hitting any aircraft in the formation below. These formations always stayed tight for mutual protection and for laying a successful bomb pattern. Tightness was the key to the success of the mission. With more than ten .50-caliber machine guns aboard each B-17, a tight bomber formation could bring a withering amount of defensive firepower to bear against any attacking fighter. (See Appendix G)

At first, I practiced and perfected my formation flying with only one other bomber. I worked hard to keep my wingtip as close as possible to that other aircraft, often as close as ten feet from the other airplane. As time progressed, more airplanes joined the training formation and the training became more demanding and rigorous. We practiced so hard and flew formations flights so often that maintaining proper formation position became second nature.

During practice flights, both student pilots and instructors took turns flying as formation leader in the lead box. In actual combat, only a qualified formation leader and lead navigator flew in that position. The formation leader and lead navigator often led massed heavy bomber formations consisting of hundreds, up to a thousand or more heavy bombers to the assigned target.

We also learned how to fly and handle various in-flight emergencies. I learned how to fly with one engine inoperative, then two engines inoperative and, finally, two engines inoperative on one side. The latter required the aspiring B-17 pilot to exhibit textbook knowledge of the proper procedures. Moreover, having two engines inoperative on one side was quite difficult physically, as the pilots needed to apply almost 140 pounds of rudder pedal force to maintain proper directional control.

On some flights, my instructor would retard both throttles on one side to idle, then gauge my reaction. Almost instinctively, I'd reach for the flight control trim tabs. "Sorry," he would say. "Shot away." I'd yell at the instructor to get on the rudder pedals and help me hold the plane steady. He'd only look at me with sad eyes, shake his head and say, "Sorry, I'm dead."

My only recourse was to turn to the flight engineer and yell, "Get this dead SOB out of the seat and help me fly this beast." Now, my instructor would smile, as this was exactly the response he wanted. He would then let me re-trim the plane, but I'd still have to fly it back to base and land it on two engines.

Later, as I gained proficiency and confidence in our emergency training in flight at altitude, the instructors would idle two engines on one side after takeoff and after the wheels had retracted. I had to maintain altitude and direction, trim the airplane, simulate the shutdown and feathering of the propellers, and line-up the airplane for landing. As before, the instructor would often play "dead" to simulate conditions in combat.

Two problems plagued the summertime B-17 transition student training - heat and humidity. Each contributed to make for a miserable flight, especially in a hot cockpit with no moving air. After takeoff, my instructor and I usually opened various windows, thus allowing a cooling breeze to sweep through the inside of the four-engine bomber.

Two other predominant problems were the hoards of hungry mosquitoes in the

morning and the hot metal surface of the bomber after baking in the afternoon's sunlight. Each contributed its own unique form of misery.

Another quiet misery was that I was always saluting somebody. There were a great number of Second Lieutenants at Hendricks Field and in the Sebring area and a considerable number of higher-ranking officers. As Second Lieutenants, our instructions were simple: every officer should salute every other officer. With the great number of Second Lieutenants and other officers in the area, we spent all our time saluting one another as we walked up and down the streets and on base. It got to be such a habit that Billie would wake up at night and discover, much to her personal amazement, that I was laying in bed asleep - saluting. No doubt my actions had become a reflexive reaction from the many days of saluting everyone in and around the area.

Another reflexive action developed, again due to a repetitive action. We flew and practiced flying the low frequency radio range for many, many hours in the Link trainer. On several occasions, I got so involved with flying the beam, the "A's" and the "N's" (or, as I heard it in my headset, the "dit-dah" and "dah-dit"), that I would lay in bed at night and turn my head to one side to get an "A," and turn my head to the other side and to get an "N." We devoted a lot of time to flying the low frequency range, both for orientation and for flying instrument approaches.

I made my initial "First Pilot" or pilot-in-command flight on August 18, 1943, which was barely ten days and thirty hours of dual instruction after my first B-17 flight. I made arrangements with Billie to be on the Lake Hamilton dock to see this first "solo." I anticipated I would be flying as "First Pilot" that particular day, so I made arrangements with Billie that I would fly a certain pattern so she could recognize me readily. I would fly out over the lake and make turns in a pre-arranged direction to convey to her I had checked out in the aircraft. Billie had no problems recognizing my B-17 from the other four-engine bombers that flew over or near Lake Hamilton that day.

My training in Sebring provided other interesting and memorable if not unusual experiences. Once, after an early morning briefing, while it was still very dark and base personnel were just beginning their daily routines, I laid on a bench while I waited for the crew to get ready to go to the aircraft. Having laid there for a few minutes, I extended my hand over the side of the bench and felt something furry underneath. Thinking that it was one of the local dogs, I rubbed it back and forth. Curious to see what kind of dog it was, I turned over to take a closer look. Much to my complete surprise, I discovered that it was an Ocelot. I continued rubbing this cat-like animal very gently until he moved on his way, hopefully back into the jungle from where he came.

Summertime weather in central Florida was fraught with many heavy thunderstorms with torrential rainfalls that gave us a lot of concern while flying. This nasty weather created another memorable flying experience.

One night while retuning from a cross-country flight, I was flying above Lake Okeechobee and flew headlong into one of these torrential rainstorms. Without any warning, my #3 engine failed. I lost complete power on this engine! I was dumbstruck! Why this one engine failed, or for that matter why only one engine failed, I have no idea. That's the first and only time I ever had an unexplained engine failure.

By this time in my training, Billie's mother and older sister had written once or twice to inquire when she was going to terminate her vacation and come back home. Neither knew Billie and I were married, but we both knew we had to soon tell them the good news.

I arranged to fly a cross-country training flight from Florida to Kentucky, Illinois and Ohio, eventually landing in Pittsburgh, Pennsylvania at the old Allegheny County Airport. These long flights were scheduled to last one or two days at most. On this training mission, I planned it so I could spend the night at my home in Steubenville, Ohio and return to Hendricks Field the next day. Often, we took with us some of the local troops who were assigned to Hendricks and allowed them to go home for an overnight visit with their families.

After my cross-country flight to Pittsburgh, I went to see Billie's mother and tell her that we were married. I was expecting to get the big blow, but that did not happen. Instead, the surprising news was very well received. I was pleased and relieved by her reaction. Though Billie had given it a lot of thought, she didn't know how she was going to tell her mother we were married.

My time in Steubenville ended all too quickly and I had to return to the Allegheny County Airport and fly the B-17 back to Florida. Upon my arrival at the airport, however, I learned to my complete surprise and dismay I had greater problems at hand.

The men I carried with me from Sebring were mostly from the Pittsburgh area and were all aircraft mechanics. True to their mechanically inclined nature, they found a multitude of things wrong with the aircraft. They removed the voltage regulators, even going so far at one point to end up with a hole in a fuel tank. Counting the time until we received maintenance support and supplies, it was three more days before we returned to Sebring. Obviously, the lads that I had with me made sure they could take full advantage of that trip home. I was happy, too, as I could spend more time with Billie's family.

I finished B-17 Pilot Transition Training at Hendricks Field on September 22, 1943, with a total of 110 hours and 15 minutes in the B-17E and B-17F. I was one step closer to combat.

Once again, Billie and I accompanied Donald Snyder and his wife on the return to Ohio. They dropped us off in Steubenville before they proceeded to their home in Wooster, Ohio.

I had a brief leave before I had to report to my next duty station in mid-October in Salt Lake City, Utah, an Army Air Forces assignment station. I spent only a few days there before being assigned to a B-17 unit based at Ardmore Army Air Field in Ardmore, Oklahoma.

In mid-1942, when Ardmore Army Air Field was activated, it was supposed to be for glider training, but evolved first into a B-26 crew training base, transformed into troop carrier training and still later into a B-17 crew training base. The area's most famous resident was Gene Autry, the popular country-western singer and actor. Autry's 1200-acre farm was barely a mile from the base's main entrance.

When I arrived at Ardmore AAF and reported for duty, the base was still a troop carrier training base and nobody had any idea why I, a bomber pilot, was there. We soon learned that the 395th Bombardment Group, a B-17 bomber unit from Ephrata Army Air Field, Washington, had been reassigned to Ardmore AAF and was scheduled to arrive soon. Within about ten days, this bomb group flew in and the base changed from a troop carrier base to a B-17 bomber base. In turn, the 395th Bombardment Group (H) became the 395th Combat Crew Training School. This new school's primary function was to train instructional personnel who, in turn, would train new B-17 combat crews at other bases. Later, the base's mission changed slightly and Ardmore trained B-17 crewmembers for combat operations.

As I was not assigned to Ardmore AAF to become an instructor, my stay at Ardmore was brief, only a few weeks. During the interim, I made only a couple of flights to maintain proficiency. I flew my first flight on November 2nd and my last flight sixteen days later. I made formation flights, day and night instrument flights, bomb runs with and without the autopilot and several routine transition flights. In all, I logged slightly more than 30 hours flying time.

I flew several flights as copilot with a gentleman named Bob Sheriff, who was from the Cleveland, Ohio area. The next time I saw Bob was in England. He was assigned to the 91st Bombardment Group (Heavy) at Bassingbourn, which was very near the base where I was eventually assigned near the quaint, English village of Nuthampstead.

During the short time I was at Ardmore, Billie decided she would come down and spend a few days with me. She rode the train the whole way, which was very difficult because the trains were so crowded with troops moving about the country. She was very fortunate that a military member was kind enough to let her have his seat. I thought her route was a bit odd because the train came into the town of Henryetta, Oklahoma, then reversed gears and backed all the way to Ardmore. Before I picked up Billie at the train station, I located a small apartment, which worked out very nicely for our brief time together in the Ardmore area.

In mid-November 1943, I received orders to report to Dalhart Army Air Field near to Dalhart, Texas for Combat Crew Training. At this school, I met my crew for the first time and I learned how to mesh my responsibilities as a B-17 aircraft commander and "First Pilot" with the duties of my team of specialists to create a formidable weapon system.

It was this crew I took into combat.

"What we anticipate seldom occurs; what we least expected generally happens."
    Benjamin Disraeli, Earl of Beasonsfield (1804–1881),
        Henrieta Temple [1837], bk. II, ch. 4

CHAPTER 5

Getting Closer to Combat Flying

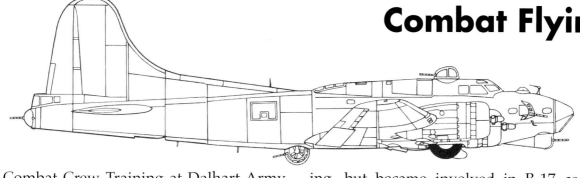

Combat Crew Training at Dalhart Army Air Field was my last formal school before I went into combat overseas. Within a few months, I would leave a world comfortable and familiar for one fraught with danger and death. I was not worried, and I believed that I fully understood the many hazards ahead of me. I washed any worry from my mind and thought of doing only my very best. I believed firmly that anything less would invite trouble, and I had no intention of making Billie or the wives of any of my crewmembers a widow.

Dalhart Army Air Field was located two miles southwest of Dalhart, Texas. Activated in September 1942, the 3,000-acre field was intended originally for glider train-

ing, but became involved in B-17 combat crew training. Sometime later, Boeing B-29 combat crew training and fighter training shared ramp and airspace on and around Dalhart AAF. The base closed in 1946 and the land went to the city of Dalhart. Today, the Dalhart Municipal Airport occupies the property.

The base personnel had to live with the aftermath of a very embarrassing incident. On July 5, 1943, the bombardier aboard a B-17 on its way to make a practice bombing run at the bombing and gunnery range miscalculated and dropped the plane's small load of 100 lb. practice bombs on the sleepy town of Boise City, Oklahoma. These bombs carried only

Three B-17s make a pass over the Headquarters building at Dalhart Army Air Field during mid-1943.
    (XIT Museum)

55

four pounds of charge and ninety-six pounds of sand; thus, there was little damage and, fortunately, there were no casualties.

Soon afterwards, a slogan made its rounds at Dalhart AAF: "Remember the Alamo, remember Pearl Harbor, and for God's sake remember Boise City!"

Dalhart proved to be a very interesting assignment for me, not so much for the flying, but more for its austere location. Florida had a constant green lushness that invited memories of a relaxing paradise. Dalhart, on the other hand, was smack in the middle of a part of the United States that seemed void of anything green and wet. It was cold, desolate and almost desert-like, definitely most uninviting.

Located in the northwestern Texas panhandle, north of Amarillo, Dalhart takes its

The area around Dalhart was flat, free of any obstructions and ideal for flying. For those of us assigned to Dalhart Army Air Field, or to one of the other nearby bases or training fields, we shared a common assessment: this part of the world was almost at the end of the world. The sun scorched the earth during the summer and the cold winds of winter compounded any seasonal misery. The wind blew constantly, and nothing stood in its way to deflect its never ending rush.

Three other airfields surrounded Dalhart. When personnel from these airfields all tried to get some Rest & Relaxation (R & R) in town, they found the entertainment to be very limited, consisting of one or two bars.

At the same time, it was very difficult for anyone to find any quarters. Thank goodness the single men were happy to stay on base, otherwise the housing situation would have been impossible for the married troops.

Billie decided to join me shortly after I was assigned to Dalhart Army Air Field. We left Ardmore on November 18, 1943 and arrived in Dalhart just as this region's inclement wintertime weather was taking hold. The outside temperatures got very, very cold.

For some reason never fully explained, I was assigned to an administrative position for exactly a two-

Dalhart was a quaint town in the 1940s, but offered limited entertainment for the many men stationed at Dalhart Army Air Field and the two other nearby training bases.   (XIT Museum)

name from the first syllables of the two counties it straddles, Dallam and Hartley. When I arrived in Dalhart in late 1943, I discovered the town's main thoroughfares consisted of two railroads, one paved street with a few dirt streets to either side.

month period before I flew. I made my first flight at Dalhart on January 18, 1944.

Once again, Billie endeavored to find us a place to live, which proved almost impossible. She did find a small, old wooden hotel where we were fortunate enough to rent one small room. There were no cooking facilities, limited bath facilities, and very little else.

Unfortunately, Billie, on one occasion, had a bad experience there. While doing laundry inside the hotel, she noticed a small package on the ironing board. When she picked it up to move it, the package felt very stiff and very hard. Curious, she unwrapped the package to see what was in it. To her utter astonishment, she found it was the landlady's recently deceased cat.

Winters at Dalhart Army Air Field were often very cold with lots of snow.   (XIT Museum)

Billie and I left that particular establishment in short order and sought accommodations elsewhere.

Meanwhile, I had purchased a nice ring for Billie. While talking to the jeweler, I mentioned that my wife and I were looking desperately for a place to stay. The jeweler kindly rented us a room in his home. Our first child, William, was conceived while I was stationed in Dalhart.

The weather was awful in the Texas panhandle. There were occasions when the snow was so deep that I had to stay on base because I couldn't get into town. In turn, Billie was holed-up in our single room by herself. All Billie had at that time was radio for entertainment, no television, so she spent her time reading magazines and listening to the radio. I, on the other hand, had my training at the base to help me pass the time. I made my first flight on January 18th and didn't fly again

until February 24th. Due to the terrible weather, I logged only three hours flying time in February. Flying began in earnest in March with a training flight on March 1st. I logged approximately seventy-five hours in both March and April.

My assigned combat crew came together at Dalhart Army Air Field and became recorded as Crew #179-9. Each crewmember, having undergone his own specialized training at various Army Air Forces bases around the United States, contributed to the greater whole of the B-17's wartime purpose and fighting efficiency.

I was working in Operations when the Operations Officer introduced me to my crew. I tried to give them a little background about me, a feel for what I had accomplished and what I would attempt to do as their commander. Moreover, I described what I expected of them as crewmembers. I had before me a diverse group of men from all walks of life and ethnic backgrounds from nineteen years of age to thirty-three. They were farmers, athletes, aircraft workers and students. Our meeting was unique as they were the very crew I would command and be responsible for their welfare. I was impressed with their attitude, their training in their respective crew positions and their overall conduct. The longer I got to know these men the more I respected them and appreciated their abilities. Every commander believes their crew is the best, and my feelings for my crew were no exception.

During this first meeting, I got a kick from a question one of the sergeants asked me when he was first assigned to my crew. He asked, "How do they determine who is the pilot and who is the co-pilot on this crew? Do they just flip a coin or what kind of action is taken?"

I smiled. I explained to him that our co-pilot had just recently graduated from flight training, having graduated from Class 44-A. I told him that I had been through B-17 transition training already and had several more

Second Lieutenant Harold Weekley and his combat crew pose together for the first time in front of *Patsy*, a well-worn B-17F while all were attending the Combat Crew Training School at Dalhart Army Air Field, Texas. Left to right, Front Row - T/Sgt Joseph W. Skarda, top turret gunner/flight engineer; S/Sgt. Gene F. Leonard, left waist gunner; T/Sgt. Ven B. Unger, radioman; S/Sgt. Robert L. Stickel, right waist gunner; S/Sgt. Joseph R. Fabian, ball turret gunner; S/Sgt. Charles "Pop" Stombaugh, tail gunner. Left to right, back row: 2nd Lt. Harold D. Weekley, pilot; 2nd Lt. Benjamin L. Clark, Jr., copilot; F/O Raymond S. Delbart, bombardier; 2nd Lt. Paul N. James, navigator (Harold D. Weekley)

flying hours in the four-engine Boeing.

As this crew's aircraft commander and "First Pilot," I had to learn the personal capabilities, shortcomings and idiosyncrasies of each crewmember. My success as an aircraft commander depended on the confidence, trust and respect the crew felt for me. Moreover, this success depended on how well I maintained crew discipline, comradeship and morale.

Additionally, I had to have a keen understanding of each man's duties and responsibilities aboard the B-17. I had to devise the ways and means of helping each crewmember perform his job more efficiently.

My copilot was Second Lieutenant Benjamin L. Clark, Jr. from Lockport, New York. Ben was pleasant to be with and was neat in appearance. I don't think he was pleased particularly to be a copilot on a B-17, as he wanted to be pilot on a B-25. Being from upstate New York, I thought he would have a distinct accent, but I never heard one. He was a diligent student before entering the military and his ability to reason through difficult subjects served him well.

The B-17's copilot was the aircraft commander's executive officer, chief assistant and second in command. A rated pilot in his own right, the copilot had to be very familiar with all B-17 flight operations and characteristics, and the duties and the responsibilities of the "First Pilot." Should the need arise, the copilot had to be able to take charge and act in the airplane commander's place at any time. Ben Clark was a fine pilot and performed his duties admirably.

My navigator was Second Lieutenant Paul M. James who came from Wilmington, Delaware. He was a dashing, outgoing young man of twenty-five when he was assigned to my crew. James was an electrical engineer before he joined the many young men going to war. He proved to be a very competent navigator, but for some reason carried the nickname "Snaffy," a variation of the acronym SNAFU, which stands for "Situation Normal All Fouled Up."

James' job was to direct the B-17's flight from departure to return. He had to know the exact position of the airplane at all times and report this information to his airplane commander when requested or required by Standing Operating Procedures. The tools and navigation methods of his trade consisted of charts, radio aids, celestial navigation, pilotage and dead reckoning, or any combination of the above. He was expected to maintain the aircraft's position within a quarter of a mile.

The navigator worked closely with the pilots to study the flight plan of the route to be flown, the weather, determine alternate airfields if needed, and any other areas of crew coordination and communication as required. In combat, the navigator kept the flight log and manned the two cheek guns in the event of a fighter attack.

James was also a keen poker player. He played poker almost every night that he had time, and he always won. He saved his money and sent it home to his wife so he could accumulate enough to open a restaurant upon his return to civilian life. (See Endnotes, Chapter 4)

My bombardier was Flight Officer (changed to 2nd Lt. in July 1944) Raymond S.

Delbart from St. Albans, West Virginia. Unlike Paul James' extrovert personality, Ray was more of an introvert with little to say and tended to keep his opinions to himself. He was employed in the chemical industry before he entered the military. Though he carried a slight West Virginia accent, neither I nor any member of my crew ever gave speech or accent any second thought as we accepted everybody for who they were and their contributions to the crew and the war.

The bombardier's job was why the B-17 was built: to deliver bombs on the target. Every other function on the B-17 was preparatory to hitting and destroying the target. The success or failure of a mission often depended upon the actions of the bombardier during the last few minutes of the bomb run.

During these anxious moments, the bombardier took over the control of the airplane for that final run in to the target and his commands were followed to the letter. He told the pilot what he needed done and when. Until the bombardier yelled, "Bombs away!" his word was law.

The bombardier had to be well versed in target identification and aircraft recognition. He had to know how to load and fuse his own bombs. He was required to understand intimately the automatic pilot as it pertained to the bombing procedure and to know how to operate all gun positions on the airplane and how to clear simple stoppages and jams of the machine guns while in flight, including operation of the nose chin turret, if so equipped. He was required to be familiar with all duties of the crew and be able to assist the navigator in case the navigator became incapacitated. Most importantly, he had to protect the secret Norden bombsight, if installed, from falling into enemy hands and be able to destroy it, if the need arose.

The Norden bombsight was a gyro-stabilized device that allowed for uncannily accurate bombing from high altitudes. Developed in an age well before computers, this mathematical wonder literally made strategic bombing from high altitudes possible. Many experienced bombardiers claimed they could "drop a bomb in a pickle barrel from 25,000 feet."

The navigator and bombardier shared the B-17's forward-most compartment. This spacious, unheated enclosure had enough headroom for a man to stand-up within it. The large, molded Plexiglas nose afforded each man an unparalleled view of the earth and sky. The navigator's seat and plotting table was located immediately behind and to the left of the bombardier's position.

My engineer and top turret gunner was Joseph W. Skarda from Hazen, Arkansas. Joe was a rice and soybean farmer with his father on the flat prairie east of Little Rock before he went to war. He was twenty-eight years old when he joined my combat crew.

Joe was the ranking non-commissioned officer in charge of the enlisted men of the crew. He required all non-coms to conduct themselves in a very military manner and discipline was never a problem. He kept a close reign on his men and required they show the officers of our crew the respect he felt we deserved. Joe conducted himself much like the First Sergeant in any unit. His bravery and dedication to our crew's welfare was exemplary and we all appreciated his guidance.

The engineer had to know more about the airplane than any other member of the crew. Trained at one of the Army Air Forces' specialized technical schools, the engineer worked closely with the pilot and copilot, often supplementing each pilot's knowledge of the airplane. The engineer was required to thoroughly understand the airplane, its engines and its armament equipment. The lives of the crew, the safety of the equipment and the success of the mission often depended upon the flight engineer's knowledge of the airplane.

On takeoff and landing, Joe Skarda stood or sat between Ben Clark and I and moni-

tored specific engine instruments on the instrument panel. If needed or briefed, he called out take-off and landing speeds.

The top turret behind the pilots' position was the engineer's "home" on the B-17. This electrically powered turret housed a pair of Browning .50-cal. machine guns and was capable of moving 360 degrees horizontally and 85 degree vertically. To man this formidable weapon, the engineer stood on a rotating steel platform attached to the turret.

Ven "Bob" Unger was my assigned radio operator and his home was Oakridge, Missouri. Ven's father was a share crop farmer and Ven worked in the fields for $5 a week. After he graduated from high school, Ven borrowed $100 to make his way to Seattle, Washington, where he got a job at the Boeing Aircraft Company building wings for the B-17.

Ven was drafted in March 1943 and was sent to boot camp at St. Petersburg, Florida. Afterwards, he took his radio training at Sioux Falls, South Dakota and gunnery training at Harlingen, Texas.

Ven was a man of unusually high moral standards, was intelligent, hard-working and had great respect from all who knew him. At the time we first met, I never knew he was a talented singer and stringed instrument player. He was quiet at our first meeting and all I knew he was a well qualified radio operator and crewmember. He became more outgoing as the crew melded together as a fighting unit.

Occupying the radio operator position, Ven Unger had his own compartment immediately aft of the bomb bay and was located almost in the center of the B-17's somewhat cramped, cylindrical fuselage. He sat on a small swivel chair at a small wooden desk on the left side of the fuselage. His compartment held the receivers, transmitters and other communication equipment, which he used to maintain and monitor incoming and outgoing communications and navigation frequencies. Ven's view outside was somewhat limited; he had only a small window at his left and right and a larger, removable Plexiglas hatch above him. The small plywood door separating this compartment from the bomb bay was normally closed to offer some small protection against wind and cold air when the bomb bay doors were open. Another plywood door separated the bomb bay from the crew compartments forward of the bomb bay.

The radio operator had several very important duties in the combat zone. He had to give position reports every thirty minutes if required, assist the navigator in taking fixes, keep his radio equipment properly tuned and in good working order, maintain a log, understand emergency and Direction Finding (DF) procedures, and understand the use of secret codes and authentication procedures. The radio operator dispensed chaff to confuse the enemy's flak or anti-aircraft artillery directed radar. Chaff was simply strips of metal about 10- inches long and were meant to disrupt the enemy's radar signal. On some occasions, the radio operator served as a mission photographer and took photographs of the bombed target for post-mission analysis. The radio operator was also a gunner. Some B-17 variants had a single .50-caliber machine gun mounted in the overhead escape hatch.

The B-17 had four gunner positions aft of the radio compartment - the ball turret, the left and right waist gunner positions, and the tail gunner position. The gunners worked together to defend the B-17 against fighter attacks. When combined with the other gunner position forward of the radio compartment, a B-17's crew could bring to bear thirteen of these deadly guns against attacking enemy fighters creating a formidable defensive umbrella.

A B-17 gunner had to be thoroughly familiar with his weapon, the Browning .50-cal machine gun. He knew how to maintain his guns, how to clear jams and stoppages, and how to harmonize the sights with the guns. He had a fine sense of timing and was familiar with the trajectory ballistics of their rounds.

The Browning .50-caliber machine gun was an extremely effective defensive weapon and had a maximum rate of fire of 750 rounds per minute. Gunners were trained to fire in short bursts, lest they expend their ammunition too quickly, overheat the gun barrels or jam their weapons. Each machine gun weighed almost sixty-five pounds and using it effectively took rigorous training, a keen eye and finesse to hit a target moving at speeds often in the excess of five hundred miles per hour.

For the waistgunners, manipulating their post-mounted .50's took brute strength and courage, especially in the killing cold temperatures at bombing altitudes, often more than fifty degrees below zero. In addition, they had to be careful not to entangle themselves in electrical, oxygen and inter-phone connections, or slipping on the brass shell casings that piled up around their feet.

Add the pilots' evasive airplane movements, the onslaught of enemy aircraft, anti-aircraft shells bursting near the aircraft and the always-present chance that a stray round or two from a nearby B-17 may hit them, the gunners had a very tough and dangerous job to perform.

Most importantly, the gunners worked as a vigilant team. They had to be proficient in aircraft identification, friend and foe alike. Their coordinated actions often determined if their airplane would or would not return home from a mission.

Joseph R. Fabian, the youngest member on my crew, manned the Sperry electrically powered ball turret on my B-17. He hailed from Penelope, Texas, a small town of less than one hundred residents located on a single highway some fifteen miles south of the more populous Hillsboro, Texas, which itself is located an hour's drive south of the Dallas-Ft.Worth area. Joe was a tall, lanky lad, barely eighteen years old when he was assigned to my crew. He also served as the armorer and was responsible for all the weapons on board the airplane.

Standing better than six feet tall, my crew and I were amazed how he - or for that matter anyone his size - could roll himself into the ball turret and stay in that position for the long missions we flew. Once confined in this small, globe-like enclosure of aluminum, steel and glass, his only exit was a small hatch located at his back.

Joe Fabian was a straight arrow. I am sure his parents were very proud of him. He didn't smoke, drink, curse or chase girls. Yet, after a few combat missions, his quiet demeanor changed 180 degrees! I am certain that when he returned home, his family's opinion of me changed considerably as I am sure they held me responsible for these changes.

Gene F. Leonard was my crew's left waist gunner and he hailed from Emporia, Kansas.

Gene Leonard was Hal Weekley's left waistgunner. This photograph shows a proud S/Sgt. Gene Leonard in August 1943.   (Norma Leonard)

Gene had an easy-going manner and he bonded well with the other enlisted crewmembers. Many of my crew considered Gene to be the best looking and he always caught the eyes of the ladies. Like the others of my crew, Gene simply addressed me as "Skipper" whenever we flew together.

Charles "Pop" Stombaugh on leave shortly before he joined his new combat crew for training in Dalhart, Texas. "Pop" Stombaugh was thirty-three years old when he joined Weekley's combat crew, making him the oldest crewmember of this fighting team.   (Pearl Stombaugh)

Robert F. Stickel of Plattsburg, New York was twenty-five years old when he joined the crew as the right waist gunner. A college hockey coach before the war, Bob was quite an athlete and was signed to play professional baseball for the Philadelphia A's, but the war prevented this career.

The tail gunner was Charles E. Stombaugh. He came from Washington, D.C. He was thirty-three years old when he joined us, making him the oldest member of my original crew. Stombaugh was fondly known as "Pop."

The tail gunner position, with its pair of .50-cal Browning machine guns, required "Pop" to kneel on the floor in a very cramped compartment and sit for hours on end on a canvas-covered bicycle seat, with no armrests or backrest. His only means of escape in an

The Browning .50-cal. machine gun was a formidable weapon. The photo on the right illustrates the B-17's right waist gun. For the waist gunners, manipulating their post-mounted .50's took brute strength and courage, especially in the killing cold temperatures at bombing altitudes.
(Boeing Model B-17G Field Service Manual)

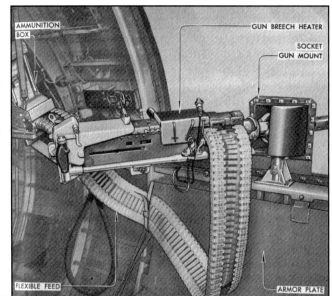

The hydraulic-driven ball turret provided defensive firepower and protection for the B-17's underside. This turret could move 360° in azimuth and from 0° to 90° downward. (Peter M. Bowers)

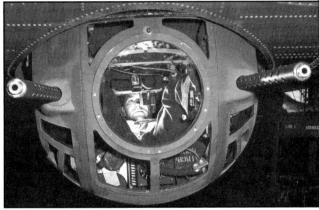

emergency or bailout was a small hatch located slightly behind and to his left.

During takeoffs and landings in inclement weather, the tail gunner handled the Altus Lamp, an electric flashlight, to guide the following aircraft.

Several members of my crew brought their wives to Dalhart and their presence boosted morale. Ray Delbart's wife, Kathryn, was there. Like her husband, she came from St. Albans, West Virginia. Joe Skarda's wife, Ruby, came from Hazen, Arkansas, her husband's hometown. Helen Stickel, the wife of Bob Stickel, was from St. Albans, Vermont.

At Christmas, Bob and Helen had all of the crew and their families at their trailer for a friendly get-together. Helen always professed that she was a poor cook, but did a very fine job on this festive occasion. This

dinner was one of the very rare occasions when the whole crew socialized together, either in the United States or during our assignment in England.

The wives of my crew looked to me, the young aircraft commander, to take care of their husbands. I was flattered by this responsibility and accepted it with a large measure of pride. During our Christmas party with all of the crewmembers present, several of the wives came to me and said, "Now, Lieutenant, I would appreciate it very much if while you're gone you would look after my husband."

I told them I would be more than happy to do so and that I was looking forward to it. As the evening progressed, the same request was posed to me several times. All of the sudden, I realized that if I'm looking after all those guys, then surely somebody ought to be looking after me.

For those on my crew subjected to the daily rigors of the Army mess hall, any cooking other than the mess hall cooking was a welcome relief. A favorite saying at the time was that the Army didn't have cooks, but chemists, because it took a chemist to make good food taste like what they dished out to the troops.

A B-17 pilot briefs his crew before undertaking another stateside training mission.   (XIT Museum)

Newly minted B-17 combat crews receive recognition for their hard work while training during graduation ceremonies at Dalhart Army Air Field.   (XIT Museum)

My crew and I continued our combat crew training in earnest. We flew our training missions from late February through April, averaging nine training flights a month in March and April. Some missions were only a few hours long, though most lasted more than six hours.

When I left Dalhart, I tallied my logbook time. Like a diary, it showed my flight time totals after one-and-a-half years in training. All of my flying time at Dalhart and Ardmore was listed as combat crew training, which added up to 189 hours and 5 minutes. My total flight time from my initial flight in the PT-17 to the time I went into combat totaled

572 hours and 51 minutes. My total B-17 flight time prior to combat was 299 hours and 20 minutes.

Billie and I left Dalhart and proceeded to Kearney, Nebraska, but I had to send Billie home prior to leaving for Europe. She boarded a train and was off to Steubenville. Our parting was very emotional.

As I walked away from the station, I kept looking at her, then turned around and would walk some more before looking back again. This parting was a very difficult time for both of us as we both realized what lay ahead. I didn't know if that would be the last time that I would ever see her. She was carrying our child and we knew that if I were lost, some part of me would remain a little bit longer.

Upon arriving at Kearney, my crew and I were supposed to be assigned the aircraft we were to fly to the European Theater of Operations, the ETO, and receive additional briefings and the necessary clothing. Instead, we learned there was no airplane to take to Europe, nor was any airplane coming to pick us up. There were a large number of crewmembers in the same predicament. Instead of flying, we boarded a troop train and everybody proceeded to Camp Myles Standish, which was near Stoughton, Massachusetts. The train's circuitous route passed through Canada and back into the United States.

My crew found it rather comical that we should come back into the U. S. and pass through Lockport, New York, the hometown of our co-pilot, Ben Clark, Jr. As we passed through town, poor old Ben looked towards the train station, saw several very attractive, young ladies standing there and said, "I don't know, but I don't remember anybody being that pretty when I was in high school."

We arrived safely at our destination and stayed there briefly until May 13, 1944 when we boarded the troop ship, SS Brazil, in Boston, which was part of a large convoy bound for England. I had no idea as to the number of personnel on board, but I knew this ship was a heavily laden troop ship and that no female of any species was on board, not even a dog. There just wasn't a female in sight on that ship.

We were able to view several other ships in that convoy, sometimes fairly close. The *SS Argentina* traveled nearby and was a sister ship to the *SS Brazil*. The *SS Argentina* had quite a number of young female nurses and Woman Army Corps on board and they would communicate by holding up signs. We, of course, would send them messages, in return. All was great fun because there was absolutely no radio contact.

Most of the troops on the ship stayed in the staterooms. Accommodations were tight and the men were stacked twelve men to a room. For sleeping, there were four rows of cots and the cots were placed three high. To pass the time, I learned to field strip and memorize every part of the Army Colt .45 automatic pistol.

The trip across the Atlantic Ocean took thirteen days and, after landing in Liverpool, England, my crew and I were taken immediately to an Army Air Forces Redistribution Center in nearby Stone. There, we spent several days waiting for assignments. *Operation Overlord*, the D-Day Invasion, occurred while we waited patiently, often doing nothing more than twiddling our thumbs. This news was very exciting and my crew and I were more anxious than ever to get into combat.

Our arrival at Liverpool was a very pleasant event with warm greetings from the English. Everyone was quite busy disembarking from the ship, getting on the train and trying to make sure everybody was together. I enjoyed hearing the local accent and we conversed whenever we had the opportunity.

We arrived in May when the countryside was green and beautiful, the best time of the year in England. I was grateful for the good weather, which at times was not the best, but much better than the crews that had to slog through Europe's atrocious winters. The English people and the beautiful countryside were great, but the weather as we would discover was seldom to our liking as really pleasant days were few and far between.

We stayed at the Redistribution Center for approximately two weeks before we learned we were among the first group of replacement crews destined for the 398th Bombardment Group (Heavy) at Nuthampstead, Hertfordshire, England, known also as Station 131. Replacement crews filled the manpower gaps created by those very few, very lucky crews who completed their combat tour and were going home and by crews lost to enemy action. Almost until the end of the war, the need for replacement crews was endless.

The 398th was a new bomb group on English soil and flew its first operational combat mission to Sotteville, France on May 6, 1944. When the month of May ended, the 398th could reflect upon an enviable record. It had flown 450 sorties in eighteen combat missions with a loss of only four airplanes, a loss of only one percent! May was kind to the 398th Bomb Group. June 1944 and subsequent months were not so benevolent.

(James B. Zazas)

"Here's a toast to the host of those who fly . . .
To the ones who will live and those who die . . .
Drink a toast, say a prayer for the next of kin . . .
For the target today is the heart of Berlin."
Excerpt from poem by S/Sgt Preston Clark, 94BG
Veteran of two missions to Berlin in May 1944

CHAPTER 6

Nuthampstead, the 398th Bomb Group and Baptism by Fire

History intrigues me. I love to study history, and I would not be disappointed when I disembarked the *SS Brazil* at the port in Liverpool, England on May 26, 1944. History speaks volumes in this part of Europe, as does a large amount of local folklore and legend. Thoughts of young men in shining armor laying down their lives for commanding ideals of government, religion and society stirred within me, and I felt a quiet admiration for their noble efforts. Centuries earlier, ancient and conquering Roman armies actually marched on or near the lands occupied by Nuthampstead, my assigned

A farmer harvesting his crop watches a B-17G from the 398th Bomb Group, 603rd Bomb Squadron, taxi out for another mission. Scenes like this were common across many parts of England. A great amount of precious farmland was used in constructing many wartime airfields, and any available farmland to grow crops was often used right up to the dispersals and taxiways.   (National Museum of the United States Air Force)

The quaint villages of Nuthampstead and nearby Anstey have changed little over time. Most homes in these villages were made of stone or brick and had thatched or shingle roofs.
(398th Bomb Group Memorial Association)

The airfield was named after the nearby town of Nuthampstead and was the nearest Eighth Air Force bomber base to London. The Nuthampstead airfield was located in the more sparsely populated northeastern part of the County of Hertfordshire. The land is a gently rolling part of England that blends into the flatter landscape of East Anglia to the north and east. The chalk range of the Chiltern Hills, with its beech woods, rolling hills, quaint villages and rich farmland, lies to the southwest and west. Cambridge and its famous university are, as a crow flies, a mere fifteen miles to the north. London is twenty-five miles to the south.

The visual landscape has changed very little over time. Centuries old stone churches are common to almost every village. Countless other structures, mostly homes made of stone and thatched roofs, dot the landscape. Waist high stone walls follow many roads and hedgerows bisect most fields. The rich soil is dark, and is masked by large fields of sugar beets, wheat, hay and other crops during the growing season, this bucolic setting highlighted by fields of green and brown as far as the eye could see. At Nuthampstead, as I am sure was true at many other English bases, local farmers grew and harvested their crops right up to taxiways and dispersal areas. Many local farmers sold the base fresh eggs, which added protein to our diets and, as I learned later, a lot of good morale.

With such idyllic and historic settings surrounding me, I found it hard to believe a war was being fought in this part of the world, with many significant and deadly

base. Within the last two hundred years, mighty industries tapped the land's natural resources and provided Great Britain the ability and military might to spread its flag far and wide around the world.

I was reminded of a poem by Henry Wadsworth Longfellow from his *A Psalm of Life*:

> Lives of great men all remind us
> We can make our lives sublime.
> And, departing, leave behind us
> Footprints on the sands of time.

I arrived at the Nuthampstead airfield with the awe and wonder of any visitor to a strange land, anxious to explore this new realm and its proud and illustrious history. My enthusiasm, however, was tempered by a much deeper resolve to do my job as a bomber pilot to the very best of my ability, fly the prerequisite number of missions without getting wounded or killed, and return home to Billie. For now, any further study of England's illustrious history on my part would have to wait, as I was now a very small cog within a much larger, more modern military machine making its own distinguished history.

battles taking place less than a couple hundred miles from my new wartime home. Continental Europe is a mere twenty-five miles from English shores, thus making the horrors of the European aerial war only a relatively short flight from the dozens of air bases that dotted the British countryside. The Battle of Britain, the most recognized and significant of aerial wartime battles, took place less than four years earlier. Barely eighteen months after this pivotal campaign, the United States entered the war and turned England into the strategic stepping stone for virtually all of the Eighth Air Force's combat missions over mainland Europe.

No land was wasted in the prosecution of this war. Military bases and airfields sprung up all over England, particularly within East Anglia, the eastern section of this historic and noble country. On a clear day, I could see a dozen or more American and British bomber and fighter bases in one glance. From here, the Eighth Air Force launched its massive bomber and fighter raids into the heart of Nazi Germany and occupied France.

Geographically, the Nuthampstead airfield was located about half way between London and Cambridge near the primary railroad system. The base's railroad stop was located in Royston, a quaint town situated about five and half miles to the northwest. Besides Nuthampstead, the other military base closest to Royston was Bassingbourn. Military personnel from both bases, including personnel from nearby Duxford, Fowlmere and Steeple Morden, used the Royston railroad station. Incidentally, an an-

cient Roman road passed near both bases, portions of which are still used more than eighteen centuries after its original construction.

The Nuthampstead airfield layout followed the Eighth Air Force's prescribed airfield plan and covered approximately 600 acres of relatively flat English countryside. The airfield's predominant feature was its three, concrete runways. The main runway was 6,100 feet long and 150 feet wide and was aligned in a northeast-southwest direction. Two other runways, each being 4,200 feet long, were aligned generally north-south and east-west respectively. One large concrete apron and concrete hardstands, or loop dispersal pads, for fifty aircraft were provided. The runways and the dispersal pads were all connected by a 50-foot wide, concrete perimeter track or taxiway.

The bombers of the 398th Bombardment Group (Heavy) - usually stated as the 398th Bomb Group (H) or 398th B.G. - were kept on these concrete dispersal pads. On most airfields, these pads were numbered in numerical order in a clockwise direction. A certain number of pads were assigned to each squadron and were known as dispersal sites. At Nuthampstead, these dispersal sites were prefixed with letters A, B, C, D and F with each squadron assigned a particular prefix.

Much of the hardcore to build Station 131 came from the rubble of the blitz-destroyed areas of London and Coventry. Ironically, the same hardcore was used to build Britain's M-1 motorway when these runways were broken-up and removed many years later.

Acres of grain growing around the Nuthampstead airfield added an idyllic quality to this station's wartime mission.

(398th Bomb Group Memorial Association)

An aerial view of Nuthampstead, England, Station 131, taken on March 15, 1944, shows this airfield's runway, taxiway and hardstand layout. At the time, Lockheed P-38s of the 55th Fighter Group occupied the base. The 398th Bomb Group (H) was assigned to this base the following month.

The 600th and 601st Bomb Squadrons were located on the hardstands in the upper portion of the photograph, and the 602nd Bomb Squadron used the hardstands in the right center of this photograph. The hardstands used by the 603rd Bomb Squadron are barely visible in the far upper left of this photograph. This airfield's technical site and its two large T-2 hangars are clearly visible in the center of this photograph. The main 05/23 runway was used for most of the operational takeoffs and landings and runs from lower right to upper left. The living areas and the village of Nuthampstead are visible in the lower half of the photograph. After the war, most of Nuthampstead's concrete runways, hardstands and perimeter track were broken up and used for highway construction and most of the land reverted to agriculture.

(National Archives, 342-FH-3A13098-69333 A. C.)

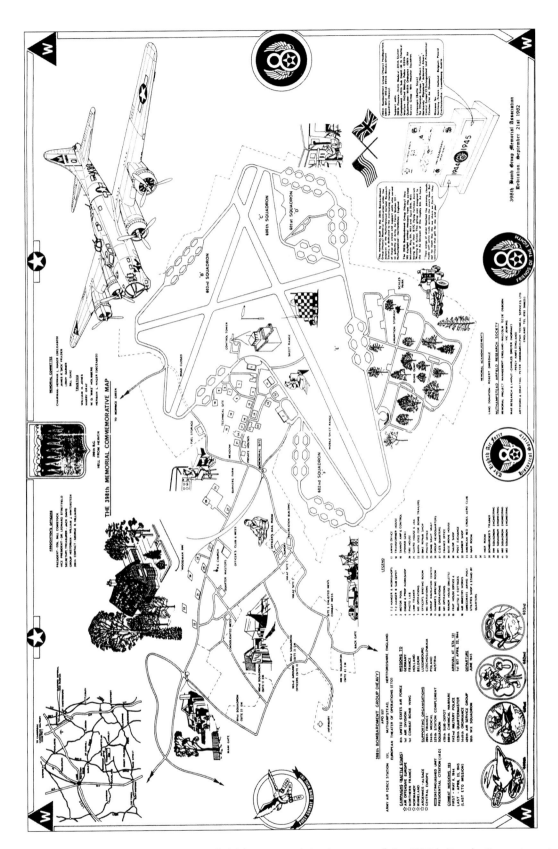

This diagram shows the Nuthampstead Airfield layout and the location of the 398th Bomb Group's assigned bomb squadrons.

(398th Bomb Group Memorial Association)

The Nuthampstead control tower was typical of Eighth Air Force control towers. Aircraft movements on the ground and in the air around the airfield were controlled from these towers.

(398th Bomb Group Memorial Association)

P-38H Lightnings of the 55th Fighter Group which moved in during September 1943. This Group experienced a high attrition rate from operational and weather-related problems. In mid-April 1944, the 55th Fighter Group moved to Wormingford in Essex. The 398th Bombardment Group (Heavy), fresh from the United States, took-up residence within days after the fighter group's departure.

The 398th Bomb Group was organized in Orlando, Florida and activated on March 1, 1943. The initial cadre came from the 34th Bombardment Group (Heavy) based in Blythe Army Air Field in Blythe, California. Six weeks later, the 398th Bomb Group and crews moved to their new home at Geiger Field in Spokane, Washington. Once again, this stay was short lived, and the base personnel, crews and planes moved to Rapid City, South Dakota on June 20, 1943. Two weeks later, the Group, which was an Operational Training Unit, was re-designated a Replacement Training Unit. Untrained crews and planes arrived quickly thereafter as the pace of combat training quickened. On January 1, 1944, the Group reverted to its original Operational Training Unit designation.

In March 1944, the 398th started preparations to leave the Rapid City Air Field for overseas duty. The Air Echelon, under the command of Col. Frank P. Hunter, left on April 7th and arrived at Nuthampstead on April 22, 1944. The 398th wasted no time undertaking local area and training flights before engaging in combat operations in early May 1944. During its entire stay in England, from May 1944 until June 1945, the 398th flew a total of 195 missions, losing 292 men and 70 B-17 aircraft in combat.

The quaint village of Anstey, with its thatched-roof homes and stone church, was only three quarters of mile from the end of Runway 23, the base's main runway. Until the war, I am sure the architectural character of most towns in England had not changed much in many years, perhaps centuries. Most of the heavily-loaded B-17s dispatched on operational missions used this runway or took-off from the opposite direction, Runway 05. I am sure this town's residents got little sleep whenever we took-off on early morning combat missions.

Two large, T-2 type hangers were built to accommodate aircraft maintenance requirements. Each T-2 hangar was 240 feet long, 115 feet wide and almost 30 feet high, and could hold three B-17 bombers. In addition, a control tower, workshops, barracks, fuel stores, ammunition stores, bomb dumps and a wide variety of other technical and utility buildings on site offered housing and work sites for almost 2,900 personnel based at Nuthampstead during its operation.

Although the base was built originally to accommodate bombers, its first tenants were the distinctive, twin-boomed Lockheed

The 1st Combat Bomb Wing (H) consisted of the three bomb groups; the 381st, the 91st and the 398th. The logo of the 1st Combat Bomb Wing was a flying eagle carrying three bombs representing these three bomb groups. (398th Bomb Group Memorial Association)

The 398th Bomb Group was one of three bomb groups attached to the 1st Combat Bomb Wing of the Eighth Air Force's 1st Bomb Division. The second was the 91st Bomb Group (H) based in nearby Bassing-bourn which was, also, headquarters of the 1st Combat Bomb Wing. The 381st Bomb Group was the third bomb group and was based at nearby Ridgewell.

Bassingbourn was a Royal Air Force Base

before it was turned over to U.S. forces, or some say "appropriated" by the USAAF. This quintessential British airbase had beautiful stone buildings as permanent quarters. The tenant bomb group received a lot of publicity during and after World War II. Various members of England's royal family, other heads of state and Hollywood movie stars visited the base frequently with eager, yet professionally polite correspondents in tow. Without a doubt, this unit's most famous B-17 bomber was the *Memphis Belle* piloted by Capt. Robert Morgan. The third bomb group in the 1st Combat Bomb Wing was the 381st Bomb Group (H) based in Ridgewell.

Each of the three bomb groups was identified by a large white letter inside a black, equilateral triangle. It was applied on the B-17's massive vertical tail fin along with the airplane's serial number and assigned call-letter stenciled in yellow or black paint immediately underneath. Additionally, the same triangle identification was applied on

Basssingbourn was home to the 91st Bomb Group (H) and was a large and very busy base. Here, 91st Bomb Group B-17s get ready for takeoff on another mission. Noteworthy in this photograph are the P-51D, the P-47D, the base's control tower and the two large hangars. The B-17G, in the foreground, without any markings painted inside the black triangle, is AAF 42-97636 (DF-P), a PFF-equipped ship. (Peter M. Bowers)

Each airplane assigned to a particular bomb squadron was identified by a squadron code painted in large, black block numbers and letters on the side of the natural metal finish airplane. In addition, each of the three bomb groups was identified by a large white letter inside a black, equilateral triangle, though some early 398th Bomb Group airplanes sported this marking in reverse with a black "W" painted inside a white or bare metal triangle.

Here, aircraft 42-102565 (3O-M), *The Ugly Duckling,* shows these early 398th Bomb Group markings very clearly. This photograph was most likely taken in the spring of 1944.　　(398th Bomb Group Memorial Association)

rope. Most new B-17Gs flown from the United States to England were ferried to a Base Depot in Northern Ireland and exchanged for aircraft already modified to combat-ready status. These same airplanes received their specific bomb group and individual squadron markings shortly after arrival in England.

In late June 1944, the distinctive red, high-visibility markings of the 1st Combat Bomb Wing were added. Both the upper and lower surfaces of the horizontal stabilizer, excluding the elevator, and the outer wing panels were painted red. In addition, a band of red, about eighty inches wide, was painted on the B-17's massive fin just forward of the rudder. The 398th Bomb Group carried these conspicuous markings until the end of the war.

the right wing's upper surface. The 381st Bomb Group was identified with a white "L" inside the triangle on the vertical fin of their B-17s. The 91st Bomb Group's B-17s were identified by a white "A" and the 398th Bomb Group was identified with a white "W." This identifying marking was commonly referred to as the "Triangle W." Interestingly, a few bombers in the 398th BG sported this marking in reverse with a black "W" painted inside a white triangle. When one takes into account the markings of all three bomb groups of the 1st Combat Bomb Wing together, they spell out the word "LAW;" the "L" being the 381st, the "A" being the 91st and the "W" being the 398th.

The original B-17s assigned to the 398th Bomb Group were unpainted, bare metal finish Model B-17Gs, the most advanced version of Boeing's ubiquitous heavy bomber already in use in combat operations throughout Eu-

The 398th Bomb Group was comprised of four squadrons: the 600th, the 601st, the 602nd and the 603rd. Each airplane assigned to a particular bomb squadron was identified by a squadron code painted in large, black block numbers and letters on the side of the natural metal finish airplane and by an aircraft code. The 398th's squadron codes were "N8" for the 600th, "3O" ("three oh," not "30" or "three zero") for the 601st, "K8" for the 602nd, and "N7" for the 603rd. These squadrons' assigned calls signs were Moorhen, Newway, Enclasp and Adorn, respectively. Squadron codes were grouped aft of the national insignia on the left side of the fuselage. On the right side of the fuselage, the squadron code was positioned aft of the national insignia and the aircraft code was positioned forward. In some case, all characters

"Bombs away!" The 398th Bomb Group drops bombs on an enemy target sometime in early 1945. This photograph shows the close formation flying that was necessary for tight bomb patterns and survival against any attacking enemy aircraft. The Group's distinctive markings show very well in this photograph.

The B-17G on the far right is AAF 43-38951 (N7-B) and was a replacement aircraft assigned to the 603rd B.S. in January 1945. It survived the war, only to be smelted in Kingman, Arizona in late 1945. Just above this airplane is the Vega-built AAF 44-8500 (K8-F) and it was assigned to the 602nd B.S. in January 1945. It also survived the war, only to be broken-up for scrap. The B-17G on the far left is AAF 42-102593 (K8-C), *Vonnie*, and was one of the original operational aircraft assigned to the 602nd B.S. in May 1944. This B-17G held the second highest number of missions for a 398th B.G. airplane. Unfortunately, this airplane was scrapped in Kingman, Arizona in late 1945.   (398th Bomb Group Memorial Association via Willis Frazier)

were positioned forward of the national insignia.

The 398th made other significant changes to their B-17Gs. According to the 398th Bomb Group's official history, the Group made some weight and balance studies of Boeing's bombardment airplane and discovered the Boeing B-17G's center of gravity was a whole foot aft of where Boeing's manuals said it should be located. An aft center of gravity caused significant performance loss at high

altitudes with a heavy bomb load, increased engine strain and wear due to higher constant power settings, increased fuel consumption, higher crew workload to stay in formation, increased airborne aborts and so forth.

In an effort to move the center of gravity closer to where Boeing's manuals said it should be located, the 398th Bomb Group and other bomb groups flying the B-17G removed the airplane's de-icing equipment, the radio

Colonel Frank P. Hunter - 398th Bombardment Group (H) Commander 1943 - 1945. He was killed in action on January 23, 1945.

(James B. Zazas)

compartment's .50-caliber machine gun, one waist gunner position and a lot of ammunition from the rear of the airplane. These changes improved the B-17G's combat performance significantly with little significant degradation of its superlative defensive firepower.

Col. Frank P. Hunter, Jr. was the 398th's commander when I arrived. He was a popular commander and the men enjoyed serving under his command. Using a self-imposed rotation schedule, he flew many missions with the four bomb squadrons under his command. Moreover, he was active in the civic affairs in the Nuthampstead area and was well liked by the local citizens. On several occasions, he brought orphan children on base where they were treated to a party of ice cream and cake, then taken on a tour of the flight line.

Col. Hunter remained the unit's commander until his death while flying his seventeenth mission on January 23, 1945. He was leading the 398th and hundreds of other Eighth Air Force bombers on a mission over Neuss, Germany (near Cologne) when his aircraft received a direct hit from an anti-air-

craft shell that sheared his left wing. Only the pilot, Lt. Frederico Gonzales, survived. Col. Frank P. Hunter, Jr. is buried at the American Battle Monuments Cemetery at Ardennes near Liege, Belgium, along with forty-one other members of the 398th Bomb Group.

Capt. Leo W. Killen, the 601st Squadron Commander, met us when we arrived at Nuthampstead. He briefed us on what he expected from us and what we could expect at the base. Shortly thereafter, we met Capt. Willis Frazier, our squadron's Operations Officer. He scheduled the crews within our squadron to specific combat and training missions. In addition, he scheduled our free-from-duty days, or "leave" as it was known. After meeting Capt. Frazier, we met the housing officer and he assigned us to our new quarters.

I was appalled by the overall dreary living conditions at Nuthampstead. Unlike the luxurious living conditions at Bassingbourn, Nuthampstead and nearby Ridgewell provided corrugated metal-covered, semi-circular Nissen huts placed on a concrete pad, each housing twelve men. These Nissen huts covered large areas of the base. Each squadron had its own set of huts to house their men, so there were a lot of olive drab painted huts on base. The officer huts were in one area and

Nissen huts were common sights at virtually all Eighth Air Force bases. Nissen huts were temporary structures that served as housing, administration and workshops for Allied forces in England during World War II. The Nissen hut was smaller than the Quonset Hut generally used in the Pacific. This photograph shows the Nissen huts in the 398th Bomb Group, Station 131, Headquarters area.

(398th Bomb Group Memorial Association)

the enlisted men were housed in huts in a different section of the squadron area not far from the officers' quarters.

Each Nissen hut was completely open inside with no walls, which meant it was often cold and drafty. Outside light entered through a few box windows. Heat came from a single, cast iron pot-belly stove. Each hut was filled with metal-framed, thin-mattress beds and wood footlockers which held a crewmember's personal effects. Though we often complained about our paltry living conditions, we were thankful for a dry bed, unlike crews based in other, more austere

Second Lieutenant Hal Weekley, far right standing, and several officer members of his crew pose with Joe Wierney's navigator, 2nd Lt. Ernie Brass, kneeling right, in front of their Nissen Hut. Note the small board placed on the right of the hut's entrance listing only the First Pilots' names of each crew, in this case Weekley, Wierney and Hornshuh.

(Harold D. Weekley)

locations who lived in tents or under aircraft wings.

Our Nissen huts had no running water. To clean ourselves, we had to use a nearby communal shower and bathing facility connected by a wooden walkway. Unfortunately, the

showers had very little hot water; thus, our early morning shower and shave were very uncomfortable, especially when we had to get up at 3:00 a.m. or earlier for a mission.

My cramped hut housed twelve officers, four from three separate crews: mine, Joe Wierney's and Merwyn Hornshuh's. A small board placed on the right of the hut's entrance listed only the First Pilots' names of each crew, in this case Weekley, Wierney and Hornshuh.

Joe Wierney and his crew trained with my crew in the states, and we had known each other for some time. Hornshuh, on the other hand, was an "old timer" and he and his crew had flown many missions before we arrived. They were most receptive to our arriving as we replaced a crew that had failed to return from a combat mission, thus casting a pall over our housing assignment. We tried to clean the area and make it as pleasant as possible.

My best friends in England were my three officer crew members and Joe Wierney and his officer crew members. For some reason, we did not become close to Lt. Hornshuh and his crew. Perhaps it was because Hornshuh and his crew had more mission totals and had developed friendships with the men they had spent more time with in combat.

Before I left the United States, I believed Europe's summertime weather would be much like the warm and balmy condition enjoyed by most of the U.S. To my surprise, the weather during my time at Nuthampstead during June, July and August 1944 was pleasantly cool and often damp. As such, we experienced a lot of foggy mornings with limited visibility. Good weather or bad, we still flew our missions.

I remember only one day during the time I was at Nuthampstead when I felt the temperature was warm enough to go swimming. I'm sure, however, the local folks were acclimated to the damp and cool weather much better than myself, and probably enjoyed it much more than I.

Any weather related misgivings I may have had at the time paled when compared to the misery the flight and ground crews faced during the winter months. We were told that the men were given only two buckets of coal a day to heat the cast iron stove in their huts. Many crewmembers slept in their heavy sheepskin flight suits to stay warm and comfortable. Many employed "Yankee ingenuity" along with a keen sense of humor to thwart the sometimes miserable English weather.

For example, we walked on wooden walkways to get from one hut to another due to the unceasingly wet ground and resulting mud. Half-joking and half-serious, many crewmembers called our base "Mudhampstead." To say the very least, the living and flying conditions were rather less than desirable.

Wartime stories abounded all around us. We were the new guys on base and there was no shortage of tales, many true and others embellished. Though I never experienced it firsthand, I heard stories of the more seasoned veterans taunting or teasing the new crews and trying to scare them. Many of the new crewmembers shrugged off these offhand comments; whereas others listened closely.

For example, when a new crew got back from their first mission successfully and alive, they'd tell the more experienced multimission veterans, "That wasn't so bad," and they'd reply, "You'll see." After their second mission, these same crews, many obviously shaken by what they had experienced, would ask the veterans, "How can you live through twenty-five of these missions?" The veterans replied, "We told you so." The seasoned crews had no malicious intent with this taunting and used these off-hand comments to assuage their own combat-related fears and concerns.

Even my Nissen hut roommates had their own stories to share, but they did not tinge their instructive comments with any sarcasm. For example, Merwyn Hornshuh and his crew flew a harrowing mission to Hamburg's oil storage and refineries on Tuesday, June 20th and returned to Nuthampstead with an airplane so badly damaged that it was eventually salvaged for badly needed spare parts. A physically exhausted Hornshuh related to me and our other Nissen hut mates how he and his crew flew their badly damaged B-17 to base. I paid close attention to his vivid descriptions, eager to learn all I could from Hornshuh's firsthand account. Everyone knew we were here to do a job and we all knew we had to make the best of a difficult situation. I do not think any one of us would have taken too kindly to anyone trying to intimidate us.

Overall, I had little contact with the more seasoned and established crews, but those few I did meet were pleased to see us and made no effort to impress us either way. My crew was among the first group of replacements and everyone seemed to appreciate our being there. My crew was very respectful to the other officers and that in itself was very gratifying. Many later expressed their appreciation of our seriousness in overall combat training and preparation and that our efforts saved lives.

Getting used to the time was another matter. During this war, wartime England played with nature's clock and used what was called Double Daylight Savings Time. Nuthampstead was near 52 degrees North latitude, which meant during the summer months the sun began to appear on the horizon around 4:00 a.m. or so. With this wartime intrusion into the natural clock, I was seeing the sun's first light two hours later, or 6:00 a.m.

My life moved at a faster pace shortly after my crew and I arrived at Nuthampstead. We entered another training phase that lasted three weeks. We received training in local communications, combat tactics, escape and evasion. We saw official, USAAF black and white training films and listened to lectures from combat-hardened officers and crewmembers. This hectic tempo was a dramatic change from the lazy, often boring times we had aboard the troop ship. We immersed ourselves in this training, as our very survival often depended upon how well we mastered our lessons.

Moreover, we quickly learned much about the "rules" while working within our host country, England, and the ongoing need to keep information secret or confidential. Posters abounded stressing the need for caution at all times in conversation. One memorable poster was captioned, "Keep Mum. She's Not So Dumb," itself emphasizing the necessity and importance of avoiding at all times the discussion of confidential and secret matters in private and public places.

We learned many new customs and terms, also. A bar or saloon was called a "Pub" and there will be no ladies drinking at the bar. Each "Pub" had a ladies lounge. A visitor might be initiated into an interesting game of darts. The favorite drink was tea, but was brewed, not made with tea bags. Beer was not iced and was called either "mild" or "bitter." The "chemist shop" replaced the drug store, and it sold no novelties or sodas. Sodas were sold at "milk bars." Favorite British games were, and remain, cricket and football, the latter being quite different from the American version. Walks were made over the "moors" and "downs."

My crew and I had barely two days to get all our gear together and organized in our Nissen huts on June 1st before we started our training, culminating in flying familiarization and formation training flights near our base and around England, often called "Grannie flights" by the instructor pilots. My crew and I made two "Grannie flights" on June 17th and 18th 1944, logging 7 hours and 10 minutes of flight time. Though I logged the date and flight time on these training flights, I did not log the Army Air Forces serial or tail numbers of the airplanes I flew.

This busy training tempo was tempered only by the letters I wrote to Billie and my family and the letters I received from home, most of it very good news. Billie always shared with me how she was doing, all she did, her feelings, how she was coping during my absence and how she felt in her pregnancy. She wrote to me about every day and shared her love for me. I was always thrilled to hear from Billie. All her letters began with "My Darling" or "My Darling Husband" and always ended with "Your Loving Wife."

Billie's letters were informative, yet none of her mail hinted she knew the combat responsibilities I had or the conditions with which I had to contend. She knew my job was hard and dangerous, as war always is, but chose to discuss more pleasant things.

My Mother and Maxine, my sister, wrote at least once a week. During this time, my mother and step-father lived at Ft. Sill, Oklahoma, where she worked in the Post Exchange and he served as a field artillery officer. My mother later sent me a lot of Hershey candy bars which I appreciated very much.

A large portion of the personal mail from the United States was photographed and sent to the combat zones in negative form. Upon arrival, it was developed and forwarded to the appropriate facility and individual. About half my mail from Billie, mother and Maxine arrived in this form. This type of mail and its government-paid delivery was called "V-Mail."

All the letters came to A.P.O. 557, the postal designation of Station 131, the Nuthampstead airfield. Mail was available at squadron office and we picked it up at our convenience.

All the letters I received were a Godsend

Government-paid "V-Mail" letters accounted for most of the mail sent to the combat zone. This "V-Mail" letter from Billie Weekley to Lt. Harold D. Weekley, with its accompanying envelope, is shown here in actual size and format.
(Harold D. Weekley)

and I was so happy and thankful to get them. Mail from home and loved ones proved to be a greater morale booster for the fighting man than anything the USAAF provided, including USO, talent shows, movies and the like.

However, one letter left me all but devastated! I received news from Billie via an Air Mail letter dated June 8, 1944 that my maternal Grandmother Johnson had been ill, then died in early June. I was born in her

Carrollton, Ohio home and stayed there for considerable periods of time when I was very young.

Billie tried to assuage my grief. Referring to the strength of our marriage, Billie added a very heartfelt, "I wouldn't give it up for the world, or you either. I'm darn glad you talked me into getting married, or I might still be single. I wish I could do it all over again." She finished this letter with a sincere, "Since this invasion has started I hope it peps things up a little, so you & all the rest of the boys can come home."

I buried my deep sorrow losing my grandmother in my continued training. I worked even harder to do the best I could in my job, and care for my crew. Reiterating what I told several of the wives who stayed with their husbands during our training at Dalhart, Texas, I had absolutely no intention of making Billie or any wife of any of my crew a widow.

During this training, my co-pilot remained out of the seat and I had an experienced pilot fly with me, a First Lieutenant Merwin Genung. He was my squadron's Assistant Operations Officer and had flown over "Fortress Europe" on many missions, including several to Berlin. He drew upon his recent combat experience to teach my crew and me the finer points of combat flying. Our combat B-17 training at Dalhart taught us the basics of combat formation flying; First Lieutenant Genung taught us how to stay alive in combat.

We learned a great deal from Lt. Genung's insightful instruction and from the intensive instruction we received from other officers. We learned, for example, that Germany's air force, the Luftwaffe, was very experienced in defending their country, and had been doing so long before my crew ever got into the European conflict. The Luftwaffe had made remarkable advances in both aircraft design and defensive maneuvers against the superior, withering onslaught of Allied air power.

The German Air Force flew mostly day-fighters with the intent to destroy the American and Allied bombers. The key role of the American day-fighters was to destroy these German adversaries whenever they rose to challenge the bombers. Fighter advocates on both sides believed they could gain the tactical advantage through attrition.

Originally, the Eighth Air Force's fighter component, the VIII Fighter Command, was responsible for bomber escort. Unfortunately, the P-47s lacked the range to take B-17s and B-24s much beyond the German border. Worse, the P-38s struggled with high-altitude engine problems. Many range-related problems with bomber escort were solved with the introduction of jettisonable auxiliary fuel tanks which stretched the P-47's range into Germany. Long-range bomber escort became possible with the arrival of the first P-51 in early 1944 and the strategic air war began shifting in favor of the Allies.

As the war expanded, the Luftwaffe lost any advantage in the skies over Europe as attacking Allied bomber and fighter forces decimated the German Air Force. This fact was evident when fewer and fewer German fighters rose to meet the heavy bombers as the war progressed, not the massed Luftwaffe formations that almost routinely attacked the bomber formations only few short months and years earlier.

Interestingly, German single-engine fighter production actually increased in the war's waning months, but most types built were outmoded models such as the Messerschmitt Bf 109. Moreover, this increase was mollified by the fact the Luftwaffe was losing their more experienced pilots in combat just as their better-trained American fighter counterparts began to fly aircraft with superior range, maneuverability and firepower. Adding to the Luftwaffe's collapse, Eighth Air Force doctrine changed that allowed the fighters to strafe assigned targets and targets of opportunity after they had escorted to the heavy bombers to their targets. Later still, many fighters were released from escort duty altogether and allowed to attack any target of opportunity. The overall result was more aircraft and personnel losses for the Luftwaffe, and a corresponding collapse of the Nazi transportation, supply and communication infrastructure.

Nevertheless, Nazi Germany and the Luftwaffe proved very tenacious and used any available manpower, equipment and technology to moderate these increasingly overwhelming odds.

Two of the Luftwaffe's primary fighter aircraft were the Messerschmitt Bf 109 and Focke-Wulf FW 190. In capable hands, these nimble fighters proved to be tenacious and effective adversaries.
(National Museum of the United States Air Force)

For example, the German Fighter Command used, by today's standards, a rudimentary radar system. Once their radar established the possible or probable target of the raiding bombers, the Germans vectored available fighters towards the bomber stream. If the Allies were bombing a major industrial, military installation or transportation depot, then the Luftwaffe attacks were intense. These German fighters fired whatever they could at the raiding bombers. Large caliber machine guns and cannons were usually employed, but so were rockets and anything else the fighters could throw against the attacking bombers.

By the time we had arrived in Europe, many bombing missions had friendly fighter escort nearby to ward off the Luftwaffe's swift fighters. Regardless, the enemy fighters always remained a major concern, especially for a crew slugging along at 150 mph indicated airspeed (200 to 240 mph true airspeed) in a four-engine bomber. The B-17's one-sixteenth inch thick aluminum skin and the many layers of heavy clothing crewmembers wore to protect them from the harsh elements of high-altitude flying afforded little protec-

tion from German fighter machine gun and cannon fire or the bone-chilling, flesh-freezing cold.

The Luftwaffe pilots changed their aerial tactics constantly to gain a tactical advantage. For example, on several occasions, the German fighter pilots attempted to divert our attention to one side of the bomber stream while they attacked the other side of the massed formation. A few fighters would do all kinds of aerobatics trying to get our crew to observe them on one side of the bomber formation, thus diverting our attention from other vulnerable areas. Meanwhile, a much larger fighter formation would attack us from the opposite side.

Similarly, German fighters would fly by the bombers attracting the attention of the escorting fighters, who would follow in pursuit leaving the bombers vulnerable to bulk of the attacking Luftwaffe fighters that would appear as soon as our friendly escort was gone.

Of course, it didn't take long for the crews to become familiar with these ruses. Though it worked for a while, most crewmembers soon became aware of what the German pilots were doing and paid attention to their task at hand. Even so, some crews got caught in this ploy, often with disastrous results.

I learned many bomber crews were annoyed when some of the German fighter pilots intentionally flew their swift planes through the middle of a bomber formation. If the German pilots could find a formation that wasn't flying good and tight, they'd pick a spot and fly through it. Their strategy was to get the B-17 gunners on either side of them to fire, thus hitting the neighboring bomber, which occasionally led to disastrous results - the wounding or killing of a crewmember, or the damaging or downing of a B-17. Needless-to-say, the bomber crews' advantage came from flying as tight a formation as they possibly could. A tight bomber formation presented a very formidable and effective defense to any attacking fighters.

Another often-used German fighter tactic was the head-on attack. The fighters would single-out a specific bomber and attack that bomber head-on with all guns blazing. Just before the fighters got to the formation, the pilots would roll over on their backs, do a Split-S maneuver and pull away from the bomber stream. This maneuver got the greatest distance between the fighter and the bombers, and afforded the German pilots some protection from the B-17's fierce firepower, as the belly of the enemy aircraft was heavily armor plated and could take a lot more damage than the top of the aircraft.

Flak was another major concern, often more so than the fighters. In fact, flak was the major concern for most of our missions. Flak was indiscriminate. It could blast an aircraft from the sky, or a near burst could bounce around an aircraft and send hundreds of lethal metal shards through aircraft aluminum skin and human flesh and bone. Many important military targets and cities were well defended by flak or anti-aircraft guns or cannons.

The word FLAK entered the English lexicon as a German acronym that comes from "FlugAbwehrKanone," which translates as "flyer defense cannons." We only knew it came from a long German word describing anti-aircraft artillery.

Even as the numbers of the Luftwaffe aircraft that engaged us decreased, the number of flak guns increased, and virtually all were aimed against the attacking Allied heavy bomber and fighter forces. Germany moved tremendous amounts of men and material from other battle fronts in any attempt to slow the incessant, almost daily attacks by hundreds, if not thousands of raiding Allied bombers.

When the war ended in 1945, some 200,000 flak guns were in service with German Air Force and Naval units. Flak guns were often manned by high school aged boys and folks too old to fight in battle. Each teenager on a flak gun meant another German solider that could be put into the field for duty. Despite their young age, these gunners used their assigned weapon deftly to shoot down a great many American and Allied airplanes during the course of the war.

The most feared anti-aircraft guns were the German Flak 36 and Flak 37. These powerful and accurate cannons were derived from their 88mm field gun and could hurl an 88mm shell to almost 49,000 feet, well above and, obviously, well within a B-17's normal operational altitudes, usually between twenty and thirty thousand feet. When multiple flak batteries opened up, the sky filled with countless popcorn puffs of black smoke hurling jagged shrapnel - quite literally iron hail - all very lethal at a hundred yards, often more. Even if a bomber survived a flak burst, the resulting damage required extensive repairs; thus, reducing the number of aircraft available for the next mission.

A significantly more lethal flak gun hurled aloft a 105mm shell. An exploding shell from one of these devastating monsters could down a bomber from a hundred yards or more.

I learned (and later experienced first-hand) some flak that had an orange center when it exploded. If they slid past my bomber at a faster and faster rate, it meant I was getting closer to these lethal blossoms. I was told flak had a high-pitched report when it exploded nearby and the resulting violent concussions could rattle the entire aircraft, not to mention the death and destruction a direct hit or nearby burst could bring upon a bomber crew and their airplane. More distant explosions possessed a deeper "WUFF... WUFF... WUFF" with the outward flying steel shards hitting the bomber and sounding like hailstones pounding a tin roof. I knew, as did every other airmen flying over Fortress Europe, the heavy flight suits and body armor we wore offered little more protection than tissue paper from a direct hit.

The German anti-aircraft gunners' goal was not to down a specific aircraft. Instead, the gunners, after determining the bomber stream's altitude, heading and, often, the intended target, would concentrate fire into "a box" (a specific area in the sky) and continue firing until the bomber stream had all passed through this area on their way to the target. This method was a devastatingly lethal way to attack the bomber stream, as everyone in the bomber stream had to fly through it. Many wartime crews related how planes would enter a portion of the sky filled with flak only to exit either in flames or rolling over out of control. To throw off the aim of the

flak gunners, the lead pilot would make a hard turn left or right and descend a thousand or more feet upon leaving the target area. I encountered this type of concentrated anti-aircraft fire on many occasions flying to and from large cities and valuable military targets.

Many flak guns were radar guided. To counter the radar's effectiveness, the radio operators dropped chaff from a small port in their radio room. Known to the British by the code name "Window" and to the Germans as "Duppel," these cardboard-wrapped, 10 - inch long strips of aluminum foil were designed to

The Flak 36 cannon was accurate and very effective in defending Germany and German-held targets. This powerful gun could hurl an 88mm shell to almost 49,000 feet, well above a B-17's service ceiling. This fully restored example is on public display at the Fighter Factory Museum in Virginia Beach, Virginia.

(James B. Zazas)

confuse the radar directed guns. On many missions, it was not unusual for the radio operator on each bomber to drop several hundred bundles of chaff. Chaff played a key role in dodging flak.

With their radar systems rendered inaccurate, the flak gunners and ground controllers often depended on information from Luftwaffe pilots who forwarded the airspeed, altitude and heading of the heavy bomber formations. On several missions over Germany, crews reported a lone B-17 or B-24 joining the bomber stream, but keeping a respectful distance from the main body. Shortly before they encountered flak, the plane left the massed formation. Only later did they learn these planes were being flown by German pilots who, in turn, relayed valuable information to waiting flak crews on the ground.

Battle-damaged B-17s and B-24s, even Allied fighters, which had gone down in Germany relatively intact, were rebuilt by the Germans. They'd put them into A-1 shape, occasionally installing heavy weapons on board and armor plate for added protection. Then they would take off from some remote field, join the bomber stream, usually just outside the range of the Boeing .50 cal machine guns, and radio to the young German anti-aircraft crews on the ground the bomber stream's altitude, course and airspeeds.

The 100th Bomb Group learned this lesson in mid-1943 when a strangely-marked B-17 joined their formation as the Group approached their target. This mystery B-17 did not communicate with the Group and kept a respectful distance from the formation where gunners couldn't fire on them. Heavy flak exploded around the 100th before the unidentified intruder turned towards some clouds and disappeared.

Quite often, the Germans used these refurbished bombers and fighters to train their fighter crews in the strengths and weaknesses of a specific airplane. In addition, German engineers studied these airplanes in detail and used the knowledge to improve their own aircraft designs.

The Germans liked to "spoof" an attacking bomber formation by relaying false course correction information over our VHF frequencies. These tactics were intended to bring one or more bombers within effective range of waiting flak gunners.

Regardless of the manner used to protect their homeland, the Germans were tenacious in their opposition to the striking Allied bomber and fighter forces.

These examples are only a few of the many important lessons of combat survival I learned before and during combat missions. Lessons etched in my mind, and were valuable throughout my military career.

After we completed the in-theater familiarization and training flights, my crew and I were ready to fly our first combat mission on Wednesday, June 21,1944, which was incidentally the 398th Bomb Group's thirty-sixth group mission. Lt. Genung was assigned to fly with me as copilot, thus bouncing my regular copilot, Benjamin Clark, from his seat for this important mission. Lt. Genung flew with many of the 398th's crews on their first mission to help get them up-to-speed on combat operations.

A notice posted on the squadron bulletin board at 1700 hours was the normal routine for announcing a combat mission for the next day. This meant the bomb group received a Field Order from Division headquarters tasking the Group to fly a mission. This notice listed the crews scheduled to fly the next day, but nothing about the intended target and bomb loads. Crews learned the sensitive information the next morning at the obligatory briefing. When the notice was posted on the afternoon of June 20th, my crew was included on the list.

During World War II, the Eighth Air Force's primary mission was the bombing of strategic targets within Europe, primarily Germany and German-occupied countries. Throughout the Mighty Eighth's campaign, its doctrine of daylight high-altitude precision bombing using massed formations of heavy bombers changed little, and actual bombing procedures varied as necessary to thwart changing enemy opposition and tactics. Regardless of the targets selected, the Eighth Air Force relied upon its vast armada of men, aircraft and material to bomb Europe.

Quite simply, the mission of the Eighth Air Force was to "Hit the target!" To this end and to the Eighth Air Force's esteemed credit, no mission was ever turned back due to enemy opposition. A highly coordinated team effort made this admirable record possible.

While I was stationed at Nuthampstead, I never knew the full story behind the incredible planning that went into each bombing mission. Only after World War II had ended did I learn how each mission progressed from detailed briefings at Eighth Air Force Head-quarters in High Wycombe, England (code named Pinetree) to preparing the airplanes for their arduous mission to the actual drop-ping of bombs on the selected target. More-over, I remain amazed how this rigorous process was accomplished time and time again with most airmen involved being barely out of high school. This finely honed process worked its way through a myriad of commands and individuals, beginning with a few ranking officers in the upper echelons of the command, eventually reaching the combat crews that flew the missions. Not to be forgotten, this process involved many other individuals, including the guys who cooked our pre-flight breakfast, the crew chiefs and maintenance personnel who kept our planes flying and the security forces who kept our bases secure.

The Eighth Air Force's general staff and senior operations officers, operating under the auspices of the Headquarters, United States Strategic Air Forces in Europe and in-cluding the Fifteenth Air Force command as of February 1944, would meet at Headquar-ters, Eighth Air Force at High Wycombe. This operations staff stood ready to brief the Deputy Commander of Operations. Potential targets were discussed while weather analysts and intelligence experts stood by to provide whatever information was requested. (See Endnotes, Chapter 6, Number 1)

With the weather and latest in-telligence information in hand, the Chief of Operations decided what targets would be attacked, the strength of the attacking force and, quite often, the ordinance require-ments. He selected targets accord-ing to the current Combined Bomber Offensive directives. Dur-ing the summer of 1944, these di-rectives included robbing

Germany's Third Reich of its oil production and storage capacity, wearing down the Luft-waffe air strength, and destroying any other means for the enemy to make war. Quite often, the Chief of Operations sent the attack-ing force towards two or three separate tar-gets. This tactic forced the Germans to spread their fighter forces and, concurrently, offered the attacking bombers a greater chance of success.

In rapid succession, other officers at Pine-tree prepared a coordinated plan of attack for the participating air divisions. Advance warning of the mission was forwarded via teletype printers to the three Bomb Division headquarters who, in turn, alerted the Com-bat Bomb Wings who, in turn, alerted the in-dividual Bomb Groups. Later, a Field Order was sent confirming the order of the Combat Bomb Wings, the Bomb Groups and squadrons within each, the times, the targets (printed in a coded form), the routes to be flown, and the final bomb loads. Generally by 1700 hours, the Operations Officer in each squadron posted a notice of who would be flying on the next day's mission.

While this beehive flurry of activity took place, bases throughout England geared up

The Officers Mess Hall played an important role in the officers' morale and health before they embarked upon their hazardous combat missions.
(James B. Zazas)

for the forthcoming missions. Tensions began to build and nervous chat led to plausible rumor. Those crews scheduled to fly quietly asked themselves where would they be going? How many bombers would be participating in the raid? Rarely, if ever, did anyone mention the unspeakable - how many crewmembers would not come back?

Anticipating a long day ahead, my crew and the others scheduled for this mission had an early dinner, and then headed for our bunks shortly after dining. Those officers and enlisted crewmembers not scheduled to fly often went to their respective clubs for relaxation after dinner.

Any sleep was fitful, at best. The constant drone of airplane engines being run-up by crew chiefs doing preflight warm-ups and tests interrupted our sleep. Worse, the public address system always broadcasted some announcement or message intended for those dedicated souls prepping our bombers for the next day's missions.

In a scene often repeated on our base and at other bomber bases, a sergeant with flashlight in hand entered our darkened barracks in the wee hours of the morning to wake-up those scheduled to fly that day. I was awakened barely an hour after midnight with a gentle tug on my arm and an accompanying, "Mission today, Lieutenant. Briefing at 0215 hours." The same cheerful news greeted my other officers.

So this was it. I was 22 years old and my baptism by fire would be today. All I learned over the last year and half would be tested today. Now, the time arrived to demonstrate my mettle in actual combat. The time arrived, also, for my crew to demonstrate their trained teamwork.

Strangely, I was not afraid, but I was apprehensive. My greatest fear was letting down my crew. I had already resigned myself to the fact I was not going to return home and I intended to inflict the greatest damage I could on the enemy. I knew I'd be very happy to complete my prescribed tour, but I had

strong doubts about that possibility. Neither I nor my crew ever discussed this possibility openly and we kept any apprehensions to ourselves.

During the whole time I was in England, I made every effort to be in the best physical condition, well rested, as knowledgeable about the operation and the target as possible and give my crew the impression I had a positive attitude as to its conclusion. No one knows the end result, but in my mind, I knew if we were to be lost, then we were going to make life for the enemy as difficult as we could.

I had fifteen minutes to dress and shave before breakfast. Because the oxygen mask had to fit tightly to perform properly, bomber crewmembers always shaved to prevent any whiskers from causing irritation and icing where the oxygen mask fitted over the face.

I joined several other officers and headed for the Officers Mess Hall for breakfast. On mission days, the flight crews were served real eggs (versus powdered eggs for non-flying crews), juice, cereal, toast, biscuits, coffee and powdered milk. On occasion, real milk was available. The meals were not particularly appealing and dining was not one of the highlights of the day.

The mess hall was always full before a mission and often noisy. The officers ate in one mess hall and the enlisted men in another. We sat at tables that accommodated about ten men. The conversation revolved around guessing the target based upon what little information we had as to the progress of the war. On rare occasions, a crewmember would be unusually quiet as he reflected upon his own destiny.

Slightly more than an hour after being awakened, my fellow officers and I filed into the briefing room, a large Nissen hut or some other structure that could seat two hundred men. On the front wall, an outsized black cloth covered a large map of the European continent. It was mounted above a low stage or platform. There were barely enough chairs for all present. Every so often, the enlisted crewmembers joined their officers for the briefing. Those enlisted crewmembers who did join the briefing had to have a special, signed pass to attend.

Anxiety ran high as we waited for the briefing officer to reveal the day's mission. Jokes and wisecracks filled the air to relieve the tension.

At 0215 hours sharp, the briefing began with a call to attention with a sharp "TennHut!" followed by a quick greeting by the Operations Officer or the Group Commanding Officer, who then signaled for us to take our seats for the actual briefing. In rapid succession, either he or the appointed briefing officer, usually the Operations Officer, stepped to the platform and lifted the black cover.

When the map was uncovered, we saw our targets for the first time. A simple piece of string marked the mission route or routes from our base to the target and back to our base.

On some days, the target routes were shown to be simple "milk runs," with the bombers striking easy targets within France, the Netherlands or some other location that presented little enemy opposition. The deeply furrowed faces of anxiety filled crewmembers eased slightly if we were scheduled to fly such an easy mission.

Other targets, especially those located much deeper into continental Europe, were cause for much concern. On those occasions, especially if the target was heavily defended, such as Berlin, there would be a muted, yet audible collective moan. Occasionally, one or more crewmembers would utter a terse expletive. These moans and comments were more a means to assuage the high anxiety of the moment than announce any legitimate complaint.

On Wednesday, June 21st, muted groans, audible gasps and a few expletive remarks filled the air in the 398th's briefing room. Pulse rates quickened considerably. All eyes

were fixed on the large map before them and the long black string that seemed to stretch forever, reaching deep into the heart of Germany itself. There would be no "milk run" today.

My first combat mission - my crew's first combat mission - would be to Berlin - the "Big B."

All eyes in the briefing hall that chilly June morning followed that simple piece of sting as it arched northeastward from Nuthampstead through England's East Anglia and across the North Sea. At a point barely twenty miles from Denmark coast, the string traced a more east-southeasterly direction, passing well north of Hamburg. As it passed over Lake Schaal, some thirty miles east of Hamburg, the string turned easterly on a route that took it well north and east of Berlin, whereupon it turned sharply southeast before turning in a more southerly direction crossing slightly inside Poland's western border. Nearing Berlin, the string made a sharp southwesterly turn over a geographical point some twenty miles northeast of Berlin. This critically important navigation point was marked in black letters as "IP" and represented the "Initial Point," the last navigation point and the beginning of the actual bomb run. From the IP, the string turned

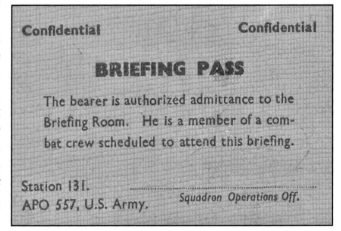

TSgt. Ven Unger's Briefing Pass. A Briefing Pass was needed for any enlisted personnel wishing to attend the officers' mission briefing as the briefing room was often very crowded and extra space was scarce.

(Ven B. Unger)

southwesterly until it was directly over Berlin, whereupon it turned more northwesterly and rejoined the inbound string over Lake Schaal. From there, our flight home was a reverse of our inbound route.

We would be flying over enemy territory for many hours on this mission, and we all knew the innumerable number of Germans

Alert combat crewmembers paid close attention to what is said at the obligatory combat mission briefing. What they learned often meant the difference between life and death during the actual mission! (National Archives, 342-FH-3A13781-26338 A.C.)

below our intended route sought to do great harm to us. Though our primary objective was to bomb Berlin, and do our assigned job well, I knew all present desired to return safely - at least alive - and tally one more successful mission that would get us closer to home.

The mission's circuitous route avoided a large number of cauliflower-shaped red scallops and circles on the wall chart. These hastily-drawn annotations marked high threat areas, mostly cities and towns well defended by flak batteries and Luftwaffe airfields. Our mission planners took great pains to avoid as many threats as possible on every mission.

This June 21st mission to Berlin was the first strike to the Nazi capital since the D-Day invasion landings on France two weeks earlier and was by far the largest Eighth Air Force attack on Berlin and its environs.

Berlin was targeted because of an unusual event that had occurred the previous night

over England. Starting that evening and lasting throughout the night, England experienced the terror from the V-1 "Buzz Bomb," a small, stubby-winged flying bomb that carried a 200 lb warhead and was powered by a pulse-jet engine. At a preset time, the V-1's engine would quit and this new terror would nose over and dive earthward. The resulting explosion on the ground would level homes and businesses. This new terror weapon was designed to inflict indiscriminate injury and death upon the British population, while aiming to rupture or break the steadfast British resolve to wage war against Germany.

When the first of Hitler's "Vengeance Weapons"(Vergeltungswaffe) started falling on England barely a week earlier, no one knew quite what was taking place and all manner of conjecture floated about us as to what was actually happening. But, as we soon learned, the V-1 - the "Doodlebug" as the British called them - was wreaking deadly havoc around England. Spectacular in concept and brilliant in deployment, a V-1 attack was a very frightening experience for anybody underneath its flight path.

Over the next year, more than nine thousand V-1s were launched against England, with one-fourth falling due to various mechanical problems and almost half destroyed by Allied countermeasures, which included anti-aircraft fire, balloon cables and fighter interception. Sadly, the one fourth that flew through this defensive shield fell on London and the surrounding English countryside killing several thousand English men, women and children, injuring thousands and leaving thousands more homeless.

Our mission briefing that chilly Wednesday, June 21st morning was virtually identical to the format used for all other mission briefings given throughout the Eighth Air Force. The Group's Operations Officer started with a general overview of the mission before he got more specific. He gave us the engine start time, the taxi and takeoff times, the time to the English coast, the time to reach the continental European coast, the time to the IP and the landing time. In addition, the briefer gave us the fuel loads, altitudes we would fly, total flying time, type and intensity of expected enemy opposition (flak or fighters), and information where and when we would get or expect fighter escort. Attacking Berlin meant we would encounter the best the Germans had to offer to protect their capital city. To this end, we knew we would encounter a lot of flak and most likely the brunt of the Luftwaffe's fury.

The importance of attacking Berlin cannot be overstated. At the start of the war in 1939, Berlin was the primary industrial and commercial center on the European continent with a pre-war population of well over four million people. Berlin was home to various government ministries and military headquarters, as well as numerous significant industrial and commercial targets arose in and around the city.

Sir Archibald Sinclair, ansard Extract, summed it best when he told the British House of Commons on December 1st, 1943:

> ...Berlin is the center of twelve strategic railways; it is the second largest port in Europe; it is connected with the whole canal system of Germany; and in that city are the AEG, Siemens, Daimler Benz, Focke Wulf, Heinkel and Dornie establishments; and if I were allowed to choose any one target in Germany, the target I would choose would be Berlin.

The 398th's mission to Berlin on June 21st was a small, yet integral part of what the Eighth Air Force called a "Maximum Effort" mission. The Eighth Air Force, following its relentless campaign of daylight precision bombing, committed virtually every available heavy bomber and fighter resource to this raid. More than thirteen hundred B-17s and B-24s and eleven hundred escorting fighters were scheduled to fly against German targets. At least sixteen B-17 and B-24 combat bomb wings were scheduled to fly over the city itself while another seven B-17 and B-24 combat bomb wings were directed towards the aircraft engine works and tank engine works on Berlin's outskirts. Other bomber formations were scheduled to attack synthetic oil production plants at Ruhland located some seventy-five miles south of Berlin. Additional forces were planned to include the 15th Air Force based in Italy, but were withdrawn.

Most of the heavy bombers involved were scheduled to return to England. I learned later other bomb groups continued to Russia after their bomb runs over Berlin, then returned to England on a subsequent mission. (See Endnotes, Chapter 6, Number 2)

The attacking heavy bombers were to be supported and escorted by eight hundred and fifty P-51s, P-47s and P-38s from the VIII Fighter Command and almost four hundred and fifty fighters from IX Fighter Command.

These fighters, our "Little Friends," provided front, top and rear cover. In simpler terms, this very welcome fighter cover kept any marauding enemy fighters at bay while we did our job.

The British threw their weight into this important mission, as well. The British Bomber Command scheduled nine hundred Royal Air Force Lancaster bombers to follow the Eighth Air Force bombers into Berlin on their first large scale daylight raid, but were withdrawn when it was deemed there would be insufficient fighter escort to take care of the slower and less heavily armed British bombers.

The 398th Bomb Group was tasked to fly the Lead and Low groups of the 1st "B" Combat Bomb Wing (CBW) box that day, an inspiring aerial armada consisting of nineteen and eighteen airplanes respectively. Thirty-seven B-17Gs, with the "Triangle W" emblazoned on their red vertical stabilizers, were scheduled to fly from Nuthampstead and join this massive raid against Germany's bustling capital, the thirteenth Eighth Air Force raid to Berlin. Rounding out the 1st "B" CBW were eighteen B-17Gs from the 91st Bomb Group occupying the High Group position.

Major Leo Killen, my Squadron Commander, was tasked to lead this mission. I was assigned to fly right wing or the number two position of the lead element in the Low Squadron of the Lead Group. My assigned ship was AAF 42-102516 (3O-H). Stations, the time we were to be in our seats and ready to fly, was fixed at 0415 hours with engine start beginning fifteen minutes later. Taxi was to begin 0440 and takeoff was planned for 0500 through 0555. Our bomb group was to assemble over the Debden Buncher beacon before proceeding to another beacon to join-up with other massed heavy bombers. The mission was to be flown between 26,300 feet and 27,000 feet, creating the distinct probability of reduced visibility due to contrails formed by the preceding combat bomb wings. As briefed, we were scheduled to bomb Berlin be-tween 1010 and 1014. Before he turned to the weather officer, the Operations Officer concluded his portion of the briefing by saying we would encounter strong fighter opposition, and potentially heavy and accurate flak. He then gave us the obligatory "time hack" to synchronize all watches. (See Endnotes Chapter 6, Number 3)

We were stirring uneasily in our seats when the weather officer stepped to the platform and gave us a detailed weather briefing. Being summertime in Europe, I expected the prevailing weather to be partly cloudy to clear except for the occasional towering cumulus clouds or thunderstorms. On this important mission, however, the weather was less than ideal. The weather was a low overcast at 700 feet with tops at 1800 feet extending to the European Continent with three miles visibility, remaining overcast through most of the route, becoming partly cloudy from the Initial Point to the target. The target forecast was unrestricted visibility. Surface winds at takeoff were 035 degrees at 18 knots.

A nimble British-built Mosquito twin-engine fighter-bomber flown by an American crew served as the weather ship. It took-off well ahead of the bombers scheduled takeoff time and flew to Germany to update the forecast. The crew reported its findings before we took-off.

On rare occasions, a nasty storm did blow in from the Atlantic Ocean or North Sea and created havoc to flight operations. Despite this inclement weather, we still took off and flew our missions with rare exception when the weather was so bad we were unable to fly at all.

Next, the Ordinance Officer stood up and briefed us on our bomb load for the day. For this mission to Berlin, the 398th carried a mixed load of 500 lb, AN-M64 General Purpose (GP) bombs, 500 lb, AN-M17 chemical cluster bombs and 100 lb, HX27 incendiary or chemical bombs. Each plane was loaded with 5,000 pounds of destruction destined for the enemy. The GP bombs had quarter-second delay fuses fitted in their tails, which guaranteed maximum destruction. A few planes carried delay-fused bombs set to go off at six, twelve, twenty-four, thirty-six and seventy-two hours after being dropped. This mix of bomb loads was designed to destroy the intended targets and create maximum hazardous conditions for the firefighting and UBX (Unexploded Bomb Ordinance) crews.

On this mission, my B-17 carried eight, 500 lb, AN-M64 GP bombs and two 100 lb, HX27 incendiary bombs.

When all was distilled, our mission orders were really quite simple: drop

Each combat crewmember had a specific task to perform during a combat mission. Here, pilots, navigators and bombardiers gather to review charts, weather, performance data and any other information deemed pertinent to the combat mission to be flown.   (National Archives, 342-FH-3A1378-B26338 A.C.)

our bombs on a bridge within Berlin, or any place west of the targeted bridge. The mandatory briefing concluded with the Base Chaplin praying for our souls and asking forgiveness for our transgressions, followed by Col. Hunter's usual, encouraging comments of "Good luck" and "See you when you return." Standing once more at attention, we were dismissed. The navigators and bombardiers stayed or went to separate huts to receive further briefings. There they received their mission boards, along with the charts, radio codes and any other materials necessary for the mission.

Each of us had specific tasks to perform. While I studied the performance charts and received any last minute instructions, my copilot went to the personal equipment room to get the escape and evasion kits for the entire crew. My navigator drew and annotated his charts and flight plans while my bombardier studied the target data and any available photographs, noting important ground and building features and check points.

The gunners received their own briefing, as well. An Intelligence Officer briefed the gunners on enemy defenses, including where they would expect to encounter fighters. Then the Operations Officer briefed them on any fighter escort, types of airplanes and rendezvous procedures. The gunner's briefing was shorter than the officers' briefings. Afterwards, the gunners went to the equipment stores to gather their flight rations, parachutes and harnesses, and heavy flight clothing, comprised of leather-covered, fleece-lined flying suits, gloves and boots, oxygen masks and "Mae West" inflatable life vests.

The radio operators received the day's codes, frequencies and information about the recall word. To prevent this valuable information from falling into the wrong hands during combat, it was printed on rice paper and sandwiched between two thin films of water-soluble plastic. Then, they would gather the necessary flight rations, flight clothing and survival equipment. If chaff was to be used, it was loaded onboard before the radio operator arrived.

After the officers' briefing and post-briefing preparation, we went to the equipment room to draw our flight rations, which included oranges and some concentrated carbohydrate candies, and equipment. Survival kits were issued which included silk hose, candies, a small compass, escape maps and some French and German money. Afterwards, we joined the balance of the crews and boarded trucks that took us to our respective airplanes. Arriving at my B-17G, I made a few mental observations. We were assigned to fly airplane #516, the *Bronx Bomber II*. The number represented the last three digits of airplane's assigned Army Air Forces' serial number, AAF 42-102516, which was painted in black block numbers on the plane's massive fin. My squadron and airplane's identifying code, 3OH, was painted in much larger block letters and numbers on both sides of bare metal fuselage.

I gave my crew a quick, yet thorough pre-flight briefing about our mission. I described our times, weather and any pertinent information about enemy opposition.

Afterwards, I made a careful preflight inspection of my "Flying Fortress" and checked with my crew chief that all was in proper working order. Together, we reviewed the fuel, ammunition and bomb load. My plane was loaded with almost 2800 gallons of flammable, high-octane fuel, enough to fly to Berlin and back. My assigned bomb load - 4,200 pounds of enemy destruction - was secured in their proper shackles with all fuse pins in place. I did not want to be part of any ground accident or mishap with so many explosive bombs secured only a few feet away from me.

The bomber crew chiefs played a vital role in every mission. They ensured that their assigned airplane was "mission ready." While the bomber crews ate breakfast and received their briefings, even as these same crews slept the night before a mission, the crew chiefs and mechanics checked and verified that all engines, turbochargers, magnetos, electric, hydraulic, oil and oxygen systems checked "OK." Afterwards, fuel, oil and oxygen quantities were topped-off as necessary. The crew chiefs' duties were indispensable and they discharged their assigned duties much in the same way a symphony orchestra conductor directs his musicians, with great care and diligence. A pilot could kick the tires and light the fires, so to speak, but it was the crew chief

After their respective pre-mission briefings, crewmembers went to the base equipment room to draw parachutes, flight rations and survival equipment. Afterwards, they joined their crews and boarded trucks and other vehicles which took them to their assigned airplanes. (National Museum of the United States Air Force)

who knew the exact status of his airplane at all times. The crew chief made the final decision about the condition and availability of his airplane.

A fully loaded B-17G, equipped with "Tokyo Tanks," carried 2,800 gallons of highly flammable 100-octane fuel. This fuel load represented one-forth of the bomber's 65,000 pound gross weight at takeoff, though this gross weight was often exceeded. Bomb loads were usually 5,000 pounds but sometimes approached 6,000 pounds. With so much flammable fuel and explosive weaponry on board, the crew chiefs and the other maintenance personal worked long hours to make sure each bomber was in the best possible mechanical condition before it took-off on a mission. Nobody relished the thought of an engine failure on takeoff with the end result usually being a horrific crash on or beyond the end of the runway.

While I talked with the plane's crew chief and undertook my own preflight inspection, my crewmembers put on the last of their high-altitude flying gear, including their inflatable "Mae West" life preservers and parachute harnesses, boarded the bomber and went about their individual duties to ensure a safe and successful mission. Lt. Genung, the instructor and First Pilot for this particular mission, readied the cockpit for flying and verified that each switch and lever was in its proper position. Joe Skarda, my flight engineer and top turret gunner, worked closely with the First Pilot during this cockpit preflight. Ray Delbart, my bombardier, checked the oxygen system and made sure the bombs were secured properly on the bomb racks before he settled into his Perplex-nosed enclosure ahead of the cockpit. Ven Unger, my radioman, secure in his small compartment immediately aft of the bomb bay and surrounded by a couple racks of crystal-tuned radios, checked his radios and set-up the necessary frequencies. He set up his radio log and noted when the first engine was started. Gene Leonard, Bob Srickel, Joe Fabian and

"Pop" Stombaugh, my enlisted gunners, made sure their weapons, the formidable Browning .50-cal. machine guns were secured and that all allotted ammunition - usually 9,000 rounds total - was aboard, plus more if they could get it!

Think about it. Each of the 13 machine guns aboard could fire 750 rounds per minute, which means that each gun had only a one minute supply of ammunition! With many missions lasting eight or more hours, the gunners had to use their ammunition wisely.

I donned my yellow "Mae West" life preserver and white parachute harness with the parachute rings on the front to attach the chest pack parachute, should the need ever arise. Underneath all, I dressed much like most of my crew on this mission, a full suit of khaki woolen underwear, a basic uniform devoid of necktie with my insignia of rank and dog tags. Unlike some crewmembers on other airplanes, I never wore an electrically-heated "blue-bunny" flight suit underneath my flight clothing. My GI-issued brown shoes were covered by an oversized pair of heavy fleece-lined boots. Leather-covered, fleece-lined pants and a heavy flying jacket completed this ensemble. The gunners wore thick anti-flak jackets over everything else. Now, fully dressed for the combat mission ahead of me, I boarded my B-17G, settled into the left seat and joined my combat crew, my fighting flying team, prepared for its first battle with a precision drilled into them by many months of diligent training.

At the appointed time, a green flare arced into the still-dark morning sky and we settled into our respective stations. I had the crew check-in on the plane's intercom. Shortly afterwards, 1st Lt. Genung and I began reading our Before Starting Engines checklists in a measured cadence honed from a year-and-half of military flight training.

Within minutes, a second green flare marked a bright path announcing the briefed time to start engines. Lt. Genung and I started the Boeing's four Wright Cyclone radial engines one at a time, manipulating starter switches, primers, mixture controls and throttles as necessary to coax each 1200 hp engine to life. Starting engines in a 1, 2, 3 and 4 sequence, propellers slowly turned before each engine belched a cloud of blue-white smoke and smoothly accelerated to idle power with a deeply throbbing roar. The dew-covered green landscape around Nuthampstead shook gently as one hundred and forty-eight engines, from thirty-seven B-17's, were warmed for taxi, takeoff and flight.

Lt. Genung released the brakes and we moved slowly, carefully from our hardstand. Our bomber's expander tube brakes squealed a noisy protest each time I gently tapped them, careful not to overtake the airplane in front of us. With choreographed precision, we joined the other 398th Bomb Group B-17s taxiing in the morning mist on the base's perimeter track. Occasionally, the bright light from a landing light stabbed the disappearing early morning darkness as a pilot negotiated a turn. For those officers standing atop the Nuthamstead control tower, the sights and sounds of our moving armada that morning must have been quite impressive.

As our bomb group's thirty-seven airplanes moved in unison towards takeoff, I knew this incredible scene was being repeated at many other Eighth Air Force bases around England as hundreds of other bombers and fighters assembled for this raid. At the time, I never entertained any thoughts of how many planes would not return. I had a mission to perform, and I was intent to do the best job possible.

As we moved closer to the runway, I saw a pair of green flares arching skyward near the control tower. The mission was on. My crew and most of the 398th Bomb Group were going to Berlin!

In the midst of all this determined activity, I had little time to ponder the fact the first American pilots over Berlin flew their mis-

sion from Nuthampstead on March 3, 1944. The 55th Fighter Group, which was based at Nuthampstead at that time and equipped with P-38 Lightnings, was tasked to support an attacking heavy bomber force. Lt. Col. Jack Jenkins led the group. Bad weather forced a recall and most escorting fighters and attacking bombers returned home, but Jenkins and his fellow pilots remained at their assigned rendezvous point and circled the outskirts of Berlin for the bombers that never came. As a result, Jenkins and his small group of Lightning pilots became the first Americans to fly over Berlin in daylight and received considerable attention from an admiring American and British press.

A day later, heavy bombers did appear over Berlin in daylight for the first time, thus obliterating German Reichsmarshall Hermann Goering's pompous boast to Hitler, "If bombers appear over Berlin you can call me Meier!" Goering later admitted he knew the war was lost the first time he saw Allied fighter escorts over the German capital in daylight.

Barely a week after this bold daylight attack, American Secretary of War Henry L. Stimson commented to the press in Washington, D.C., "American attacks on the capital indicate to the Nazis that no target is now safe day or night."

The task at hand jerked me to reality. I looked at the aircraft in front of me as they slowly disappeared in the early morning haze as each bomber made its takeoff. Only the eerie glow of the white-hot superchargers gleaming under their silver wings revealed each airplane's presence.

Strangely, I wasn't at all nervous as I maneuvered our heavily laden bomber into position on the runway. I reached towards the center console and put the cowl flaps into the trail position. Lt. Genung set the directional gyro. I called for the tailwheel to be locked and Lt. Genung responded with a crisp, "Tailwheel locked. Light's out!"

The morning sun was announcing its

daily presence over the distant horizon as I held the brakes hard and pushed our Flying Fortress' throttles forward until all four engines reached full takeoff power and 2500 RPMs. The noise was intense, even through our well-padded earphones. The big Boeing trembled mightily. Lt. Genung and I made a last, quick scan of the engine instruments to make sure all was in order. Satisfied, I took my feet off the brakes and the plane lurched

with better performance than the 80 octane fueled training B-17s we flew back home.

On takeoffs, the pilot does not look at the airspeed indicator but rather relies on the copilot or flight engineer to call out the airspeed, "Sixty… sixty-five… seventy… seventy-five… eighty…eighty-five… ninety…" Past ninety, we were too fast to abort safely. At "one-oh-five," our B-17 came off the ground slowly, lifting smoothly from the runway. When a

With engines running, the *Tar Heel Lemon*, AAF 44-6157 (N8-W), prepares for takeoff on another combat mission in a scene reenacted at Nuthampstead nearly two hundred times between May 6, 1944 and April 25, 1945. Other aircraft identified in this photograph include AAF 44-8044 (N7-X), AAF 42-97746 (K8-T), AAF 44-8031 (3O-K) and AAF 43-3786 (N8-T).   (398th Bomb Group Memorial Association)

forward as the four, massive Hamilton-Standard propellers grabbed the air. My eyes fixed forward, looking down Nuthampstead's 6,000-foot concrete runway and I concentrated on keeping our bomber on the runway's centerline. Building speed, I commanded "Lock throttles!" and Lt. Genung responded with a crisp, "Throttles locked!" The heavily-laden Boeing accelerated slowly at first but gained speed rapidly. This was a combat aircraft and set-up for 100 octane fuel

positive rate of climb was established, I commanded "Wheels up!" Reaching forward, Lt. Genung raised a red cover and toggled a switch to raise the electrically driven landing gear. Both main wheels and the tail wheel retracted smoothly. Shortly afterwards, I called for "Climb power!" TSgt. Skarda, my flight engineer and top turret gunner, and Lt. Genung set the power. We scanned the engine instruments and the vents on the wings for any sign of trouble. Spotting none, I started a slow climb. Almost effortlessly, my crew and I settled quickly into a routine borne of endless hours of rigorous Army Air Forces training.

Fifty-four airplanes from the 398th Bomb Group and 91st Bomb Group formed at the briefed Debden Buncher beacon in relatively clear skies before joining the main bomber force. Once assembled, this considerable show of force continued a slow and gradual climb over the cold, choppy waters of the North Sea. (See Endnotes, Chapter 6, Number 3)

Heading in a northeasterly direction and climbing constantly, our group was one small part of a massive bomber stream that stretched for a hundred miles or more. Long, white contrails streamed behind the massed, higher formations, marking the bomber stream's position against the azure sky above for all to see, including the enemy below us. Sometimes, an altitude change of a few hundred feet was all that was necessary to avoid making contrails, but such change was often impractical with large formations. To see so many airplanes in one place at one time was truly awesome and decidedly inspiring. On this day, America and her Allies were striking deep into the heart of the German war machine.

Once we flew above 10,000 feet, and according to standing operating procedure, we donned our oxygen masks to prevent hy-

poxia and commenced our intercom check-ins. Each man responded with his position and a simple "Roger" or "O.K." Not long afterwards, Lt. Genung cleared each man to check his weapon. An incredible din filled the airplane as the gunners cleared their guns with a short burst from their .50-cal. machine

Though beautiful for photographs, exhaust condensation was a real problem for World War II heavy bomber crews as it marked their position quite well for enemy forces. A change of a few hundred feet higher or lower was often all that was necessary to avoid making contrails, but such change was impractical with large formations.
(Peter M. Bowers)

guns, the rounds falling harmlessly to the earth and water below us. Our radio operator monitored his radios for any recall messages or mission changes. All in order, we continued on the mission.

We flew into a brilliant, rising sun that morning on the inbound leg to Berlin. For most of the mission, we flew over a solid undercast. I knew if we encountered any enemy aircraft, they would be waiting for us in the sun's glare.

Climbing slowly through 20,000 feet or so, we crossed the North Sea and into enemy airspace over southern Denmark. I am sure many Danes were quietly happy to hear the constant, thundering drone of our armada flying eastward and the unparalleled opportunity to see, if the prevailing weather allowed, the contrails left behind a thousand or more bombers bringing the war into the heart of Germany.

I am sure, also, German radar had spotted us and commands were being issued to various Luftwaffe units to intercept us. We were over enemy territory. Pulse rates quickened and anxious eyes scanned the skies for enemy fighters. Strangely, I was not afraid, but I knew some level of real fear gnawed within the gut of every man on that mission.

About this time, the entire formation went into a more rapid climb to our briefed bombing altitude. Joe Skarda was manning the top turret, so Lt. Genung and I advanced the throttles and adjusted the turbochargers to maintain full power. We used the large trim wheel on the left side of the center console to ease the physical workload manipulating the elevator flight control. Unlike the modern warplanes of today, many that possess sophisticated hydraulically actuated flight controls and computer-generated flight displays, the B-17 was flown by brawn and brains, and we used a lot of both during each mission.

The trip was rather uneventful until around 0930 hours when the lead elements of the bomber stream were attacked near Muritz Lake by almost 75 enemy aircraft, mostly Messerschmitt Me 410s. We were some 60 miles north northwest of Berlin and fifteen minutes from the Initial Point when attacked. In the ensuing melee, I observed several heavy bombers and enemy aircraft going down. Airplane parts - engines, tails and wings - fell from the sky. Bodies fell, too. White silk parachutes quickly filled the sky below us. Concurrently, a few of the attacking enemy aircraft turned their attention on our combat bomb wing box.

The 91st Bomb Group occupied the combat bomb wing box immediately ahead of us and the enemy fighters mauled them. On their first pass, the nimble German fighters, flying two and three abreast, sliced through the 91st Bomb Group. They returned quickly attacking individually or in pairs from all directions around the clock. At least four B-17 Flying Fortresses fell to earth north of Berlin. Incredibly, I did not see any of our fighters in the target area or at the time of the enemy attack on the preceding combat bomb wing.

I didn't know until later that a good friend from flight school, Eddie Waters, was among the bombers and crews lost that particular day. He was co-piloting a B-17G named *Sleepy Time Gal* (AAF 42-102527, LG-H). I learned later that he and three others of his crew were the only survivors. They were captured and imprisoned. Fortunately, Waters and the surviving crewmembers returned to the United States after the war.

My first experience with any enemy activity was a head on view of Messerschmitt Bf 109, Me 110 and Focke-Wulf FW 190 fighters, the mainstay of the German fighter forces. When I saw these fighters for the first time, I observed some strange lights on their wings' leading edges blinking at me and was somewhat mesmerized by this unusual sight. I realized suddenly and to my horror that those little lights on the leading edge of the wings were actually the machine guns and cannons firing at me! These people were trying to do away with me! My crew! My airplane!

Bob Stickel manned the right waist gunner position and he fired quick bursts from his .50-cal. machine gun at the opposing fighters. The *Bronx Bomber II* trembled with each burst. Joe Skarda manned the top turret; Joe Fabian was snug in the ball turret and "Pop" Stombaugh manned the tail turret, and all four returned fire. Even Ray Delbart, my bombardier, fired off a few rounds from the chin turret. My crew's intercom chatter was slow, deliberate and professional as they called out targets to each other. Occasionally, a brief comment or interjection was made when they saw an enemy plane or a B-17 go

Flak—murderous enemy anti-aircraft fire—endangers airplanes of the 398th Bomb Group as they fly to their target. The aircraft in the upper right is AAF 42-97317 (N7-P) and was named *Little May*. It landed on the Continent near Merville, France after the mission of March 2, 1945. Repaired by the Service Command, it did not return to the 398th Bomb Group.

(398th Bomb Group Memorial Association)

down.

We had learned that the heaviest enemy aircraft action often occurred just prior to reaching the Initial Point or IP. From the IP to the target, we maintained a constant heading, a constant air speed and a constant altitude to give our bombardiers the very best stable platform to drop their bombload. The typical run-in from IP to the target lasted five to six minutes, sometimes longer. It was during this period we were most vulnerable to flak and the Germans knew it.

The first time I saw the target was while we approached the IP. I asked Paul James, my navigator, where the IP was and how far we were from the target.

He advised me in a calm voice, "Well, Skipper, if you will just look to the right you'll see a large black cloud. Well, that black cloud is anti-aircraft fire and immediately under that black cloud is the target." Seeing that

large black cloud of flak was not a pleasant experience! The flak over Berlin was intense and accurate.

As we approached the target, the ground visibility improved, but a broken cloud cover obscured much of Berlin, not exactly the good weather that was briefed. Moreover, the thick contrails left by the preceding combat bomb wing further hampered our visibility. The Wing leader came over the radio and advised we would be dropping by PFF, or via Path Finding Force equipment. His aircraft was especially equipped to find the target through clouds, whereas our plane was not. Thus, when my bombardier saw the leader's bombs start to fall, he would toggle our bomb release. (See Endnotes, Chapter 6, Number 4)

About the time we turned from the IP towards the target, the attacking fighters made a couple more passes before they pulled up and away from the bomber stream. They did not want to get caught-up in the murderous flak that was being sent towards us.

As we flew over Berlin, Ray Delbart, my bombardier, had a ringside seat to the city below him. Looking through the black rubber eyepiece on his Norden bombsight, Ray could see all of Berlin slip by the bombsight's hairline-thin crosshairs. Being a former professional athlete, he was particularly awestruck to see the famous 1936 Olympic stadium pass by. It was only then the sheer magnitude of what we were doing really hit home.

Some men pause at this point to reflect upon their measure in history. Not me. I did

Heavy bombers from the 398th Bomb Group release their deadly bomb load over an enemy target during the summer of 1944. The airplanes nearest the camera were assigned to the 601st Bomb Squadron of the 398th Bomb Group. The airplane on the center right is AAF 42-102516 (3O-H), *Bronx Bomber II*, and is being flown by Lt. Harold D. Weekley. The airplane to the immediate left is AAF 42-97401 (3O-T), *Stinker Jr.* This airplane was reported MIA after operations of October 17, 1944. Noteworthy, this airplane carries reversed 398th B.G. markings, a black "W" on a white triangle. The B-17G on the far left is AAF 42-102565 (3O-M), *The Ugly Duckling.* This airplane and crew were lost on a mission on November 26, 1944 and crashed near Zwolle, Netherlands, after being hit by flak. (Harold D. Weekley)

not entertain these thoughts because I was too busy doing the best job I was trained to do, and concentrating on getting back to England in one piece with my crew safe.

Were we ever afraid? Yes, I am sure fear was there, but we never discussed it amongst ourselves, at least the crew did not share any of their fears with me. We did our job the way we were trained and the best we could do.

We pressed onward, preparing for our first drop in enemy territory. Lt. Genung maintained a vigilant scan outside for fighters and inside of the engine instruments, looking for any telltale sign of impending

trouble from any one of the four Wright engines. Everything went fairly smoothly until we were literally seconds from dropping our bombs on our briefed target. The lead aircraft in our bomb group took a crippling anti-aircraft hit in its number three engine only seconds from "bombs away," yet somehow managed to salvo its bombs. The Deputy Lead took over quickly and dropped his bombs visually, the targeted bridge being visible in a large hole in the clouds. Meanwhile, the stricken airplane dropped suddenly on his left wing, lost altitude rapidly and started heading in our direction. A midair collision

This combat strike photograph shows a B-17 from the 452nd Bomb Group crossing Berlin, Germany on a March 22, 1944 mission. The Templehoff Aerodrome passes near this heavy bomber's right wing.

(National Archives, 342-FH-3A20825-50903 A.C.)

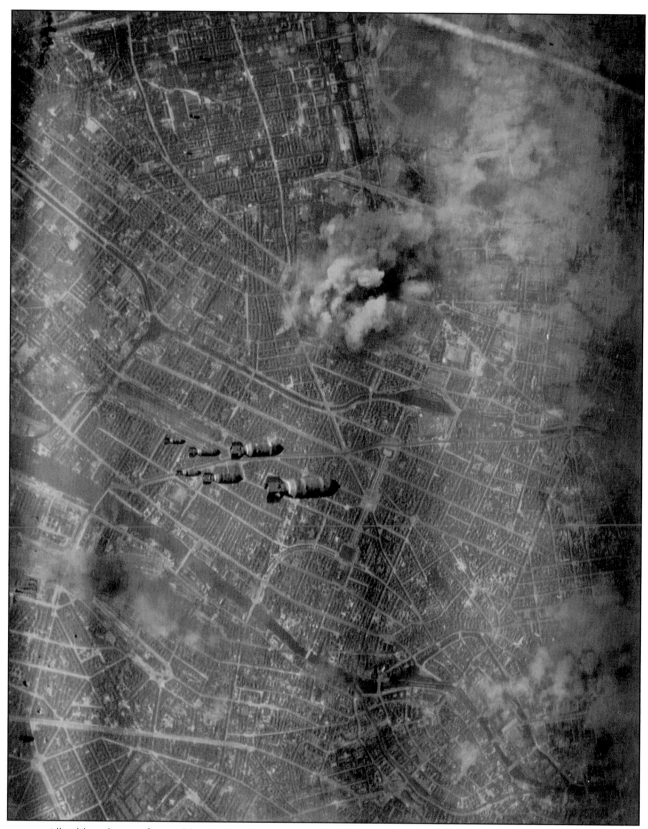

Allied bombs are framed by Berlin, Germany as they begin their deadly plunge towards a target.
(National Archives, 342-FH-3A20837-52109 A.C.)

Berlin, Germany being bombed by Boeing B-17 Flying Fortresses dropping their lethal loads through a five to seven tenths cloud coverage using PFF.   (National Archives, 342-FH-3A20839-53024 A.C.)

Much of Berlin, Germany was reduced to rubble after repeated aerial bombings by Allied bombers. This photograph shows only one small section of this destroyed city.   (National Archives, 342-FH-3A20807-116497 A.C.)

LEAD GROUP (Over Target), 1st "B" CBW

Killen
Rohrer
PFF 7686-L

Darner
2599-U

Falkenbach
Gustaves
7190-L

Dalton
2607-F

Davis, J.H.
2565-M

McCarty
7203-Z

Binger
7338-C

Taylor
7103-A

Wierney
2445-R

Weekley
2516-H

Cobb
7387-H

Scott
2543-Z

Fritog
2592-G

Rudrud
2511-P

Lowe
2600-Z

Reed
2519-A

Brown
2593-C

Richardson
2463-Z

Fairbanks
7365-X

LOW GROUP (Over Target), 1st "B" CBW

Latson
Hopkins
2476-B

Sleaman
7789-H

Cullinan
7348-R

Stoll
7186-L

Howen
2469-Q

Engel
7317-P

Lassegard
2570-F

Willard
2487-F

Dwyer
2579-C

Durtschi
2508-J

Menzel
2390-X

Floger
7218-T

Radnedge
2610-Y

Searl
7114-L

Goodwin
7138-T

Ryan
7855-A

Lovelace
7249-P

Slaven
7399-H

The 398th Bomb Group occupied the Lead and Low Groups of the 1st "B" Combat Bomb Wing on the June 21, 1944 mission to Berlin, Germany. This graphic shows the positions of the 398th aircraft and pilots that flew over the target that day.   For quick identification of assigned pilots and planes on a particular mission, most mission graphics paired together only the last name of the assigned First Pilot, the four digits of the aircraft serial numbers and the last digit of the individual squadron letter on the plane's tail. Additionally, mission reports, day-to-day record keeping and radio communication used this abbreviated serial number and letter combination to identify a particular plane. In this graphic, Second Lieutenant Harold Weekley flew aircraft AAF 42-102516, 3O-H (2516-H) in the right wing of the lead element in the Low Squadron of the Lead Group.

was imminent!

We were flying in the Low Squadron of the Lead Group and as the organization's newest First Pilot, I was flying off the right wing of the formation. Incredibly, as this riveting event unfolded, my attention was diverted momentarily to observe something on my left and I missed initially what was unfolding. Lt. Genung, an experienced and always vigilant pilot, saw what was happening and he got my attention immediately. We made a rapid control movement and narrowly averted a midair collision.

Sadly, this stricken plane AAF 42-97686 (DF-L) supplied from the 324th Bomb Squadron of the 91st Bomb Group continued its mortal earthward plunge, its crew bailing out. We later found out that the pilot was Major Leo Killen, our Squadron Commander. He was captured along with First Lieutenant Richard Rohrer, his copilot, and his crew. All were interned as prisoners of war at a P.O.W. camp somewhere in Germany. Major Killen had given our orientation lectures at the group headquarters just several days earlier. He was a West Point Officer, a fine pilot and a real fine gentleman.

The bombardier yelled "bombs away" when we released our bomb load and the radio operator made an appropriate notation in his radio log. When the bomb racks were clear, the radio operator reported "bombs all gone." Whenever the bomb bay doors opened or closed, he'd also report that information over the intercom. The bomb bay doors had barely closed when our gunners began reporting approaching enemy fighters.

German fighters hit our bomber stream again after we left the target, but not as many fighters attacked the returning bombers as on the inbound leg. Most enemy fighters concentrated on the aircraft in-bound from the Initial Point to the target. Though the enemy sought to divert as many bombers from Berlin as possible, we did not hesitate or falter in our resolve to bomb the target.

As we left the target area, fuel consumption quickly became a primary concern for several pilots, a very valid matter, especially if there was a fuel leak caused by some manner of combat damage. Though we had the proper indoctrination about fuel consumption on a mission, some people became concerned about the amount of fuel they had on board. At the time we released our bombs, our fuel tanks were less than half full. We had climbed during the entire route, with a heavy bomb load, and consequently we had used up at least half of our fuel before we had arrived at the IP, generally at our highest altitude along the whole route. However, a simple analysis revealed we were in decent shape, if we had no fuel leaks. The ride back to England was a power reduction and it was all down hill. Though never a real problem, it was a minor psychological disadvantage to think we were so far from home with less than half a tank of fuel.

A favorite saying among the bomber crews was, "We work for the government while we get to the target and destroy it. After we drop our bombs, we're working for the wife and kids." The trip home was the easiest part, as we knew we had done our best. From this point on, the chances of returning home improved greatly.

The balance of the return flight on this mission was fairly uneventful, at least until we arrived at Nuthampstead, which was still overcast with low clouds. Returning to the home field for the first time with a group of almost three dozen aircraft nearby performing the prescribed instrument letdown to the runway created a memorable experience. Once again, the Army Air Forces' rigorous training paid handsomely and everyone landed safely and without incident.

At many other bases, the scenes unfolding were neither as pleasant nor as uneventful. Ground personnel gathered on or near the control tower while they "sweated out" the return of the airplanes. They scanned the skies for their aircraft, all anxious to see their crews and planes return safely home. Apprehensive eyes looked skyward and counted the returning heavy bombers. One, two or more could be missing.

Local townsfolk would watch also from their villages and homes. Many of our friendly neighbors counted the planes when they made their takeoffs. Now, these same folks counted the airplanes that returned, often looking for the familiar markings of a specific aircraft carrying a favorite crew or crewmember.

Each missing bomber meant nine or ten men were not coming home, nine or ten men killed, prisoner of war or missing in action, which meant no one knew what happened to them. Every lost or missing airplane meant nine or ten families back home would soon

receive the dreaded telegram beginning with "The War Department regrets to inform you that…" Three stars at the top of the telegram meant the military member was "Missing in Action." Four stars conveyed the loved one was "Killed in Action." On many missions during the course of the war, dozens of planes and their crews were killed or were missing - an appalling tragedy that represented hundreds of men lost or missing in action.

Screaming engines could be heard while a pilot, or another crewmember, fought valiantly to keep a crippled bomber aloft for a few minutes more. Two, three or more airplanes would appear with red flares arching skyward announcing they had wounded on

In a scene repeated countless times, a weary B-17G combat crew unload their airplane after a combat mission and await transportation to debrief while other returning B-17s fly overhead.

(National Archives, 342-FH-3A9108-56141 A.C.)

board. Some planes landed with one or more propellers feathered. Others had major pieces of their structure gone, blown away by the ferocity of the earlier air battle. Others landed with dead crewmembers.

Even as planes and crews neared the safe bosom of Mother England, Death waited patiently its due. For those planes known to have wounded or dead aboard, base medical personnel and ambulances waited anxiously at a particular bomber's parking hardstand. Other personnel and ambulances waited nearer the base's control tower to assist in the aftermath of any belly landing, landing gear collapse, and the usual subsequent fire or explosion.

Soon, the day's tally of what was gained against what was lost would be recorded.

We landed at 1347, exactly eight hours and thirty minutes after our 0517 takeoff. Engine start to engine shutdown accounted for nine hours and ten minutes. Five of those hours were on oxygen. Though we were tired physically, we were elated to be alive.

Shortly after landing, we boarded trucks or other means of transportation and were taken immediately to a post-mission intelligence debriefing. Once at debriefing, we passed the Red Cross table and those wonderful, cheerful and attractive ladies that served us donuts, cake, canned milk, hot chocolate and tea. The base doctor or one of his associates was near to offer something with more kick, shots of liquor for crewmembers who needed one. Most of my crew drank hot chocolate, and we took our warm mugs and some donuts with us to the debriefing table where a young, middle-aged Intelligence Officer gathered us around his table.

The intelligence debriefing was a simple matter of telling the Intelligence Officer all we could remember about the mission. Basically, we would relive the mission. We described everything we had seen relative to the types and the numbers of the enemy aircraft, the amount of anti-aircraft fire that we had encountered and the number of B-17s and fighters we saw go down. For some crewmembers, the intelligence debriefing meant reliving the horrors of the day's mission.

We tried to give them as much information as possible as it was all to our benefit. At the next mission briefing, it was most helpful to know the location and concentration of fighters and anti-aircraft fire. The information we provided often meant the difference between a bomber crew living or dying the next day. Several crews reported seeing barrage balloons over Rendeburg, Germany, and the flak reports went from heavy and accurate over the target to light and inaccurate elsewhere. Some crews reported seeing smoke screens whereas other crews saw fires still burning in Hamburg. Jamming of certain radio frequencies was also reported. A few crews used this debrief to gripe about the morning's breakfast, the "piss poor" crew transportation or some other insignificant item not related to the mission.

Many crews, including mine, reported seeing Major Killen's bomber go down, but the information differed as to the number of crewmembers seen bailing out and the subsequent number of parachutes in the air. Some crewmembers reported they saw eight parachutes, others reported nine. One crew even reported they saw a body exit the stricken bomber, but no parachute opened during its long descent to the ground.

I learned well after the war that all of Major Killen's crew bailed-out successfully and became prisoners of war. At the war's end, all were repatriated.

When the day's missions were tallied and the crews debriefed, the official Army Air Forces records recorded any missing airplanes and crews as "Failed to Return." On occasion, a simple "FTR" or "MIA" (Missing in Action) was placed besides the pilot's name and aircraft in the bomb group's records. Major Killen and crew were listed as MIA. Only one member from another 398th crew was wounded.

History of that day's mission tally revealed a much greater story. Six hundred and six B-17 and B-24 bombers of the First, Second and Third Bomb Divisions attacked the city of Berlin. Another three hundred forty-three B-17s and B-24s attacked various targets of opportunity and assigned industrial targets in the Berlin area. Some twenty-three hundred tons of bombs fell. Tragically, forty-five heavy bombers were lost with at least two landing in neutral Sweden and their crews interned. Another five hundred and eight heavy bombers sustained damage to varying degrees. At least twenty-three bomber airmen were killed-in-action (KIA) and another thirty-five are listed as wounded-in-action (WIA). At least three hundred forty airmen were shown as missing-in-action.

The 398th did not come away unscathed. Outside of losing Maj. Killen and crew, no other personnel were seriously wounded or killed on this mission, but ten bombers experienced minor flak damage and seven bombers were recorded as sustaining "major" flak damage. Fortunately, none were damaged beyond repair and had to be salvaged for parts. Obviously, the crew chiefs and the maintenance crews had a busy night ahead of them preparing their bombers for another mission the following day.

The day's tally was tough on the fighter escort. Of the one thousand one hundred and seventy fighters that participated on this mission, four fighters and their pilots were lost or were listed as missing in action.

Walking wearily to my Nissen hut, I took measure of my place at Nuthampstead, the war and history in general. A deadly history was unfolding around me, and I was an active participant. My crew and I had completed one mission successfully. We needed twenty-four more before we could rotate home.

We had received our baptism by fire and joined an elite group of fliers who were rightful combat veterans. We had joined an even more elite group who had flown a mission to wartime Berlin…and survived. It was a real indoctrination that our first combat mission and enemy encounter was over the city of Berlin with a determined and potent German military machine trying to protect it. I was now a combat pilot and, following USAAF tradition, I could wear my silver pilot wings on a blue background.

We were only beginning to leave our footprints on the sands of time.

This Boeing data plate, shown here in its original size, was usually placed on the left side of the instrument panel. An example of the data plate's placement is shown on page 47. (Jon Wm. Aldrich)

"Men, the cards are dealt. Good luck to you. And may there be enough luck for all of you."

Col. Frank P. Hunter, Remarks made at a
398th Bomb Group briefing prior to
a combat mission (circa 1944).

CHAPTER 7

Adding to the Mission Count

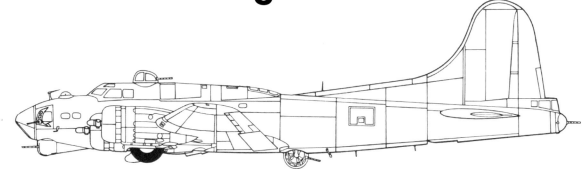

I flew my first combat mission on June 21, 1944, which was the thirty-sixth group mission of the 398th Bomb Group. Thus, during my combat flying time in England from June to August, the 398th Bomb Group flew thirty-two group missions of which we flew twenty, leaving only twelve group missions in a two-month period that we did not fly. Except for a couple of crewmembers, my originally assigned crew flew with me on every mission.

During this busy period, our flying and rest schedule was either feast or famine. During one period, we logged five straight missions without any intervening rest. I grew very tired, as did many of my fellow crewmembers, of getting up at three o'clock - or earlier - in the morning for the ten to twelve

hour missions. Except for a very few afternoon bombing missions, this rigorous schedule changed little over the next two months.

Though we were young, some no older than eighteen, we did not believe ourselves to be invincible. Despite any previous misconceptions, we were not afraid of dying in combat. Many of us believed we would die in the skies over Europe. Death over wartime Europe was often fast, violent, decisive and always indiscriminate.

How would we die? What would we feel? A brief instant of pain, tinged with a pleasant memory or quiet regret? Our views were neither fatalistic nor based on conjecture or gut feelings, but were rooted in cold, hard facts.

Statistically, the most dan-

Second Lieutenants Ben Clark, Hal Weekley and Ray Delbart pose together shortly before embarking upon another mission. Their fleece-lined clothing offered little protection against the numbing cold they experienced at most combat bombing altitudes.

(Harold D. Weekley)

gerous place for an American to fight in World War II, either on the ground or in the air, was in a bomber over Europe. The average probability of completing a combat tour in the Eighth Air Force was less than 50 percent. Statistically speaking, a combat crewmember was flying on borrowed time after flying his tenth mission.

Moreover, the air was cold at most of our bombing altitudes of twenty to thirty thousand feet. This bitter cold was neither a refrigerator cold nor snowball cold, but was a frostbite-producing cold, a body numbing cold, a cold that incapacitated and killed without discretion. This cold jammed guns and made engine oil run thick like molasses.

On occasion, oxygen masks froze over and became useless, the insidious effects of oxygen starvation often not noticed until a crewmember was rendered unconscious. Crew check-ins at regular intervals and ascertaining their status were normal procedures.

The B-17's cardboard thick, 24ST aluminum alloy shell and the fleece-lined leather-covered gear we wore offered little protection from the elements or enemy action. Though enemy action extracted a terrible toll, so did the rigors and dangers of flying in a non-pressurized, unheated environment at altitudes often exceeding 30,000 feet. Frostbite accounted for more aerial combat casualties than did enemy action!

Fortunately, my gunners had electrically-heated flight suits underneath their gear, which worked fine and presented no problems unless there was a short circuit or the aircraft lost electrical power. Similarly, many crews had electrically heated oxygen masks. Though we lost an engine or two during our time in combat, we never lost electrical power during any mission.

Other concerns crossed my mind and I'm sure the minds of other heavy bomber pilots. Takeoffs were always of some concern due to the length of the runway and the heavy loads we carried, especially into fog, mist or low ceilings. A visible sun was always a welcome

relief. Moreover, we had to contend with propeller wash and wake vortices during takeoff from proceeding aircraft. After takeoff, our climbs, on occasion, could be nerve-wracking, including flying through unexpected turbulence and not knowing the origin.

Joining the bomber formation was a source of concern and several pilots displayed a serious lack of professional airmanship while assembling. There was quite a difference in pilot expertise and formation assembly was one area where these deficiencies were quite obvious. Even after assembly, other formations flew through our formation at thirty to forty-five degree angles, all very scary. Add clouds or marginal weather, and formation assembly would be challenging for any pilot. Some crews aborted due to their inability to find the lead aircraft. Pilots welcomed formation assemblies in sunny skies.

We worked hard to maintain formation position during our missions. I always believed one should use whatever control pressures were necessary to stay in proper position. Upon "bombs away," I never noticed much of a "bounce" partly because I reacted almost instinctively on the controls to any altitude or position change. In later missions, I flew as lead and assume I did a good job of keeping the guys behind me in position. Any inclement weather merely compounded our problems and, of course, made formation flying much more difficult.

One of my main concerns during the bombing run was making sure there were no bombers beneath me. Our missions were difficult enough and we did not need to add to our losses due to "friendly fire," though I know of several bombers lost due to bombs falling on them from an airplane overhead.

Enemy fighters were always a concern, and this concern began at the European Continent and did not end until we left. Some bomber bases experienced fighter attacks in the traffic pattern, so the gunners could never relax until they were safely on the ground.

Even after we dropped our bombs, we

had to consider enemy fighters, flak, mid-air collisions, fuel states, weather at the base, delays in landing and taxi congestion due to the narrow taxiways to the small dispersal pads or hardstands. We kept our guard up from the time we entered the briefing room until we cleared the Intelligence debriefing at the end of the mission. There was so much to consider, and my crew and I had to be on our toes at all times.

Despite these and many other hazards, we went about our job in the most professional manner possible. Yes, we made mistakes, and for those who lived through the experience, we learned from those mistakes. We all hoped to return from each mission, adding to our individual tally before we earned the right to go home, alive.

My mission to Berlin on June 21st was a small part of the Allied Strategic Bombing Campaign. This and other bombing missions against Axis forces were designed to grind the Nazi Germany war machine to a halt. Thus, the target lists were long and varied. The Luftwaffe factories and airfields, oil and petrochemical plants, Axis heavy industry, transportation infrastructure, communications and even cities themselves were all primary targets.

In the months prior to *Operation Overlord*, the Allied Invasion of Europe on June 6, 1944 (D-Day), U.S. Strategic Air Forces (created to coordinated the strategic-bombing efforts of the British-based Eighth Air Force and the Italian-based Fifteenth Air Force) and Headquarters Eighth Air Force commanders and mission planners, working closely with their British Bomber Command counterparts, opted to concentrate on the Luftwaffe and transportation targets. After the Allied landings at Normandy, these directives changed to favor targets that would further the Allied advance into France and Europe. Missions were still planned and bomber raids were still flown to other strategic targets deep within enemy territory.

To disrupt the German transportation system, the bombing mission planners targeted the railroads, railroad stations and marshalling yards. Quite often, when Allied bombers were unable to bomb their primary targets, the railroad repair shops often became secondary targets or targets of opportunity. Thus, many of the targets I bombed were intended to hasten collapse of the transportation system that, in turn, hastened the collapse of the German Army.

To cripple and destroy the Luftwaffe, Allied planners paid close attention to the German manufacturing capability and sent bombers to attack airfields and aircraft production plants. Any plant or activity engaged in Luftwaffe support or supply was targeted. Despite the daily and nightly onslaught of Allied bombers, the German war machine continued to produce war material at a prodigious rate. Some high-priority targets, such as the heavy industries in and around Berlin, Munich and Leipzig, were attacked repeatedly to slow and eventually stop this production.

Almost from the start of air operations over Europe, Eighth Air Force mission planners learned that the B-17 and the B-24, without proper fighter escort, had a difficult time defending themselves adequately against the withering onslaught of attacking Luftwaffe fighters. These planners believed strikes against the aircraft manufacturing plants would decrease the number of airplanes the Luftwaffe had to bear against the bombers.

The sad truth was the German war machine actually increased aircraft production during the middle to latter part of the war by moving production factories into smaller, interlinked facilities that did not draw the attention of a long-range bomber mission. However, Germany was losing its experienced pilots faster than they could train them, a significant factor that tipped the scales of aerial combat in the Allies' favor.

The Nazi oil industry was another keen target of the Allied Strategic Bombing Campaign. Whereas attacks on oil fields in Romania held the American public's attention,

Ugly Duckling, AAF 42-97338 (3O-C), begins a slow climb after takeoff from Nuthampstead on another mission.
(398th Bomb Group Memorial Association)

notably the Ploesti missions, bombers from the Eighth and Fifteenth Air Forces attacked many other oil industry targets, including synthetic oil production plants in Germany, Poland and Czechoslovakia. Stop the flow of oil, and Germany could not hurl its instruments of war against Allied forces. The German war machine proved tenacious, indeed, and oil continued to flow until the waning months of the war.

Other targets were attacked repeatedly due to their military value. The research and test facilities at Peenemunde, Germany, for example, were targeted again and again because of their secret and devastating "vengeance weapons" work.

The Allied bombing campaign was meant to slow and eventually stop the German war machine, but the price the Eighth Air Force paid was enormous! Some 43,742 airmen were killed or reported missing. More than 11,000 airplanes fell over enemy territory. Never again will such resolve be demonstrated in modern warfare.

As the Allies gained air superiority, particularly over western France, German fighter opposition decreased substantially. Notwithstanding, enemy fighter aircraft re-

mained a credible and lethal force, though they rarely attacked in the massed waves that ripped through bomber formations early in the war. German fighters attacked the bomber formations when priority or high-value targets were threatened or the German commanders believed air superiority was possible.

Anti-aircraft fire, better known as flak, became an increasing concern. During the three months I flew in the European Theatre of Operations, I experienced comparatively little direct fighter opposition, but I encountered flak on almost every mission, sometimes with devastating results.

Knowing the very small, yet important role my crew and I were to play in this bombing campaign, we embarked on our second mission on Thursday, June 22nd. Thirteen 398th Bomb Group airplanes, each carrying twelve, 500 lb, AN-M64 General Purpose (GP) bombs, formed and climbed to 25,000 feet indicated altitude. Our primary target was La Vaupaliere, France. The weather was forecast to be clear to and from the intended target with unrestricted visibility. My assigned airplane was AAF 42-97338 (3O-C), nicknamed *Ugly Duckling,* not to be confused with another 601st Bomb Squadron airplane called *The Ugly Duckling* (AAF 42-102565, 3O-M).

The lead airplane took-off at 1630 and we were over the target at 1951. No enemy fighter's were seen, but flak started appearing in random bursts, increasing in intensity as we approached our target. Smoke on the ground reduced the visibility somewhat, but not enough to cause any real concern.

On this and virtually all missions, Ben Clark, my copilot, flew the plane from assembly until we came under attack when I relieved him. I always flew the ship when we were under attack or on the bomb run, otherwise I tried to split the flying chores as much as possible.

"Enemy flak so thick you could walk upon it...!" was a popular cliché of combat crewmembers. Each one of those black bursts could severely damage or shoot down a heavy bomber. (Peter M. Bowers)

Without a doubt, the hardened combat crew saying, "Flak so thick you could walk on it!" was in order that day!

On the second run to the target, the lead aircraft's bombsight wiring was damaged by flak rendering the unit's intervalometer inoperative. The pilot called for the deputy lead airplane to take the lead position, but not before some bombs had been dropped by a ship in the High Squadron. The squadron leaders were instructed to

Upon reaching the Initial Point, the lead ship was unable to open its bomb-bay doors, so the pilot led the whole group in a 360-degree turn while a crewmember tried to manually open them. Ultimately, due to his many problems over the target, the lead aircraft returned with his bomb load aboard. The enemy flak gunners didn't get an accurate bead on our bombers on the first run, but they did our second. Flak exploded all around us with an incredible fury with its distinctive and reverberating orange-center explosions. More and more black clouds slid past us, some quite close. Several of the big Boeing bombers near me rocked from the concussions like an old car driving over a set of railroad tracks at a high speed. Lethal metal shards hit the sides of the bombers and sounded like hailstones hitting a metal roof.

form on the deputy lead for another run over the target. In the confusion that followed, many of the airplanes in this attacking force, upon seeing the bombs falling from the ship in the High Squadron, toggled theirs. The few airplanes that did not release their bombs during this confusion did so shortly afterwards on a nearby target of opportunity, a powerplant near La Houline, France.

Very few bombs fell on the intended target that day and the results were recorded as "poor." We did not do a very credible job in slowing the German war machine.

All told, some nine hundred twenty-two

The Ugly Duckling, AAF 42-102565 (3O-M), stands ready to fly another combat mission, most likely during the spring or early summer of 1944. This aircraft was lost on a mission to Misburg, Germany on November 26, 1944 after being hit by flak and crashed near Zwolle, Netherlands killing all aboard. (398th Bomb Group Memorial Association)

B-17s and B-24s attacked various targets throughout northwestern France, with ten heavy bombers falling to enemy action. Fortunately, none were from the 398th.

Paul James, my navigator, was intent on sending a message to Hitler on this mission. He relieved himself in a candy box and advised the crew he was going to dump its contents on Hitler. Flying over German-occupied territory, he threw the box out the nose hatch. Unfortunately, the box and its contents spread itself over the ball turret. Joe Fabian, our ball turret gunner, was not at all happy and he had to endure this unsettling scene all the way back to England. After landing, Joe and Paul had the messy job thoroughly cleaning the ball turret.

On Saturday, June 24th, we flew our third combat mission. Pilots and crews of the 398th were briefed to attack *Noball* targets near Belloy Sur Somme. *Noball* targets were V-1 and V-2 "vengeance weapons" sites on the northwestern French coast near Pas de Calais. The Eighth Air Force used the code name *Noball* for these sites. Medium bombers, such as the B-26 Marauder, had been used against these sites for some time, but now the Allied mission planners deemed the heavy bombers - the B-17 and B-24 - could add their weight to the V-1 flying bomb offensive.

I was assigned to fly AAF 42-102469 (N7-Q), a nameless and well-worn B-17G assigned to the 603rd Bomb Squadron, in the number two position of Low Group's Low Squadron. Capt. Willis Frazier, the 601st's Operations Officer, assigned us to the airplanes and missions we flew that day as on many other occasions. The weather was briefed to be CAVU (Ceiling and Visibility Unlimited), so a visual bombing was planned. Each of our airplanes carried eighteen, 250 lb, AN-M57 cluster bombs.

The 398th took off into a glorious morning sunrise, assembled over the field at 1,500 feet, then climbed to 20,000 feet as we circled the Debden Buncher beacon. Once assembled, we flew towards our target in France.

When we arrived over the assigned target, we found it obscured by low clouds with only a few breaks, but not enough where we could pick-out a target of opportunity to bomb.

Following instructions from the Wing Leader, the thirty-six 398th airplanes returned to Station 131, in clear weather, with their full load of bombs aboard except for any delayed-fuse bombs, which were jettisoned over the English Channel.

The fighter support over the European Continent that day was very good, and I tip my hat to them for keeping any enemy fighters at bay. Unfortunately, the weather refused to cooperate and our mission was for naught.

I was dejected!

Records show the 398th Bomb Group's effort that day was a significant part of an impressive armada that included seventy-four 1st Bomb Division B-17s and two hundred sixty-five 2nd and 3rd Bomb Division B-24s sent to attack targets in central and northwestern France. Three heavy bombers fell to enemy fire that day but, again, none from the

398th. Three hundred and seven VIII Fighter Command fighters provided escort for the morning heavy-bomber missions. One fighter and its pilot were lost.

My crew and I returned to Nuthampstead exhausted. We had flown three missions in four days. Consequently, we were given two days to rest. Many of us stayed in the Nuthampstead area and rested. For others, London proved to be an irresistible escape, with its many pubs and historic attractions. For a few crewmembers, the Woodman Inn, a quintessential English pub that was located less than a hundred yards from the aircraft dispersal area of the 602nd Bomb Squadron, provided their solace. I spent my time resting and writing letters to Billie, my mother and Maxine, my younger sister.

The Woodman Inn was a popular pub located just off base and was not far from the skeet range, the combat mess hall and the 602nd hardstands. Many crewmembers sought solace from the war's rigors at this pub.
(James B. Zazas)

During the time my crew and I rested, the 398th flew one mission as part of a greater raid against airfields, transformer stations and other targets in France. Unfortunately, the Bomb Group's luck did not hold and one 398th B-17 airplane (AAF 42-102463, K8-Z), commanded by Lt. John K. Godwin, was lost to anti-aircraft fire and crashed near Cornebarriou, France, which is about seven miles northwest of Toulouse. The navigator died when he slipped from his harness as he parachuted to earth. Eight other crewmembers bailed out successfully and became prisoners of war (POWs). This meant more empty beds in Nuthampstead that night, more telegrams with four and three stars sent to loved ones back home and more calls from the Group's Operations Officer for replacement crews.

Rested from our leave, my crew and I flew our fourth combat mission on Tuesday, June 27th. My assigned airplane was AAF 42-102607 (3O-F), which carried the odd moniker, *Lodian*. The bomb load consisted of ten 500 lb, AN-M64 General Purpose (GP) demolition bombs, and our briefed target was construction works, most likely a V-weapon site near Biennais, France. Enemy fighter opposition was expected to be light, but flak was expected to be a credible threat. Weather for takeoff was briefed to be broken clouds at 2000 feet with visibility better than six miles underneath the clouds and unrestricted visibility above the clouds. Weather over the target was briefed to be marginally better. Takeoff was to commence at 1530 hours.

Twenty-two B-17s from the 398th and two Pathfinder B-17s, one from the 303rd Bomb Group and the other from the 384th Bomb Group, took-off and assembled at the Deben Buncher beacon at 1733 hours, forming the 398th Lead and Low Groups of twelve airplanes each. One crew aborted when they were unable to find the formation due to an inoperative radio compass. Though we were briefed to assemble at 20,000 feet, we had to climb to 23,500 feet to get above the clouds. My position was the right wing of the Low Squadron in the Lead Group on this late afternoon mission. We left the English coast at Selsey Bill at 1821 hours and crossed the enemy coast twenty-three minutes later.

Weather over the target was poor, almost completely overcast. Our problems compounded when Pathfinder GEE-H navigation/bombing equipment problems plagued the Lead Group's lead aircraft over the target at 1900 hours. The lead pilot ordered a 360-degree turn before dropping bombs on the second bomb run. The High Group made two 360-dgree turns over the target before this group released their bombs. (See Endnotes, Chapter 7, Number 1)

Coming off the target, we were unable to close our airplane's bomb-bay doors. I looked over my right shoulder and saw Joe Skarda using the hand crank to close the two clamshell doors. Unknown to me, a greater story was unfolding behind me.

While Joe cranked the doors closed, the oxygen tube from his mask came loose from the oxygen bottle that was clamped to his parachute harness and he started to get dizzy from the lack of oxygen. Ven "Bob" Unger, our radioman, realized his friend was in trouble when Joe started to move unsteadily towards the radio room. Ven went out on the bomb-bay catwalk, grabbed Joe's harness and jerked him into the radio room. There, he reconnected his oxygen mask to another oxygen supply source. Undoubtedly, Ven's quick thinking saved Joe's life, yet he always denied it to be so.

This was not the first time Joe Skarda ventured out on the bomb-bay's narrow catwalk to assist in completing a mission successfully. During another later mission, with bomb-bay doors open, Joe walked on the catwalk between the bombs and used a screwdriver to release them from an inoperative bomb shackle. He did this terrific feat suspended in the open air at 25,000 feet in mind-numbing cold!

My group, the Lead Group, returned to England alone, crossing the English Coast at Beachy Head (near Brighton) at 1931 hours. Let down was made through broken clouds and we took spacing for landing at Nuthampstead, the familiar pastoral landscape coming into full view. We landed at 2039 hours and boarded trucks to go to the Intelligence debrief shortly thereafter. Even though we had been flying for a little less

than five-and-a-half hours, all of us were very happy to see the always-cheerful Red Cross girls with the hot coffee and delicious cake snacks they had prepared for us. Several airmen from other crews opted for the long shot of Irish whiskey from the flight surgeon or one of his assistants.

When the final numbers were tallied, the 398th Bomb Group placed almost forty-eight tons of bombs, but the bombing results were not observed due to cloud coverage. Several planes returned with full or partial bomb loads aboard. Two hundred and fifty-one Eighth Air Force B-17s and B-24s were dispatched against *Noball* sites that day, including one hundred ninety-five escorting fighters from the VIII Fighter Command. At least five B-24s and two P-51s were lost or posted as MIA.

The enemy directed a moderate amount of anti-aircraft flak against the massed Flying Fortresses that day and except for one airplane, none came very close to our planes. Many 398th crews commented in the Intelligence debrief that it seemed as if the flak gunners were firing blindly through the overcast. The altitude was correct, but the bursts were wide right. Most planes dropped a lot of chaff that day and I am sure these thin metal strips confused the enemy's radar-directed flak. Best of all, crews reported seeing very few if any enemy aircraft coming through the clouds to engage the raiding bombers.

One crew was quite upset by the 360-degree turns and commented at the Intelligence debrief that the Lead bombardier should be prepared for this event by making a change in heading and altitude. Making a 360-dgree turn over the target increases the chances of being shot down, which added a lot of anxiety. Additionally, encountering flak on a mission added enough stress for all and numbing fear for many. Adding enemy fighters whose only purpose is to blow you from the sky only multiplied the gut-wrenching apprehension.

My crew and I enjoyed a much needed

rest for a day before we flew our fifth mission on Thursday, June 29th. We participated in an important mission to Leipzig, Germany, one of Germany's most culturally and economically important cities, where trade fairs date back to the Middle Ages and near where Napoleon was defeated by a combined army force of Swedes, Russians, Prussians and Austrians in the Battle of Nations in 1813, eventually leading to his exile on Elba Island.

The 398th put forty-two airplanes into the air to support this bombing effort, including two PFF-equipped airplanes from the 91st Bomb Group. Unfortunately, we never reached our briefed target. For that matter, we never departed English airspace. Shortly after takeoff, we encountered worse-than-briefed weather.

The 398th spent at least two hours and fifteen minutes trying to join another formation assembling at the Bassingbourn Buncher beacon. Planes kept getting scattered and lost during assembly, so the Group tried assembling at the Mundesley Buncher beacon but this, too, failed. We encountered clouds that kept building higher and higher. It seemed the higher we climbed, the higher the clouds and the greater the condensation built-up. In reality, we were building our own clouds from the hot engine exhaust emitting into the cold air, which quickly made the flying environment hazardous. The chance for a mid-air collision was great.

England and Europe as a whole often experienced cloudy and foggy summertime days in 1944 and this inclement weather created many problems for takeoff, group assembly, and bombing targets. In addition, the abnormally cool weather during June, July and August exacerbated another unique problem - engine exhaust condensation. The long contrail left behind each airplane marked its position quite well. Add several hundred bombers in the miles-long bomber stream, and this condensation problem was magnified many times.

While we attempted assembly on this par-ticular day, our combat bomb wing flew through a B-24 combat bomb wing that was assembling at another nearby assembly beacon. We were at the same altitude as the Liberators, but used a slightly different heading. Either through luck or divine intervention, there were no mid-air collisions. We merely passed each other with the B-24s and the B-17s crossing each other at a ten-degree angle. We spread out as much as we could under the circumstances and everyone continued without any further difficulty.

Eventually, things got too dangerous and the mission was recalled. We returned to Nuthampstead with a full load of 500 lb, AN-M64 GP bombs. We consumed a lot of precious fuel on that aborted mission. Everyone was shaken by this event and there was a lot of lively conversation once we returned safely to solid ground. Despite the generous amounts of cake and coffee available at the Intelligence debrief, I am sure the flight surgeon's on-hand supply of Irish whisky took a hit before many of us dug into whatever the cooks had prepared for us in the mess halls.

Reviewing this day's figures, some one thousand one hundred and fifty Eighth Air Force heavy bombers were dispatched to hit targets within Germany, mostly on or near Leipzig, and The Netherlands. Seven hundred and seventy-nine VIII and IX Fighter Command fighters were dispatched as well. Of this attacking force, more than four hundred heavy bombers aborted due to the heavy weather. The balance of the heavy bombers managed to attack their assigned targets or targets of opportunity.

The toll on man and machine was heavy and deadly that day. At least six B-17s and nine B-24s were tallied as "Missing in Action" or "Failed to Return." The VIII and IX Fighter Commands lost three airplanes and their pilots. In uncompromising terms, almost one hundred fifty crewmembers were killed, missing in action or became prisoner of war. All of these men and planes were lost on one mission on one day in one theater of an aerial

A 398th Bomb Group B-17 awaits its crew prior to another mission. Crew chiefs made every effort to insure their planes were in the best possible mechanical condition before they departed on a combat mission.

(Harold D. Weekley)

war that still had another year to run before it ended!

Replacement crews filled the manpower void and the empty beds at the bases, but not the broken hearts of loved ones back in the United States. To their heroic credit, Eighth Air Force crews kept flying their missions as ordered, despite this loss and other greater combat losses.

The 398th did not fly any combat missions for the next five days. During this down time, we did not rest, but, instead prepared for the next round of combat missions. Though crews got a much-needed respite from the almost daily rigors and stress of combat flying, many attended obligatory briefings and other courses designed to increase their chances of survival in case they were shot down. The airplane crew chiefs and mechanics used this down time to fix their bombers and prepare them for the next round of combat missions, which surely would result in many damaged airplanes. Our Wing and Squadron Commanders consulted with their superiors and Eighth Air Force mission planners at Pinetree to ensure the 389th Bomb Group was ready for any mission it was tasked to perform.

Much like other bomb groups in England, the 398th provided its crew a multitude of leisure activities and organized athletics to occupy one's free time and relieve combat stress. Baseball, softball, volleyball and boxing were available. Movies, called motion pictures in those days, played many of Hollywood's latest releases. Many officers listened to the Soldiers Band play at the Officers Club. Other individuals escaped to the quiet solitude of the Woodman pub.

I used this time to write letters to Billie, mother and Maxine. I wrote to them on "V-Mail," single-page letters sent to loved ones at home at government expense, but read beforehand by Army Air Forces censors on base to ensure no classified information was contained within them. Once cleared, they were sent to the intended recipients. One of my many duties included censoring crewmembers' letters. So, in order to let Billie know how many missions I had flown, I devised a little system to get by the censors whereby I'd put a figure in the return address area of the letter. Thus, Billie knew when I was due to complete 25 missions and, afterwards, rotate back to the United States. I wrote about three letters a week.

I never wrote anything to Billie about the missions I flew or the dangerous conditions I faced. She was pregnant at the time with our first child, William Deane Weekley, and I did not want to concern her in any manner with my perilous situation. Billie obtained most of

Ben Clark, Paul James, Hal Weekley and Ray Delbart pose together while on leave in England. With minor exceptions, the officers from Hal Weekley's crew would travel to London together, but would normally go their own way once in town.
(Harold D. Weekley)

her information about what was happening in Europe through the newspapers and radio broadcasts back home.

During this time in England, my association with the enlisted crewmembers was strictly military with no socializing allowed. During any leave or passes in England, the officers went one way and the enlisted men went the other. With minor exceptions, the officers from my crew would travel to London together, but we would normally go our own way once in town. Sometimes we would have dinner together, other times we would go separately.

During one of our forays into London, three of the officers got drunk. I had one in one arm and two in the other arm. I told them I'd get them back to the hotel, but the first SOB that threw up on my shoes I'd drop in the gutter and he'd have to fend for himself.

On Saturday, July 1st, my crew and I flew a two-hour navigation and transition training mission. I gave Ben Clark, my copilot, the opportunity to make several landings for proficiency and he did a very credible job. The weather was good and we enjoyed the opportunity to see more of the idyllic English countryside under less stressful circumstances.

We flew our sixth combat mission on Tuesday, July 4th, which was the 398th's forty-first Group Mission, to attack a hardened target south of Paris. I was assigned to fly aircraft AAF 42-102445 (3O-R), another nameless B-17G, in the number six position in the Low Squadron of the Lead Group. Major Robert K. Simeral, the 398th Bomb Group's Operations Officer, and Capt. Gene L. Douglas, the plane's pilot, would lead the 398th on this early morning mission. Lieutenant

Merwin Hornshuh, one of my Nissen hut roommates, flew as our squadron leader. 398th airplanes formed the Lead and Low Groups of the 1st "A" CBW. The Lead Group was briefed to bomb from 25,000 feet with all other aircraft taking formation position and spacing as trained on this early morning mission. The lead airplane was scheduled to takeoff at 0430 hours. Zero hour, the time we were scheduled to be overhead our assigned target, was set at 0630 hours. Weather on departure and assembly was briefed as being good and over the target briefed as having broken clouds. Reality, however, proved otherwise and no PFF or GEE-H equipped airplane was assigned to the 398th for this mission.

On this day, at least five hundred and fifty eight Eighth Air Force heavy bombers were assigned to attack seven airfields and other targets north, west and southwest of Paris on this important mission. Additionally, six hundred and thirty-two VIII Fighter Command fighters, consisting of one hundred ninety-nine P-38s, one hundred eighty-nine P-47s and two hundred forty-four P-51s, were assigned to provide escort and to attack airfields and other targets within France.

The 398th's assigned target was a very old, very strong concrete bridge in Tours, France. In order to bomb this reinforced bridge effectively, each airplane carried two, 2000 lb, AN-M34 General Purpose bombs. Each B-17 could carry only two of these powerful weapons because each of these one ton bombs filled up one side of the bomb bay. These one ton bombs were ideal for busting-up strong structures, such as this concrete bridge.

Twenty-four 398th airplanes took-off between 0429 and 0442 hours, assembled at the Debden Buncher beacon and left the English Coast at Selsey Bill as briefed.

Unfortunately, the Fickle Finger of Fate rode with the Group that morning and offered its mischief. Shortly after assembly, the Wing Leader's B-17 experienced a blown cylinder in the number two engine which, in turn, caught fire. Worse, the pilots were unable to feather the propeller. Unable to keep up with the Group, the crippled bomber left the formation to return to base and the Deputy Wing Leader assumed the lead.

Then the rapidly deteriorating weather became our concern. Though the weather over England was as briefed to be good, the weather over France was not. The Initial Point was completely covered by clouds, as was the primary target. Worse, the secondary target was also covered completely. There were no breaks in this thick blanket of clouds in any direction. Unable to see the ground that day denied us any chance to hit any target of opportunity such as a road or railroad bridge, an enemy column or convoy, or a large concentration of troops or equipment.

When we bombed in France, we were not allowed to bomb the target unless we had the target in sight (or recorded we had the target in sight) and had it positively identified. Moreover, the target could not be adjacent any populated areas. Thus, we were not allowed to drop our bombs whenever there was a low cloud cover. As was the case on July 4th, we couldn't drop our bombs on either our primary or secondary targets. Consequently, we returned to Nuthampstead with our bomb load intact.

The returning bombers set up a landing pattern at Nuthampstead in such a manner as to have twenty-three aircraft pass over the runway at one time and have the last bomber make a sharp turn over the runway. Thus, the last aircraft in this pattern would be the first to land, so the turn had to be sharp and crisp.

As it happened that day, my airplane was the last aircraft in the formation and, consequently, we were the first one to pitch out for the landing. I told Ray Delbart, my bombardier, to advise me immediately as soon as the nose of our B-17 was over the end of the runway, whereupon I would make a rapid and definite pitch to the left so that we could get on the ground immediately.

I didn't wait for Ray to make the call. Just prior to the nose getting over the end of the runway, and confident I was on the mark, I went ahead and pitched out, remembering we still had 4,000 pounds of bombs and a substantial amount of fuel on board. After the pitch-out, I landed the heavily-laden Boeing about as far down the runway as possible to allow the remaining aircraft sufficient runway to land. We landed shortly before noon. We were in the air for slightly less than seven hours.

At the earlier Intelligence debriefing, I vented a simple frustration I carried within me since we shutdown our engines and turned the airplane over to the crew chief. Though we were the first airplane to land, we were the last crew to be picked-up by transportation. The Intelligence Officer duly noted my terse comment "transportation too slow" on the official interrogation form. At least one other crew agreed with my observation.

Comments from other crews were more instructive. "Ammunition was cut down to 400 rounds." "Lead was right - men want full load." "Friendly fighters had yellow noses." "Gunners coordination was piss-poor." "10/10 coverage at target." "Few breaks, worse than briefed."

During the post-mission critique, Col. Frank Hunter, Jr., our Group Commander, discussed the fact that we did not get all twenty-three aircraft on the ground on any one particular pass. Laboring the point further, he said he didn't think we were pitching out hard enough, steep enough and soon enough. He then asked, "Who was the first man on the break?"

I stood up and exclaimed, "This is Lt. Weekley, Colonel, and I was the first man to pitch and there is nobody that can pitch any sharper or any harder than I did!"

He nodded appreciatively and said, "That is fine. Who was the second man to break?" With that question, our little discussion ended.

Shortly after our return to base, we learned Maj. Robert K. Simeral and his crew

were the ones that experienced the blown cylinder leading to an engine fire on their way out over the English Channel. They released their bombs over an open field near West Chiltington in Sussex before bailing-out and parachuting to safety. Their B-17G, AAF 42-107114 (N8-L), crashed at Truleigh Manor Farm near Edburton in Sussex County, just north of Brighton. All ten crewmembers returned to base with lively stories to share. Except for this one unfortunate incident, all other 398th airplanes returned to Nuthampstead safely.

The weather created havoc on all missions that day. Only sixty-one 1st Bomb Division and two hundred fifty-two 2nd and 3rd Bomb Division heavy bombers managed to bomb their targets or targets of opportunity. The balance of the heavy bomber attacking force, more than three hundred and fifty airplanes, was thwarted due to weather and mechanical difficulties. At least sixty-three fighters aborted for similar reasons. Moreover, more than ninety B-17s and B-24s were listed as damaged due to hostile action.

This mission proved to be a most unusual flight for my crew and me. By some manner of navigation, and I have no idea how it happened, the formation's lead navigator flew us right over Paris. We could look down and see Paris and its famous landmarks very clearly. Of course, that was quite a shock to me to be in such a position.

During the war, Allied bombers made every attempt not to bomb Paris. It had been declared an "open city" during the first part of the war, a neutral sanctuary. If any of the aircraft had been forced down, it would have caused extensive damage in and around the Paris area, something the Parisians did not want to happen to their proud city.

There was no adverse reaction to our Paris overflight and there was no enemy action. We returned to our home base without incident.

My crew and I had a brief respite from combat flying on July 5th, but we flew nevertheless. Once more, we went aloft to fly a local training navigation and copilot transition flight lasting slightly more than three hours. As was the norm in wartime England, if the bomber crews were not flying missions, they were almost always doing some sort of training in the air or on the ground.

Ground training was an important part of our flight operations training. We'd cover such subjects as navigation, procedures for operating in the United Kingdom's airspace, ditching procedures, emergency Air/Sea Rescue (ASR) operations, Buncher and Splasher Beacon training, hand-to-hand combat techniques, and escape and evasion procedures. On occasion, a crewmember from another bomb group - who was an actual evader - would come to our base and describe how he evaded capture and made his safe return to England.

In addition, we'd cover subjects not taught during my training in the United States, such as aircraft handling with structural damage, how to lighten the aircraft (such as jettisoning the ball turret and .50 caliber guns), emergency procedures over England and so forth.

I paid close attention to these ground sessions. I wanted to know intuitively how something worked or how it was to be done. If I could explain to the instructor how something worked or was supposed to be accomplished, then I understood the covered system or procedure completely.

Learning a hard lesson from the weather-related mission debacle of only a day earlier, the 398th gained two permanently-assigned PFF aircraft. Now, the 398th did not have to rely on other nearby bomb groups to provide these specially-equipped and vitally important B-17s.

We flew our seventh combat mission on Thursday, July 6th. Once again, I flew the *Bronx Bomber II*. My assigned position was left wing of the Low Squadron of the Lead Group, one small part of a thirty-five airplane 1st "C" CBW formation. Lt. Melvin Horn-

shuh, one of my Nissen hut roommates, flew as my squadron leader. Col. Hunter and Capt. Willis Frazier, our squadron's Operations Officer, led the entire formation. Our assigned target was a *Noball* site near Cauchi D'Ecques, France. Each heavy bomber carried eighteen, 250 lb, AN-M57 General Purpose bombs, ideal for smashing these high-value targets. Weather for takeoff was briefed as partly cloudy with four mile visibility and light surface winds. We were scheduled to takeoff at 0730 hours and land three-and-a-half hours later.

Leaving the mission briefing, everyone agreed this mission would be a "milk run," an easy mission. We expected little or no enemy opposition. Unfortunately, the enemy rarely acted as we expected.

We took-off into a bright morning sun and immediately began our timed, turning climb to assemble over an awakening English countryside. Group assembly took place over the Nuthampstead beacon and the Wing assembled over the Graves End Buncher beacon an hour and twenty minutes after takeoff. We left the English Coast at Beachy Head twenty minutes later, crossed into enemy airspace shortly thereafter, making an easterly turn at the Initial Point before we proceeded towards our assigned target at 25,000 feet.

Unfortunately, the Initial Point and assigned target were obscured by smoke, so the Lead and Low Groups flew around Northern France and Belgium looking for any targets of opportunity. Following the prescribed Eighth Air Force dictate of not bombing any target in France until it was positively identified, the 398th Lead and Low Groups made several 360-degree turns over the target area trying to find their target, but were unsuccessful. The smoke obscured the target or it was camouflaged too well. The High Group, meanwhile, continued forward and bombed what they thought was their target. (See Endnotes, Chapter 7, Number 2)

Eventually, the Lead Group bombed an airfield near Nuncq, France and the Low

The B-17G, AAF 43-37527 (N7-X), *The Prowler,* assigned to the 603rd Bomb Squadron, 398th Bomb Group, is shown here on a training flight over England during the summer of 1944.
(398th Bomb Group Memorial Association)

This same B-17 is shown after its crash-landing at RAF Penhurst upon returning from the mission on July 6, 1944. The pilot was 2nd Lt. H.J. Sleaman. All of the crew escaped injury. This B-17 never flew again and was salvaged for parts.
(398th Bomb Group Memorial Association)

Group bombed an airfield near Dunkirk.

Within minutes after releasing our bomb load, our bomber formation made a diversionary turn to the southeast prior to turning towards Ostend, Belgium and home. We were north of Rouen, France when we encountered heavy and accurate anti-aircraft fire, most of it exploding just under our formation.

Ven Unger, my radio operator, was throwing out chaff at the time and he saw the flak exploding below him. He decided to take off his flak jacket and place it on the floor to offer some protection. In the next instant, a flak blast rocked our airplane and some shrapnel hit Ven in the hip, the impact knocking him to the floor.

Ven tried to call me on the intercom to tell me of his dire situation, but his intercom cord was disconnected. Now in great pain, Ven reconnected his intercom cord and called me to say he was hit. I called Bob Stickel, our waist gunner, to help Ven. Bob grabbed a first aid kit and tended to Ven's wound, administering morphine as needed.

Returning to Nuthampstead, I sent Ben Clark, our copilot, to stay with Ven until we were close to landing. When we arrived in the Nuthampstead traffic pattern, Joe Skarda, our flight engineer, fired red flares from the Very pistol we carried to alert medical personnel on the ground we had wounded on board. After landing, we cleared the runway as quickly as possible and shutdown our engines. The attending medical personnel carefully removed Ven from the airplane and took him to the base hospital.

During this three-and-a-half hour mission, several 398th bombers encountered intense and accurate flak. No enemy aircraft were sighted and all 398th bombers returned safely, except for one airplane (AAF 43-37527, NX-7, *The Prowler*) piloted by 2nd Lt. H.J. Sleaman that made a successful crash-landing at RAF Penhurst in Kent. All crew emerged unhurt. In turn, this bomber was salvaged for parts several days later.

So much for a "milk run" mission!

At the Intelligence debriefing, the aircrews griped about the greasy morning food, being awakened too late for breakfast and the "piss poor" transportation. Other crews complained of not receiving enough 50-caliber ammunition, whereas others noted problems with modified or poor-fitting oxygen masks.

The flak reports were the most important. Most crews reported encountering barrage flak. Lt. D.L. Foster, who flew in the lead element of the Low Group, commented "Flak burst looked unusually large. Flak was very near yet the usual yellow flame was not visible." Lt. Hunshuh and his crew said it best when they reported, "Big black stuff!"

Back at the base hospital, Ven Unger's injury was deemed severe enough that he was transferred to a larger regional hospital where he stayed for seven months. He re-

Ven Unger, right, recuperating from his wounds, poses with two of his wartime buddies.

(Ven B. Unger)

mained in bed for the first seventy-three days recovering from his wounds, his feet never touching the floor.

This mission was the last Ven flew as a combat crewmember. He was an excellent radio operator and an outstanding crewmember, and we were never the same after he was wounded.

Technical Sergeant Louis Buchsbaum was assigned to my crew as the new radio operator prior to our next mission. Louis was the radio operator on Capt. Allan Arlin's crew, another fine group from the 601st Bomb Squadron, and he had logged several missions before being reassigned to my crew. Older than most of his contemporaries, Louis joined the service when he was 30 years old. He was fluent in German and this language skill served him well during his short military career. T/Sgt. Buchsbaum flew the radio position for the balance of our combat missions.

Reviewing the Eighth Air Force record for July 6th, some six hundred and eighty-nine B-17s and B-24s from the 1st, 2nd, and 3rd Bomb Divisions participated in these morning raids throughout central and northwestern France, including two hundred and twenty-four fighters dispatched from the VIII Fighter Command for escort. Eighteen *Noball* sites in or near Pas de Calais, France were targeted. Three B-24s failed to return home and two hundred and twenty heavy bombers were damaged, including the one 398th B-17 that crash-landed at RAF Penhurst. At least two airmen were killed in action and three were wounded, including Ven.

July 6th was also Billie's birthday. Shortly after my safe return to Nuthampstead, I wrote her a letter to celebrate it. Letters were the only means for service members to maintain contact with our loved ones at home. We did not have the luxury of today's marvelous satellite-linked communications, so every letter from home was just as sweet and meaningful as any telephone call or computer e-mail.

I was posted to fly the next day with an early wake-up. This meant another long mission lay ahead. I thought little about the planned target while I had a quick dinner and retired early. My thoughts were on Billie.

Our eighth mission, and the 398th's forty-fourth Group Mission, was on Friday, July 7th. We were assigned a relatively new, unpainted B-17G, AAF 42-107080 (3O-S), which carried the odd moniker *OXO*, and flew in the number five position of the Low Squadron of the Lead Group. General William Gross, Commander of the 1st Combat Bomb Wing of the 1st Bomb Division, flew the Group's lead aircraft and led the 1st Bomb Division on this vitally important mission. Col. Hunter flew the Deputy Lead position. Thirty-seven 398th Bomb Group airplanes launched for the mission, but one bomber returned early due to mechanical problems.

Our assigned target was the Allegemeine Transport Anlagen Gmbh aircraft factory three miles north of Leipzig (Mockau), Germany, which is located geographically about a hundred miles south of Berlin. This bustling plant produced fuselages for Junkers Ju 88 airplanes and other components for Heinkel aircraft. As briefed, we knew this mission would be particularly tough as it meant a deep penetration raid into Germany, and we were guaranteed to encounter the brunt of German flak and enemy fighters on this run.

The Eighth Air Force's attacking armada scheduled that day was impressive! One thousand one hundred and twenty-nine B-17s and B-24s and six hundred and fifty-six fighters were dispatched to attack three synthetic oil plants, eight aircraft assembly plants, marshalling yards at two locations, an equipment depot, several railway repair shops and two aerodromes. The attacking bombers were scheduled to release their deadly salvo between 0959 and 1057 hours. Most fighters were assigned escort duties while other fighters were tasked to strafe airfields and rail targets.

Takeoff went smoothly, but weather quickly became a concern as we assembled at 8,000 feet over the Bassingbourn Buncher Beacon. The weather closed in west of Bassingbourn, which forced the High Group to a lower than briefed altitude. Compounding our problems, especially for our navigator, the lead pilot decided to change the briefed flight plan and omit a turn point. The Group departed the English coast at 12,000 feet, but a few minutes early. To get back on the briefed schedule, the Division Leader made a few "S" turns and short dog-legs before reaching the enemy coast. We crossed the enemy coast at 20,000 feet, still climbing.

More problems lay ahead for us. The leader in the second element of the Low Group blew a cylinder head on an engine and was forced to abort. Then, the PFF (Path Finding) equipment on the Lead aircraft failed. Fortunately, the weather cleared over Europe and the Lead aircraft radioed we would drop our bombs visually. The fighter escort was excellent and we had no serious enemy fighter opposition inbound to the target. We were forming no contrails at 25,000 feet, so the lead pilot decided to bomb 1,000 feet higher than briefed.

As we approached the primary target, we discovered it was obscured by heavy smoke from ground-based smoke screens. Our problems compounded when heavy smoke was observed over the secondary target. Quickly accessing the deteriorating situation, the pilot in the lead aircraft radioed the MPI (Main Point of Impact) was changed to a railroad marshalling area.

By now, the flak was heavy and accurate and two 398th airplanes were shot down almost immediately, the first being 2nd Lt. Boyd Nisewonger's crew in AAF 42-102508 (N7-J). They were hit in the number three engine only two minutes from bombs away. A tremendous explosion quickly followed that sheared its right wing with the wreckage falling on or near the Liebschwitz railway station near Gera, Germany some thirty miles

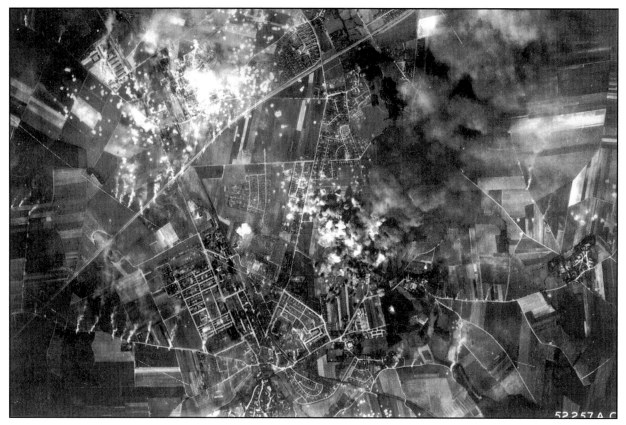

This combat strike photograph shows the Taucha Aero Engine Works being bombed near Leipzig, Germany on July 7, 1944. One thousand one hundred and twenty-nine B-17s and B-24s were dispatched to attack three German synthetic oil plants, eight aircraft assembly plants, marshalling yards at two locations, an equipment depot and two aerodromes.　(National Archives, 342-FH-3A21825-52257 A.C.)

southwest of Leipzig. All but one of the crew escaped alive and became prisoners of war.

The second B-17 lost was AAF 42-107218 (N8-T), *Agony Wagon II*, commanded by 2nd Lt. Roger A. Folger. His plane was hit just after "bombs away" and was last seen descending earthward under control. I learned after the war that Folger and his crew made a successful crash landing, but destroyed a tenement house in the ensuing crash. Folger and his crew emerged unhurt and were taken prisoner almost immediately. Tragically, the copilot, 2nd Lt. Raymond Hopp, was killed while trying to escape.

Adding to our woes, many crews saw German Me 410 twin-engine fighters take off three at a time in the Leipzig area, but for reasons unknown they did not attack our bomber stream. These formidable fighters carried a lethal combination of machine guns and cannons that wreaked deadly havoc on

B-17 formations.

Worse, the Wing circled several times southwest of Leipzig and picked-up the High Group, which had somehow separated itself from the Low and Lead Groups. Similarly, the Low Group lost the Lead Group in this circling and, likewise, attached itself to another attacking Combat Bomb Wing before it was able to contact the Lead Group some seventy-five miles west of the target.

I did not appreciate this circling one iota!

We left the target battered and bruised, and Leipzig had been dealt a massive blow. I learned later that two large workshops received direct hits with a third workshop getting three direct hits. Additionally, two concentrations of GP bombs and one concentration of incendiary bombs burst within the target area. At least two large fires were started from our bombing.

Homeward bound, we crossed the enemy

coast at 18,000 feet and received a radio message warning of heavy icing over England at 10,000 feet. The lead airplane dropped quickly to 1,000 feet and returned home with all groups in trail (single file formation). We made individual instrument approaches and landed at Nuthampstead in very poor visibility.

Though the mission to Leipzig and other German targets was successful, the toll in Eighth Air Force aircraft and men lost that day was high. A total of thirty-seven heavy bombers, including the two 398th airplanes, failed to return. Another three hundred ninety bombers were damaged. Of the eighteen total crewmembers in the two 398th airplanes listed as missing in action, at least two were killed-in-action and the rest became prisoners of war. At least six escorting fighters and their pilots from VIII Fighter Command were shown as MIA.

Leipzig was quite a long way from Nuthampstead and we were on oxygen for a long period of time. We were in the air a total of eight hours and thirty minutes. Fortunately, nothing unusual happened to us personally on this mission, which was quite a relief from the previous day when Ven Unger was wounded.

At the Intelligence debrief, a few crews groused about dirty windows, poor transportation, not enough flak suits and "too much bugle blowing-disturbs the crews." Several crews reported seeing a B-17 go

These 398th Bomb Group B-17Gs drop bombs on an enemy target. The aircraft in the foreground is AAF 42-102610 (K8-Y), *Boomerang*, and was assigned to the 602 B.S. This aircraft was lost on December 30, 1944 when it crashed into the English Channel with all aboard. The other aircraft pictured are AAF 42-97387 (K8-H), *Maude Maria,* and AAF 44-8398 (K8-Q). (National Archives, 342-FH-3A20919-57548 A.C.)

down with a fire between the number three and four engine, eventually blowing-up. Only five or six chutes were seen afterwards.

Other observations were more significant. One crew reported seeing a large convoy with twelve ships moving northbound. Another crew reported seeing two catapults with two planes mounted on each. Other crews reported seeing fifty to sixty airplanes parked in the target area.

I included the emphatic comment "making circles over the target not appreciated" on our Interrogation Form.

My crew and I did not fly any combat missions for the next few days, though the 398th continued to do so. On Saturday, July 8th, the first of twenty-four 398th Bomb Group aircraft took off at 0400 hours to bomb bridges and tunnels at Humieres and Fresnoy in France, one small part of an overall attack force that consisted of one thousand and twenty-nine heavy bombers and seven hundred and fourteen fighters, yet only four hundred and sixty-two bombers actually bombed their targets. The balance aborted due to bad weather, mechanical or other problems.

What were supposed to be "milk runs" proved tragically otherwise. During this mission, the 398th lost four airplanes. These losses were grievously high, as four crews were killed, wounded or became missing in action.

Two 398th B-17Gs, AAF 42-102445 (3O-R) commanded by 2nd Lt. George F. Wilson and AAF 42-107096 (3O-K) commanded by Capt. Kearie L. Berry, were hit by heavy and accurate flak over the target area. Wilson's plane fell to earth and crashed near Rouen, France killing the pilot. All but one of the surviving crewmembers became POWs, with one evading capture. Berry and his crew managed to fly their severely damaged and burning airplane as far as the English Channel before Berry ordered everyone to bailout. British Air/Sea Rescue picked-up Berry near the English Coast and S/Sgt. Manuel Ray, the tail gunner and the only other survivor, near the French coast. All other crewmembers from Berry's plane were lost. In all, thirteen crewmembers from these two airplanes were listed as "Missing in Action."

As for the other two 398th airplanes lost on July 8th, one was commanded by Lt. Curtis D. Lovelace and the other by Capt. Tracy J. Peterson. Lovelace and crew bailed out at 17,000 feet near Southminster in Essex near the English coast. This pilotless airplane (AAF 42-97380, N8-R), flying on only two engines, flew for almost thirty miles before crashing near Chelsworth in Suffolk. The other bomber, piloted by Capt. Tracey J. Peterson, crash-landed successfully on a beach near the quiet village of Sandwich in Kent. Once again, another lucky B-17 crew survived a close brush with catastrophe without grievous injury or death.

Capt. Peterson's crash-landing is particularly interesting and speaks highly for the B-17's ability to keep flying even after sustaining severe combat damage. Leaving the protective umbrella of the formation shortly after bombs away, Capt. Peterson and his copilot, Capt. Hal Lamb, managed to nurse their crippled, Vega-built B-17G (AAF 42-97855, 3O-A) towards the English Channel, all the while losing precious altitude. They left the French coast with two engines inoperative and a third engine losing oil pressure.

Two of Peterson's crewmembers were injured by flak, but they did not tell their fellow crewmembers of their grim situation until after they were on the ground. The crew tossed out everything they could to lighten the load and slow or arrest the B-17's gradual, constant descent. Guns, ammunition and any loose equipment were given the heave-ho, including the ball turret. As they neared the English coast, the airplane began to vibrate wildly from one of the runaway propellers, the engine throwing sparks as they descended. Fearing the vibrating bomber might explode at any moment, Capt. Peterson and his copilot had just enough altitude to set down their damaged bomber on the first available spot on English soil.

As unfortunate luck would have it that day, they landed on a sandy beach peppered with mines. Peterson and his copilot made a wheels-up landing on the water's edge, but had to lift the left wing to clear the mine sticks

Second Lieutenant Harold D. Weekley and his crew pose at the tail of the *Bronx Bomber II,* AAF 42-102516 (3O-H) on July 8, 1944. The strain of flying combat and fatigue shows clearly in each of their faces.
Left to Right, Back Row - 2nd Lt. Harold D. Weekley, pilot; 2nd Lt. Benjamin L. Clark, copilot;
2nd Lt. Paul N. James, navigator; F/O Raymond S. Delbart, bombardier
Left to Right, Front Row - T/Sgt. Joseph W. Skarda, top turret gunner/flight engineer; S/Sgt. Gene F. Leonard, left waist gunner; S/Sgt. Robert L. Stickel, right waist gunner; S/Sgt. Charles "Pop" Stombaugh, tail gunner.
(National Archives, 342-FH-3A9286-C59252 A.C.)

protruding from the water, then had to lift the right wing to avoid the mine sticks on the beach. Their sliding airplane came to rest in front of a barbed-wire barricade only yards from one of England's finest golf clubs. A shaken crew emerged from the wrecked Flying Fortress.

Though I never heard otherwise, I certainly hope the English golf club members were proper gentlemen and offered each crewmember a well-deserved drink.

While this aerial drama unfolded, an Army Air Forces photographer was at Nuthampstead taking 398th crew photographs. I gathered my crew, some of us dressed in flying gear after a brief maintenance or training flight, at the tail of the *Bronx*

Bomber II, AAF 42-102516 (3O-H), so the photographer could take the obligatory photograph. When this black and white photograph was printed and distributed, the strain of flying combat and fatigue showed clearly in each our faces. Most of us, barely into our late teens and early twenties, looked many years older. It was difficult for us to conjure a smile for the photographer. We were too tired.

On Tuesday, July 11th, the Eighth Air Force began a series of bombing missions, spread over a five day period that targeted marshalling yards and aircraft factories in or near Munich. These were deep penetration raids with each mission lasting nine or more hours. Guided by H2X radar, one thousand

Lieutenants Harold Weekley, Benjamin Clark, Paul James and Raymond Delbart pose together after receiving their first Air Medal on July 10, 1944. This ceremony gave Hal Weekley and his officers a brief respite from the daily grind of war.   (Harold D. Weekley)

forty-seven heavy bombers attacked their targets, escorted by six hundred and ninety-nine P-38s, P-47s and P-51s. Before the day was over, the toll on man and machine was high and at least sixteen B-24s, four B-17s and four escort fighters were lost. Another one hundred thirty-one heavy bombers were damaged with at least four damaged beyond repair. Worse, twelve crewmembers were killed in action and another nineteen were tallied as wounded in action. Many more airmen were listed as missing in action.

Twenty 398th Bomb Group airplanes paticipated in this Munich raid and all but one bomber returned safely to Nuthampstead. This bomber landed at another base, but returned safely later in the day.

Neither my crew nor I flew on this important mission and, instead, spent the time on base. I used my free time enjoying my promo-

tion to First Lieutenant and writing a long letter to Billie. How I missed her so! Even as I pinned the rank's single silver bars on my uniform, I had little time to celebrate this well-deserved promotion. I was posted to fly and embarked upon my ninth combat mission the following day, Wednesday, July 12th.

The briefed mission was another deep penetration raid to Munich, Germany, to bomb the marshalling yards and other important industrial and airfield targets in the surrounding area. One thousand two hundred and seventy-one heavy bombers and eight hundred three escorting P-38, P-47 and P-51 fighters were dispatched on this raid, including thirty-six B-17Gs from the 398th and 91st Bomb Groups. The 398th provided the Lead and Low Groups, while the 91st comprised the High Group. These combined groups made up the 1st "B" CBW on this significant mission.

My assigned aircraft was, once again, the *Bronx Bomber II*. Our bomb load consisted of four, 500 lb, AN-M64 bombs and six, 500 lb, AN-M17 chemical cluster bombs with delayed fuses. Really nasty stuff! All other 398th airplanes carried a similar bomb load that day. I was assigned to fly in the number two position, or the right wing, in the second element of the Low Group.

The first airplane took-off from Nuthampstead's 6,000-foot long main runway at 0900 hours. The last airplane lifted off sixteen minutes later. My airplane had some mechanical problems and we did not get airborne until 1027 hours. Weather created havoc for us and we flew for almost two hours trying to find the formation and join up at the Bassingbourn Buncher beacon, all the while consuming precious fuel. Unsuccessful, I aborted and returned to base with my bomb load still on board. I was not alone as two other crews and planes also aborted and returned to Nuthampstead with their 5000 lb, bomb load and a lot of fuel onboard. None of us received credit for this mission.

I sighed. We still needed to fly sixteen more missions before we could rotate home.

Despite these weather and assembly problems, the remaining thirty-three airplanes from the 398th and the 91st Bomb Groups joined the other B-17s and B-24s dispatched to bomb their targets inside Germany. The raiding bombers crossed the enemy coast at 21,000 feet, and immediately encountered 9/10ths cloud coverage all the way to the target. Unable to drop visually, the attacking force dropped their bombs using Pathfinder/H2X airborne radar with unobserved results.

Though fighter support was judged as excellent by many crewmembers at the Intelligence debriefings and flak was stated to be moderate in intensity and inaccurate, the actual story revealed a more tragic tally; the Eighth Air Force lost two dozen heavy bombers on this mission and another two

hundred and ninety-seven were damaged to varying degrees, with at least four damaged beyond repair. There were a lot of empty beds that night as two airmen were killed in action, seven were wounded and at least two hundred sixteen airmen were shown as missing in action. Fate, however, waved its fickle hand and spared the 398th Bomb Group from any losses that day.

On Thursday, July 13th, my crew and I were airborne once more, but we did not fly much further than the Nuthampstead traffic pattern. We flew the *Bronx Bomber II* for two hours, mostly to give my copilot some valuable training.

I had a little program in which I practiced landings extensively with a number of co-pilots. For some reason, a lot of the 398th's aircraft commanders, or First Pilots, did not allow their co-pilots to make any landings. Maybe there was a lack of confidence in their own abilities to correct for any copilot deviations or variations on landing. Personally, I thought the copilot's ability to land the airplane was a very important and a prudent judgment call because you never knew when you might be wounded and had to depend on the co-pilot's ability to land the aircraft. Following my own edict, I gave Ben Clark several landings.

While I was giving Ben Clark some proficiency takeoffs and landings, the 398th flew another mission to Munich, the Group's forty-ninth mission. Thirty-six airplanes were dispatched to bomb the Aero Engine Works in Munich. Eighteen B-17s from the 398th Bomb Group formed over the Bassingbourn Buncher beacon before proceeding to the Debden Buncher beacon, where they joined eighteen other B-17s from the 91st Bomb Group.

The whole of the Eighth Air Force's attacking force consisted of three hundred and fifty-six 1st Bomb Division B-17s and one hundred and thirty-nine 3rd Bomb Division B-17s attacked Munich while another one hundred B-17s from the 3rd Bomb Division

Boeing-built AAF 42-102516 (3O-H), the *Bronx Bomber II*, makes a go-around at Nuthampstead during a training flight in the summer of 1944. The tents in the background are believed to be the dispersal areas for the 600th and 601st Bomb Squadrons.

Lieutenant Harold Weekley believed the copilot's ability to land the airplane was a very important and prudent judgment call, and he allowed his copilot to make several landings during these training flights. In combat, Weekley and his crew never knew when they'd have to depend upon the copilot to land the aircraft.

This aircraft's uniquely painted black nose shows up very well in this photograph.

(398th Bomb Group Memorial Association)

hit an aircraft engine plant near Munich. At least twelve B-17s attacked targets of opportunity. The B-24s threw in their bombing weight and two hundred and ninety-eight B-24s attacked a marshalling yard at Saarbrucken. Heavy clouds covered Germany and H2X radar was used to locate the targets.

When this mission ended nine hours later, only one 398th heavy bomber failed to return and was recorded as "missing in action." This missing aircraft (AAF 42-97348, N7-R) piloted by Lt. Thomas K. Foster, was hit in the rear fuselage by flak near Brussels and exploded before most of the crew could bailout. Only one crewmember survived.

The Eighth Air Force tallied at least nine B-17s and one B-24 lost on these missions. Another three hundred sixteen heavy bombers were battle-damaged to varying degrees. Of the five hundred and forty-three P-38, P-47 and P-51 escorting fighters, at least five airplanes and three pilots were lost. Worse, at least thirty-one airmen were killed that day and another seventy-six were

wounded, not to mention the many crewmembers listed as missing in action.

For loved ones back home, this meant more War Department telegrams sent to stunned and grieving families, more letters of sympathy and concern from Base Chaplains mailed to loved ones and more three or four stars hung in windows. This daily toll of destruction and death continued unabated.

I flew and completed my ninth combat mission on Sunday, July 16th on another raid against the Munich Aero Engine Works in Munich, Germany. Munich was a long, high flight from Nuthampstead. Each bomber was provided with seven-and-a-half hours of oxygen, though the average flight time from takeoff to landing was eight-and-a-half hours. My assigned B-17G (AAF 42-97401, 3O-T) for this difficult mission carried the moniker *Stinker, Jr.* I was assigned to fly in the number two position of the High Squadron of the Low Group.

Munich was a major Allied target and had been hit numerous times. The Royal Air Force bombed the city at night and the Eighth Air Force bombed it during the day. I know Munich was hit as many as seven days in a row in an effort to cripple the German's expansive industrial and airplane production capability in this area.

Two hundred and thirteen 1st Bomb Division heavy bombers participated in this particular raid, including thirty-six B-17Gs from the 398th Bomb Group. For the day, the Eighth Air Force dispatched one thousand and eighty-seven heavy bombers to bomb Munich and hit other targets within Germany. Seven hundred and twelve P-38s, P-47s and P-51s were dispatched as escort.

Each 398th airplane carried 2 1/2 tons of 500 lb, AN-M64 General Purpose bombs and AN-M17 fragmentation bombs plus a full load of fuel, which made for a very slow climb. Following a common practice, a spare airplane took-off ready to join the formation in case of any ground or airborne abort, but it was not needed and returned to Nuthampstead. About fifty miles from the IP, we encountered some bad weather and climbed to 28,000 feet to clear the clouds. The inclement weather and the persistent contrails from our aircraft only added to our difficulty maintaining formation. Arriving over the briefed target, we dropped our bombs upon the Wing Leader's command.

Shortly after bomb release, a dozen German Messerschmitt Bf 109 fighters raked our bomber formation with cannon fire, making three head-on passes in all. Our gunners were quite busy defending their respective airplanes from this ferocious, murderous onslaught. Cannon shells, .50-cal. bullets and pieces of riddled B-17s and attacking fighters filled the skies high above Germany. Several bombers took evasive action to avoid falling debris. One enemy fighter was seen to lose control and enter a flat spin before its pilot bailed out. Several B-17 crews continued to shoot at the spinning Messerschmitt, including the gunners aboard a severely damaged B-17 that was later reported at debrief to

depart the formation and fall earthward.

I learned later that despite the gunners' best efforts, one 398th airplane (AAF 42-102476, N7-B) was lost to enemy fighter action. The ball turret was blown to pieces by an attacking Messerschmitt Bf 109, killing the gunner. A fire started in the left wing and the crew bailed out. Eight crewmembers exited, but only seven parachutes opened. Furthermore, I learned that it was most likely Lt. Raymond J. Gallagher's crew that shot down the attacker as they themselves were being shot down.

Not long after Gallagher's B-17G began its fatal plunge, Lt. Curtis D. Lovelace's aircraft (AAF 42-102599, N8-U) was lost to flak. Ironically, this crew was the same crew that bailed out of their crippled B-17 near Essex, England eight days earlier. Of the nineteen crewmembers aboard these two airplanes, four crewmembers were killed, including Lt. Lovelace, and the balance became prisoners of war.

The Wing Leader's PFF-equipped B-17G (AAF 42-97740, K8-Q) was not without its own problems. The attacking fighters had shot out the airspeed indicator, some flight control cables and the oxygen system. Struggling to stay aloft, the Wing Leader relinquished formation lead to the Deputy Leader about 100 miles after striking the target. After struggling to stay aloft for several more hours, this courageous crew and their aircraft made a safe landing at Nuthampstead, obviously relieved to make it back to their English base alive.

Other than a few holes caused by flak, my crew and I returned to Nuthampstead with comparatively little overall damage to the airplane. Other 398th aircraft were not as lucky and several B-17s sustained heavy combat damage. A long night awaited the crew chiefs and the sheet metal repair mechanics.

Once again, the post-mission Intelligence debriefing revealed much about what was on the hearts and minds of the weary crews.

"Keep kitchen serving room open so we can get a drink before mission," "Relief tube in radio compartment leaks, needs repair," "Officers didn't get fresh eggs," and "Men were ill because the food served at breakfast - too greasy."

Other comments were much more germane to the mission flown and revealed much about the gritty, often heartless reality of day-to-day combat operations. "No flak suits - not enough to go around," "Saw B-17 ditch. Saw one dingy. About ten crewmembers out," "Saw enemy fighter shot down, went into spin, saw wisps of smoke, parts seen falling out. Straggling ship shot him," "Contrails - persistent at target. About 50 miles to target and 200 miles from target," "One B-17 observed in trouble, one engine (no. 4) smoking 13 min after target, 8 chutes seen bailing from a/c."

What does the official record show regarding the enemy fighter losses that day? Enthusiastic bomber crews claimed five fighters destroyed, three probably destroyed and three damaged. In reality, I am sure these numbers were somewhat less.

More somberly, the record also shows the Eighth Air Force lost eleven heavy bombers and at least three fighters. More empty cots at the Eighth's bomber and fighter bases, more letters sent home, more gold stars in windows.

My next sortie was on Monday, July 17th, which was my 23rd birthday. Unfortunately, I didn't get to stand down on that day, but at least I was not assigned a combat mission. Instead, I flew a local area navigation and formation lead crew training flight that lasted two hours. I don't know how it was for the fighter side of the house, but the bomber pilots were always flying training flights and working with new crews. I returned to my Nissen hut satisfied and confident my crew performed well this day. I had a few free minutes to pen a letter to Billie before I retired early for my next mission.

I flew my tenth combat mission on the

Tuesday, July18th against the Luftwaffe's experimental stations at Peenemunde, a high-value target located on a little island in northeastern Germany on the northwestern end of the Usedom Island, which itself was in the River Oder estuary. History dates Peenemunde to 1282 as a fishing village. Four and a half centuries later, this remote location proved ideal for the research, development and testing of Hitler's terrible "V" missile and rocket weapons that rained terror on England.

With what was becoming a routine early morning tug on the sleeve and the customary "'Morning, Lieutenant, mission today," my crew and I embarked upon another mission in the *Bronx Bomber II*. Nearby, Joe Wierney and his officer crewmembers got the same tug on their sleeves. Mel Hornshuh was not scheduled to fly on this mission and he and his crew were able to catch a few more winks of treasured sleep.

This aerial raid on Peenemunde was the first time the 398th had struck this Baltic Sea town and the obligatory briefing revealed to all assembled just how far we would fly. The round-trip flight time from Nuthampstead to Peenemunde and back was almost nine hours and thirty minutes and we would fly a distance of almost 1,300 miles. Undoubtedly, this mission was one of the farthest missions flown by the 398th thus far. We would be on oxygen for at least three hours. Stations was set at 0410 hours with the Pathfinder ship beginning its takeoff forty-five minutes later. The first of the 398th airplanes would begin its takeoff roll at 0510 hours.

Thirty-six 398th aircraft formed the Lead and Low Groups of the 1st "A" CBW, which included a Pathfinder airplane from the 91st Bomb Group. The 91st occupied the High Group.

I was assigned the number six position in the Low Squadron of the Lead Group. Joe Wierney would fly on my right. Each bomber in our combat box carried ten, 500 lb, AN-M64 GP bombs and we were scheduled to be over the target at 1004 hours bombing from altitudes between 22,500 and 25,700 feet, depending upon position within the High, Low or Lead Groups.

In all, eight combat bomb wings formed the Division formation for this mission, including some three hundred seventy-seven heavy bombers from other participating bomb groups. Besides the experimental stations at Peenemunde, other strategic targets included the scientific headquarters at Zinnowitz and the marshalling yards at Stralsund. At least nine hundred and thirty-five heavy bombers and four hundred and seventy-six fighters groups were dispatched to hit other tactical targets throughout France and Germany.

My crew and I took-off at 0515 hours and we settled quickly into the job at hand. We assembled in relatively clear air at the Bassingbourn Buncher beacon at 8,000 feet at 0604 hours, then followed our growing formation towards a more powerful Splasher beacon where we formed-up with the Division thirty-five minutes later. When everyone was in position, this massed armada turned east and began a slow climb towards our assigned target.

The weather was good at the start of the mission with scattered clouds and a three mile visibility, but became mostly undercast as our planes flew towards the enemy coast. Fortunately, the cloud cover thinned as we approached the target area, which allowed us to bomb the intended target visually. We encountered comparatively little anti-aircraft fire, except for some moderate yet inaccurate barrage type flak over and near the target area before and just after "bombs away." Best of all, we encountered no enemy fighters. Even when we flew over Peenemunde itself, there was little opposing enemy action, which was most unusual for such a high-value target. Friendly fighter support was good.

I consider this mission to be one of the finest "milk runs" I ever had.

Unfortunately, other participating bomb groups and fighter units did not fare as well

on this mission and other crewmembers did not share my enthusiasm. Of the three hundred seventy-seven aircraft that attacked Peenemunde, sixty-four were damaged by flak and three bombers were lost. At least three P-51s were lost.

The Intelligence debriefings tallied several instances of intense and accurate flak. In all, some thirty-seven flak guns were counted near the target area. Fortunately, none of the thirty-six bombers from the 398th that participated in this raid were damaged substantially, and no one was either wounded or killed.

The bombing results, however, were outstanding! The Lead Group's bombs fell directly on top of the targeted hydrogen peroxide plant. The bombs from the other groups and wings fell directly on or very near this vital target.

Lieutenant General Carl Spaatz, Commander of the U.S. Strategic Air Force (USSTAF) in Europe and a prominent aerial bombardment tactician, took great pride in the Peenemunde bombing mission of July 18th. Upon viewing the results of the mission, he commented that it was "one of the finest examples of precision bombing I have seen." He sent a congratulatory message to all participating units.

Overall, this mission worked out very well for us. We got plenty of flying time, we dropped our bombs on target, and we didn't encounter much enemy action. Best of all, we got another combat mission notched on our belts.

Most Intelligence briefings given to bomber crews prior to a mission offer a general overview of the operation but, in many instances, these briefings did not go into detail as to the specific activities undertaken at the intended target. Such was the case of Peenemunde. Though we were briefed of Peenemunde's importance prior to the mission, I did not learn of this installation's far-reaching significance until after the war. This very secret and well-hidden facility was

LEAD GROUP (Over Target), 1st "A" CBW

Daily
Douglas
PFF 7632-L

Ford
2467-J

Markley
Chase
PFF 7746-Q

Nelson
7214-V

Wheeler
6157-W

Lowe, D. B.
2600 -Z

Heintzelman
7098-Y

Bestervelt
2487-B

Taylor
7401-T

McCarthy
7509-J

Mezel
2418-M

Slavin
2519-A

Davis, J. H.
7385-X

Davis, J. R.
2565-M

Weekley
2516-H

Wierney
7203-Z

Farnsworth
2607-F

Falkenbach
7889-B

LOW GROUP (Over Target), 1st "A" CBW

Ross
7103-A

Ryan
7387-H

Hough
2543-B

Richardson
2568-N

Dollar
7094-M

Driscoll
2597-V

Novak
2553-K

Woodson
2593-C

Engle
7317-P

Howden
8083-P

Roderick
7337-R

Rudow
2610-Y

Dwyer
2562-G

Kaufman
2469-Q

Foster, D. L.
2570-F

Sleaman
7138-T

Fisher
7078-U

Cobb
7150-K

The 398th Bomb Group occupied the Lead and Low Groups of the 1st "A" Combat Bomb Wing on the July 18, 1944 mission to Peenemunde, Germany. This graphic shows the positions of the 398th aircraft and pilots that flew over the target that day. On this mission Hal Weekley flew in the number six position, in the Low Squadron of the Lead Group.

where the Germans undertook V-1 and, more notably, V-2 research and development. The V-2 advanced rocket bomb was developed by Dr. Wehrner von Braun, the same Dr. von Braun who later came to the United States and was instrumental in getting our fledgling space program off the ground in the 1950s and our Apollo astronauts to the moon a decade later.

The V-2 was a devastating weapon. Within its 50-foot long body, it carried a 2,000 lb warhead and a rocket motor that could propel it to a maximum speed of 3,500 mph. When a V-2 hit a target, it did so without ever being heard as it was travelling at supersonic speeds at impact. Thus, there was absolutely no warning of a V-2 attack. From early September 1944 until late March 1945, more than eleven hundred of these V-2 "vengeance weapons" were aimed at London, all meant to demoralize the population and wreak havoc upon the city's infrastructure. At least five hundred seventeen V-2s reached the city with the balance falling elsewhere.

A couple months later, I experienced a V-2 attack personally and learned firsthand the destructive power of this very formidable weapon.

The V-2 was only one of several rocket-powered weapons developed at Peenemunde. The Germans used Peenemunde to develop the Messerschmitt Me 163, a swept wing, rocket-powered airplane. This relatively small aircraft was capable of very high-

speed flight, but suffered from a very limited range. The Me 163's swift speed made it virtually impossible for any bomber gunner or escorting fighters to shoot one down. Fortunately, it was most vulnerable when it was landing and several were shot down.

Many Me 163 pilots and ground support personnel died while this airplane was being developed and flown operationally, mostly during ground operations. The plane's rocket engine fuel was notoriously unstable, haz-

The German V-2 ground-to-ground rocket was a devastating terror weapon and could destroy whole city blocks with no warning. Most V-2 research and development took place at Peenemunde, Germany. This photograph shows a V-2 on a mobile launcher. Once raised into the vertical position, this rocket could be fueled and fired. (National Museum of the United States Air Force)

ardous and prone to explode. Worse, human flesh literally dissolved when it came in direct contact with this exotic fuel.

The 398th's mission against Peenemunde on July 18th was a small part of *Operation CROSSBOW*, the Allied bombing campaign against the German V-1 and V-2 weapon sites. Though the first V-1 "Buzz Bomb" was launched against London in mid-June 1944, the U.S. Army Air Forces had lost some seventy-nine aircraft in sorties against these sites before the first V-1 was ever launched.

At British Prime Minister Winston

Much of the development work on the German V-1 (Fieseler Fi 103) flying bomb or "Buzz Bomb" was done at Peenemunde, Germany. Hundreds of these terror weapons were launched against London beginning in mid-June 1944. Considered by military planners as a high priority target, Allied bombers and ground forces destroyed virtually all V-1 (Noball) sites.
(National Museum of the United States Air Force)

The Messerschmitt Me 163B Komet was a rocket-powered interceptor developed at Peenemunde, Germany during the summer of 1941. On August 16, 1944, the Me 163 made its first contact with B-17s without success. Some 300 Komets were built, but scored only nine confirmed kills and two probable kills during its brief time in Luftwaffe service.
(National Museum of the United States Air Force)

Churchill's urging and Supreme Allied Commander Dwight D. Eisenhower's concurrence, Peenemunde remained a high-priority target from mid-1944 through the end of the war. The Eighth Air Force returned to this sprawling German complex on many other occasions. In time, we returned there, as well.

Our eleventh mission was on Wednesday, July 19th to Lechfeld, Germany and, again, I flew the *Bronx Bomber II.* Lechfeld was Germany's test and training facility for the new Messerschmitt Me 262 jet powered airplane, a very formidable aircraft just beginning to enter service.

On this day, one thousand and eighty-two heavy bombers from the 8th and 15th Air Forces, supported by six hundred and seventy escorting fighters, launched coordinated attacks against a wide array of military targets, including marshalling yards, aerodromes and various industrial targets throughout western and southwestern Germany, even into Austria, including a massed raid directed against Lechfeld and Munich. The 398th dispatched thirty-six airplanes on the Lechfeld mission, including one spare. I was assigned to fly in the number two position of the Low Group's Low Squadron. The bomb load that day consisted of forty-two, 100 lb, AN-M47 incendiary bombs. No problems were encountered on takeoff and we assembled as briefed. The weather was clear enough to make a visual run to the target. Flak was light to moderate, but accurate.

Our formation was tight, ideal for a compact bombing pattern. If the Lead bombardier was very good, then the target would cease to exist. If not, then most bombs would land on nearby farm fields and only by chance would a few bombs would come near or hit the target.

During this mission, several 398th crews, including mine, observed a number of P-51 Mustangs engage some enemy fighters, but they were too far from us to determine if they were successful in shooting down any airplanes. We did observe a P-47 Thunderbolt shoot down a German twin-engine fighter, either a Messerschmitt Me 210 or Me 410, which elicited a few joyous comments from my crew.

The Lechfeld raid damaged or destroyed several of the new Me 262 jet powered aircraft sitting on the ground. Unfortunately, the main jigs and a substantial amount of tooling remained intact enough that the Germans were able to build more Me 262s and quickly put this terrifying new airplane into frontline service.

On a later mission, I saw one of these swift, twin-engine jet fighters in action. I was amazed, dumbfounded and scared. This swift fighter's sleek aerodynamic design allowed for then unheard of speeds. Its formidable firepower could and would create havoc among raiding heavy bomber formations. Much like the Me 163 rocket plane, the Me 262 was most vulnerable on landing, though many were shot down while taking off.

Fourteen B-17s and three B-24s were lost to enemy action on July 19th. At least five combat-damaged airplanes turned south towards the reassuring safety of neutral Switzerland, with at least two B-17s making emergency landings there, whereupon these crews were interned for the duration of the war. Another B-17 crew bailed out over Switzerland and they were interned, as well.

Apparently, this B-17, which came from the 91st Bomb Group, was involved in a mid-air collision with another B-17 from the same bomb group only seven minutes from bomb release. The first of the two B-17s involved in this tragic mid-air collision encountered the propeller wash or turbulence from an aircraft in front of it and slipped to the left, its left wingtip striking the second B-17 on the horizontal stabilizer in the tail causing the entire tail section to break off. This aircraft rolled over, plunged earthward and crashed in Germany. Only one crewmember survived. The first B-17 continued flying with its crew bailing-out successfully over Switzerland.

Other B-17s lost on the Lechfeld raid included a 398th Bomb Group airplane commanded by 2nd Lt. Dallas A. Hawkins, a personable young lad from West Virginia. At 1030 hours, two minutes from "bombs away," his aircraft was hit by flak and subsequently blew-up killing all but one on board. This particular loss was quite disheartening for the 398th Bomb Group, especially as the gruesome details became known.

During the bomber stream's approach to Lechfeld, an anti-aircraft battery with six Flak 37 88mm guns based at Scheuring opened fire. One or more flak shells found Hawkins' B-17. At least one flak shell hit just inside the number one engine, exploded and the left wing folded. In rapid succession, another flak shell struck AAF 42-102511 (K8-P) in the fuselage, the subsequent explosion ripping Hawkins' aircraft in half with the blazing wings and forward fuselage falling to the ground five miles north of Lechfeld, the bomb load exploding upon hitting the ground. Incredibly, Staff Sgt. Doyle Borchers, the waist gunner, was thrown clear of the exploding aircraft, survived and was eventually taken prisoner by the Germans. Meanwhile, the intact aft fuselage and tail section floated earthward with an alive, but badly injured tail gunner still aboard. He died within thirty minutes after German ground troops arrived at the crushed aircraft sections. Except for Borchers, the rest of the crew perished.

The loss of this crew was particularly tough on my crew and me. The officers of this crew, with the exception of Lt. Hawkins, shared the stateroom with me and my other officers during our voyage to England on the *SS Brazil*. Their regular First Pilot, 1st Lt. Leland L. Zimmerman, was sick the morning of this fateful mission and Lt. Hawkins stepped-in to fly the mission. When we returned from this mission, Zimmerman was at the Intelligence debriefing to meet his crew, and we had to tell him they were all gone. It was quite a traumatic experience for all of us. As could be expected, Zimmerman blamed himself for their loss. Despite his deeply personal tragedy, Zimmerman flew many more missions with the 398th.

My crew and I had arrived at Nuthampstead barely six weeks earlier. During this brief interval, at least ten 398th Bomb Group airplanes and crews had been lost to enemy action. The Eighth Air Force, meanwhile, had lost many dozens of airplanes and crews from other England based bomb groups. Replacement airplanes and crews streamed into England to fill the growing void.

My crew and I had only a few hours to relax from this mission, as we were posted to fly another mission the next day. No rest for the weary!

I flew my twelfth combat mission, and the 398th's fifty-third Group Mission, on Thursday, July 20th. Once more, I piloted the *Bronx Bomber II*, as my crew and I went to Dessau, Germany. Each of the thirty-six 398th airplanes dispatched on this raid, as well as most of the other three hundred sixty-five heavy bombers involved, carried 5,000 pounds of AN-M64 General Purpose bombs. More than one thousand heavy bombers attacked a broad array of targets inside Germany that day, including Dessau. Other targets in central and western Germany included arms factories, aerodromes, ball-bearing plants and an optical instruments factory. Four hundred and seventy-six VIII Fighter Command fighters escorted the heavy bombers and they proved very effective in keeping Luftwaffe fighters from attacking the bomber stream.

The first Nuthampstead bomber made its takeoff at 0641 hours and was piloted by Col. Frank P. Hunter, our Group Commander. This particular aircraft was a recently assigned PFF (Pathfinder) aircraft and the 398th was most happy to receive it. The rest of us took-off in one to one-and half-minute intervals behind Col. Hunter. My takeoff was twenty-four minutes later as we were sequenced behind at least twenty-one other aircraft in the takeoff flow, climb and formation assembly. From my assigned slot in the number two position of the High Squadron in the Low Group, I had an excellent overall view of our combat box and of the whole of the Division formation forming and enroute to the target.

Following the times specified by the mission's detailed Field Order, our Bomb Group formed at the Debden Buncher beacon at 0745 hours with the 1st Combat Bomb Wing assembling at the same beacon twenty minutes later. Division assembly took place near the Felixstowe Splasher beacon thirty-five minutes after Wing assembly. We crossed the Dutch coast around 0920 hours at 15,000 feet climbing to 20,000 feet. We crossed the German border west of Dusseldorf, whereupon we made a course change towards the southeast with Cologne passing to our left. Our route took us past a lot of enemy flak guns and fighters intent on defending these prominent German cities and we did not want to tangle with these lethal forces. Regardless, we saw a lot of flak in the distance and at least two groups of enemy fighters that came up and intercepted a combat bomb wing flying to our right. Twelve minutes from the IP, at least two heavy bombers in that bomber group were savagely attacked and went down before friendly fighters could engage them. At least one of the B-17s shot down was actively engaging the enemy, shooting down at least one fighter.

USAAF P-51s - "Little Friends" as heavy bomber crews affectionately called the friendly fighter forces - arrived and joined the murderous melee. Their timely arrival kept any marauding enemy fighters from attacking our formation. Thank you "Little Friends!" I am sure the tight formation we flew and the arrival of our P-51s spared our bomb group from any further losses from these attacking enemy fighters.

White silk parachutes, bodies, and tumbling and burning airplane pieces filled the sky. Several bombers had to take evasive action to avoid this rain of men and metal. Smoke and haze obscured the trail of crashed and burning bombers below our path. I had seen scenes like this on numerous other occasions, but I was too busy maintaining a tight formation to even think about, much less look at the human carnage below us.

Thirty miles north of Frankfurt, our combat box turned northeasterly and started a slow climb to our briefed bombing altitudes. We flew northwest and north of Leipzig, keeping this historic German city and its deadly flak batteries on our far right. Shortly thereafter, my combat box made a sharp left turn to a 270 degree heading. We arrived at the IP twenty-three miles from the target.

Approaching the IP, Col. Hunter and his lead bombardier, Capt. C.J. Strickrott, realized a visual bombing run was impossible due to 5/10ths cloud coverage and haze, so they radioed the other bombers to make a PFF run. For Ray Delbart, my bombardier, his job was simple; release our bombs when he saw the lead airplane release its load. For me, I would hand-fly the aircraft rather than turning on the C-1 autopilot as I normally did at this part of the mission and let the bombardier "fly" the airplane from the IP to bomb release, usually a run of about seven or eight minutes. At the morning's briefing, much emphasis was placed on flying a tight formation for the best possible bomb pattern, so I concentrated on maintaining my formation position as best I could. If I had flown any closer, I am sure I could have reached out and touched the right waist gunner on the B-17 beside me.

I could see dozens, if not hundreds of B-17s flying ahead of me, their white contrails marking their presence against the summer's blue sky. The bomber stream stretched for miles. On some missions, these heavy bomber streams stretched for hundreds of miles and I could see aircraft inbound to their targets while I was on my way outbound. I was always awestruck by this unforgettable spectacle, and enthralled that America and the USAAF could bring so much aerial firepower to bear against the enemy.

Flying at 150 miles-per-hour indicated airspeed, or almost 200 miles-per-hour true airspeed, the lead aircraft began bombing the target at 1139 hours from an altitude of 26,000 feet followed by the other heavy bombers in our Combat Bomb Wing box, flying between 24,500 and 27,000 feet, with the exception of one bomber that released its load near Nordhausen, Germany.

Moderate to heavy flak met us over the target. Angry, orange-centered black puffs appeared all around us and I could hear the jagged metal hit our airplane. Our B-17 bucked and bounced every time one of those shells exploded nearby, sending hot metal through its thin aluminum skin. Incredibly, none of these lethal shards hit anyone onboard my plane.

Bombs away, the formation turned for home. Behind us, German targets were in flames.

Seventy percent of the attacking Flying Fortresses were flak-damaged to varying degrees, with two crewmembers wounded, including the Low Group's lead navigator. The bombardier on that airplane tended to his wounded comrade and navigated the balance of the mission. In all, twenty-two 398th airplanes received flak damage reported as light to substantial.

Later, at the mission Intelligence debriefing, I learned that most of the 398th Bomb Group's bombs fell short of the intended target. In addition, I heard later the Combat Bomb Wing flying ahead of the 398th did not fare as well as we did and at least three airplanes were lost to enemy action. Overall, at least eighteen heavy bombers failed to return from their assigned missions that day. Another three hundred seventy-two are damaged to varying degrees. The 91st Bomb

Group was particularly hard hit as eight of their B-17s fell to enemy action. Eight of the escorting fighters failed to return home.

One of the fighter pilots who failed to return that day was Lt. Col. Francis S. Gabreski, the highest scoring ace of the European Theater of Operations. While strafing an airfield, the massive propeller of his rugged P-47 hit the ground. Unable to stay aloft, he bellied in the crippled fighter without injury. Gabreski managed to evade capture for several days but, eventually, was taken prisoner.

He was fortunate, as strafing ground targets was a leading cause of death among American fighter pilots.

This day was also significant in history because there was an unsuccessful attempt against Adolf Hitler's life. The maniacal dictator extracted an incredible revenge on his soldiers and population as retribution for the attempt on his life.

The 398th Bomb Group "stood down" on the July 21st and 22nd. Bad weather over the Continent hampered any significant aerial combat operations. Moreover, the Eighth Air Force was gearing-up for another series of significant operations, and this gave planners, commanders and even aircraft crew chiefs time to prepare for events in the days ahead. I was grateful for this brief respite for my crew as we had been flying constantly over several days and everyone was fatigued. We welcomed this rare chance to rest and relax. I wrote a long letter to Billie while I enjoyed reading and rereading the many letters she had sent to me.

During this particular stand down period, I placed an order with Base Supply for some bulletproof windshields and side windows for the *Bronx Bomber II*, remembering how Ven Unger, our radio operator, had been wounded. We were given the bulletproof windows and windshields but, unfortunately, no maintenance personnel were available to make this installation. Impatience wellsprings resourcefulness, so I took Ben Clark and Joe Skarda with me to the airplane

to do our own installation. We took out the old windows and installed the new bullet-proof glass windows ourselves.

During a later mission, these window replacements saved my copilot and me from harm. An 88mm anti-aircraft shell exploded on the right side of the airplane, knocking off a large piece of the right windshield glass. The replacement glass did its job and deflected the shell fragments. Had the older glass been in place, the projectile would have passed through it and hit me.

About the same time, the pilots began to receive flak suits or body armor. The gunners already had flak suits issued to them and these bulky suits had proven their worth on many occasions. The suit came in two major parts with a large piece or apron that protected your lap, so to speak, and another much larger piece that protected the chest. In my position as pilot, I took the lap piece and put it underneath my seat. Thus, if there was flak burst or hit from the bottom of the airplane, the lap apron afforded me some protection in an area of my body I dearly wanted to protect.

On Sunday, July 23rd, the weather cleared enough that I was able to do some formation flying and training with other co-pilots. In addition, I did some Lead Crew training. I guess the commanders thought I was ready to lead a squadron, perhaps the Group on a future mission. I looked forward to this new responsibility and renewed my desire to perform to the best of my ability. Flying in a lead position added a lot of prestige and personal satisfaction. Best, I would no longer endure the long drudgery of formation flying. I logged a little over five hours that day.

Barely a day later, my crew and I, including a lot of heavy bomber groups were involved in a couple of missions that would have a profound effect on how heavy bombers would be used in this and future wars.

1. A-11 Gloves
2. A-4 QAC Parachute Harness
   (attachable chest pack not shown)
3. A-14 Oxygen Mask
4. B-8 Goggles
5. A-11 Flying Helmet
6. B-15 Jacket
7. B-4 "Mae West" Life Vest
8. A-11 Trousers
9. A-6 Boots

This type of clothing and body armor was the customary dress for many Eighth Air Force crewmembers during 1944.

(Used with permission from Charles Taylor, *Iowans of the Mighty Eighth.* Copyright 2005.)

Having made it through English coastal defenses, a V-1 "Buzz Bomb," dives down on its deadly mission over Piccadilly Section, London, England on June 22, 1944. Near the end of World War II, Germany used the self-guided, pulse jet-powered V-1 and other "vengence weapons" (Vergeltungswaffe) against the Allies to strike terror into civilian populations and disrupt military operations.   (National Archives, 342-FH-3A6395-60033 A.C.)

This London pub was demolished by a V-1"Buzz Bomb" attack on June 17, 1944.

(*Impact: The Army Air Forces' Confidential Picture History of World War II,* Vol. 2, No. 8, August 1944)

"It is not a field of a few acres of ground, but a cause, that we are defending, and whether we defeat the enemy in one battle, or by degrees, the consequences will be the same."
Thomas Paine (1737–1809), *The American Crisis, no. I*
[December 23, 1776]

CHAPTER 8

Hell from Heaven: The War Continues

The 398th Bomb Group released the majority of its bombs on enemy targets in France during June and July 1944. Though a virtual "round-the-clock" bombing of strategic targets in France and Germany by Allied aircraft was proving effective, more bombing was needed to soften a stiffening enemy resistance positioned ahead of the advancing Allied forces sweeping into the European Continent since the June 6th D-Day landings and, concurrently, slow the retreat of enemy forces returning to Germany. Since this invasion, the Normandy beachheads had been won and the skies over Western

AAF 42-97317 (N7-P), *Little May,* far left, was one of the original operational aircraft assigned to the 398th Bomb Group in April 1944. It had flown over eighty missions when it was forced to land near Merville, France, where it was salvaged by the Service Command and returned to flight status, though not with the 398th. This bomber returned to the United States at the end of the war only to be broken-up as scrap at Kingman, Arizona in 1946.   (James B. Zazas)

France nearly so, but German opposition inland remained fierce and bloody on a broad front. On orders from Hitler, German commanders were told to order their troops to fight to the death. Allied military planners acknowledged more firepower was needed to thwart the fierce German resistance. Artillery alone would not suffice.

On the evening of Friday, July 7th, 1944, English Field Marshal Sir Bernard Montgomery called in 450 Royal Air Force Wellington heavy bombers to drop a carpet of bombs on elite German Panzer tank units entrenched ahead of his troops. Attacking shortly before midnight, the British bombers dropped their bombs, a carpet 4,000 yards wide and 1,500 yards deep, in front of Montgomery's British Second Army that was advancing against German army units south of Caen, France. The results were devastating. These heavy bombers cleared a path through German opposition in a manner unattainable by massed artillery and Montgomery's forces pushed ahead the next morning.

At first, Sir Arthur Harris, the British Bomber Commander, resisted using his bombers against enemy emplacements so close to British ground troops, but acquiesced. When the results proved acceptable, he saw such operations had merit, if planned carefully as not to bomb friendly forces.

General Omar Bradley, the U.S. Army's First Army Commander, recognized the value of such aerial attacks and drafted his own breakthrough plan several days later. Bradley called his plan *Operation COBRA*. Quite simply, he called upon the Eighth Air Force to lay down the most massive artillery barrage ever conceived. As one participant later reported, this mission was "a rain of fire and steel without precedent in the annuls of human conflict."

In much the same way Montgomery used British bombers to soften or destroy entrenched enemy resistance, Bradley believed American heavy bombers could support and achieve a breakout for his infantry by virtually obliterating any enemy opposition through carpet bombing, an intense concentration of bombs placed in a few square miles of battleground. To prevent any Allied troops from being bombed inadvertently, Bradley believed well-defined ground references would assist the bomber crews in identifying American lines from the enemy lines, in this case the Periers St. Lo highway, a long and straight road in northwestern France. The German's elite Panzer Lehr Division held one side of the road, and troops of the American First Army held the other side. (See Endnotes, Chapter 8, Number 1)

In his original plan, General Bradley

wanted the bombers to make their bomb runs laterally or parallel to his army's front lines. Furthermore, he deemed only relatively light bombs would be used so as not to create large craters, thus avoid hindering the rapid advance of his troops after the bombardment. In addition, he laid out a rectangular target area south of the highway roughly 7,000 yards wide and 2,500 yards deep. To protect his own troops, Bradley incorporated a narrow 800 yard safety zone in his original plan.

In his memoirs, Bradley later wrote:

Indeed, it was this thought of saturation bombing that attracted me to the Periers road. Easily recognizable from the air, the road described a long straight line that would separate our position from the German. *The bombers, I reasoned, could fly parallel to it without danger of mistaking the front line.* [Italics Bradley.]

Upon being briefed of Bradley's plan, the service Air Chiefs, including General "Tooey" Spaatz, Commander of U.S. Strategic Air Force, and Air Chief Marshall Trafford Leigh-Mallory, commander of the Allied Expeditionary Air Forces, believed a lateral bomb run would cause a great amount of congestion and confusion over the target area, and the time allotted would hamper the attack. These Chiefs told Bradley the bombers should approach their targets from the north, fly over the heads of the Allied troops, and use the Periers - St. Lo highway as a clearly distinguishable "no bomb line."

Furthermore, they insisted on a 3,000 yard safety zone for Allied troops. Bradley balked at this number, but agreed to a 1,200 yard safety zone, with the heavies striking no closer than 1,450 yards from the ground troops. The remaining 250 yard interval would be covered by fighter-bombers which, theoretically, could attack and bomb more accurately at lower altitudes.

Believing every one was in agreement, Bradley gave the "go ahead" for this mission.

Very quickly, the mission planners at Headquarters, Eighth Air Force at Pinetree took General Bradley's plans for *Operation COBRA* and used all means available to assist the General's infantry bogged down by slowly retreating yet doggedly determined enemy troops. Prior to *Operation COBRA*, strategic targets that could be bombed from high altitudes, such as railroads, vital roads and bridges, were priority targets to hamper German troop and supply movements. Now, these planners faced a fundamental change in the deployment of heavy bombers - close tactical air support of troops on the ground.

With orders in hand, the Eighth Air Force embarked upon a very risky series of combat missions for which none of the heavy bomber crews had neither trained nor practiced: precision, tactical bombing of enemy targets just ahead of advancing American soldiers. Considering most bombs dropped from heavy bombers at altitude rarely fell closer than 1,000 feet to their assigned target, these close-in tactical operations raised the ire of many Eighth Air Force commanders and officers, including Lt. General Spaatz. He voiced his strong objections to General Eisenhower about using heavy bombers on such missions, but was overruled. Even though Eisenhower had dismissed the use of heavy bombers for ground support only weeks earlier, he changed his mind when he realized heavy bombers could achieve certain desired results for advancing troops on the ground.

As mission planning unfolded, the air support dedicated to *Operation COBRA* included all available Eighth Air Force B-17s and B-24s, and all of the medium bombers and fighter-bombers of the Ninth Air Force, including IX Fighter Command P-47s and P-51s. Fighters from the VIII Fighter Command and the RAF would fly protective cover.

The Allied battle plan called for a sustained bombardment of enemy troops and equipment lasting two-and-a-half hours covering a target area of six square miles. Al-most 5,000 tons of high explosive, jellied gasoline and white phosphorus bombs would be dropped on German troops, tanks and antitank guns massed very near the Allied lines. Once this murderous bombardment was complete, waiting Allied ground troops would breakthrough the freshly created gap in the German lines. Simple in concept and impressive on scale, military planners and commanders recognized there was little room for error on this risky mission.

Operation COBRA was scheduled to begin on Friday, July 21, 1944, but bad weather postponed the offensive for three days. Then, on Monday, July 24th, weather cleared sufficiently to start this ambitious operation. As events unfolded, hell came from the heavens for both German and Allied troops.

The Eighth Air Force dispatched one thousand five hundred and eighty-six heavy bombers and VIII Fighter Command dispatched six hundred and seventy-one fighters to support the U.S. First Army's offensive. The 1st Bomb Division's 94th Combat Bomb Wing was tasked to lead this historic and noble mission, followed by bomb groups from the 41st CBW, the 40th CBW and the 1st CBW. The 2nd and 3rd Bomb Divisions followed the 1st Bomb Division. Each participating bomb group committed thirty-six to fifty-two airplanes on this vital mission.

The 1st Combat Bomb Wing's bomber strength was divided into three separate combat boxes, denoted on the Field Order as the 1st "A" Force, 1st "B" Force and 1st "C" Force consisting of the 91st, the 398th and the 381st Bomb Groups respectively. Each bomb group dispatched at least fifty-two airplanes, with the 398th and the 381st Bomb Groups tasked to supply one spare aircraft per combat box.

Similar to other participating bomb groups, the 398th's bomber strength was subdivided into four individual groups, twelve to fourteen airplanes in each group. All four of the 398th's squadrons participated in this raid. The 600th Bomb Squadron occupied the

1st Group, 1st CBW

Markley
Douglas
7892-L

Ford
2467-J

Bestervelt
7157-W

Baker
7399-H

Chase
2487-B

Searl
2507-F

Wheeler
7249-P

Menzel
2390-X

Lowe, D.B.
2536-C

Slavis
Pappas
7192-K

Fritog
2519-A

Elwood
7846-T

Reed
7214-V

2nd Group, 1st CBW

Lamb
Frazier
7874-W

Dalton
7190-L

Davis, J.H.
7203-Z

Heintzelman
7908-M

Hornshuh
7385-X

McCarthy
7509-J

Weekley
2516-H

Wierney
7401-T

Davis, J.A.
2565-M

Binzer
7889-B

Taylor
2600-Z
(Spare)

Farnsworth
2607-F

Fairbanks
7080-S

3rd Group, 1st CBW

Dunlap-
Berry
7874-W

Ross
2593-C

Bochme
7337-R

Hough
2543-B

Cobb
7150-K

Clarks-J
7509-J

Roderick
7374-X

Driscoll
7401-T

Ryan
2610-Y

Woodson
7094-W

Rudrud
7789-N
(Spare)

Dollar
2506-L

Rudow
2597-V

4th Group, 1st CBW

Cullinan
Scott
7223-A

Latson
2568-N

Dwyer
2579-C

Stoll
2562-G

Kaurman
2469-Q

Slaeaman
7825-J

Durtichi
7977-R

Spitzer
7401-T

Howden
7317-P

Novak
7186-L

Fisher
7078-U

Fahrenthold
7138-T
(Spare)

Lassegard
2570-F

Weather Ship Davidson, 7205-F

This graphic shows the 398th Bomb Group formation as briefed for the mission to St. Lo, France on July 24, 1944. Lieutenant Harold Weekley and his crew flew the *Bronx Bomber II* in the number two position of the Low Squadron of the Second Group.

first group, the 601st Bomb Squadron occupied the second group, the 602nd occupied the third and the 603rd occupied the fourth group of dispatched bombers.

The call signs that day were "Swordfish Able" for the 91st Bomb Group, "Swordfish Baker" for the 398th and "Swordfish Charlie" for the 391st. In turn, each of the four groupings of bombers within each combat box was identified as "Swordfish Able One," "Swordfish Able Two," "Swordfish Able Three," Swordfish Able Four," etc.

The bomb load was a mix of fragmentations bombs and General Purpose bombs, the bombers' intervalometers set at 150 feet for the fragmentation bombs and 100 feet for the GP bombs. The 94th CBW Force and the first half of the 41st CBW Force loaded fragmentation bombs. The balance of the attacking 1st Bomb Division bombers each carried thirty-eight, AN-M30, 100 lb General Purpose bombs, ideal for attacking massed troops and equipment, but not powerful enough to leave deep craters that would hinder advancing troops from the U.S. First Army.

We were briefed to bomb our targets between 15,000 and 16,500 feet, depending upon our formation position. Other bomb groups had slightly higher bombing altitudes. The key objective was to release a very compact pattern of bombs. Navigators were cautioned not to bomb short "as the penetration route is directly over friendly troops and the targets are 1500 yards south of the forward line." We were briefed to commence the release of chaff at the French coast and continue for twelve minutes. Friendly ground forces were tasked to conduct counter battery artillery fire against enemy flak positions throughout the entire mission.

Moreover, the 2nd and 3rd Bomb Divisions would be close by, especially in the target area. Our TOT (Time Over Target) had to be precise, or we would create tremendous timing and spacing problems for the following Bomb Divisions. Spacing between each attacking force was set at one minute!

The weather was briefed to be overcast until the English coast with tops at 7,000 feet and unrestricted visibility above. Cloud coverage was briefed to improve to broken to scattered clouds as we flew towards our targets. Takeoff and landing visibilities at Nuthampstead were briefed to be less than three miles, unrestricted above 7,000 feet and three to four miles vertically over the target area.

Once again, I flew the *Bronx Bomber II* and was placed in the number two position of the Low Squadron of the Second Group. 1st Lt. Merwyn Hornshuh, one of my Nissen hut roommates, would fly lead in this squadron. Flying time to and from the European Continent was scheduled to be less than six hours. Takeoffs were scheduled to commence at 0952 hours with the weather ship taking off an hour earlier.

The Field Order was most specific with respect to the overall conduct of this high-visibility and risky mission:

1. All aircraft will open their bombays before arriving at the French coast as a precaution against any faulty release, and will keep them open to the target.

2. Utmost caution will be observed so no bombs will be dropped through another formation.

3. Routes, timings, and corridor assigned will be strictly adhered to.

4. The 91st will circle Bassingbourn Buncher to the north.

5. The 398th will circle Debden Buncher to the south.

6. Bombardiers are again instructed not to drop bombs short because of the nearness of our own troops.

All 398th aircraft got airborne with little difficulty, but traffic congestion and the resulting propeller turbulence from so many airplanes added a few anxious moments for us as we assembled at the Debden Buncher beacon, then we climbed to between 15,000 and 17,000 feet, our briefed bombing

A 601st Bomb Squadron B-17G flies in formation with other 398th Bomb Group airplanes. This airplane, AAF 43-37889 (3O-B), carried no known nickname and flew on the missions to St. Lo, France on July 24 and 25, 1944. This heavy bomber was posted as MIA on the January 20, 1945 mission to Ludwegshafen and Manheim, Germany. *(398th Bomb Group Memorial Association)*

altitudes depending upon our formation position. We climbed through an overcast sky at 4,000 feet and topped the clouds at 6,500 feet. As we neared the English coast, the weather ship reported a one-half or greater cloud cover near the target.

In order to avoid conflict with other traffic, we flew an assigned corridor which took us on a southwesterly direction from Nuthampstead, with London on our left. We left the English Channel at Selsey Bill and crossed the French coast well east of Cherbourg as we flew south, then turned westward toward our targets. After bombing, we were to fly toward the English Channel, keeping the Channel Islands on our right before turning north and our return route to Nuthampstead.

The fickle European weather deteriorated rapidly as the mission progressed. Most of the attacking bombers were recalled before reaching their assigned targets, almost two-thirds of the aircraft that were dispatched. Many heavy bombers never received the recall and continued on the mission. Some bombers from other bomb groups were already overhead their targets when they received the recall, and wisely withheld

releasing their bombs because they could not see their targets visually. Most airplanes obeyed the recall and returned to their respective bases. The 398th Bomb Group was not recalled and we proceeded to our briefed targets.

Arriving at the Initial Point, the 398th's First Group of the 1st "B" CBW discovered a visual bomb run was impossible due to extensive cloud coverage over this part of France. However, once the group approached the target, they found a break in the clouds and made a visual bomb release. My group, the Second Group, followed close behind and bombed visually, as well.

The 398th's Third Group leader experienced an inadvertent release of one rack and, as a result, the other aircraft in this formation released their bombs upon seeing the leader's release. Incredibly, both the pilot and the bombardier were unaware of this early release, the pilot because his Bomb Release Light was inoperative. Thinking he still had his original bomb load, the bombardier continued on his run with the remaining bombs.

Only the Fourth Group of the 1st "B" CBW did not release their bombs, due in part that the lead navigator was unable to pinpoint his position exactly once over the coast. Then, when he saw the MPI (Main Point of Impact) through a break in the clouds, there was not enough time for the bombardier to make a bomb run. The thirteen 398th airplanes in the Fourth Group did not release their bombs and returned to Nuthampstead with their bombs aboard.

The murderous onslaught continued as dozens more heavy bombers from other bomb groups followed close behind. Most bombs fell harmlessly in a no-man's area between opposing armies, but some did not.

Notwithstanding the earlier recall and the accurate bombing of briefed targets by some Bomb Groups, including the 398th, the destructive toll on the ground was profound and very distressing. Due to an unfortunate combination of errors, bad luck and other serious miscalculations by airborne crews and by staff and operations personnel of all participating Bomb Wings, many errant bombs fell on Allied troops who were 2,000 yards north of the Periers - St Lo highway. Twenty-five infantrymen were killed with one hundred and thirty-one were seriously wounded.

An infuriated General Omar Bradley demanded an explanation. Much to his horror and outrage, Bradley discovered many of the American heavy bombers flew a north to south route, which placed the bombers' flight path perpendicular to the ground landmarks, not the lateral east to west route he envisioned in his original plan. Bradley asked Air Chief Marshall Sir Trafford Leigh-Mallory, head of the Allied Expeditionary Air Force, why the bombers did not fly parallel to the Periers - St. Lo highway. Leigh-Mallory told Bradley it would take more than two and a half hours to funnel almost fifteen hundred heavy bombers along a narrow path such as a road, not including the time required to fly the hundreds of fighters and medium bombers in the same operation. He was then told the mission planned for July 25th would have to be scrubbed to brief the heavy bomber crews on the new approaches to the

targets. (See Endnotes, Chapter 8, Number 2)

Rather than postpone *Operation COBRA* any further and lose any advantage against the enemy troops massed south of the highway, Bradley consented to the bombers using the north-south route. Once more, the heavy bombers' approach would be perpendicular to the Allied lines.

On Tuesday, July 25th, the same operational plan was put into effect once more, but with some variation as detailed in the day's Field Order. Zero Hour, the commencement of bombing, was set for 1000 hours. The base bombing reference altitude was set at 15,000 feet with other aircraft adjusting according to formation position. A weather reconnaissance plane from the 2nd Bomb Division, carrying an air commander, weather forecaster and a lead-qualified bombardier, would fly over the target area two hours prior to the scheduled bombing and report if the weather conditions and visibility were adequate for aerial bombardment. This air commander would report to the Eighth Air Force Headquarters, Pinetree, not less than two hours from the commencement of bombing, on "his estimate on the feasibility of carrying out the operation as scheduled or make such recommendations based upon his weather forecast for a delay or cancellation of the zero hour."

The Field Order continued:
Providing suitable bombing conditions are not forecasted (sic.) for the assigned target time, PNT (Pinetree) will notify 1st, 2nd, 3rd Divisions and fighter command by zero hour minus 90 minutes in case a delay in zero hour is deemed necessary. Group leaders will be prepared to delay zero hour up to 90 minutes after aircraft have become airborne.

Assault troops of the 1st U.S. Army will start advancing into the target area at zero plus 60 minutes. All bombing in the target area will cease, repeat, will cease at zero plus 55 minutes. Aircraft arriving over the target area after zero plus 55 will attack secondary and last resort targets positively identified as being south of the designated target area.

This same Field Report defined secondary and last resort targets as:

> ...any aerodrome, any marshalling yard, any railroad bridge, any road bridge, any enemy column or convoy on the road, any concentration of troops or equipment. All targets must not be adjacent to a built-up area, must be positively identified as one of the aforementioned objectives and must not be inside the current bomb line and a visual sighting must be made.

In order to prevent a repeat of the horrendous events of a day earlier, the Field Order's Special Instructions stated:

> Bombardiers will be cautioned not to bomb short as the penetration route is directly over friendly troops and targets are 1500 yards south of the forward line. Red smoke will be laid down by the artillery along the St. Lo-Periers Road at one mile intervals. North boundary of the area will be marked at 2 minute interval from zero hour minus 5 to zero hour plus 50. No second bomb runs will be made.

These Special Instructions concluded with the chilling:

> Some a/c (aircraft) on mission run 24 July dropped short. American troops were killed and many wounded.

The overall plan was quite detailed and, once again, committed all available resources of the Eighth and Ninth Air Forces. Eight fighter groups from the IX Fighter Command would precede the bombers. They would attack at three minute intervals and in groups and squadron strength, continuing to strafe and bomb an area 250 yards wide and 7,000 yard long just to the south of the Periers - St. Lo highway. Then the heavy bombers would follow and bomb an area one mile wide and five miles long. Immediately after the departure of the heavy bombers, the Ninth Air

Force's A-20s and B-26s would saturate the target area with 250 lb and 500 lb high explosive bombs. The U.S. First Army's ground offensive would begin just as the heavy bombers began their scheduled bombing.

Once more, the Eighth Air Force and VIII Fighter Command committed at least one thousand five hundred fifty heavy bombers and five hundred fighters, respectively. Of this force, the 398th again sent fifty-two airplanes, again divided into four groups of thirteen aircraft, with each airplane carrying thirty-eight, 100 lb, AN-M1A1 fragmentation bombs. As used in the previous day's mission, the same call signs were used with only the lead group of each CBW using "lead" in the call sign, e.g. "Swordfish Baker Lead" to avoid any terminology confusion of using "one," as was used the day earlier. All other following groups in a CBW still used the previously-used numeric call signs, e.g. "Swordfish Baker 2," "3" and "4," respectively.

The 1st Bomb Division was tasked to hit the same target areas as the day earlier, a heavily-defended area west of St. Lo and south of the Periers - St. Lo highway. The 2nd and 3rd Bomb Divisions were tasked to hit areas adjacent the 1st Bomb Division's targets.

Though takeoff weather was not much better than the day before, the weather over the target area was briefed to be better. Visibility for the planned 0750 hours takeoff was briefed to be 3000 yards with scattered clouds at 5,500 feet and a thin overcast at 10,000 feet. Weather over the target for 1053 hours was briefed to be a thin overcast at 12,500 feet with a five mile vertical visibility in haze. On our return between 1250 and 1320 hours, we could expect a trace of clouds at 3,500 feet and a thin overcast at 20,000 feet. Visibility was forecast to be four miles with surface winds 160 degrees at 18 miles per hour.

Once more, I flew the *Bronx Bomber II* on this, my fourteenth combat mission and again flew in the #2 position in the Low Squadron of the Second Group.

Almost from the start, the fickle European weather created havoc for the young bomber crews. After assembling over the Debden Buncher beacon, the First Group of the 1st "B" CBW - "Swordfish Baker Lead" - received a message from the weather ship and several proceeding bombers that reported a cloud base at 14,000 feet over the target. Once again, the weather was not as briefed. A weak frontal system had apparently strengthened and created a host of weather-related problems.

Despite these weather problems, the attacking heavy bombers continued forward. The 398th's First Group, "Swordfish Baker Lead," descended from 16,000 feet and remained at 14,000 feet outbound from England. The weather worsened and the Group descended to 13,000 feet to avoid a cirrus type fog. Bombardiers quickly recomputed their bombing calculations in flight, mindful the American and Allied forces were positioned north of the Periers - St. Lo highway and the Germans south.

Upon arriving at the IP, the Isle St. Marcouf about five miles off the coast of the Cherbourg Peninsula, the weather continued to cause problems and "Swordfish Baker Lead" turned to remain clear of the preceding bomb groups, then made a couple "S" turns to maintain the briefed bombing interval. We were still flying inbound to the target when the first wave of attacking fighters and heavy bombers hit the St. Lo target area, a bomber stream that was almost eighty miles long.

Ernie Pyle, perhaps the most respected combat journalist of his time, stood witness to the approaching bombers and wrote of this mission for his rapt *Stars and Stripes* readers in his popular and widely read "Straight From the Front" column:

"And then a new sound gradually droned in our ears. The sound was deep and all encompassing with no notes in it - just a gigantic faraway surge of doom. It was the heavies. They came directly behind us and

first they were merest dots in the sky. You could see clots of them against the far heavens, too tiny to count individually. They came on with a terrible slowness. They came in flights of 12 - three flights to a group. And in the groups stretched out across the sky they came in "families" of about 70 planes each.

Maybe these gigantic waves were two miles apart, maybe they were ten miles. I don't know, but I do know they came in constant procession and I thought it would never end. What the Germans must have thought is beyond comprehension. The march across the sky was slow and steady. I've never known a storm, or machine, or resolve of man that had about it the aura of such ghastly relentlessness. You had the feeling that even had God appeared beseechingly before them in the sky with palms outward to persuade them back, they would not have had within them the power to turn from their irresistible course.

I stood with a little group of men ranging from colonels to privates back of some farmhouse. Slit trenches were all around the edges of the farmhouse and a dugout with a tin roof was near by, but we were so fascinated by the spectacle overhead that it never occurred to us we might need the foxholes.

The first huge flight passed over our farmyard and the others followed. We spread our feet and leaned back trying to look straight up until our steel helmets fell off. We'd   cup our fingers around our eyes like field glasses for a clearer view, and the bombs came.

They began ahead of us as a crackle of popcorn and almost instantly swelled into a monstrous fury of noise that seemed to destroy all the world ahead of us.

From then on for an hour and a half that had in the agonies of centuries the bombs came down. A wall of smoke and dust erected by them grew high in the sky. It filtered along the ground back through our own orchards, it sifted around us and into our noses. The bright day grew slowly dark from it.

By now everything was an indescribable cauldron of sounds. Individual noises did not exist. The thundering of the motors in the sky and the roar of the bombs ahead filled all the space for noise on earth. Our own heavy artillery was crashing all around us, yet we could hardly hear it."*

The earth around St. Lo shook furiously as the first of more than fifteen hundred B-17s and B-24s dropped more than 3,500 tons of bombs in the *COBRA* area. After the heavies left, B-26s and other medium bombers pressed their attacks and dropped over 650 tons of high explosive and fragmentation bombs. Fighter-bombers contributed their share to this offensive and dropped more than 250 tons of bombs and jellied gasoline (naplam).

Once more, hell rained from the heavens.

In the midst of changing altitudes and headings, word came over our headsets on the "C" channel that some bombers preceding the 398th were dropping their bombs short as much as 3,000 meters. Word was passed quickly via radio to drop their bombs over and beyond the briefed targets, but many crews could not or were unable to authenticate this message. Worse, too many planes were arriving over the target at nearly the same time which only added to the confusion.

I didn't have time to reflect upon the importance of this last message, but its implications were clear. For whatever reason, bombs were falling on Allied troops, again! Most of the bomber crews whose bombs fell short never knew of the indescribable carnage taking place on the ground below them. Only later did they learn of the horrible destruction that occurred.

The heavy bombers of the 398th's First Group of the 1st "B" CBW found their aim point visually, which was one mile beyond the smoke line, and dropped their bombs as briefed from 13,000 feet at 150 miles-per-hour on a magnetic heading of 304 degrees.

*Used with permission from *Stars and Stripes*. Copyright 1944, 2006 *Stars and Stripes*.

Shortly afterwards, "Swordfish Baker Lead" made a rapid descent to 8,000 feet and headed towards Nuthampstead.

"Swordfish Baker 2" was the 398th's Second Group of the 1st "B" CBW and was comprised of bombers from my squadron. We received the same message as the Lead Group and encountered the same weather problems while assembling and flying towards the IP. The Lead Group was still in and out of clouds upon leaving the coast, so we let down to 13,000 feet while still over England. Encountering lower clouds over the English Channel, we dropped down to 12,000 feet for bombing. The vertical visibility was still four to five miles and the assigned MPI was located and bombed.

The Third Group, "Swordfish Baker 3," took-off and assembled as briefed. The Third Group leveled at 11,000 feet to maintain formation integrity and to stay clear of clouds. This Group dropped their bombs at 11,000 feet with excellent results. A good, tight formation made the bomb pattern compact. During its descent, "Swordfish Baker 3" fell in line behind "Swordfish Baker Lead" on their return to England.

"Swordfish Baker 4," the Fourth Group in the 1st "B" CBW, consisted of thirteen formation aircraft plus one spare. This group assembled at 11,500 feet and dropped their bombs visually from this altitude with results reported as good. Just after "bombs away," this group let down to 9,000 feet, then continued to 3,000 feet to avoid flying in clouds on their return to England.

All 398th airplanes returned to Nuthampstead intact with no casualties. Much as occurred the previous day, there was no fighter opposition and very little flak, most of it seen near the Jersey Island in the English Channel. This lack of enemy fighters gave us reassuring evidence of the Luftwaffe's decline.

The story on the ground, however, was very different and decidedly ghastly. A wind change allowed the artillery smoke markers used for troop identification to drift back

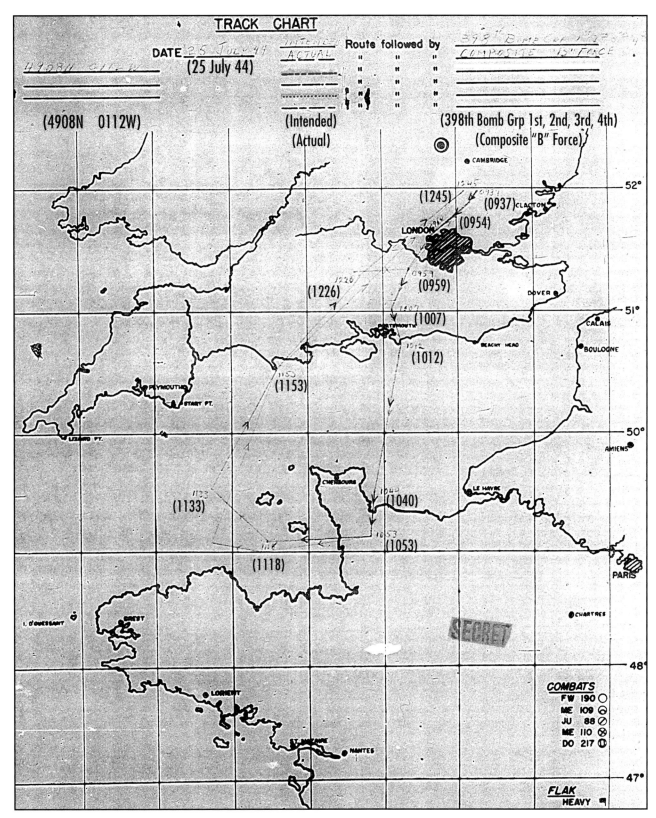

This enhanced reproduction of the original 398th Bomb Group Track Chart shows the intended and actual tracks the 398th Bomb Group flew during the mission to St. Lo, France on July 25, 1944. In addition, the times over key navigation references are shown. (To add clarity, times and other items are annotated in parenthesis.) These Track Charts became an important part of the Group Commander's Report, a summary detailing a bomb group's specific mission. Today, these reports remain an invaluable historical reference source.   (Harold D. Weekley)

over the troops, thereby identifying them as the target for one or more of the bomb groups preceding the 398th. Adding to the mayhem, large clouds of smoke and dust obscured the briefed ground landmarks. Worse, when the lead pilot from another bomb group ordered his bombs released, all planes in his formation released their loads. The accumulated errors in weather, winds and judgement killed one hundred two soldiers and wounded three hundred eighty, most of who were with the U.S. First Army's 30th Infantry Division.

Lieutenant General Lesley J. McNair, fromerly Commanding General of the U.S. Army Ground Forces, died that day. He was to observe the bomb drop, to learn what went wrong on the previous day and how it could have been prevented. To everyone's stunned disbelief and horror, several of the errant bombs fell on his location. General McNair was the highest-ranking American officer killed in action during the war.

In the end, enough bombs fell on the entrenched German forces to render them immobile and senseless. Heavy tanks and many other vehicles were either blown to bits or overturned completely. The cratered battlefield was corpse-strewn. Surviving terrified, crazed and dazed German troops later recounted the sheer volume of bombs falling upon them as Bomben- teppich - "carpet of bombs." (See Endnotes, Chapter 8, Number 3)

General Bradley and the U.S. First Army troops achieved the much-sought break-through - known as the St.-Lo Breakout - but the terrible toll was seared in the minds of those involved in its planning and execution. Despite these losses General Dwight D. Eisenhower, Supreme Commander Allied Expeditionary Forces, was impressed by the overall results achieved, i.e., the Break-through, and would again use heavy bombers in tactical support of ground troops in future bombing operations. In the mean-time, the Eighth Air Force's heavyweights, the B-17s and B-24s, returned to bombing strategic objectives in France and Germany.

The aerial photograph shows the widespread destruction of the bombing missions to St. Lo, France .   (Natonal Archives, 342-FH-3A19189-55586 A.C.)

Upon our return to Nuthampstead, very few of us talked of what had transpired only hours earlier. We dutifully answered the Intelligence Officer's questions and reported what we saw, not what or how we felt, though I am sure some bomber crewmembers carried deeply personal thoughts of the ghastly results of this mission, and the previous day's mission as well. I am sure most, if not all, of us realized our actions saved a great number of our own boys and hastened the final collapse of the German Army, or at least its war-making participation in Normandy, France.

The weather turned decidedly sour for several days after these appalling missions, which virtually grounded all Eighth Air Force operations. The whole of the Eighth Air Force needed this time to rest and reflect upon the events of the last week, and prepare for a new round of strategic bombing missions. Aircraft maintenance was especially important.

My crew and I spent the next five days attending classes on base, traveling to London for a day, visiting the nearby Woodman Inn or preparing for the next round of missions. We caught up on much needed sleep. I wrote more letters to Billie, sharing what I could with her without incurring the wrath of the military censors who screened our outgoing mail. In addition, I enjoyed reading the many "V-Mail" and regular Air Mail letters she had sent me. Back then, air mail letters used a 6-cent stamp. I had a lot of letters with 6-cent stamps on them waiting in my Nissen hut to be read again and again.

During this interim, the 398th lost a bomber on Wednesday, July 26th during a routine training flight to upgrade the crew's copilot to First Pilot, or the Aircraft Commander pilot position. AAF 42-102553 (N7-K), *Lil 8 Ball*, crashed while the copilot attempted to takeoff from Nuthampstead's shorter, 4200-foot long Runway 17. The crew's regular copilot was in the left seat and the First Pilot was in the right seat with another pilot standing between them serving as the check pilot. During the takeoff roll with the copilot at the controls, the B-17 veered left and departed the runway before the First Pilot could regain control of the errant heavy bomber. The plane hit a tractor, went into the woods at

Mechanics often worked under difficult and primative conditions. Here, 398th Bomb Group mechanics change the number two engine on a B-17. (James B. Zazas)

Maintenance was vitally important during wartime operations. Here, Corporal Frederick J. Lang, standing right, and an unidentified mechanic repair a Wright R-1820-97 engine in the 601st Squadron area during 1944. The aircraft is believed to be AAF 42-102596 (3O-N), *Doodit.*

(398th Bomb Group Memorial Association)

Corporals Ed Howell, Jimmy Fong, Frederick J. Lang and an unidentified mechanic install a waist gunner Plexiglas window on AAF 42-102596 (3O-N), *Doodit.*

(398th Bomb Group Memorial Association)

the end of the runway and caught fire. Though the most of the crew escaped with minor injuries, the right waist gunner received burns serious enough to prompt his return to the United States.

Though comparatively little was said of this accident, I did not waiver from my belief that copilots must maintain proficiency in takeoffs and landings, long runways or short.

The 398th lost another B-17 and crew on the July 28th mission to Munich, Germany. Lt. Wilber S. Dwyer and his crew were flying AAF 42-102579 (N7-C), nicknamed *Stinker*, when this airplane was observed with its number three propeller feathered. Dwyer had problems keeping up with the formation. He was seen to restart this engine, but it was smoking. He dropped further behind the for-

mation, eventually breaking away to his right. The crew was shown as "Failed to Return" from this mission. Later, I learned all nine crewmembers bailed out over Belgium, with seven of the nine taken prisoner-of-war. The other two evaded capture.

The 398th resumed combat operations on Monday, July 28th; however, I did not participate in either the July 28th mission to a synthetic oil plant near Merseburg, Germany or return mission to the same target the following day. Instead, I closed out July by flying a combat mission to Munich, Germany on Monday, July 31st. This combat mission was my fifteenth and the 398th's fifty-eighth Group Mission.

In all, some five hundred and sixty-seven B-17s participated in this raid to bomb an aircraft engine factory at Allach industrial works and marshalling yards in and around Munich. More than twelve hundred heavy bombers were dispatched by the Eighth Air Force to hit targets in Germany and airfields in France that day. Seven hundred P-38, P-47 and P-51 fighters from VIII Fighter Command provided escort. Before the day was over, at least sixteen Eighth Air Force bombers and three fighters were lost, with

The Shady Lady, a Boeing-built B-17G (AAF 42-97385, 3O-X), was assigned to the 601st B.S. on May 4, 1944 and was one of the original aircraft assigned to the 398th Bomb Group in April 1944. This airplane took-off on the raid to Munich on July 31st, but returned to base before reaching the formation. (Harold D. Weekley)

This same aircraft (right) made a successful forced landing on the Continent near Rechicourt, France on August 9, 1944 after experiencing serious mechanical problems during a mission. Its eventual fate is clouded in mystery as some records state it was destroyed by Allied fighters and other records state it was salvaged by the 5th SAD. (Harold D. Weekley)

another five hundred and twenty-one bombers sustaining damage. At least six airmen were killed in action and another twelve were wounded. Many more airmen were listed as missing in action.

The 398th fielded thirty-six bombers on this mission and they flew as part of the 1st "B" Combat Bomb Wing. I flew as leader of the Low Squadron of the Low Group. Twelve bombers were in our group, with twelve aircraft in the Lead Group and thirteen airplanes in the High Group. From my vantage point, I had an incredible view of the Lead and High Groups flying ahead and above me. Our formation was tight and the pilots did a great job maintaining position flying to and from the target.

This mission was the first time I had the aircraft up to 31,000 feet. Flying a B-17 this high was unusual, at least for me, as we normally flew to our targets between 23,000 and 25,000 feet indicated altitude; however, due to the towering clouds along our route, we slowly climbed our way up to 31,000 feet. Several of the heavily-laden bombers wallowed slightly in the rarified air.

Nearing our target, we descended to our briefed bombing altitudes to drop our bombs. I am sure many crews did not like giving up all that life-saving altitude, but the bombardiers needed the lower altitude for bombing accuracy.

Clouds still covered the entire area, so before the group reached the IP, the group leader ordered his planes to drop their bombs on the lead PFF aircraft's command. A nine-minute bomb run from the IP to the target was made using H2X ground-scanning radar. From the IP inbound, the flak was intense and several 398th airplanes sustained damage, though none were lost.

Flying at 150 mph indicated airspeed (about 200-mph true airspeed), we dropped our bombs around 1300 hours from an indicated altitude of 26,000 feet. Within minutes, three hundred and forty-one 500 lb, AN-M64 General Purpose bombs found their assigned targets. Almost ninety tons of bombs fell from 398th airplanes.

At the post-mission Intelligence debrief, returning crews stated enemy opposition was mostly flak and was judged to be from heavy to moderately heavy in intensity. No fighters were seen in the target area. This mission lasted about eight hours and thirty minutes and created some lasting and memorable experiences.

The first occurred when the number two engine picked up a small piece of flak that punctured a push-rod housing. Though it was a very small opening, engine oil pumped through that hole and continued to do so for some time. I elected to keep the engine running and had Joe Skarda, our flight engineer, keep an eye on it.

We were deep in enemy territory and I did not relish the thought of flying on three engines, especially in the midst of all the heavy fighter aircraft they had in this part of Germany. Stragglers were prime targets for German fighter planes and I worried about this as the faltering engine continued to pump away its life's blood. We were a long way from home.

About an hour after we departed the target, the oil pressure flickered and we immediately shut down the engine by feathering the propeller. We were able to remain in formation because, having dropped our bombs, we were light enough to maintain our position and stay in formation all the way back to England. Though the base's crash trucks and other emergency vehicles awaited our arrival, we made an uneventful landing at Nuthampstead.

The other unusual event on

this mission involved a close encounter with a Bf 109 fighter. This German fighter came from high above us and passed through the bomber formation that was above and ahead of us. As he hurtled earthward, he passed through a small cloud. When he popped out of that cloud, he was looking at our formation head on. He was literally eyeball to eyeball with me! I looked up and saw the black crosses on the wings and on the fuselage. I looked into his cockpit and saw him clearly.

As he crossed over our left wing between number one and number two engines, I called on the intercom and said, "I didn't hear anybody shoot at that 109".

A few of the fellows came back with a simple, "What 109, skipper?"

Nobody in our plane had seen the German fighter except ME!

History shows the 398th Bomb Group concluded July 1944 with seventeen group missions and 572 sorties flown. Seven airplanes were listed as missing in action and at least another four airplanes shown as other operational losses. At least thirteen heavy bombers either assigned or attached to the 398th were struck off as missing in action or salvaged due to accidents.

On a more social and recreational level, the 398th's official record shows at least one USO show, two American Red Cross Shows and one soldier talent show came to Nuthampstead during July. Moreover, at

The Officer's Club offered a much-welcome and needed respite from the physically and emotionally draining rigors and stress of combat flying.

(Peter M. Bowers)

"Look out below!" Three 398th Bomb Group heavy bombers drop bombs on enemy targets, probably on August 1, 1944 during Group Mission #59 to attack an airfield near Melun/Villaroche, France. The lead aircraft is AAF 42-102592 (N8-G) and the second aircraft is AAF 42-102506 (K8-L), *Contrary Mary*. The rear aircraft is AAF 42-107103 (K8-A), *Marie Notre Dame*. Aircraft N8-G was salvaged following a landing accident at Nuthampstead on January 29, 1945 upon return from an aborted mission, whereas aircraft K8-L was damaged by flak, landed on the Continent following a mission on February 25, 1945 and eventually salvaged. Aircraft K8-A was reported MIA on September 10, 1944 on a mission to Stuttgart, Germany. The aircraft was hit by flak between the radio room and the ball turret and was seen going down north of the target area.   (398th Bomb Group Memorial Association)

least six dances were scheduled and an excellent band played at the Officer's Club every Monday night. The ball field and the seven volley ball courts saw a lot of use. All of these activities offered a much welcomed and needed respite from the physically and emotionally draining rigors and stress of combat flying.

August did not begin on a very auspicious note. On Tuesday, August 1st, the 398th dispatched thirty-six aircraft on a mission to attack an airfield at Melun/Villaroche, France. Fortunately, my crew and I did not fly.

Right from the start, everything went wrong. One aircraft blew a tire while taxiing. The Lead and Deputy Lead airplanes were airborne in instrument condition when word was received the Zero Hour was delayed an

hour; thus, keeping other airplanes on the ground to conserve precious fuel. These two aircraft had to stay aloft until the new assembly time consuming precious fuel. During the actual mission, one aircraft had to abort due to engine problems. The pilot jettisoned his bombs over the English Channel and returned to base.

Later on this mission, the Lead and Deputy Lead aircraft sustained severe flak damage while flying towards the target. The Lead airplane (AAF 43-37892, N8-L), flown by Col. Frank P. Hunter, our Group Commander, and Capt. G. L. Douglas, had one engine burning, two more damaged and producing partial power, and various controls shot-out. Somehow, they managed to remain in formation until "bombs-away," then left the formation to return to England. He and his crew made a successful crash-landing at RAF Merston located on the English Channel between Brighton and Portsmouth.

Our sixteenth combat mission came on Thursday, August 3, 1944. The black string on the wall map at briefing showed us bombing targets near Saarbrucken, Germany, specifically the marshalling yards. Saarbrucken lay just north of the border shared by Germany and France, and was about a hundred miles southeast of Frankfurt, Germany. I was slotted to fly as lead in the Low Squadron of the Low Group. My assigned airplane for this mission was called the *Kentucky Colonel*, AAF 42-97394 (3O-P).

All 398th airplanes on this mission carried twelve 500 lb, AN-M64 General Purpose bombs. The Group Leader took off at 1100 hours for a mission briefed to last slightly longer than seven hours. My takeoff was normal and I joined the other 398th Bomb Group's Flying Fortresses assembling at 14,000 feet over the Debden Buncher beacon. In the post-mission debrief, several pilots commented this assembly could be judged as only fair because the lead aircraft arrived late due to some malfunction.

The Group departed the assembly point on time and on course, joined the Wing and, shortly thereafter, the Division in the correct battle order. Climbing at 350 feet-per-minute, the Division crossed the enemy coast at 21,000 feet indicated altitude. A lone Fw 190 passed under our bomb group, but the German pilot did not press an attack. Instead, he and his fighter disappeared into a cloud, not to be seen again.

Our formation reached the IP at 23,000 feet. A scattered to broken cloud layer was over the target allowing a visual release, so the Wing Leader radioed instructions to us to bomb the target visually. The bombardiers had enough ground references for a visual bombing, but finding these references on short notice in a heavy bomber bouncing in turbulence and avoiding flak was difficult at best. Even though the bomber stream en-countered moderate but accurate flak over the target with my airplane taking its own share of minor hits, I did not and could not hear the exploding metal ricochet off my airplane. Instead, I heard through my cushioned earphones the professional chatter of my crew doing their job under high stress and anxiety.

Leaving the target, the Wing Leader descended our group to 21,000 feet and maintained that altitude to the coast. Crossing the English Channel, he led us down to 9,000 feet and crossed the English coast at this altitude. Forty miles from base, the Wing Leader dispersed us for landing at Nuthampstead. My crew and I were exhausted. We were in the air seven hours and ten minutes. Bombing results were reported later as being good to excellent.

Reviewing the Eighth Air Force's activities on that fateful day, sixty-two 1st Bomb Division B-17s participated in this morning raid to the Saarbrucken marshalling yards, including thirty-six airplanes from the 398th, one small part of more than six hundred and seventy-two heavy bombers dispatched to attack various targets throughout Germany and France. Three hundred fifty-two fighters were dispatched by VIII Fighter Command.

Though all 398th bombers returned to Nuthampstead safely, six heavy bombers and six fighters from other bases did not return to theirs. At least ninety-eight heavy bombers were damaged due to hostile action. Nine airmen were KIA, nine were WIA and fifty-four were MIA.

These figures included one wounded 398th crewmember and at least five 398th airplanes put out of commission due to major flak damage. Several more sustained only minor battle damage. Major battle damage required extensive structural repairs whereas minor battle damage required mostly skin patches of holes punched by flak.

The next day, Friday, August 4th, was Billie's and my first wedding anniversary. Coincidentally, I had been flying or training to fly the B-17 for exactly one year. I celebrated both events with another long mission to Peenemunde. I wrote a letter to Billie upon my safe return. My personal combat mission count was now seventeen and I made note of this number in the return address section of the "V-mail" letter I sent to her.

My previous mission to Peenemunde on July 18th had been a "milk run," an easy mission with little or no enemy opposition. But, unlike the earlier one to Peenemunde, this mission was not. The Germans were waiting for us with Flak guns and fighters, the latter engaged by our escorting fighters.

One thousand three hundred seven heavy bombers and seven hundred forty-six fighters were dispatched to strategic targets in Germany. Of this attacking force, two hundred twenty-one were B-17s from the 1st Bomb Division.

I was assigned to fly AAF 42-102596, nicknamed *Doodit*, with 3O-N emblazoned across both sides of the bare metal fuselage. I was lead pilot in the High Squadron of the High Group. Joe Wierney, one of my Nissen hut roommates, flew AAF 42-102565 (3O-M), nicknamed *The Ugly Duckling*, below me and to my left as the lead pilot of the High Group's Low Squadron. Each airplane on this mission carried five, 1000 lb, AN-M65 bombs. These very large bombs were ideal to destroy the assigned target, another hydrogen peroxide production plant. Though this mission was planned to last eight and a half hours, some airplanes actually remained airborne nine or more hours. The Low Group would bomb from 23,000, the Lead Group from 23,500 and the high group from 24,500 feet.

Thirty-six B-17 airplanes, including a loaned PFF aircraft from Ridgewell's 381st Bomb Group, took-off in very poor weather (500 feet overcast and less than a mile visibility) and assembled over the Debden Buncher beacon as briefed. None of these B-17s had any difficulty joining the Division and the growing bomber stream. The flight over the North Sea was uneventful, but the bomber stream had to negotiate some towering cumulus clouds while flying to the target. Visibility improved to fifteen to twenty miles as we approached the coast of Denmark. Visibility was even better over Peenemunde. We had an excellent view of our target below us, including lots of enemy flak trains beginning to take aim at us.

Though we left no contrails, the flak gunners on the ground had an excellent view of us flying high overhead and they aimed their guns carefully. As soon as we approached the IP and continued towards the assigned target, the German flak trains were in position to create all sorts of mayhem for us. These trains were full of anti-aircraft guns, mostly the notorious German 88s. As soon as we flew overhead, the Germans dropped down the sides on those flak trains and attempted to blow us out of the sky.

This intense enemy action was a complete reversal of what we had anticipated from the briefing, mostly because we had encountered nothing at all the first time we had flown to Peenemunde. Murderous puffs of black flak exploded all around us ripping jagged holes in several airplanes. I could see the angry orange centers and feel the reverberations from these deadly aerial explosions. The initial flak bursts were low on our approach, but the Germans corrected and found their targets immediately after "bombs away." The anti-aircraft fire was particularly accurate upon the 398th's High Group.

We dropped our bombs on target shortly after 1500 hours from altitude between 22,500 feet and 24,500 feet with good to excellent results. Most bombs fell directly on or very near the target.

Just as we departed the target, I felt my airplane surge violently upward. "Christ! What was that?" My first thought was we had taken a devastating flak hit on the bottom of our airplane and my mind went into overdrive wondering what the hell happened. My mind found its answer and in the split second before I could check on the con-

A combat strike photograph of Peenemunde, Germany taken on August 4, 1944, shows this test facility's hydrogen peroxide plant being bombed. Characteristic circular embankments protected several of this facilities hydrogen peroxide plant. The center embankment was complete and the object of numerous strikes. The top embankment was complete but not used. Preliminary work began on the lower unit. After the August 4th attack, these units were abandoned.
(National Archives, 342-FH-3A22243-54885 A.C.)

This combat strike photograph shows a B-17G from the 401st Bomb Group (H) bombing the V-weapons research establishment at Peenemunde, Germany on August 25, 1944. The photograph shows a tight concentration of bomb bursts on the V-2 rocket fueling installations. (National Archives, 342-FH-3A-22236-53553 A.C.)

This combat strike photograph shows targets near Peenemunde, Germany being bombed by heavy bombers on the August 4, 1944 raid.   (National Archives, 342-FH-3A2246-54888 A.C.)

dition of my bomber and crew, I realized the B-17 flown by one of our new crews, commanded by a young Second Lieutenant pilot named John S. MacArthur, took that direct anti-aircraft hit and blew-up immediately underneath us. Death came quickly for all aboard. They never had a chance to bail-out.

In one instant, Lt. MacArthur, his crew and his airplane (AAF 42-107186, N7-L) were safely positioned within our formation. In the next instant, there was a fiery detonation with nothing left except broken bodies and airplane pieces, twisting and tumbling as they fell to earth. The Germans recovered only some small aircraft and body parts from the water below.

But our troubles were far from over.

Upon leaving the target and starting our return to base, Major E. B. Daily, who was leading our Combat Bomb Wing box, headed straight for Kiel. Kiel had been bombed many times and the Germans made great efforts to protect this city with numerous anti-aircraft guns. When Paul James, our navigator, advised me of our position, I broke radio silence and merely said, "Kiel straight ahead." I expected the lead aircraft to turn the Group on to a more southwesterly direction to keep us from harm's way.

When the lead did not make the turn, I radioed the same comment again and still the lead aircraft kept flying towards Kiel. I turned to Ben Clark, our co-pilot, and told him if there was no change in heading soon I was going to leave the formation with my squadron in tow.

About this time, the lead aircraft made the course correction. Nothing further was ever said of this part of the flight and I never learned of the lead's intentions if, indeed, he had one.

We got out of Germany, but in pretty bad shape. We left the enemy coast at 1604 hours and arrived at Nuthampstead at 1810 hours. Taking spacing, I landed at 1848 hours.

At the Intelligence debrief, everyone expressed their surprise at the amount of anti-

aircraft fire and commented they did not expect such intense German reaction. At least eight airplanes suffered minor to major combat damage. Many crews reported the MacArthur loss in chillingly vivid details. "MacArthur blew up over target. No Chutes" and "Copilot saw ship explode. No chutes seen." Many crews saw MacArthur's airplane blow-up, searing this tragic event in the weary minds of every witness.

Besides the MacArthur and crew loss, another 398th airplane was lost to enemy action on the same mission, a B-17G (AAF 42-107098, 3O-Y) commanded by 2nd Lt. Nigel B. Carter. He and his crew were from my squadron, the 601st, but I did not know Carter or any of his crewmembers. For whatever reason, Carter departed the formation shortly after he dropped his bombs and was last seen in a level descent. At debrief, many crews, including myself, believed Carter was making an attempt to fly towards Sweden. The 398th recorded the MacArthur and Carter crews as "Failed to Return." Sometime later, I learned Carter and his crew either bailed out or crash landed near Sweden and were interred for the balance of the war.

In addition, I learned many years after this mission that Dr. Wehrner von Braun suffered a broken arm during our bombardment of Peenemunde. Our bombs hit this strategic target hard, and we obviously got very close to the scientists who created Germany's terrifying "vengeance weapons."

The Eighth Air Force lost fifteen bombers that day with another four hundred thirty-three damaged, plus another nine damaged beyond repair. At least fifteen fighters were lost with two pilots killed in action. Moreover, at least six bomber airmen were KIA, another ten were WIA and at least one hundred forty-three were MIA. The requests for Replacement Crews continued unabated.

I flew my eighteenth combat mission on Saturday, August 5th. The briefed target was a synthetic oil plant at Dollberg, Germany, near Hanover. This very important plant possessed one of the five largest fuel storage facilities in Germany and had a reported capacity of 147,000 tons of fuel, precious fuel we aimed to destroy to keep from Germany's war machine. I flew aircraft AAF 43-37874 (3O-W), later nicknamed as the *Georgia Peach*, though I don't remember if it carried this moniker at that time or not. I was assigned to fly as the lead pilot in the Low Squadron of the Lead Group.

Thirty-six airplanes from the 398th, including one B-17 from the 91st Bomb Group serving as the lead PFF aircraft, comprised the 1st "A" CBW combat box that day. Capt. Willis Frazier, our Squadron Operations Officer, flew as lead pilot on this mission. Capt. Tracy Peterson, the same Capt. Peterson who crash-landed his B-17 on an English beach near a golf club a month earlier, was the Airborne Commander and led this mission. A PFF-equipped aircraft would fly in the Deputy Lead position. Each heavy bomber carried twenty, 250 lb, AN-M57 General Purpose bombs, except for the two PFF aircraft. They carried eighteen, AN-M57 GP bombs and two Sky-Markers.

Capt. Peterson presented a detailed briefing. Stations time was set at 0730 hours, engine start at 0800 hours, taxi commencing ten minutes later and the first B-17s scheduled to take-off at 0815 hours. Group and Wing assembly was set at 0930 at the Debden Buncher beacon with Division assembly taking place fifty-five minutes later. Actual bombing was to begin between 1317 and 1319 hours from 21,000 to 22,000 feet at 150 miles-per-hour indicated airspeed. After bombing, we would return to England, crossing the English coast at Lowestoft. Letdown would begin shortly afterwards with landings set to begin at 1545 hours.

Capt. Peterson emphasized that each twelve airplane box must exercise excellent formation procedures over the target to insure a good bomb pattern. When he completed his briefing, the weather officer told us the weather would be overcast at takeoff,

clear over the Continent and partly cloudy with good visibility over the target. A weather airplane would be sent ahead of the main bomber force to report on actual weather conditions near and over the target.

Everything was uneventful until assembly, whereupon the flying got a little busy. Group, Wing and Division assembly went well, except for a few "S" turns we had to make so we would not overrun the combat bomb wing box assembling ahead of us. We arrived at the enemy coast six minutes late, primarily due to these spacing turns. Since the weather scout relayed word the weather over the target was good enough for a visual drop, we set-up for a visual bomb run from 22,000 feet indicated altitude. Two minutes from the IP, the Lead Group notified the High and Low Groups to take proper intervals so as not to over run each other as we approached an intense barrage flak area immediately ahead of the three groups near Hanover. We avoided this flak easily.

Bombing results were judged good to excellent, at least for the Lead Group. My radio operator had carried a camera on this mission, one of several bombers on this mission so equipped, and the post-strike photographs showed the Lead Group's bombs fell 50 yards beyond the Main Point of Impact. The Low Group's bombs fell some 75 yards beyond the Main Point of Impact. The High Group, on the other hand, had to answer to Col. Hunter, our Group Commander, why their bombs fell approximately 225 yards short.

Overall, the bombing results were good and no 398th crewmembers were killed or wounded. In addition, no airplanes sustained any combat damage, much to the delight of the crew chiefs. At the post-mission Intelligence debrief, crews judged the fighter coverage as excellent. P-51 Mustangs provided close and front support, whereas P-47 Thunderbolts flew rear support.

Unfortunately, other bomb groups participating in this raid did not share the 398th's mission euphoria of August 5th. During this day, at least five hundred and forty-three Eighth Air Force heavy bombers of more than eleven hundred dispatched made effective attacks on oil refineries, airfields, factories and other strategic targets in and around Hannover, Brunswick and Magedeburg, Germany. The rest aborted due to bad weather and other causes.

Accurate anti-aircraft fire, intense fighter opposition and a variety of mechanical problems exacted its usual, terrible toll as seventeen aircraft, bombers and fighters, failed to return and at least half the attacking force was damaged in some manner. At least fifteen airmen are killed in action, eighteen are wounded in action and many more were missing in action.

At the Intelligence debrief, my crew and I commented we thought we saw a prisoner of war camp below us when we flew over Zwolle, Netherlands. Though our report was forwarded to higher authorities, we did not hear anything further about our unusual observation.

By now, my crew and I were quite tired as this was the third consecutive day we had flown a combat mission. Other crews were also tired, but the Eighth Air Force maintained an unrelenting schedule. There was no rest for the weary during wartime and the mission board showed our names posted for another mission the next day.

I flew the *Bronx Bomber II* (AAF 42-102516, 3O-H) on what started out to be our nineteenth combat mission on Sunday, August 6th. The briefed target was a large aircraft and engine plant at Brandenburg, Germany near Munich. Intelligence reported this plant manufactured Heinkel twin-engine bombers. I was assigned to fly the lead aircraft in the Low Squadron of the Low Group of the 1st "C" CBW. Our bomb load was forty-two, 100 lb, AN-M47A2 incendiary bombs. We took-off on instruments - the weather was a low overcast - and assembled over the Debden Buncher beacon with the other thirty-five 398th airplanes assigned to this raid.

About two hours out over the North Sea, we encountered a most unusual circumstance that forced me to return to Nuthampstead as quickly as I could. While we were maintaining a loose formation profile, the navigator in the B-17 off our right wing thought he would test his airplane's left cheek gun. He pulled off a few .50-caliber rounds without looking to see where the gun was pointed.

Almost immediately and much to my complete surprise and utter dismay, I learned Charles "Pop" Stombaugh, my tail gunner, had been hit by an errant bullet from this reckless navigator's actions and was badly wounded. "Pop's" left knee was shot off and he was in severe pain. Worse, he was quickly losing a considerable amount of blood. I knew from the description of the wound that "Pop" would die from the loss of blood if we continued on the mission.

I advised Maj. P. J. Rooney, the airborne mission commander, of what had happened and described my tail gunner's grievous wound. Without hesitation, he told me I should return to base. I pulled out of formation and flew back to base.

The Nuthampstead control tower wasn't expecting me. Upon return arrival, I contacted our control tower, whose call sign was "Moorhen," and asked for the weather conditions. I was advised they could not give me that information because, at that time, they couldn't confirm who I was. They did inform me, however, that the weather was the same as it had been at takeoff. With that in mind, I continued and landed. Medics removed "Pop" from the airplane and took him to the base hospital for medical care and recovery. That was the last time anyone on my crew saw Charlie "Pop" Stombaugh in England.

We were in the air for only two hours and, of course, did not get credit for this mission. We did not replace "Pop" as we had Ven Unger. Instead, I moved Gene Leonard, my left waist gunner, to the tail gunner position.

At least one other 398th airplane also

returned early. AAF 42-107191 (N8-K), nick-named the *Tomahawk Warrior*, returned to Nuthampstead due to extensive damage inflicted by flak upon passing the enemy coast. Another 398th B-17, AAF 42-102467 (N8-J), the *Agony Wagon III*, was hit by flak about the same time and this plane and crew failed to return. Piloted by Lt. Isaac N. Alhadeff of the 600th Bomb Squadron, this plane was last seen peeling away from the formation with one propeller feathered and losing altitude rapidly. We learned later the crew bailed-out and were reported as prisoners of war.

Of the one thousand one hundred eighty-six bombers and seven hundred forty fighters dispatched by the Eighth Air Force that day, twenty-four bombers and eight fighters were lost. At least five hundred twenty-two were damaged. At least seventeen airmen were killed in action and another twenty-six were wounded. Two hundred thirty-six airmen were shown as missing in action.

The strain of combat was unrelenting. Any diversion or respite from this almost daily rigor was welcome. Occasionally, crews performed maintenance and flight test functions. My crew was no different. On Tuesday, August 8th, we were tasked to perform various engine runs and timing, not exactly a glamorous job, but one necessary to keep the bombers flying in good condition.

We did not participate in the 398th's combat mission to bomb enemy troop and material concentrations near Bretteville Le Rabet in France in support of friendly forces. Despite special instructions issued to prevent bombs falling onto the friendly troops, errant bombs from Eighth Air Force bombers fell short and killed 25 Canadian soldiers and wounded another 131 soldiers.

August 8th also proved to be a disastrous day in the 398th's combat record history. At least three airplanes were lost to enemy action and one was forced to crash-land in Normandy.

The first airplane lost was being flown by Capt. John M. Baker. His airplane, AAF 42-

97399 (N8-H), was hit by flak in the left wing between the number one and two engines only seconds before "bombs away." The wing separated between these engines and the mortally damaged airplane rolled over on its back and was seen spinning earthward. Only two crewmembers were able to bailout successfully and became prisoners of war.

The second 398th B-17 lost that day was AAF 42-107223 (N7-S) flown by Capt. Lawrence L. Hopkins and Capt. Meyer C. Wagner. Their plane was hit by flak about three to five minutes before reaching the target. The crew bailed-out successfully near friendly lines, but enemy ground troops fired upon the descending crewmen, killing at least two. The surviving crewmembers were taken prisoner, but two crewmembers wounded by flak were left to the advancing American forces for their care and later returned to the United States.

The third 398th loss occurred when Second Lieutenant Wallace H. Blackwell, Jr. was flying the *Kentucky Colonel,* AAF 42-97394, (3O-P). His B-17G was hit by flak in the tail, which blew off most if not all of the rear fuselage, with the wreckage coming down in Allied occupied France. The tail gunner was killed and the rest of the crew bailed-out successfully behind friendly lines.

The fourth and last 398th airplane that "failed to return" on August 8th was piloted by Lt. Charles V. Cobb. He landed his flak damaged airplane, AAF 42-107150 (K8-K), at strip A13 at Tour-En-Bessin, a friendly airfield in Normandy. His airplane earned the dubious distinction of being the first 398th airplane to land on the European continent.

The 398th flew another mission on August 9th, but neither my crew nor I participated in this planned mission to bomb Allach, Germany. Bad weather intervened and the eleven 398th aircraft bombed a target of opportunity, the marshalling yards at Saarbrucken, Germany. The 398th lost no airplanes that day, though the Eighth Air Force lost eighteen bombers and three fighers to hostile action.

Two days later, I ferried a flak-damaged B-17, most likely an aircraft that had participated on the disastrous August 8th mission, to the 2nd Strategic Air Depot facilities at Little Staughton near Alconbury, East Anglia, England. This large facility, like several other aircraft depots located throughout the United Kingdom, could repair or recondition a damaged aircraft and return it to combat flying. Only the most damaged or combat fatigued airplanes were stripped of parts to support flying aircraft. Workers at these facilities were not immune from the horrors of war while working on combat-damaged aircraft. On many occasions, they faced the grim task of washing out human remains with high-pressure hoses before undertaking their assigned tasks.

In addition, these Air Depots prepared new aircraft for combat units. Bomber aircraft flown across the Atlantic were often ferried to a base air depot, such as Langford Lodge in Northern Ireland or Alconbury in England for necessary inspections and modifications before being turned over to the assigned unit for combat operations. Virtually all of the 398th's airplanes that arrived from the United States were inspected and modified at the Langford Lodge Air Depot.

I flew my nineteenth combat mission on Saturday, August 12th, which was the 398th's sixty-seventh Group Mission. The briefed target was the wide, grassy meadow that comprised the Buc Airfield near Versailles, France. I piloted AAF 42-102565 (3O-M), *The Ugly Duckling*, and led the Low Squadron of the Low Group. Joe Wierney, one of my Nissen hut roommates, was assigned to fly as leader of the High Squadron in the Low Group. Thirty-six 398th airplanes were tasked to fly on this mission in the 1st "B" CBW consisting of three, twelve aircraft groups. For this airfield raid, each 398th B.G. airplane carried thirty-eight, 100 lb, AN-M30 General Purpose bombs, ideal for chewing-up sod and grass runways. The black string

Jimmie Fong painted the names on many of the 398th Bomb Group's airplanes. Here, he applies the finishing touches to AAF 42-102565 (3O-M), *The Ugly Duckling*, a Boeing-built B-17G.
(398th Bomb Group Memorial Association)

this day stretched from Nuthampstead across the English Channel to this idyllic airfield west of Paris, France, with a return route that virtually overlaid the inbound route.

As a lead pilot on this mission, my day began very early. I got my wake-up call at 0130 hours. The mission briefing was held at 0230 hours, stations at 0530, engine start at 0545, with taxi beginning ten minutes later. Takeoff for the Lead and Deputy Lead airplanes was planned to commence at 0615 hours. This mission was briefed to last eight-hours and, according to the Intelligence brief, was supposed to be fairly uneventful with respect to flak or enemy fighter opposition. P-51 Mustangs from the 352nd, 359th and 364th Fighter Groups were tasked to provide close support.

During the prerequisite briefing, we learned the daily Field Orders contained a welcome addition: "Emergency landings are permitted on any suitable a/d (aerodrome) north of the Loire River and west of zero degrees avoiding the immediate vicinity of Brest, Lorient and St. Nazaire." Now, we had the option of landing on the Continent instead of fighting our way back to England with a badly damaged airplane or wounded crewmember aboard.

The weather over the base and England as a whole was atrocious, poor visibility and thick clouds, so the Group had a difficult time assembling at the Debden Buncher beacon. We encountered solid clouds from 10,000 feet extending to 30,000 feet. In an effort to ease the deteriorating assembly congestion at the assigned Buncher, Group assembly moved to Splasher #11 at Rogate near Southampton at 18,000 feet. During most of our climb, visibility was less than a quarter mile!

Due to mission aborts and the bad weather, only nine airplanes comprised the Low Group. One airplane, AAF 42-102596 (3O-N), *Doodit* never received word of the change in assembly and returned to Nuthampstead. The second airplane that aborted entered a spin due to ice accumulation on the wings. The pilots, 1st Lt. John Falkenbach and 2nd Lt. Filbert Arbogast, managed to recover their spinning aircraft (AAF 42-107080, 3O-S), but not before the bombs aboard were shaken loose.

Lady Luck did not ride with one 398th heavy bomber assembling that morning and the Bomb Group suffered another appalling casualty. During the extended assembly in the marginal weather, AAF 42-107191 (N8-K), nicknamed *Tomahawk Warrior*, collided with a B-24 Liberator from the 392nd Bomb Group. The Liberator crashed at Cheshunt in Hertfordshire with all personnel lost. *Tomahawk Warrior* crashed near Penn in Buckinghamshire with pilot 1st Lt. Charles J. Searl and his crew of eight killed.

Ironically, this same aircraft was involved in another mid-air collision three months earlier, on May 4, 1944, during a practice mission. Both the crew and the aircraft returned to Nuthampstead safely with damage to the vertical stabilizer.

Weather over the target was hazy, but clear enough to drop the bombs visually. At bomb release, the Group was indicating 150 mph at 24,500 feet indicated altitude. More than three hundred seventy bombs from 398th airplanes rained to earth and landed on or near the intended target. Fortunately, no fighters or flak interrupted the bomb run and we returned to Nuthampstead safely.

Once again, the post-mission Intelligence debrief provided a lot of valuable information. One crew reported "railroad yards northwest of Paris showed evidence of being heavily bombed - still being used." Other crews reported a large number of ships in the English Channel.

The Eighth Air Force dispatched five hundred and seventy-seven heavy bombers that day, including four hundred thirty-six fighters, to make visual attacks on marshalling yards and airfields in central and eastern France. Before the day was over, at least three bombers and three fighters are lost. At least nineteen airmen were killed in action and another sixteen were wounded.

The air war over Europe witnessed other significant losses that day, as well. Lt. Joseph P. Kennedy, Jr., USN, the eldest son of the former ambassador to the United Kingdom and brother of the future president of the United States, was killed with his radio-control engineer when their U.S. Navy PB4Y-1 Liberator drone, exploded prematurely at 2,000 feet over Blythburgh, England. Loaded with almost 20,000 pounds of high explosive, they were undertaking a secret mission to bomb the V-site at Mimoyecques, France. Subsequent investigation pointed to a fault in the electrical system and automatic guidance system that was switched on before the crew could bailout.

We believed that our next scheduled mission on August 13th - our twentieth - would be as easy and uneventful as our nineteenth.

We soon learned how wrong we were.

August 13th was a Sunday. Several of my crewmembers were Catholic and they normally attended a small service the priest had for the crewmembers prior to departure. On this particular day, the crew asked me if I would go along with them. I said, "Sure."

I knew Father Sullivan, the priest, as being one of our active chaplains on the base. He approached me and said, "Harold, I can't say too much as far as the Methodist religion is concerned since I'm Catholic. And I can't give you the same rites as I do with the Catholic boys, but after I'm finished, if you will just come up here, we will say a few words to try to insure your safety during this mission".

I was surprised and comforted by these words, as this was the first time this type of meeting had happened during my time at Nuthampstead. As events came to be, this meeting became and remains a source of deeply personal contemplation.

© 1944, The Studebaker Corporation

"We all have faith in those engines!"

THE pilot of a Boeing Flying Fortress wrote the following about his bomber and the Studebaker-built Wright Cyclone engines that power it:

"I fly one every day and think there is no other ship her equal. We all have faith in those Cyclone engines."

Studebaker, famous for its peacetime motor cars and trucks, has already built tens of thousands of the mighty power plants with which the Flying Fortress has winged its way to world-wide victories.

But Studebaker realizes that this great four-engine Boeing bomber is merely part of an all-star team of other bombers, fighters, seaplanes, transports and observation planes that makes America's air might so effective.

All the valiant men and women of the Army, the Navy, the Air Forces, the Coast Guard and the Marine Corps know that the success of America's armed forces depends upon teamwork.

There is glory enough in decisive victory to give everyone who helps a share. And so Studebaker workers proudly and steadfastly keep on producing Wright Cyclone engines for the Boeing Flying Fortress— big, multiple-drive military trucks—and other vital war matériel.

Look ahead with Uncle Sam and buy more War Bonds now. Every Bond is a safeguard for the future... your country's future and your own.

Studebaker BUILDS WRIGHT CYCLONE ENGINES FOR THE BOEING FLYING FORTRESS

(*Saturday Evening Post* - May 13, 1944)

> *"The man of virtue makes the difficulty to be overcome his first business, and success only a subsequent consideration."*
>
> Confucious (551–479 B.C.)

CHAPTER 9

The Loss of a Friend, and the Beginning of Many New Friendships

My life at Nuthampstead had settled into a routine. The war was still significant for my crew and me and it affected everything I did and saw on and off base. Flying the B-17 had become second nature and I performed my duties almost instinctively. When I wasn't in the air, I was generally doing something to improve my flying skills or support my airplane and crew.

Sunday, August 13, 1944 was another mission day for me, and it began like most of my other combat missions. I was awakened early by the dutiful sergeant with the flashlight in hand and made the usual rush to shave and shower before breakfast. After sitting through the almost routine briefings of who and what we were going to bomb, and where and when we were going to let our bombs

This photograph shows the *Bronx Bomber II's* unusually painted, black nose to a good advantage. This paint was applied to prevent further deterioration of the aluminum around the nose area caused by "scare flak." (Harold D. Weekley)

fall, the weather brief and ordinance brief, I went to my plane, loaded, armed and ready to fly. After climbing aboard my heavily laden B-17 and making sure everyone was set and ready to go, I started engines, taxied and took-off to fly my mission as briefed, without any qualms, reservation or hesitation. For me, this day was just another day to fly another combat mission.

August 13 was a significant day in Allied ground and air operations. Any day in which troops fought bravely and were wounded or killed was significant. On this day, like many before it and many that would follow, Allied ground forces raced to capture tens of thousands of German Army soldiers in France's Falaise Pocket while the Eighth Air Force launched a pummeling blow to close transportation chokepoints

The 398th Bomb Group's primary target on August 13, 1944 was the large railroad bridge at Le Manoir, aimed as an effort to frustrate enemy troop withdrawal from this area in France. This photograph, taken many months after this particular mission, reveals the bridge's stout construction made it a difficult target to destroy.

(Harold D. Weekley)

in the area between Paris and Le Havre. In the air, approximately thirty combat bomb wings, consisting of seven hundred and ninety-eight B-17s and four hundred and sixty-six B-24s were dispatched to attack railroad bridges, coastal batteries and important highways over a large area on both sides of the Seine River between Le Havre and Paris. Six fighter groups from the VIII Fighter Command escorted the bombers.

This coordinated effort was a part of an ongoing mission to destroy as many transportation routes from France to Germany as possible, thus blocking any retreat by the German forces. The Germans were trying to return to their homeland to make a last stand within their nation's boundaries and our job was to prevent them from doing just that.

On August 13th, a total of 2,701 tons of bombs fell from American bombers on the assigned targets between the hours of 1257 and 1421. During this fateful day, seven B-17s and five B-24s were lost in Eighth Air Force operations. One B-17 crash-landed in France. Another B-17, one from the 91st Bomb Group based in Bassingbourn, crashed some five miles from its intended target.

The 398th Bomb Group's assigned target was a large railway bridge over the Seine River to the northwest of Paris, near the community of Le Manoir in the Normandy region. Our objective was to prevent the withdrawal of some nineteen German divisions from the Normandy front. Thirty-six aircraft were in the 398th's formation. Almost twice that number of heavy bombers were

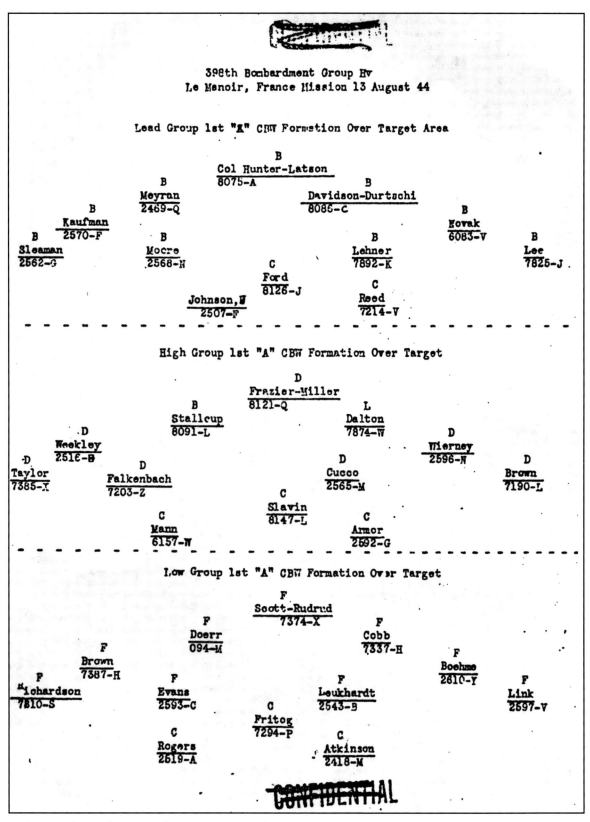

398th Bombardment Group Hv
Le Manoir, France Mission 13 August 44

Lead Group 1st "A" CBW Formation Over Target Area

B
Col Hunter-Latson
8075-A

B
Meyran
2469-Q

B
Davidson-Durtschi
8085-C

B
Kaufman
2570-F

B
Novak
6083-V

B
Sleaman
2562-G

B
Mocre
2568-N

B
Lehner
7892-K

B
Lee
7825-J

C
Ford
8126-J

C
Reed
7214-V

Johnson,W
2507-F

High Group 1st "A" CBW Formation Over Target

D
Frazier-Miller
8121-Q

B
Stallcup
8091-L

L
Dalton
7874-W

D
Weekley
2516-B

D
Wierney
2596-N

-D
Taylor
7385-X

D
Falkenbach
7203-Z

D
Cucco
2565-M

D
Brown
7190-L

C
Slavin
8147-L

C
Mann
6157-W

C
Armor
2592-G

Low Group 1st "A" CBW Formation Over Target

F
Scott-Rudrud
7374-X

F
Doerr
094-M

F
Cobb
7337-H

F
Brown
7387-H

F
Boehme
2610-Y

F
Richardson
7510-S

F
Evans
2593-C

F
Leukhardt
2543-9

F
Link
2597-V

C
Fritog
7294-P

C
Rogers
2519-A

C
Atkinson
2418-M

CONFIDENTIAL

The 398th Bomb Group formation as briefed for the mission to Le Manoir, France on August 13, 1944. Lt. Harold Weekley was leading the Low Squadron of the High Group on this mission when he, his crew and his airplane were shotdown by flak. This graphic is a reproduction of the actual mission flimsy.

(Harold D. Weekley)

This combat strike photograph shows bombs falling on and around the targeted railroad bridge of the 398th Bomb Group's mission to Le Manoir, France on August 13, 1944.
(Harold D. Weekley)

dispatched to attack the Le Manoir bridge.

On this day, Col. Hunter, our Group Commander, led the 398th on this "milk run". I was assigned to lead the Low Squadron of the High Group of the 1st "A" Combat Bomb Wing. From this position, I could most effectively maintain formation position by flying in the co-pilot seat, which is exactly what I did. Once again, my assigned airplane was the *Bronx Bomber II*, now a well-worn, if not battle-weary Boeing B-17G.

In retrospect, the plane's name did not relate to anyone on my crew at all. Another crew named this Boeing bomber before it arrived in the European Theater of Operations.

Months earlier, my crew and I were supposed to go to Kearney, Nebraska, to pick-up a factory-new B-17 to bring to Europe and into combat. As events unfolded, we picked up this well worn airplane in England, instead. Overall, I was quite pleased to fly the *Bronx Bomber II*. It performed rather nicely and the maintenance personnel who worked on it were well qualified.

We flew the *Bronx Bomber II* on our first mission and, eventually, a total of eleven times. It seemed like we always came back with some sort of damage and there was always some repair work that needed to be done.

The *Bronx Bomber II* was a uniquely marked aircraft. The entire nose of the airplane was painted black all the way to the cockpit. The reason for the black paint was that it had flown through some "scare flak." Scare flak was something that the Germans experimented with for some time and it did just exactly that, scare the bomber crews. The Germans fired large shells high above a formation and the chemical makeup of the contents of the shell was such that when it exploded, it would just look like liquid fire pouring from the sky. For many crews, it gave the impression that a bomber was going down.

As happened on one occasion, the *Bronx*

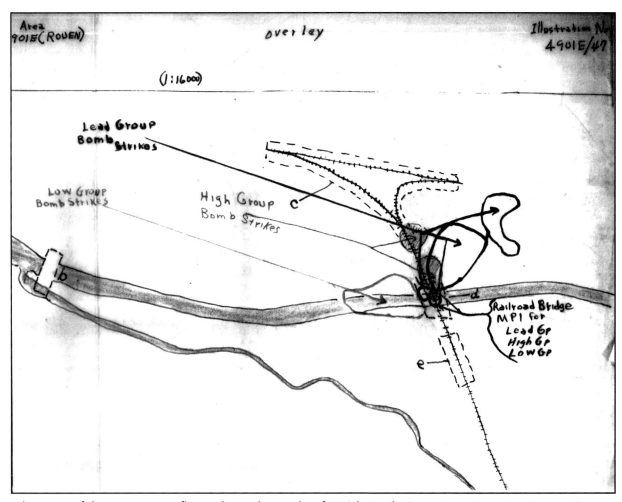

This copy of the post-mission flimsy shows the results of 398th Bomb Group's mission to Le Manoir, France on August 13, 1944. The various notations were made at the post-mission debriefing.   (Harold D. Weekley)

Bomber II flew through some of this scare flak chemical. In turn, the aluminum on the nose began to deteriorate noticeably. The scuttlebutt was the aircraft would be flown back to the United States in the near future and analyzed by the chemists to get some more information on the corrosive effects of the chemical. In the meantime, the nose was painted black and the *Bronx Bomber II* continued to fly missions.

The mission takeoff and formation assembly on August 13th was fairly uneventful. Each airplane carried six, 1000 lb, AN-M65 bombs, ideal for attacking a hardened or well-built structure such as the large, steel railroad bridge near Le Manior, France. This railroad ran to Rouen.

The day was generally warm and clear with only an occasional towering cumulus cloud here and there. Flying in the High Group, I kept my position flying at 150-mph indicated airspeed at 20,500 feet indicated altitude. The Lead Group was below me at 20,000 feet and the Low Group was 500 feet below them. The route from England was normal except the entire Group was compelled to make a slight detour to avoid a B-24 wing that intersected our flight path. Flying inbound to the target, we encountered the expected amount of flak, which was generally light and initially inaccurate.

Approaching the target, we made a turn from the IP to the target that put us on a northeasterly heading. Flak intensity increased considerably during the two-minute bomb run. Deadly, black cotton-ball puffs filled the air. The Germans were as intent on protecting the railroad bridge at Le Manoir as we were intent on destroying it.

Thirty seconds from the bomb release, the Lead Group's bombardier's bombsight malfunctioned resulting in a dry run. The Lead Group had no choice but to make a 360-degree turn and try once more, with the High Group in tow. The Deputy Lead took over for the second run. The Low Group, however, continued forward on the bomb run. The first airplane in the Lead Group made a series of "S' turns so that the other airplanes in the Lead Group and my group, the High Group, could catch-up. This wild maneuvering caused the entire formation to become spread and somewhat scattered. Somehow, everybody managed to return to the target and release their bombs, but on totally different headings than briefed.

A German antiaircraft gun crew, much like the one shown in this photograph, was responsible for shooting down the *Bronx Bomber II* on August 13, 1944.
(Harold D. Weekley)

Despite this "S" turning, the flak gunners on the ground had found their marks. Angry, lethal black puffballs exploded all around the scattered formation, forcing everyone to get as far away from this murderous mayhem as they could.

Without any warning, all hell broke loose inside the *Bronx Bomber II* and my otherwise routine mission ended quickly! Fate intervened and, as if it had a malevolent personality, reawakened me to war's harsh reality and said, "Your turn!" just as a tornado of deadly fury exploded around me.

We took numerous anti-aircraft hits throughout the aircraft. A fire erupted in the tail gunner's position and in the radio compartment causing us to lose all of our radios and intercom. I couldn't ascertain the status of my crew and they couldn't hear my commands.

The hydraulic system - located behind the copilot's seat - was shot out, spraying its contents around the cramped cockpit confines behind me. When I looked down and back to my left, I saw a large amount of red fluid splattered about the cockpit. I wasn't sure if it was hydraulic fluid or blood. Fearing blood, I thought for a brief instant that Joe Skarda, my flight engineer and top turret gunner, was seriously wounded. To my immediate relief, I realized it was, indeed, hydraulic fluid.

The number one engine was on fire, so I feathered it immediately. My actions were swift and methodical, almost a reflexive action developed from months of intense Army Air Forces training. The number two engine was on fire and the number three engine was running away. I had to get it feathered quickly or risk loosing the propeller entirely. I had just feathered the number one engine, so things got pretty bad very quickly. The aforementioned was only the least of our problems.

My wingmen spread a little wider from me than standard formation. They saw the fire coming from my aircraft and anticipated an explosion. They didn't want to be near if and when the *Bronx Bomber II* did explode. Our wingmen tried to contact us and tell us of our rapidly deteriorating situation. Since our radio was out, we had no knowledge of our precarious state.

Within minutes, Joe Fabian, the ball turret gunner, came out of his ball and advised Louis Buschbaum, our radio man and Joe Skarda, our flight engineer, that we had a large fire in the fuel cell between the number two engine and the fuselage. My briefing to my crew from the beginning of our combat operations was that any time you had a wing fire, it was an automatic bailout.

When this information was given by word of mouth to the flight engineer, he passed it on to me. I turned around and looked aft through the fuselage. The crew in the rear was looking at me. I waved my hand to get out and they wasted no time leaving our stricken bomber.

I engaged the autopilot, which put our airplane into a relatively stable flight long enough for my crew and me to bailout. I scrambled out of my seat and reached under it for my parachute, but it was not there. I must have had a look of panic as I turned around looking for my parachute. During flight, I wore only my parachute harness and kept the chest-mounted parachute under my seat. The rest of the crew followed a similar procedure. Relief swept over me when Joe Skarda handed me my chest pack, a 24-foot diameter silk parachute. Afterwards, he proceeded toward the back of the aircraft. Ben Clark, my co-pilot, went down and into the nose to tell Paul James and Ray Delbart, our navigator and bombardier, that they should evacuate the aircraft immediately.

Paul and Ray were already trying to open the forward hatch located just behind the navigator's station, but the hatch was jammed. They even tried kicking it with their feet and jumping up and down on it, but to no avail. Fighting panic, they proceeded toward the rear of the aircraft to bailout. Despite the very close confines in this area of a B-17, they had already managed to move past me as they headed toward the tail.

I followed close behind Ben to make an attempt to jettison this escape hatch. I pulled the handle, which is supposed to release the nose hatch door, but for some reason it didn't

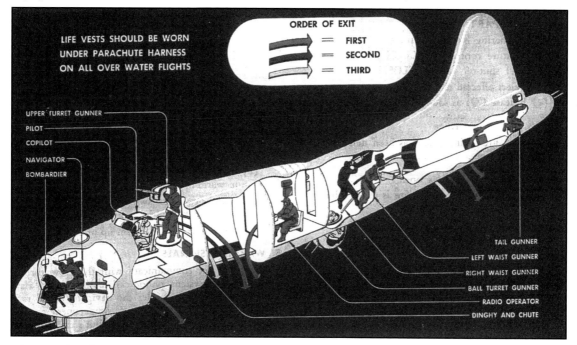

This graphic depicts a B-17G's recommended emergency escape routes.

(Model B-17G Army T.O. No. AN 01-20EG-1)

work. Eventually, I was able to work it free enough to hold the hatch door open, but was unable to jettison it. At four miles above the earth, I held it open as best I could against the rushing slipstream. I motioned for Ben to precede me and evacuate. Seeing Ray and Paul moving hastily toward the bomb bay, I wasted no time and followed Ben out through the nose-hatch.

When Ben went out, his chute opened almost immediately. As such, he was in the air for quite a long time. But Ben faced another, greater danger. Our now-abandoned aircraft made several slowly descending circles with each round getting closer to Ben. He became quite concerned until on the third circle, the airplane blew up and fell to the ground.

Having no knowledge of what conditions existed as far as enemy activity in that particular area, I delayed opening my parachute as long as possible. I planned to open my chute between 3,000 and 4,000 feet. I fell on my back and shoulders in a head-down position with my feet pointed upwards. Everything was surprisingly calm. The only noise to tell me I was falling was the sound of my flight suit flapping around my legs.

I looked to one side and saw the English Channel. We got so close to the channel, within forty miles. It would have been nice if we could have made it and possibly ditched, but considering the poor condition of the aircraft, a ditching would have been impossible with little chance of survival.

Considering the magnitude of my difficulties at the moment, it is hard to imagine some of the things that go through one's mind during such a time. When we bailed-out, one of my first thoughts was of my personal effects back at Nuthampstead. "The SOBs will get my candy!" flashed through my mind.

I know that's an odd thought, and some explanation is necessary. As mentioned earlier, my mother and my stepfather were at Fort Sill, Oklahoma. He was in the field artillery school there as a Second Lieutenant

and my mother worked in the PX. On occasion, she sent me large Hershey candy bars, which at that time were about a pound or 3/4 of a pound of delicious chocolate, and cost about 25¢ apiece.

I put several of these coveted candy bars and a couple of other valuable sweets into a Musette bag, which is like a little knapsack, and hung it from the rafters of my Nissen hut at Nuthampstead. I wanted to keep it from the ground where, hopefully, if there were any rats, they wouldn't be able to get into it.

Now that I had gone down, I thought of the crewmembers from the other two crews that shared our Nissen hut and of the visitors that came by from time to time. I frowned at the thought they would get all that good candy I'd been saving.

This thought didn't last too long because I had to get back to more important, immediate things. My most important consideration was to try to locate some of my other crewmembers. I looked left and right hoping to see some of them under canopy. Unfortunately, I didn't see anyone in parachutes because we had bailed-out over quite a large area.

My next consideration was trying to get myself safely on the ground. I began to think I wasn't in a very good position in which to be falling and believed there would be quite a snap to my body when I opened my chest pack, possibly injuring my back. I feared, also, I'd lose my boots in the opening shock. Since the second or third mission, I had been flying with a new issue of British escape boots and I certainly didn't want to be in enemy territory or in the woods without any footwear.

I made a conscious effort to get myself falling in a feet-first position. In doing so, I got my body into a spin, something I did not want to happen. At the time, I did not know I could adjust my attitude by simply adjusting my body position, much in the same way skydivers today maneuver themselves into position. When I got myself into a spin, I made an immediate effort to correct the situation. I put both my arms out to one side against the spin. The spin stopped and I resumed my descent head and shoulders first.

I fell almost four miles before I opened my parachute. I feared some enemy action would come from the ground and that I'd be an easy target. Once I hit the ground, I knew I'd have to quickly find a place to stay away from the German soldiers or unfriendly civilians. In various parts of France, and in almost all of Germany for that matter, a man descending in a parachute was fair game for anyone wanting to kill him, including some enemy fighter pilots or soldiers on the ground. Regrettably, some civilians on the ground went after downed fliers with small arms and personal weapons, such as pitch forks, shovels, clubs, etc. With that idea in mind, and not knowing the locals' attitude towards me, delaying the parachute opening was probably the best of all of the alternatives available.

When I was getting close to what I believed was two or three thousand feet above the ground, I pulled the D-ring on the parachute. (Unfortunately, I failed to retain the D-ring, crucial evidence needed to join the famed Caterpillar Club…those who have successfully bailed-out of an aircraft as the result of an emergency.) I was a bit surprised by the opening shock. It wasn't really as hard as I had anticipated and it appeared that I was where I had wanted to be, about 2,000 feet above the ground. After all that had happened in the previous fifteen minutes, I was lulled into a little bit of complacency by the mild opening.

Gently rocking under a good canopy, I saw I was coming down at the edge of the small town named Brametot. There was a small, triangular shaped field outside the village, lined with tall trees on two sides and a small road along the third side. Luckily for me, there was no wind whatsoever.

I thought a lot about the landing fall positions that I should make (e.g. feet first with knees bent slightly, then roll towards a hip and shoulder). Still thinking of the mild opening shock, I thought my landing would be softer than it was, but without any wind, I came straight down and landed hard. I didn't fall to either side and my only comment was a curt, "Jesus Christ!" The only comparison I can make is that the landing was the same as jumping out of a second story window. Immediately, I began to recover my chute.

About that time, two young boys, approximately eleven or twelve years of age, came out of the woods, and assisted me in recovering my parachute and, working together, we got it all rolled up into a ball. I asked where the Germans were located and the boys pointed in one direction. Wasting no time, I took off immediately in the opposite direction as fast as my feet could take me.

Just as I started to leave, they indicated they would take care of the parachute. Then they pointed to a church steeple and indicated I should return to that church after dark. We parted company never to make contact again.

I quickly entered a large, wooded area. It was approximately 1:45 p.m. on a sunny Sunday afternoon and I knew that I'd best get into hiding and remain there until after dark.

When I thought I was in a secure position, I took off the suntan summer shirt that I had underneath my flight suit and put it in a place in the thicket where I thought would be a good place for me to hide. Then I stepped back into the nearby open area again to see if I could see that shirt in the thicket. When I couldn't, I went back into the woods, put my shirt back on, my flight suit back over the top of it, and sat back down to relax and think.

I tried to put my mind at ease. To keep myself occupied, I thought of a variety of things. I thought of a plan to get me back to base as soon as possible. Of course, this plan was twofold: I wanted to get out of Europe safely, and I wanted to let my family know I was safe.

I knew the War Department would be sending them information very shortly to say

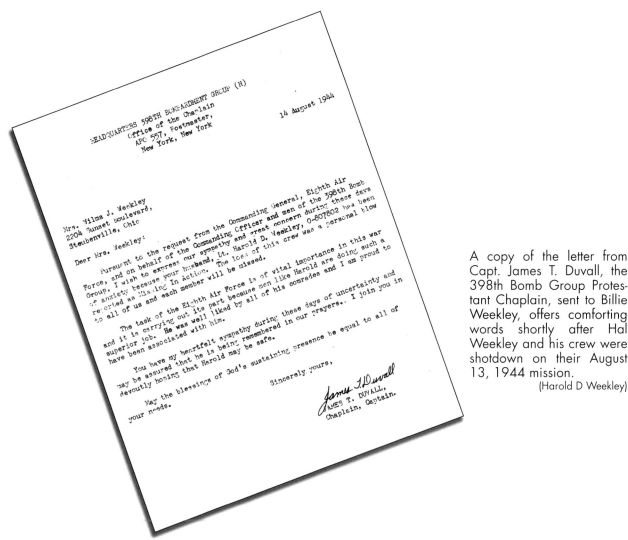

A copy of the letter from Capt. James T. Duvall, the 398th Bomb Group Protestant Chaplain, sent to Billie Weekley, offers comforting words shortly after Hal Weekley and his crew were shotdown on their August 13, 1944 mission.
(Harold D Weekley)

I was missing in action. I wanted to keep their hopes alive and let them to know I was alright. Circumstances allowing, I wanted them to know I was on my way back to either my home base or the United States.

I was frustrated. I wasn't doing anything productive for the war effort sitting on the ground. I became more upbeat when I re-assessed my situation and developed a more positive attitude.

There were several hours of daylight remaining till it got dark. I replayed the events of the day in my mind. I thought of my crew and of their wellbeing. I didn't know where they were or their current situation.

I thought of the aircraft that we had just lost. Our "Queen of the Skies" held together well, I hoped long enough for my crew to es-

cape safely. I regretted the loss of this fine machine.

While I took stock of my situation and tended to a cut caused by Flak, I was startled by the unusual sight of another B-17 flying near me at a low altitude, probably in the neighborhood of 1,000 to 1,500 feet above the ground. Just as it flew by my position, it blew up!

The bomber exploded with such a tremendous force that all I could see were just the two wingtips dropping from the sky. Everything else - including engines, propellers, the aluminum skin and armor plate, and the turrets - absolutely disintegrated! Nothing but two wingtips floated down to the ground. To this day, I do not know where that plane came from, to which base it was assigned or its target. I didn't see any identification marks on it. All I could do was hope the crew had bailed-out sometime earlier and that this airplane behaved like ours and had proceeded on course on autopilot for just a short period before it blew up. I never learned the fate of this crew or from where it was based.

I returned to my hiding place and continued to contemplate my situation. Once again, I recounted my blessings and gave consideration to what my next actions would be. I would not let personal anxiety and loneliness take command of my situation.

I was rudely awakened from my thoughts when I heard a large amount of .50-caliber machine gun fire, its loud staccato barely muffled by the foliage around me. Though I didn't know it at the time, my supposedly secure location was within a few hundred yards of a V-1 "Buzz Bomb" launch site. The site was being attacked by P-51 Mustang fighters of the VIII Fighter Command.

The Mustangs made repeated passes and worked over the V-1 launch site pretty doggoned well. I sat in silent disbelief and thought this would be one heck of a way to go. I made it through this much of the war, survived the bailout, landed on the ground in fairly safe circumstance, only to get shot up by a bunch of friendly P-51s trying to destroy an enemy V-1 "Buzz Bomb" site.

The Mustangs soon left the area. The pilots were probably content with the destruction they wrought that day.

When it got dark, or at least dusk, I headed to the church that the two young boys had indicated to me earlier. I got there and waited for awhile, expecting they would show up. They never did and I never found out why.

I started walking down a little road where I encountered a man walking with his wife and little girl. I still had on my suntans, having discarded my flight suit in the thicket because I didn't see any more use for it. They recognized me as a downed flier and ad-

dressed me as "parachutist." I wasn't sure I wanted to be identified as a parachutist as I was unsure of their intentions. I did know that some paratroopers on both sides were pretty tough troops and had some pretty tough reputations.

Likewise, I didn't want them to think that I was an armed combatant at the time; I wasn't. At one time, we each had been issued a Colt .45-caliber semi-automatic pistol carried in a shoulder holster. Some months before we were shot down, we were told to turn in these weapons with no explanation given. Thus, when my crew bailed-out, we parachuted unarmed.

When I indicated that I was unarmed, he motioned I should come with them. We started down the road together.

This chance meeting was a very critical point in my time on the ground. I knew there were some collaborators in the area who were well aware of the value of an American flyer to the Germans. These collaborators would turn the flyer over to the Germans and, in return, get a pretty good reward, around $500. My mind questioned, "Do I think this fellow is working for our side or the other side?" I decided that he looked like a pretty decent individual with a nice looking family and their actions were sincere and honest. I decided to go along with them.

We walked back into the little village of Brametot. This kindly family took me to the home of the Mayor, Monsieur Dubuc. There, I met the Mayor and his wife and they tried to communicate with me as best they could. Because I was the only parachutist that had come down in the vicinity of their town that day, there was no doubt I was an Allied flyer. Despite our problems communicating, it was clear to me they were going to try to protect me from the Germans and, eventually, get me back across the Allied line which, of course, was exactly what I sought to do.

The mayor and his wife had a large house. Very quickly, they took me upstairs to a small room in the attic. Apparently, it had been

Brametot, France in mid-1944. Hal Weekley spent his first couple of nights in enemy territory in the home of Monsieur Dubuc, the mayor of this small French village.
(Harold D. Weekley)

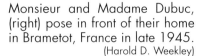

Monsieur and Madame Dubuc, (right) pose in front of their home in Brametot, France in late 1945.
(Harold D. Weekley)

used before for this same kind of clandestine activity. The entire room was painted white and it was just as clean as it could possibly be.

I stayed in this small room for two days. During that time, I had very little to do other than to exercise quietly and contemplate my next move. My growing boredom eased when a young couple came to the house and visited with me. Fortunately, they spoke better English and everyone was able to communicate more easily.

During my brief stay in the Mayor's home, I was able to provide my hosts a cou-

ple of photographs of me wearing ill-fitting civilian clothes. These photographs were the "escape and evasion" photographs I had taken at Nuthampstead some time earlier and were a key part of the survival kit each crewmember carried. They were about the size of a driver's license photo used today. In turn, my hosts created official identification papers for me. These papers showed me to be a Frenchman named Ernest Bourdoy who owned a house in the town of Criquetot. Without proper identification papers, there was no way I could travel on the roads in

France at that time. I found out later that the Germans knew what bomb group the captured airman belonged to by the tie he wore in the escape photograph, as we all wore the same tie for these photos.

Most fortuitously, on missions over France, we carried in our possession several copies of these photographs, as well as escape money, French francs, all brand new bills. We were instructed to give the French people copies of these photographs, as necessary, and use the money as needed.

During my stay at the house, I learned of a lady that lived next door who's son had been taken to Germany to work at one of the forced labor camps. Her son and I were about the same size, so I took some of my escape money and bought some of her son's clothes. All that remained to identify me as Allied Forces was my hack watch, which I put in my pants pocket, my dog tags, which I hid on my person as well, my identification bracelet, and my British escape boots.

With proper French identification in hand and wearing my new change of clothing, I was ready to proceed south to try to get back across the lines to the Allied side.

Local citizens of nearby Lammerville, France, inspect the relatively intact right wing of the *Bronx Bomber II*.
(Harold D. Weekley)

The *Bronx Bomber II* exploded in flight, severing the left wing between the number one and number two engines. The left wing landed in an upright position with the number one engine still attached. Note the propeller is feathered in this photograph.

(Harold D. Weekley)

The remains of the *Bronx Bomber II's* center section and right wing, bomb bay and left wing root rest in a wooded area not far from Lammerville, France. Note the remnants of the number two engine nacelle are still attached.

(Harold D. Weekley)

The *Bronx Bomber II's* severed left wing rest in an upright position with the number one engine still attached.
(Harold D. Weekley)

A light, wintertime snowfall covers the wreckage of the *Bronx Bomber II* several months after it was shot down. The remaining structures of the right wing, the bomb bay and the left wing root can be seen in this photograph.
(Harold D. Weekley)

The *Bronx Bomber II's* number two engine landed some five miles away from the main wreckage.   (Harold D. Weekley)

Assigned as a 389th Bomb Group replacement aircraft on August 15, 1944, Boeing-built AAF 43-38064 was given the 3O-H call-sign of the 601st Bomb Squadron within days after Lieutenant Harold Weekley, his crew and the B-17G Flying Fortress they were flying, 42-102516 (30H), were shotdown.   (398th Bomb Group Memorial Association)

"One's home is the safest refuge to everyone."
  Sir Edward Coke (1552–1634), *Third Institute* [1644]

CHAPTER 10

Safety with Friends

My departure the next day was very emotional, with much handshaking and hugging. Everyone wished me a safe return to the Allied lines. My escort was a middle-aged gentleman named Pierre Basire from Vittefluer, France. We were given bicycles, which we rode south along a moderately busy road.

Before we parted ways, I gave my identification bracelet to Pierre as a small gesture of my sincere appreciation for all the efforts he and his family took to protect me from capture. I know I would have been in very different hands if it were not for this family's unfailing courage to protect and shelter me from harm.

Pierre was very grateful and expressed great pleasure receiving this gift. Now, all I had on my person to identify me as a

member of the United States Army Air Forces were my dog tags, hack watch and the British flight boots.

Leaving Brametot, Pierre and I encountered several German officers and many German troops along the road, some in cars, some walking, and some riding bicycles. We ignored them and, in turn, the Germans ignored us as we proceeded on our bicycles. To our great fortune, everything remained uneventful for a couple of hours.

I hadn't ridden a bicycle for several years and I started to get tired quickly. Aching muscles aside, I had to be very cautious in Europe or, at least, in that part of France. Pierre recognized my fatigue and instructed me on the proper way to ride a bicycle. He taught me when the riding got tough or I came to a hill,

A close-up of Hal Weekley's AAF identification bracelet which he gave to Pierre Basire in appreciation for the efforts Pierre and his family made to protect Hal from capture.   (James B. Zazas)

I shouldn't stand up. He told me to remain seated on the bicycle seat the entire time. This wasn't the way I had learned to ride a bicycle in the United States. When I got to a hill, I stood up so I could apply greater pressure on the pedals. But in this part of France, such an action was a dead giveaway that I was not a Frenchman.

I had one real scare during the time we were riding. Pierre held back for just a moment, stopping briefly to pick up something on the road, then caught up with me quickly. He handed me my identification papers. Somehow, my papers had fallen out of my pocket and onto the road. He had noticed it, picked them up and returned them to me. That was quite a scare for me because I knew that if I was checked by any of the German officers or guards and I didn't have my papers, I would have been in deep trouble, and so would Pierre.

Many German soldiers were trained to look out for evaders because there was a lot of aerial action in that part of the country and many airmen were shot down. Consequently, there were a number of us on the ground all seeking to return to friendly lines.

While very few of the Germans could speak any English whatsoever, at least as far as normal communication was concerned, most of them were taught several key phrases designed to trip-up an Allied evader. One of these English phrases was, "Show me your papers." If, by chance the evader let down his guard and reached for his papers, this action alone cast immediate suspicion on him. It took only a few more queries before the Germans learned the evader was a downed airman. Therefore, one had to be very much aware of the often innocuous tricks they pulled to try to catch the evader in transit.

Pierre and I soon came to the town of Criquetot. This was just a stopover point, a rest stop, in the residential quarters of a bakery/pastry shop. The shop was owned and run by Pierre Basire's friends, truly lovely folks. I spent a couple of hours there resting and trying to converse, which was often very comical. Neither my hosts nor I could speak the other's language very well, nevertheless we managed to carry on a lively conversation. Despite the differences in language and customs, we became good friends because they were Allies.

I learned they were very concerned about my safety, well being and care. I was concerned for their well being, as well. These lovely people jeopardized everything they had - their livelihood, their lives, and their families' lives - to help the Allied cause and the Allied airmen. Words do not express the most sincere appreciation we downed airmen had for these courageous folks. All of us very much appreciated their efforts.

Many years after the war, when I returned to Europe and visited their home, I discovered that the chair that I sat in had printed on the bottom "Lieutenant Weekley sat here on 15 August of 1944," which was quite an honor for me.

Criquetot is a small town not far from Brametot, located in a political division of France called Seine-Inferieure, which is comparable to the counties in the United States. The geographic area where I found myself was within an area that lies east of Le Havre, France, which is a large seaport on the English Channel and the Atlantic Ocean.

After we spent some time visiting various people in Criquetot, Pierre and I rode further down the road to a farm on the outskirts of Yvetot, a town slightly larger than Criquetot. We arrived in the early evening hours. Shortly thereafter, Pierre Basire bid farewell and left me on this farm.

The farm was rather large with many outbuildings. Most structures, including the barns and all of the sheds, were constructed of stone and were very old. A large area in the center of the compound had several large, leafy trees. Much to my dismay, I soon discovered the Germans put those large trees to very good use.

The owner and operator of the farm was a

Monsieur Durmaney. He had a very nice wife, two sons, about 13 and 14, named Pierre and Michelle, and a couple of younger daughters that were of school age. With very few exceptions, my stay at this farm was a very pleasant experience. For a brief moment, the ravages of war seemed so far away.

I was brought quickly into the reality of the times. My first encounter with any Germans or German material on the farm occurred the next morning when I looked out my small window and saw some farm wagons under the trees. In an effort to try to compensate the farmer for my lodging and my food, I thought I'd try to go out and give him a hand.

I walked out the door of the farmhouse to the area of the wagons. Though I didn't notice any individuals around the wagons, I did notice that the wagons had large boxes on them. Each box had terribly long words printed on them. Much to my personal horror, I realized immediately that the labeling was in German.

During the daytime, German troops pulled their wagons off the main road and hid them under the farm's large trees. The skies above me were saturated with Allied fighter-bombers that flew up and down the roads shooting up all the transports and other targets on the highway.

A young Pierre and Michell Durmaney risked their lives and the lives of their family to help Hal Weekley evade enemy forces during Hal's stay on the Durmaney farm outside of Yvetot, France. (Harold D. Weekley)

I realized quickly I had placed us in a precarious position. Moving so slowly as not to draw any attention to myself, I eased my way toward the farmhouse. Opting not to go through the entrance, I slid over a low stone windowsill, sat there for just a few moments listening, then cautiously eased myself into the house. When I got back to my room, I stayed there until somebody came to get me. I was very fortunate I wasn't observed by any of the Germans. From that moment on, I decided that I would wait to be asked to help, anxious to assist whenever I had the opportunity. But I wasn't going to jeopardize either the farmer or myself in the future.

I acclimated quickly to family life on the farm. Life was very tough for the French people during the war and food became scarce which only compounded their difficulties. One ate what was available.

While I was on the farm, we were in a period when green beans were being harvested. As a result, we ate green beans in every way imaginable. It took me a long time after I got back to the United States before I could enjoy green beans again.

The family invited me to sit with them at their dinner table and I ate exactly what they ate, carefully observing their etiquette and traditions. One custom I found most interesting involved the family's patriarch. The old man sat at the head of the table with a great big, round loaf of bread. He held the bread against his chest, took a big, sharp serrated knife and cut off pieces of bread which he passed to each of us.

I grew up accustomed to putting butter on my bread, but butter was scarce in France during the war. Nevertheless, the bread tasted quite fine without it. When the meal was over, we each ate another piece of bread and this time there was butter on it. The buttered bread was in lieu of dessert.

On occasion when we were having dinner, German troops either individually or in groups of two to three would come off the

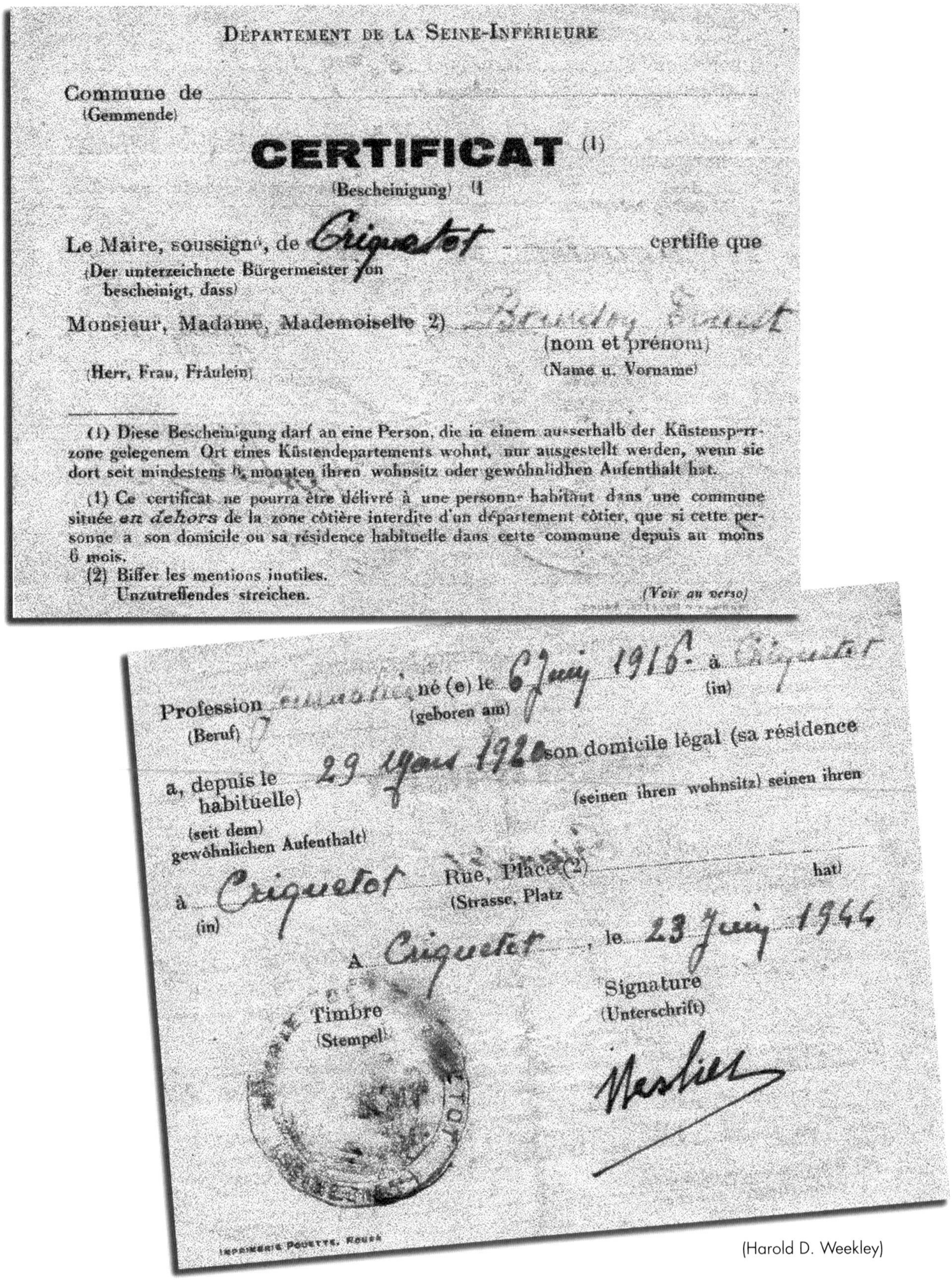

DÉPARTEMENT DE LA SEINE-INFÉRIEURE

Commune de ....
(Gemeinde)

CERTIFICAT (1)

(Bescheinigung) (1

Le Maire, soussigné, de *Criquetot* .... certifie que
(Der unterzeichnete Bürgermeister von
bescheinigt, dass)

Monsieur, Madame, Mademoiselle 2) *Beustry Ernest*
(Herr, Frau, Fräulein)   (nom et prénom)
      (Name u. Vorname)

(1) Diese Bescheinigung darf an eine Person, die in einem ausserhalb der Küstensperrzone gelegenem Ort eines Küstendepartements wohnt, nur ausgestellt werden, wenn sie dort seit mindestens 6 monaten ihren wohnsitz oder gewöhnlichen Aufenthalt hat.

(1) Ce certificat ne pourra être délivré à une personne habitant dans une commune située *en dehors* de la zone côtière interdite d'un département côtier, que si cette personne a son domicile ou sa résidence habituelle dans cette commune depuis au moins 6 mois.

(2) Biffer les mentions inutiles.
Unzutreffendes streichen.   (Voir au verso)

Profession .... né (e) le *6 Juin 1916* à *Criquetot*
(Beruf)   (geboren am)   (in)

a, depuis le *29 Mars 1920* son domicile légal (sa résidence
habituelle)
(seit dem)   (seinen ihren wohnsitz) seinen ihren
gewöhnlichen Aufenthalt)

à *Criquetot*   Rue, Place (2) .... hat)
(in)   (Strasse, Platz)

A *Criquetot* , le *23 Juin 1944*

Timbre   Signature
(Stempel)   (Unterschrift)

(Harold D. Weekley)

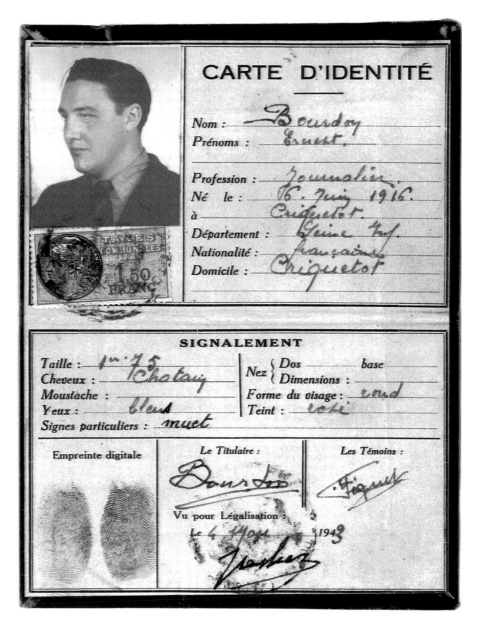

(Above and opposite) Lt. Harold Weekley's forged identity papers were made by the French Underground and used one of the Escape and Evasion photographs the Harold Weekley carried with him into combat. These documents, shown here in their original size and format, show him as Ernest Bourdoy, a 28 year old journalist and homeowner living in Criquetot, County of Lower Seine, France. His height is shown as 1 meter, 75 centimeters, hair is chestnut color, eyes are blue, and complexion is pink. The special markings entry located above the fingerprints describe him as being a "mute."

(Opposite) This document notes: "This certificate may only be issued to a person living in a coastal county but outside the restricted coastal zone when they have made this their permanent or normal residence for 6 months." In addition, this same document describes Ernest Bourdoy as having "made his legal residence since 29 March 1920 in Criquetot."

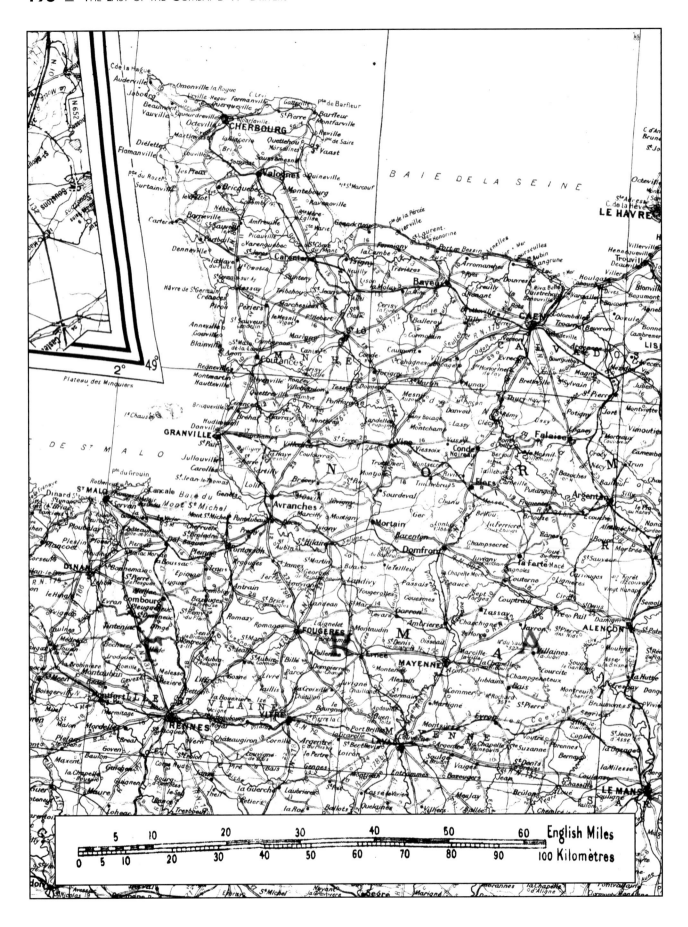

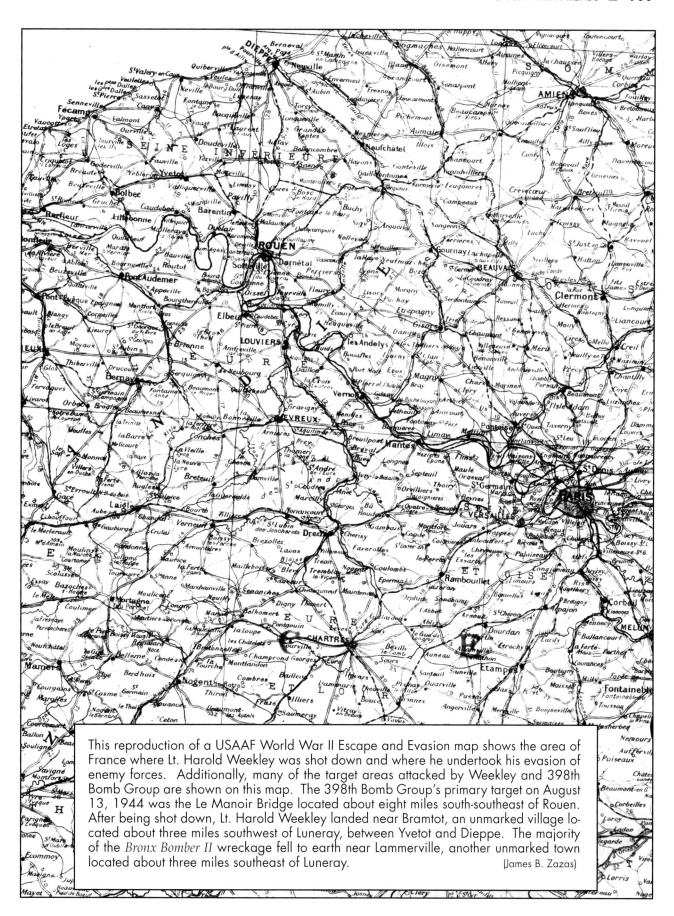

This reproduction of a USAAF World War II Escape and Evasion map shows the area of France where Lt. Harold Weekley was shot down and where he undertook his evasion of enemy forces. Additionally, many of the target areas attacked by Weekley and 398th Bomb Group are shown on this map. The 398th Bomb Group's primary target on August 13, 1944 was the Le Manoir Bridge located about eight miles south-southeast of Rouen. After being shot down, Lt. Harold Weekley landed near Bramtot, an unmarked village located about three miles southwest of Luneray, between Yvetot and Dieppe. The majority of the *Bronx Bomber II* wreckage fell to earth near Lammerville, another unmarked town located about three miles southeast of Luneray.

(James B. Zazas)

road to seek something to eat. They would come into the house and indicate what they wanted. Being in an occupied country, the family had no choice but to comply with their desires. They had the weapons; the family did not.

The soldiers would sit down at the table wherever the family and I could make space for them. Invariably, they'd look at me and wonder what I was doing there. The old man of the house would always give them some kind of a song and dance about why this young fella, 20 to 23 years of age, was sitting at his table. Fortunately for me, the Germans never pursued the questioning any further.

I learned very quickly I had to be very careful of my actions and mannerisms. First, I had to learn how to look and act like a farmer and not to walk around like an officer with my shoulders erect and a snappy step. Mr. Durmaney brought this problem to my attention. I had to train myself to walk with my shoulders hunched somewhat, kicking the gravel and rocks in front of me, as I walked down the road. At first, this action was a bit difficult, but it soon became second nature with little forethought.

Secondly, I was still wearing my British escape boots which I would polish regularly or at least wipe off the dust to try to keep them looking halfway decent. My host advised me not to wipe my boots clean. I learned that I shouldn't be walking around with brand new looking boots because no one else in the area had anything like that. At that time in France, there was very little leather available. The Germans had taken almost all it and used it for their boots, harnesses for their horses, and for other military requirements. Due to this acute shortage of leather, many people in France had shoes soled or made with wood. It behooved me to immediately rough up my boots somewhat so that they were not so obvious.

Thirdly, I learned quickly that fear shows up immediately in one's eyes. Instead of looking at these troops with fear in my eyes, I leaned more towards hatred and looked at them with very strong emotions. My hard looks sidetracked them, at least to a degree. I never had any problem with any of the troops who joined us for meals.

Perhaps most importantly, I couldn't speak either German or French and I learned quickly to keep my mouth shut!

However, I did run into a problem on one day after my host, his sons and I had been in the fields harvesting wheat. We were sitting on a little mound of earth in the center of the compound refreshing ourselves when a German officer came over and started to ask us some pointed questions about my identity. I was sitting on the ground and Mr. Durmaney was standing nearby. His two sons were sitting near me.

This German officer was exactly what I'd expect a German officer to look like; he was bald, short, stocky and very arrogant. The day was warm and he was naked from the waist up.

He put one of his shiny boots in between my two escape boots and stood there so that I wouldn't possibly get up. He proceeded to question Mr. Durmaney about who I was. Convinced I was no one he would be interested in, the German officer proceeded back to his unit.

I realized, of course, that had I been identified, the Germans would have executed the farmer and his family. Obviously, this episode made our hearts beat a little faster.

Harvesting wheat was a hot, dusty and very dirty job. Every time we returned to the center of the compound and put the wheat into the barn, we showered ourselves in dirt. The dirt came from bombs that had been dropped in the fields we harvested and the resulting explosions showered everything with dirt. Thus, every time we threw one of these sheaves of wheat up into the loft of the barn, it rained dirt upon us.

Mr. Durmaney and I took short walks after dinner. Often, we would go into the barnyard or into the garden where he tried to teach me a little bit of French. Though I tried my best to learn the language, I had little luck. After a while, he just gave up, looked at me with an air of resignation in his eyes and indicated to forget the whole thing. From that point on, we used charades to communicate. He told me to just play deaf and dumb.

Not too long afterwards, I had to leave the farm. I learned the farmer's younger children who attended school were very proud of the fact their family was aiding an American airman. They told their friends I was staying with them at their home. In telling their school friends about my status and my whereabouts, everybody involved in my safety was put in jeopardy. Everyone was concerned because one never knew who they told, whether they talked to a friendly individual or to the children of a German collaborator. If the latter had happened, then everyone was in danger.

Just as my hosts made arrangements to transfer me to another residence, German military moved into the farm's large compound. This time, the majority were the feared *SS* (Schutzstaffel) troops and officers.

During this particular phase of the war, a lot of German soldiers were retreating towards Germany in a somewhat organized withdrawal effort. Though it wasn't anything of magnitude, nevertheless a lot of men and material were underway.

Any individual or airman captured along the way would be in deep trouble because these Germans were not anxious to take prisoners back to Germany. On many occasions, prisoners were killed on the spot.

Shortly after the *SS* officers moved into the downstairs portion of the main building, I gathered what very little I had and in the night started down the narrow stairs. Light for the stairs was provided by narrow windows, which were open during the summertime. When I reached the bottom of the stairs, I stepped through one of these windows, which could not be seen from the courtyard of the compound and went into the woods. I remained there for two days and three nights.

The *SS* troops and officers soon moved out and, in turn, I eased back into the compound area. I let Mr. Durmaney know my whereabouts. Arrangements were quickly made for me to transfer into the city of Yvetot.

I was taken to the residence of Monsieur Fern Raoult, who in the early part of the war had been a French fighter pilot. Now, he had returned to his civilian profession as the district attorney of the Seine Inferieure in Yvetot. He was a very knowledgeable man and he carried much respect with the people in his area of jurisdiction. I knew I would enjoy my stay with this gentleman.

Fern's home was quite nice. During the day, I remained in my room with the door locked. I read to pass the time. In the evening, when Fern came home, he would unlock the door. Afterwards, we would sit down and talk while we enjoyed a glass of wine together. Because Fern spoke very good English, we had some fine conversations.

He had a housekeeper who took care of the chores around the house. She fixed the evening meal and departed just before Fern came home. Before she left, she would leave the dinner on the stove for us to enjoy.

Fern would go to the kitchen and prepare our evening meal. He would handle each course individually, starting off with a soup in most cases. At the completion of each course, he'd return to the kitchen and heat up the next course until we had had our full dinner. This took some time, and between the reheatings, we'd sit and have a glass of wine or several glasses of wine or, sometimes, champagne. Our meals took many hours. We filled our time with wonderful conversation.

When I first tried champagne in his home, I told Fern I wasn't accustomed to either wine or champagne. Since the French drink wine much like one would drink water, I was at a disadvantage. At the time I was shot down, I hadn't developed a taste for either wine or champagne, so I drank well water instead.

When I worked in the fields, or came in to discharge my load into the barn, the young girls of the family would bring out refreshments. These refreshments included a bottle of wine for their father and brothers, and a little yellow pitcher of water for me. Every time they brought this pitcher to me, they called me by the pet name they had given to me, "Donald Duck." They got this name from the cartoon character.

Fern got a big kick out of this story. After a few days in Fern's company, I developed a taste for both wine and champagne.

Fern was a fighter pilot at the beginning of the war in Europe and he had many stories to share late into the night. I told him of my experiences on the farm just outside of Yvetot and shared other events that happened to me during my time in Europe.

I learned that Fern had been a ham radio operator for several years but, because of the war, he no longer possessed a radio operator's license or the equipment. The Germans had confiscated all of it. All of the ham radios and personal radios, AM radios at that time, were housed in a jail cell in the courthouse in Yvetot.

Even though he no longer had his own radios, Fern knew of several people in the area who had kept their ham and AM radios. On two separate occasions, he took messages from me and tried to have them transmitted back to the United States to let my family know that I was well and healthy. Upon returning home, I learned that none of these messages were received.

While sitting with Fern and talking into the evening, I told him another story that happened to me just before I arrived at his home. I told him of my experience when the *SS* soldiers moved into the farm where I was staying. Fearing capture, I had to leave the farm's comfort and stay in seclusion for a couple of days. My departure was quite hasty and I didn't carry any food or water with me. After a day or so in the fields and woods, I got pretty hungry, so hungry I considered eating

more of the green beans in the fields, which in a pinch, would have been an acceptable food. August in France is quite hot and I got thirsty quickly. I looked around my immediate area for something suitable to drink. All I could find was a little stagnant pond that had green scum all over the surface. At this point, I had few options and decided to give it a try. I took my hand and wiped scum and algae from the surface of the water to get at the cleaner water underneath. Fortunately, there weren't too many creatures in it to make me ill and I managed to get a little refreshment that way.

As the conversations progressed, I told Fern about the terrifying V-1 attacks in England and related how I had personally experienced one of initial attacks the night before my first mission. I told Fern how the German V-1 "Buzz Bombs" came over London and, when they ran out of fuel, started into a steep glide and destroyed whatever they hit. I related how people would stand on the ground and watch them fly overhead in a morbid awe knowing that when the V-1's pulse-jet engine cut out, something beyond them would be destroyed.

Furthermore, I explained to Fern how these "Vengeance Weapons" became more sophisticated and deadly. The Germans reconfigured the pulse-jet engines on the "Buzz Bombs" so they would not cut out before their deadly glide and, instead, would actually go into its descent prior to the engine being starved for fuel. Worse, many V-1's were programmed to make a turn towards the end of their lethal run. Now, instead of going straight ahead, as they did initially while under power or during their final glide, they would make an unnerving turn. Many V-1s would go beyond where one was standing, make a turn and come back towards the observer. Consequently, those on the ground were never sure what the V-1s would do and no one could consider themselves safe, regardless of where they were standing or sheltered during a V-1 attack.

Another story I shared with Fern was my first encounter with the Me 262 jet which, incidentally, was about the first time American bomber crews had encountered this swift twin-engine fighter. Except for some scant intelligence passed along to the bomber crews, we were neither fully briefed nor warned of the Me 262's formidable performance, mainly because no one had any valid or usable knowledge about this jet airplane whatsoever. So it came as quite a surprise to see this new German fighter coming straight up at the bellies of our B-17s. Defensively, the B-17's underside was the most vulnerable part on our airplane because there were only two .50-cal. ball turret machine guns, which could be directed at anyone coming straight up.

I told Fern how this episode put quite a scare into everyone, including myself. When we returned to the base and prior to our obligatory intelligence debriefing, I went to the Red Cross table and took about three quick shots of liquor instead of my customary hot chocolate. Several others in my crew followed my example.

When the intelligence people and other returning crewmembers observed our actions, all raised their eyebrows and agreed, "This ought to be very interesting. This one really got to old Weekley and I'm sure that we'll have some very interesting information come out of this."

We discussed the military and political philosophies of World War II, the war's progress, and our respective families. We developed a very strong, close friendship.

One night after we had just finished dinner and I was still downstairs in the dining room, there was a knock on the door. This was the first time that ever happened during my stay with Fern. At the first knock, I saw the surprised look in Fern's eyes and he probably saw the equally surprised look in mine. I immediately headed back to my room and locked the door from the other side.

Fern answered the door and was greeted by a German officer who exclaimed he needed a place to spend the night and he had decided Fern's house was where he was going to spend it. Fern and the officer exchanged a few pleasantries before the officer retired to the bedroom located immediately adjacent to my room. I could hear him grunting and snoring throughout the night. The following morning the German got up and departed without saying goodbye or thanking Fern. All he did was steal Fern's camera and go on his way.

My room in Fern's modest home was on the second floor. I spent most of my time in this room, but I was not bored. I exercised several times a day, quietly of course, to try keep my muscles limber and to try to maintain some semblance of muscle tone.

A problem I faced while staying in the room was the lack of toilet facilities. Fern was good enough to provide me with a chamber pot, as they called it, which I used during the day, but his housekeeper couldn't empty its contents. I had to take care of emptying its contents when she was away from the house.

This chamber pot posed its own unique problem, particularly when the German officer was sleeping in the room adjacent to me. It had a metal bottom and a metal lid. Thus, when I replaced the lid after use, I had to be very, very careful not to make any noise, particularly in the dark. I am sure, had this officer heard any noise, he would have investigated further, which could have been disastrous for Fern and myself.

I had a fairly decent view from my single window. I could see a large area to the east towards Rouen, a city that possessed a good sized river port. From my unobstructed vantage, I observed the enemy activity in the area, including the movements of some German soldiers staying in a home just behind where I was staying.

I could see the ongoing Allied efforts, as well. On several occasions, I observed Republic P-47 Thunderbolt fighter-bombers operating in the area. One day Fern came home and told me excitedly that one of these fighter-bombers had been hit by ground or anti-aircraft fire on his bomb run and had crashed on the steps of the Cathedral of Rouen.

I kept track of the daily German troop activity and soon noticed a small reduction in the numbers of Germans remaining in the vicinity. Since the successful D-Day Invasion a few months earlier, I knew Allied troops were regaining German occupied territory in France. As a result, most of the Germans were easing their way back to their homeland in one way or another.

The number of German troops remaining in Yvetot decreased as well. There was very little need for them to remain there; the only value of Yvetot was that it was at a crossroads. The town was not convenient for the transport of any large equipment or war material, as it was not on any important railway or waterway.

Fern knew several people who were Allied sympathizers and about every third day he would bring one or two by the house to visit with me. These visits really kept my spirits high. Most of them spoke very good English. Because the town was close to the English Channel, the better-educated in the area spoke English quite well.

During these visits, I related that I wished to become aware of any German troop concentrations and activity, principally in the Le Havre area. I knew Le Havre was a big seaport and would be of considerable importance to the Allies as the war progressed.

Cherbourg, a good-sized seaboard town, which was further west on a peninsula, had been involved in a big battle. The Allies' success there secured a badly needed seaport in which to supply the ground forces, which were moving toward this area. I recognized there would be a positive need for supply support in the Le Havre area and, as such, tried to obtain as much information as possible, which later proved to be very beneficial.

I continued my observations of the number of German troops in town and their movements. Each day, the number decreased until, eventually, there were no more troops in evidence.

One evening, while enjoying our after dinner conversation, Fern told me that it appeared that all the troops had left the town. To test this theory, Fern retrieved from his garage a small, French motorcycle, which he taught me to ride in a very short time. Then he instructed me to cruise around the town and see if I could see anyone that might be associated with the German military. I proceeded into town, cautiously at first, but soon discovered any fears I may have had of being caught were for naught. The town was completely void of any German troops or activity.

I returned to Fern's house and told him that it appeared that all of the German troops had vacated the city. He smiled his approval, whereupon he and I proceeded to the city building that housed the jail. He told a small crowd assembled there that we had scoured the area and found no Germans remaining. Of course, everyone was overjoyed by the news.

The good news spread rapidly and the local people started to come to the town's square to celebrate. AM and ham radios, confiscated by the Germans and held in the city building, were returned. People were very happy to be able to get some kind of outside communication, which was cause for celebration.

Plans were set in motion to have a large party or festival in the city. But these plans were put on hold when word came that some retreating German soldiers were heading towards town. Wishing to protect his American friend, Fern decided that I should vacate his house and head towards another town a few miles south of Yvetot.

I bid a very fond farewell to Fern and the many other good people that I had become acquainted with in the area.

"We, too, born to freedom, and believing in freedom, are willing to fight to maintain freedom. We, and all others who believe as deeply as we do, would rather die on our feet than live on our knees."
Franklin Delano Roosevelt (1882–1945), *On receiving the degree of Doctor of Civil law from Oxford University [June 19, 1941]*

CHAPTER 11

Freedom's Cry

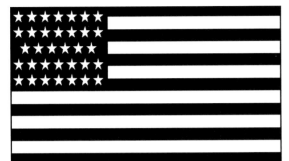
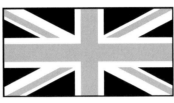
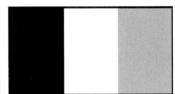

It had been almost three weeks since I bailed out of my B-17 and now I was headed for the Allied lines. I proceeded towards the river town of Caudbec, which was located several miles down the road. My transportation was a girl's two-wheel bicycle, the only conveyance that could be found for me at the time. The bicycle was geared differently than most bicycles I had ridden and I tired quickly. I realized that I was doing a lot of peddling, but wasn't getting anywhere fast. I was grateful for the time I spent exercising in my small room at Fern's house and, now, my good physical condition kept me going a little farther.

During the ride south, I tried to observe and mentally record all that I saw. My observations took on an almost surreal quality. I viewed the remains of several crashes, both of Allied and German aircraft, several vehicles - trucks mostly - and one Panther tank that had been burned out. I noticed the crumbled or crushed remains of a few French homes and other buildings. On rare occasion, the air carried a curious and very faint mixture of burned rubber, fuel and human flesh.

My solo journey across the picturesque French countryside took me up and down a series of rolling hills. The single-geared bicycle I was riding utterly wore me out. Just when I thought that I couldn't go much far-

ther, I saw the top of another hill and said to myself, "If I can make that hill, I think that's about as far as I'll be able to go."

I am glad I kept riding. Upon reaching the hill top, I looked down at a most wonderful sight; there were no more hills to climb and the road meandered downhill to the town of Caudbec and the Seine River. A tremendous wave of relief swept through me. I coasted most of the way to Caudbec and, shortly thereafter, the Seine River itself.

My timing could not have been more fortuitous. As I reached the river, I met advance troops from the Canadian Army. A part of the British 8th Army, they had just crossed the river from the south. Excitedly, I called to them and joined them on the Seine River's northern shore.

On Thursday, August 31, 1944, I enjoyed my first taste of freedom in almost three weeks.

Wasting no time, I approached the commander of the unit and identified myself as an American airman who had evaded capture. I was very excited to be with friendly troops and chatted with the commander for a few moments.

During our brief discussion, I tried to tell him my observations regarding potential enemy resistance, if any, he and his troops might encounter in this part of France. He listened intently, then directed me towards the rear echelon, whereupon I was escorted to the Intelligence section of the British 8th Army.

After a short discussion with them, the Major in charge of Intelligence took me to see the General and his staff. Entering a good-sized room filled with maps and charts lining the walls, all depicting the Allied advance in this part of France, I was impressed.

Arriving in civilian clothes and rather disheveled from my bicycle ride, I must have presented quite a sight to the General and his staff. But neither cared about my appearance, they wanted to know what information I had to offer about enemy troop activity in the area.

Wasting no time, I gave the General and his staff the information about the number of enemy troops, the type of fortifications and the supply conditions in Le Havre. The officers listened intently to my report.

Upon ending my briefing, the General requested me to escort the Major from the intelligence section back across the river and show him some of the area from which I had just arrived.

The Major and I returned to the General's headquarters some hours later and together, briefed the General on what we saw. We had very little to add to my earlier briefing.

Being totally exhausted from the ordeals of my day, I was given a place to sleep for the night, my first night behind friendly lines in almost three weeks. I slept without dreams as my body relinquished itself to a very deep sleep.

Awaking early the next morning, my British hosts told me that I was to be transported further south to another area designated for former prisoners of war and evaders. The British were attempting to gather all former POWs and evaders at an old abbey for medical treatment and debriefing, as necessary. Coincidentally, the Germans had vacated this abbey very recently and

fires, set by the Germans shortly before they departed, still smoldered in one section. Fortunately, only a small portion of the abbey had been damaged.

In a very short time, perhaps only a few days, a great number of POWs and evadeers came together. Downed airmen, soldiers lost from various Army units, even tank crewmembers, all gathered at the abbey. As the Germans retreated from outlying areas, Allied officers and enlisted men came forth to rejoin friendly forces. The large number of men returning to freedom was sobering, several hundred at least. I was quite stunned to see so many others who had evaded capture.

While I waited further disposition and eventual transportation back to England, I met another pilot, a young fellow named Robert M. Littlefield from Carmel, California.

During our lively conversations, I learned that my new friend was a P-51 Mustang pilot from the 55th Fighter Group based in Wormingford, England and that, ironically, he had been shot down by anti-aircraft fire near Rouen, France the same day as I, on August 13th. For all practical purposes, I believed this Mustang pilot and I were probably in the air under our respective parachutes about the same time.

I shared with Bob a piece of salami and a chunk of bread that Fern had given me. While we enjoyed our meal together and talked of our experiences, we heard a large number people walking down one of the wide hallways in the abbey. More from curiosity than anything else, I asked Bob, "How about sticking your head out there and hollering to see if there's anybody from Weekley's crew." He did and the result stunned me.

I heard a voice come back and say, "Here's Ben Clark." Ben was my copilot and he was just arriving with the newest batch of returnees. I was very happy to see Ben and to see that he was in good health. Within minutes, Ben brought me up to date on his activities since we had been shot down.

Ben told me that while I was in the relative safety in the thicket of the woods far from Brametot, he had been in the air for quite some time. In an incredibly convenient twist of luck, Ben landed near Bacqueville-en-Caux, a small town east of my position. When he landed, a Frenchman named Mlle Blondelle helped him hide his parachute.

Unfortunately, Ben was spotted by some German troops who then chased him out through a wheat field. After he had gained a little bit of distance - I guess fear will do that - he couldn't find any place that looked safe to hide except some stacked shocks of wheat. He got inside of one and buried himself as best he could. While doing so, he watched the German troops come down through the field with bayonets fixed on their rifles. They were shoving their bayonets into these wheat shocks in an effort to find him.

Of course, Ben was very lucky that they didn't approach the one he was in. When the German soldiers departed the area, Ben was able to escape to a little bit safer location.

Ben made contact with some local Frenchmen, possibly members of the French underground, and he was quickly placed in the care of a the family of Pierre Rique, his middle-aged wife, an older son, a young daughter named Simone and a younger son named Jean Francois. This gracious family gave him some civilian clothes and kept him in hiding. Ben remained in this idyllic location from the time since he had been shot down until he came to the abbey. This family was helped by a close friend named Marcel Gesse. Ben later learned this Frenchman had once served in the English Navy.

Ben related his only concern was that the Rique's teenage son was very active in the local guerrilla and underground effort and was apprehensive that the teenager's activities might draw Germans to the home. As a result, Ben often feared he would be captured, and possibly shot, for being associated with a member of the French Underground Resistance movement.

The organized Underground that oper-

ated in France, I learned very quickly, possessed two heads - the French Underground, which served the Allied cause, and, the German Underground, which served the German cause. Both operations had a very efficient communications network.

The French Underground Resistance existed to clandestinely disrupt the German war effort. Operating in small groups called "cells," they proved effective in many parts of France. By its very organization, this "cell" hierarchy usually preserved the identity of other members should one or more members of particular cell be captured, tortured or killed.

The German Underground was much more dangerous and insidious. Often, local citizens volunteered or were recruited to supply the Germans with information. On many occasions, members turned against their family, under threat of death, to supply information. Quite often, this information included the whereabouts of downed Allied crewmembers.

Being a part of the French Underground in occupied France was a risky proposition. If the location of evaders was revealed, German collaborators would inform the Germans who would move in and capture everyone.

The Germans took the Allies prisoner and, in almost every instance, executed all those who had helped them. Neither Ben nor I became involved with any part of the French Underground. After the war, we did learn that a few downed crewmembers had joined in French or other Allied nation underground activities, with a few being captured and eventually shot as spies.

Ben and I shared a common goal - to get home. Not long after our reunion, Ben, Bob and I left the abbey's meager comfort and boarded trucks to be transported further south. We were told that we would be taken to an airfield where, eventually, we would be flown to England.

We remained at our new location for a couple of days. Once again, we encamped in

E. & E. REPORT No. *1/94*   **TOP SECRET.**
                                                              I.S.9 (WEA)

(Applies to all BRITISH, CANADIAN, U.S. & ALLIED PERSONNEL)

EVADED CAPTURE/~~ESCAPED FROM~~ (Name of Country) *FRANCE*

For All Personnel.

1. No. *O-807802*   Rank *1st LT.*   Name *HAROLD D. WEEKLEY.*
    (U.K.: Acting, Temp. or W/S)

2. Decorations: (U.S.A.A.F.: No. of missions) *AIR MEDAL   20*

3. Were you wounded? Give details *NO.*

4. Ship (Navy), Unit (Army), Sqn. (Air Force) *601 Sqn.*

5. Div. (Army) or Gp. (Air Force) *398 Bomber.* 6. Job (Pl. Comd., Rfn., etc.) *PILOT.*

7. Date of Birth *17 July 1921*   8. Length of Service *2 yrs.*

9. Peace time occupation *AIR MECHANIC* 10. Private address *2204 SUNSET BOULEVARDE*
    STEUBENVILLE   OHIO. U.S.A.

11. Did you carry any form of identification, or photograph? *IDENTITY DISCS. 3 FULL FACE*
    6 PROFILE.

12. Do you speak French, or any other foreign language? *NO.*

FOR R.A.F. ONLY.

13. No. and location of O.T.U.

14. No. and location of Conversion Unit

FOR ALL AIR FORCE PERSONNEL AND/OR AIRBORNE OR PARACHUTE TROOPS

WHO BALE OUT

15. Post in Crew *PILOT*

16. Other members of crew, and information about what has happened to them.

    N.B.—Airborne and Parachute Troops: list below names and units of other occupants of plane, including R.A.F.
    and U.S.A.A.F.

    PILOT *PILOT. NARRATOR*

    CO-PILOT *BENJAMIN L CLARKE*   *Baled out.*

    NAVIGATOR *PAUL H JAMES*   *do*

    BOMBARDIER *RAYMOND S DELBART.*   *"*

    RADIO OPERATOR *LEWIS BUCHSBAUM*   *"*

    TOP TURRET GUNNER *JOSEPH W SKARDA* *"*

    BALL TURRET GUNNER *JOSEPH R FABJAN.*

    WAIST GUNNER (R.) }
                        ROBERT F STICKEL *"*
    WAIST GUNNER (L.) }

    TAIL GUNNER *GENE F LEONARD*   *"*

17. Type of aircraft, place, date, time of departure *B-17 G. NI. NUTHAMPSTEAD.*
    10.00 hrs. 13th August.

18. Where and when did you come down? *BRAMTOT 063540 (Sheet 8 E/2.   13.30 hrs.*

19. How did you dispose of your parachute, harness and mae west? *Disposed of my friends.*

20. Were all secret papers and equipment destroyed? *A/C exploded in air.*

(National Archives, Records Group 498)

TOP SECRET.
I.S.9 (WEA)

APPENDIX "C" TO E. & E. REPORT No. *1/94*

If further circulation of this information is made, it is important that its source should not be divulged.

No. *O-807802* Rank *1st LT.* Name *HAROLD D WEEKLY.*

Date of Interview *1st September 1944.*

MAP USED FRANCE 1:50,000 Sheet 8E/2 & 8E/2.

1. *MAYOR OF BRAMETOT 063543. Sheet 8E/2 Fed and sheltered me from 13-15 August. Arranged. civilian clothes.*

2. *PIERRE BRASOIR. BRAMTOT. Worked in conjunction with the Major.*

3. *M. DURAME St. CLAIR sur les MONTS 982342 Sheet 8E/4 Fed and sheltered me for 11 days.*

4. *M. Roualt YVETOT 5J 9634 Sheet, 8E/4 Attorney General. of town. Look after me for 5 days.*

5. *LUCIEN, surname unknown. St. CLAIR SUR LES MONTS aged about 28 yrs. Had us when Germans occupied opposite house to his own in which I was living*

(National Archives, Records Group 498)

These two pages and the next two pages show Harold Weekley's original Escape and Evasion Report (No. 1/94), his signed War Department Security Certificate, a form that he had been debriefed by an Intelligence Officer in France, and a Movement Order for Evacuation to UK (American) from France. Of special interest are the repeated misspellings of Weekley's name on several documents.

RESTRICTED

WAR DEPARTMENT
The Adjutant General's Office, Washington

AG 383.6 (31 Jul 43) OB-S-B-M   6 August 1943   KLS/el-2B-939 Pentagon

SUBJECT :   Amended Instructions Concerning Publicity in Connection with Escaped Prisoners of War, to include Evaders of Capture in Enemy or Enemy-Occupied Territory and Internees in Neutral Countries.

TO :   The Commanding Generals,
           Army Ground :
           Army Air Forces :
      The Commander-in-Chief, Southwest Pacific Area :
      The Commanding Generals,
           Theaters of Operations :
           Defense Commands :
           Departments :
           Base Commands :
      The Commanding Officers,
           Base Commands :
      Director, Bureau of Public Relations.

     1.   Publication or communication to any unauthorized persons of experiences of escape or evasion from enemy-occupied territory, internment in a neutral country, or release from internment not only furnishes useful information to the enemy but also jeopardizes future escapes, evasions and releases.

     2.   Personnel will not, unless authorized by the Assistant Chief of Staff, G-2, War Department General Staff, publish in any form whatever or communicate either directly, or indirectly, to the press, radio or an unauthorized person any account of escape or evasion of capture from enemy or enemy-occupied territory, or internment in a neutral country either before or after repatriation. They will be held strictly responsible for all statements contained in communications to friends which may subsequently be published in the press or otherwise.

     3.   Evaders, escapees, or internees shall not be interrogated on the circumstances of their experiences in escape, evasion or internment except by the agency designated by the Assistant Chief of Staff, G-2, War Department General Staff, or the corresponding organization in overseas theaters of operations. In allied or neutral countries, American Military Attaches are authorized to interrogate on escape, evasion and internment matters.

     4.   Should the services of escaped prisoners of war, evaders, or internees be deemed necessary for lecturing and briefing such services will be under the direct supervision of the agency designated by the Assistant Chief of Staff, G-2, War Department General Staff, or the corresponding organization in overseas theaters of operations.

     5.   Commanding Officers will be responsible for instructing all evaders, escapees, and internees in the provisions of this directive which supersedes letter, AG 383.6 (5 Nov. 42) OB-S-B-M, 7 November 1942, subject : Instructions concerning Publicity in Connection with Escaped Prisoners of War and other previous instructions on this subject.

     By order of the Secretary of War :

                           /s/ J. A. ULIO
                             J. A. ULIO
                             Major General,
                           The Adjutant General.

---

     1.   Information about your escape or your evasion from capture *would be useful to the enemy* and a danger to your friends. It is therefore *SECRET*.

     2.   *a*   You must therefore not disclose, except to the first Military Attache to whom you report, or to an officer designated by the Commanding General of the Theater of Operations, or by A. C. of S., G-2, W.D.

           (1) The names of those who helped you.
           (2) The method by which you escaped or evaded.
           (3) The route you followed.
           (4) Any other facts concerning your experience.

       b   You must be particularly on your guard with persons representing the press.

       c   You must give no account of your experiences in books, newspapers, periodicals or in broadcasts or in lectures.

       d   You must give no information to anyone, irrespective of nationality, in letters or in conversation, except as specifically directed in Par. 4.

       e   No lectures or reports are to be given to any unit without the permission of A. C. of S., G-2, W. D., or corresponding organization in the theater.

CERTIFICATE

     I have read the above and certify that I will comply with it.

     I understand that any information concerning my *escape* or *evasion* from capture is *SECRET* and must not be disclosed to anyone other than the agency designated by A. C. of S., G-2, War Department, the corresponding organization in overseas theaters of operations, or to the Military Attache in a neutral country to whom I first report. I understand that disclosure to anyone else will make me liable to disciplinary action.

Name (Print)   HAROLD D WEEKLY   Signed _Harold D Weekly_

Rank   1st LT.   A. S. N. O-807-807   Dated   1st September 1944.

Unit   601 Sqn. 398 Bomber Gp.   Witness   D. C. De Cat Capt RA

(National Archives, Records Group 498)

CONFIDENTIAL.

CERTIFIED THAT:

No. O-807802 Rank 1st LIEUT.

Name (BLOCK LETTERS) HAROLD D WEEKLY

Unit 601 Sqn. 398 Bomber Gp.

has been fully/briefly/interrogated by an Intelligence Officer of I.S.9(WEA) on 1st Sept. 19 44

and has signed a Security Certificate.

He should/should not/be re-interrogated.

[stamp: GENERAL STAFF I.S.9. ★ 1 SEP 1944 1/94 WESTERN EUROPEAN AREA]

[signature] CaptRA.

for Major.

IMPORTANT.

THIS CERTIFICATE MUST BE RETAINED AND HANDED TO (BRITISH) AN OFFICER OF M.I.9 OR (AMERICAN), AN OFFICER OF PW. & X. DET. M.I.S. ON ARRIVAL IN U.K. OR U.S.A.

(National Archives, Records Group 498)

1416

MOVEMENT ORDER FOR EVACUATION TO UK (AMERICAN)

No. 080782 Rank. Lieut Name Weekly, H.D.

You are directed to travel by the route and method which will be indicated to you

and to report immediately to an officer of the P.W. & X. Det. M.I.S. 63 Brook St.

LONDON W. This Movement Order together with Medical Report will be handed to

the Officer Commanding, L.D.A.C. upon arrival.

Bearer is still in possession of AB 64 Pts. I and II AF B 2606 Form 1250

[stamp: GENERAL STAFF I.S.9 ★ 3 SEP 1944 WESTERN EUROPEAN AREA]

Office Stamp

[signature] Lieut.

I.S.9 (WEA)
First Cdn Army

This Officer has not been medically examined

[signature]

(National Archives, Records Group 498)

a British Army facility. While the British continued to coordinate the transportation efforts for the many former POWs and evaders who arrived on a daily basis - many came from the woods and hedgerows where they had hidden. Others marched or straggled in from the nearby villages. Very few had escaped their captors. All basked in their new-found freedom.

Though I did not look much like an officer, and most of us didn't as we were all a bit ratty at the time, we were granted the privilege of eating at the British officers' mess. We generally kept to ourselves and had very little contact with the British.

The British moved Ben, Bob and me further south to an airfield. By the time we arrived there, we had about fifteen to twenty individuals in our ever-growing group. While we waited for an aircraft to take us back to England, we shared our stories as an evader or prisoner of war. Some of these stories were very interesting, whereas others were best left with the men who experienced them.

One airman in our group told us a particularly hair-raising story. After bailing out and parachuting safely to the ground, he was chased by German troops. Eventually, he ran into a farmer's house with a German soldier following very close behind him.

As the airman entered this French home, he stepped behind the door and found an ax standing there, which he grabbed immediately. Almost at the same time, the German chasing him - with a machine pistol in hand - came through the door, only to be greeted by the airman swinging the ax. The German caught the ax's blow in the mouth. The airman escaped to the rear of the house and was able to remain free until he made contact with the Allied troops.

Another airman in our group told us how he had the misfortune of landing on the outskirts of a German occupied airfield after bailing out of his crippled airplane. He had few escape options as many people near the

airfield saw him come down. Most fortunately, he landed in a small recess on the ground, which partially hid him. A German soldier approached, indicated that he should stand up and be taken back to the airfield. The Allied airman tried to communicate that he was injured, even though he wasn't. The German soldier leaned over to offer the airman his hand to aid him in getting to his feet. Meanwhile, the airman had been laying on a Colt .45 automatic hidden under his body. As soon as he raised the slightest amount and freed the weapon, he killed the German soldier and was able to make an escape. Eventually, he worked his way to the Allied lines.

Another interesting story came from a Royal Canadian Air Force (RCAF) gunner who had been flying on a Lancaster doing night bombing raids when his aircraft was shot down. During the course of our discussion, I learned that he was located in a small village not too far from mine. Rather than try to work his way to the south, he favored staying in one location. Thus, instead of trying to go to the Allies, this fellow decided to let the Allies come to him. To my amazement and amusement, this plucky airman played a little ruse on the French and Germans alike. He would sit in the park in the middle of this little village and make faces and funny sounds at the passers by, thereby trying to impress everyone that he was the village idiot. Apparently it worked, because he was with our group and awaiting transportation back to England.

One bailout story was rather comical and involved another RCAF airman who had been on a bombing mission during a bright, moonlit night. The aircraft was shot up badly. One of the gunners' parachutes had been hit repeatedly by flak and there were several holes in it. When they were forced to evacuate the airplane, the unlucky airman grabbed the damaged parachute and, soon, he was descending at a more rapid rate than the other crewmembers. Though he could see his other descending crewmembers clearly in the moonlight, he was unable to determine exactly why he was descending faster. In jest, he shouted at the other fellows, "Hey, guys, you're in real trouble because it looks like you're going the wrong way."

There were many ways that people survived in, and escaped from, German occupied territory. The preceeding stories are only a scant few of the more interesting ones I heard.

Our little storytelling session ended when a Douglas C-47 Skytrain arrived loaded with fuel drop tanks for fighter aircraft. The crew told us if we would help unload the drop tanks, the crew would take most of us back to England. We were more than happy to help, especially if it hastened our return to England and, eventually, home!

When I saw those drop tanks for the first time, I was stunned. They were made of papier-mâché! I soon learned that in the early part of the war, fighter drop tanks were made of aluminum. Every time one of these fighters dropped its fuel tanks in combat, it was the same thing as dropping a Cadillac, which at that time was very expensive, averaging about $5,000.

Papier-mâché was considerably less expensive and lighter than regular, external aluminum fuel tanks. A fighter pilot never returned with the papier-mâché tanks. As soon as the fuel was used in these tanks, or if he was engaged in battle, the pilot would dispatch the tanks immediately.

The only problem with papier-mâché tanks was that the fuel, after a prolonged period of time, attacked the glue holding the tank together, in turn, deteriorating the structural integrity. If the tanks were kept on the aircraft too long, they would deform and become more ball-like in shape than an aerodynamically streamlined item.

After unloading the drop tanks we jumped on board the Skytrain. Within min-

Fiber auxiliary fuel tanks for P-51 fighters are offloaded and stored.   (National Museum of the United States Air Force)

utes, we were airborne and heading toward England.

Our route took us over Caen, France, which had been the location of a tremendous tank and ground battle. Looking through the Skytrain's small windows, we could see many assault gliders and other aircraft that had crashed in the area during an earlier airborne assault. Caen itself was devastated. All that remained of the town was one wall on the side of a church.

The transport pilots flew low-level on the way back to England, mostly to avoid any stray enemy fighters, flak batteries or Allied aerial operations being conducted at higher altitudes. As a result, our flight was quite turbulent and caused a couple of conspicuous problems.

Foremost, the turbulence presented a problem when using the limited toilet facility,

A Douglas C-47 Skytrain, similar to the one shown in this photograph, flew Lt. Harold Weekley, other repatriated evaders and former prisoners-of-war from France to England.

(National Museum of the United States Air Force)

which was located in the tail of the C-47. The toilet itself was a large bucket filled with oil. The rough air made the tail swing back and forth, up and down in some wild gyrations which, in turn, made the oil in the bucket slosh around a bit.

When I went to relieve myself, I wound up with my bottom covered in oil. There was no toilet paper in evidence, so the only thing I could do was take off my shoes and use my socks to wipe off my backside. Afterwards, I rejoined the others, sans socks.

The steady drone of the C-47's two radial engines made us all a little sleepy. Taking advantage of the opportunity to catch-up on his sleep, Bob Littlefield lay down and stretched-out on one of the canvas and aluminum seats attached to the side of the airplane. Bob was a fighter pilot and I thought I'd have a little fun with him. At the point when I thought he had had some good rest, I shouted in his ear, "Break left!" Bob moved quickly to his left, and rolled right out of his seat onto the floor. Shaking the last remnants of sleep from his

body, he looked up and could only give me a puzzled look of "What happened?"

The trip to England was uneventful, for which we were all very grateful. German fighters were still active in this part of France and coastal warnings of enemy fighter activity were still being posted at all Allied airfields. Even though the ride was rough at low altitude, those of us on the C-47 gladly traded comfort for safety as we knew we would be an easy target for any German fighter. Everyone had been through enough already and we didn't want to come this far only to be shot down or killed over the English Channel.

Our concerns were well-grounded because we were flying not far from Abbeyville, France, the home base of the "Abbeyville Kids," an elite group of Luftwaffe fighter pilots. Better known as "Goering's Yellow Noses" because the fighters they flew sported noses painted yellow. The pilots of this unit were tough, aggressive and very courageous. Handpicked for this assignment, rumor had it that a Luftwaffe pilot wouldn't be accepted into this elite unit until he had at least twenty confirmed "kills." Such rumors and other incidents increased the "Abbeyville Kids'" notoriety to almost mythical proportions.

One incident involving the "Abbeyville Kids" involved an often reported feud that they had with the 100th Bomb Group of the Third Air Division of the Eighth Air Force. This bomb group flew B-17s identified by a black letter "D" on a white square on the tail, called a "Square D." Many stories abound about this feud, but I think the one that is probably most often told concerns a battle that took place between a 100th B.G. B-17 and some attacking German fighters.

In the early days of the war, an uncommon chivalry existed between Allied and Luftwaffe pilots. When a bomber became disabled and could no longer sustain flight enough to make it back to England, the pilot would lower the landing gear, which was the sign of surrender, similar to a foot soldier holding his hands up in the air. Upon seeing this signal, the German fighters would back off and stop their attack. Instead, they would escort the crippled bomber to the nearest Luftwaffe base where the crew would be taken prisoner.

The story goes that in the early part of the war a disabled bomber from the 100th Bomb Group lowered his gear to signal his intentions to surrender. One of the "Abbeyville Kids" came up alongside to escort him to a Luftwaffe airfield, whereupon the gunners on the disabled B-17 shot down the yellow-nosed German fighter.

Word of this presumed and appalling act spread quickly, especially among the Luftwaffe pilots. Thereafter, the "Abbeyville

Kids" would fly the length of the bomber stream looking for any B-17 with the "Square D" marking on its tail. Then, they would center their attack on this hapless bomber or bombers. These actions were regrettable because there was enough grief to go around without having to be singled out by the enemy on every mission.

Though the story of this feud was often told, the truth is questionable. A more accurate story would be that the 100th Bomb Group was involved in many difficult missions and ferocious air battles. As a result, they suffered horrendous losses, an unsettling pattern that began with the missions to Regensburg and Munster in 1943.

100th Bomb Group tail markings.

(Peter M. Bowers)

This hard-luck bomb group lost fifteen B-17s on the initial Berlin raids of March 1944 earning the bitter "Bloody Hundredth" epithet. Many crewmembers in other bomb groups considered the 100th Bomb Group to be the "jinx group," even though the losses of other bomb groups, notably the 91st and 96th, exceeded that of the 100th.

When my crew and I first arrived in England, we heard about the 100th Bomb Group's hard luck while we were in the Redistribution Center at Stone, England prior to assignment with the 398th Bomb Group. At the time, all of us felt very fortunate that, while we didn't know anything about the 398th, we knew we weren't going to the 100th Bomb Group.

The flight to England allowed us time to think and reflect upon our many individual experiences and consider the activities, debriefings and other things that were going to occur in the near future. I was very concerned about my crew and except for my copilot, Ben

Clark, did not know how many had survived, whether they had been captured, whether they were still evading capture or whether they were in prison camps.

I wanted to get back to my base and finish flying my last five required missions to complete the rest of my tour. Though I knew I wouldn't be flying with my own crew, I knew I would have the opportunity to fly with other outstanding men. I trained for quite a long time to do a job and, for me, I certainly felt that the job was not over. I still wanted to do my duty for my country.

I couldn't possibly hope for a crew that was any better than the one I had. My crew had some of the finest men I've ever known in my life and I considered it a privilege to know them, work with them and fly with them. I was hoping everyone would be able to get back to the United States and that everyone would be in good shape.

As I learned later, everyone in my crew survived. Even though a couple of them were taken prisoner, everyone returned safely to their home.

I reminisced about the missions we had flown together and recalled certain details. I remembered times when we had almost 2000 airplanes on a mission. We would take off in the morning and there were aircraft ahead of us for as far as I could see. On my way outbound from the target, I could see aircraft still on their way inbound. The bomber stream stretched for a hundred miles or more. With that amount of activity, I knew a tremendous number of bombs were being dropped on the enemy.

We always encountered enemy opposition of some kind. We would frequently encounter enemy fighters either above us or in the sun. Flying from west to the east in the morning hours, the sun was in our eyes and the enemy fighters took advantage of the sun's glare to shield them as they made their initial attacks. Then, when we returned to England, we had a bright sun in the western sky, and once again, the German

fighters waited for our return using the sun to shield them.

More often than not, we didn't see the enemy fighters hiding and waiting for us in the sun's glare. Most of us in the bomber stream were too busy flying formation. If we were lucky, we had a group of friendly fighters escorting us.

When our fighters, particularly the P-51 Mustangs, came in close to escort us, they were well aware of the bomber crews' apprehension about any single-engine fighter approaching the bomber stream and were quick on the draw to shoot anything resembling an enemy fighter. To lessen the bomber crews' concern, the escorting fighters would join the bomber stream in a skid so that they weren't pointing their nose towards the bombers. When they came in sideways like this, we knew they were friendly and there was no need for us to take retaliatory action.

I thought of Billie and the letters I sent home to her. I wondered how she and my family were coping with my situation, if they even knew I was an evader.

As we continued on our flight to England, I thought of the happier times we had in England. I recalled one particular event when I went over to nearby RAF Bassingbourn, home of the 91st Bomb Group. They were having their 100th mission party. Bob Sheriff, a good friend from my earlier flight training days in Ardmore, Oklahoma, invited me to join the party.

Bob Sheriff was the Operations Officer for the 91st Bomb Group. The party I attended was held at General William Gross' quarters with several other ranking officers attending. General Gross was the commander of the 1st Combat Bomb Wing of the 1st Bomb Division of the Eighth Air Force. The day was beautiful, ideal for a party.

As my friend and I stood in the General's quarters, located on the second floor of a small two-story structure, we observed all sorts of local people entering and leaving the base. Bob told me that many folks came onto the base to enjoy better food than they could find in the local economy. Others came to enjoy the company of the young men.

The General observed all this activity and remarked, "We have these people on the base now and I don't know if we're ever going to get them off because once they get here it's very difficult to get everyone out of the barracks."

I know this to be true. It was not uncommon for us to go into the latrines to use the facilities, shave or brush our teeth, only to be standing there and have one or two young British ladies come in, use the latrine, brush their teeth or comb their hair. Afterwards, these local visitors returned to the barracks as if they had found themselves a new home.

One day, not too long after the party, the General put out a memo stating that the local residents had to get off the base and return to their homes. As generous as the Eighth Air Force was to wartime England, it couldn't provide that level of subsistence. Everyone regretted the loss of the companionship, but life on base did get back to a more normal military routine a few days after the General issued his memo.

I remember, also, reading a book by Ernie Pyle called, *Here is Your War*. Before he was killed in the Pacific Theater, Pyle was a very well known, World War II war correspondent and author, and he spent most of his time writing about the "GI Joe," the "grunt," and "the man in the foxhole." Pyle's newspaper columns were widely read and he wrote several outstanding books.

One time, Pyle had the opportunity to fly on a bomber mission. When he returned, he purportedly stated, "Well, it's pretty much the same all the way around. There's one or two differences, those being that a bomber crew member or an airman, when they get killed, at least they die with a clean shaven face and a full stomach, if that's any consolation."

My flight from France to England soon ended and we landed at an airfield near Lon-

don on Sunday, September 3rd. Army Air Forces personnel, security people and Military Intelligence greeted the flight. We boarded buses that took us to London where we were housed in a very fine hotel for a couple of days to be debriefed. (See Endnotes, Chapter 11, Number 1)

The day after our arrival, we were debriefed individually. My debriefing officer was a Major White. I gave him all the information that I could possibly recall. I described my activities, the enemy troop activities I observed, the location of enemy personnel in the Le Havre area, specifically around Caudbec, Yvetot and Rouen.

Military Intelligence was keenly interested in what I had to say and my debriefing was lengthy. Afterwards, I signed statements that I would maintain the secrecy of the information I had provided. Shortly thereafter, I was told that I would be going back to my bomb group, but only for a very short period of time until transportation could be arranged to send me back to the United States. My days flying combat missions over Europe were over and I would not be allowed to complete my tour. Obviously, I was disappointed and I soon learned why I could no longer fly combat missions.

If I had returned to flying combat missions and was unfortunate enough to be shot down behind enemy lines, I could be shot as a spy for having knowledge of enemy activities in another country and passing it on to Allied forces. More significantly, I would have been tortured by the Germans to provide the names of the French who had helped me to escape. In turn, the Germans would have executed the families. Therefore, for my own protection and the protection of the French citizens who sheltered me, I was going home, though not to my initial liking.

Strangely, I received the news that I was going home with mixed emotions, but as I was about to become a father I looked forward to being home for that very special occasion and to be with Billie. I remained in

London another day before I was transported to Nuthampstead.

I expected a peaceful night sleeping, but was rudely awakened by the wail of a city air raid siren and by the reverberating sound of tremendous explosions. The siren was just outside my window and it was one of those large, city sirens that the Defense Corps used in case of an enemy raid. London was under a German V-2 attack, one of the very first of those frightful events.

Several V-2 rockets plummeted into London and the surrounding area with devastating results. Whole city blocks were destroyed. They literally disappeared, totally eliminated from the face of the earth. I witnessed this devastation firsthand.

The morning after this V-2 attack, I boarded a train to Royston, the station nearest Nuthampstead. There, I disembarked and rejoined the 398th Bomb Group. A lot of new faces greeted me when I arrived on base.

I didn't know it at the time, but I was the first 398th Bomb Group aircrew member to have been shot down, evaded capture and returned to the group. Ben Clark returned to the 398th shortly after my arrival as part of another group of returning airmen.

My return created quite a stir among the crews on base. There were numerous new crews assigned to the bomb group, none of which I knew. As such, except for very few officers, nobody really knew who I was. This fact was highlighted by an experience I had in the chow line on my first day back on base.

I was standing in line with a group of officers ahead of me when one turned around to talk to another pair of officers standing be-

Little of this London church survived when a German V-2 rocket fell.
(National Archives, 342-FH-3A6390-B-58306 A.C.)

hind me and commented, "Have you heard? Weekley is back at the base. He made it back!"

The ensuing conversation centered on someone they had heard about, but they didn't have any idea who Weekley was or what he looked like. Obviously, they didn't realize that I was standing right there.

I left Nuthampstead with many good feelings. I had made a positive imprint on the 398th' Bomb Group's overall operation and people were aware that I had been there.

During my debriefings, I learned I could claim damages for any personal property lost during the time I was behind the lines. An intelligence officer assigned to the case said it was very easy to remember my situation because I was the first one to return to the 398th Bomb Group after being an evader. He worked hard and quickly to recover what was due to me.

As was the normal custom, when a crew was shot down, those individuals that remained in the Nissen hut had the option of going through the downed person's effects, and if anything fit, they were welcome to it. What little remained would be reviewed by base supply personnel to see if there was anything that would be harmful to the family, such as phone numbers, addresses and, possibly, photos of local girlfriends. Afterwards, all was packed-up and sent back to the next of kin. Army Air Forces policy was to remove a missing man's personal property as soon as possible to prevent any unnecessary brooding over his loss.

Those lucky individuals that remained in the huts went about the grim and often repeated task of rearranging their quarters. Memories of the names and faces of those crewmembers missing, killed or prisoner of war blurred quickly as they went about their business and prepared for another mission. For many crews, these names became a distant dream, often all but quickly forgotten. With death in combat an almost daily occurrence, making close friendships was tough for some crewmembers, and virtually non-existent for others.

Despite the losses within our group, and the fact many personal effects were being shipped routinely to the United States, I decided to pay a visit to see what had became of my own personal equipment. I had no uniforms, nothing I could wear to show that I was a member of the United States Army Air Forces.

Much to my total surprise, I discovered that everything that had been in my quarters was still located in the base's supply building. All of my clothes and other personal items were boxed up. Everything was still intact.

I was curious why my belongings were still being retained in unit supply and hadn't been distributed by the other aircrew members within the officers' group. When I asked, many of them told me that they felt that if anyone could get out of Europe, it would be me and they darned sure didn't want to be wearing my clothes upon my return. Consequently, no one got into my personal effects and everything was taken to unit supply. The base's unit supply kept all of my personal gear intact in storage.

Of course, I was very fortunate and very

pleased that everything assigned to me was in place. Soon, I was in proper uniform and I was back in business. The only things missing were my bag of candy, the chocolate and a few other goodies.

I spent a short time with my Bomb Group before I boarded a train to Prestwick, Scotland where I caught transport to the United States. My train ride to Prestwick that night was one of the worst train rides I ever had in my life! The train cars were hooked together with big chain links and each car had steel bumpers on each of the four-corners, which caused the cars to bounce against each other like balls in bumper-pool. Combined with the uneven railroad beds, we were jolted all over the place.

At one point, I thought, "Of all the things that I've been through, I surely hope that I don't get killed in a train wreck on the way back to the United States." I had the same uneasy feeling when the P-51 Mustangs attacked the V-1 site close to my position on my first day in France.

I arrived safely in Prestwick, whereupon I caught a ride to the nearby Army Air Base to be bedded down in a large barracks maintained for the transient crewmembers and soldiers. These long barracks probably housed a hundred men or more. Each bunk had a name printed on it. I found my bed, a bottom bunk. I was very tired and I fell asleep quickly.

About four o'clock in the morning on Wednesday, September 27th, 1944, the Charge of Quarters came through the barracks with his flashlight. I was lying there awake reflecting on my journey when he came down the aisle between the beds. I asked him who he was looking for. He said he was looking for Weekley and I replied, "Well, you found him."

I left for the United States that morning. For some reason, I was the only person in that whole barracks that left for home on the morning flight.

*"So it's home again, and home again, America for me.
My heart is turning home again, and there I long to be."*
Henry Van Dyke (1852–1933),
America for Me [1909], st. 2

CHAPTER 12

Back Home in the U.S.A.

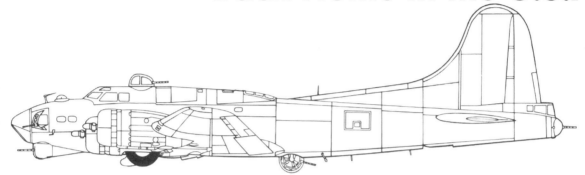

I rose quickly, gathered my things, packing all in my olive drab B-4 flight bag, and made myself as presentable as possible. Shortly thereafter, I boarded a four-engine Douglas C-54 transport that was bound for Washington, D.C. It was a long flight in the droning C-54, but I didn't care at all. I was going in the right direction - west towards the United States of America and home almost exactly three months since arriving in England!

The plane made refueling stops in Reykjavik, Iceland, and Stephenville, Newfoundland, before making that last, long leg to National Airport in Washington, D.C. I kept a small log recording the takeoff and landing times. It was early morning on

Thursday, September 28, 1944 when I arrived. I looked out the transport's small window and saw the Potomac River as we came in to land.

I thought we were awfully low on the final approach and said to myself, "Okay, let's stay on the ball up front because this is the last leg and the last landing that I need to get back home." Of course, the landing was very well done and there certainly was no cause for alarm.

Being this close to home, I didn't want anything to ruin my return.

I was met at the aircraft by a Lt. Colonel from the Pentagon and was taken promptly in his personal staff car to the Pentagon for another debriefing.

The Douglas C-54 was one of the USAAF's airlift workhorses.
(National Museum of the United States Air Force)

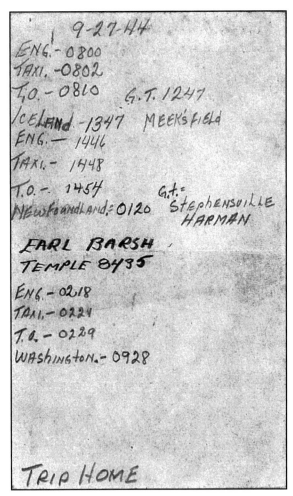

Hal Weekley kept a time log during his return home. It is reproduced here. (Harold D. Weekley)

I spent the entire day at the Pentagon and told my debriefers everything I had told Major White previously in London.

Based on the information that I had provided and the work that I had done behind the lines, I was advised I would be recommended for a Silver Star decoration. I was credulous and was sure my interrogators were very busy and had more important things to do than process my award. As I expected, that decoration never came to pass.

After being debriefed, I was given a short leave. I didn't call Billie, my mother or my father to let them know that I was in the United States. I was so close to home that I just decided to get there.

I went down to the Pennsylvania Railroad station and boarded a train for Steubenville.

It was a beautiful, though chilly late autumn evening when I boarded the train. The journey took all night. I traveled through Pennsylvania and West Virginia before coming to the Ohio River that separated West Virginia and Ohio. I crossed the Ohio River at the Fort Steuben Bridge, big, old auto bridge that spans the river at Steubenville just south of the Steubenville Lock. At that point, I realized that I had made it. This was probably the most trying time for me emotionally. When I crossed that steel bridge, I knew I was back in Ohio and home.

The train pulled into the station around four o'clock in the morning. I immediately called Billie and told her I was getting a cab. I wanted to make sure the front door was unlocked and that everyone knew I was on my way. Billie was breathless to hear my voice!

My homecoming was memorable in every way, with lots of embracing hugs and tears of joy, but a bit shocking as well. The last time I had seen Billie, she was a beautiful woman of twenty-two years of age with a perfect figure. Now, as I greeted her, she was still the beautiful woman, but seven months pregnant with our first child. During my trip home I had tried to imagine or visualize how she would look pregnant, but I was still surprised.

Billie and I talked for some time. After having been awake all night, I was quite tired. In fact, I hadn't slept since I left Scotland. I had to excuse myself to get some needed rest. That slumber lasted only a few hours. At about eight o'clock in the morning, Harding Junior High School, located approximately two blocks away, summoned their students with a siren, not the customary bell as in most schools. I had forgotten this fact completely and I awoke with a start.

In the span of one week, I had gone from enemy territory to debriefings in London and the associated air raid and sirens to base at Nuthampstead to Washington, D.C. and, eventually, home. The sound of a siren was quite a surprise and I literally flew from my bed. It took a moment for me to realize what was going on, and it took a long time for me to accept the Harding Junior High School siren every morning.

Billie and I shared many stories of what each of us had been doing during my time overseas. Billie told me one story that astonished me and reminded me of how fortunate I was to be married to her.

Just before Bille left on a ten-day vacation to Canada with her mother, brother and his wife, she received a telegram from the War Department referencing me. After she opened it up, the first thing she saw was that the telegram had three stars on it. She called her mother and said, "Mother, it's not too bad. He's only missing in action."

Three stars on the War Department notification meant the service member was missing. Four stars reported a death. The same was true for small pennants many families hung in a window in their home. In some instances, a gold star indicated a death.

Billie and her family went on their vacation and enjoyed themselves. On their way back home, Billie commented to her mother that she felt sure she'd hear something from me after they returned. As it turned out, I returned home about two weeks after they returned from their vacation. The telegram notifying Billie that I had been found alive in Europe arrived about three or four days after I arrived home in Steubenville.

My brief leave ended and I had to return to duty. However, just before leaving, Billie and I went down to Wheeling, West Virginia on a shopping tour. Shortly after we came home, Billie started experiencing labor pains. I took her to the hospital.

Our first son was born at approximately 9:26 p.m. on October 25th, 1944, which was exactly a month prior to his expected arrival time. We were both overjoyed and, yes, somewhat surprised that he came so early.

Born prematurely, he weighed five pounds and one and a half ounces. His conditioned worsened and within just a couple

A very happy Billie Weekley holds her first child, William Deane Weekley.

(Harold D. Weekley)

of days his weight dropped to three pounds and twelve ounces. His condition remained very critical for quite some time and for the most part, he stayed in the hospital's incubator until we brought him home on January 2, 1945.

Fortunately, I was granted an extension on my leave for a few days so I could take Billie home, even though our son remained in the hospital.

We named our son William Deane Weekley. William is the masculine form of Wilma, which was Billie's given first name. We used my middle name of Deane.

My leave soon ended and I had to return to active duty. I went to the Redistribution Center in Miami Beach, Florida to be reassigned. During my few days there, I received a thorough physical examination. The doctors determined that I needed a short, additional period of non-duty, so they sent me to Fort Logan near Denver, Colorado, which was a rehabilitation base.

Fort Logan was located outside of Denver, in Aurora, Colorado. I stayed in an open bay barracks with several other officers, all former combat crewmembers. Of the approximately twenty officers in that barracks, only two were B-24 crewmembers and the rest, B-17.

During my stay at this rehabilitation center, it struck me as sort of odd that crewmembers were separated with little time given for any socializing, perhaps to keep individuals from reliving war-related experiences. I did strike up a friendship with a young fellow named Earl Fry from Oregon, Wisconsin. He was a B-24 pilot. For some reason, I had believed that more B-24s were lost in combat than B-17s. I really don't know where or how I got that idea, possibly based on some information I had at the time. I asked him if my information was correct and he replied that he knew a lot of B-24s were lost as well as a lot of good men, perhaps more than the B-17s, but he wasn't really sure either.

Like many others at the center, I spent a good amount of time working on various projects, including a re-education program. Everything we did was meant to get us stabilized and ready to return to duty.

I stayed at the rehabilitation center until Christmas Eve, December 24th, 1944, whereupon I was granted another leave. I returned to Steubenville and traveled east on the *Burlington Zephyr*. I got the last seat on the train, which happened to be in the club car near the bar. In this comfortable seat, I was able to put my feet up on the bar rail, which made for a very enjoyable trip back to Chicago and then to Steubenville, arriving in time for Christmas.

I enjoyed my brief time at home over the holidays before I had to leave for my next assignment. Being an evader, the Army Air Forces allowed me to choose my next assignment. USAAF Commanding General Henry "Hap" Arnold considered evaders to be his "good fellows," and made it clear that any ex-prisoner of war or evader would have the

assignment of their choice. I opted to be a B-17 instructor at Lockbourne Army Air Field, which was located near the town of Lockbourne, Ohio, about ten miles south of Columbus. I chose assignment because it kept me within 150 miles of home.

I reported for duty in early January and soon started to train pilots in the B-17. For a few brief moments during the cold winter, I questioned why I requested this assignment, especially in an airplane that never had anything close to a good heater, but I was close to home and my family and that was all that really mattered.

Lockbourne grew from the area's rich farmland. Some 1,600 acres in size, Lockbourne was an ideal location to train B-17 pilots, though initially the base was used to train glider pilots. In October 1942, the glider school left for Stuttgart Army Air Field in Arkansas. Training started shortly after the arrival of several B-17s from Hendricks Field in Sebring, Florida. This training school started officially on January 15, 1943.

Flying and instructing at Lockbourne often proved challenging. The nine-week transition course had changed very little from the B-17 course I had taken at Hendricks Field a year earlier; it still consisted of 105 hours of ground and flight instruction, including fifteen hours in a Link trainer. A resourceful base staff made instructional aids from parts of crashed or derelict airplanes. Items included engines, instruments and aircraft systems.

Interestingly, the base became a unique part of the Women Airforce Service Pilots (WASP) program in late 1944 when several WASPs were selected to train in the B-17. An experimental program was set up and each WASP selected went through a program similar to their male counterparts. Of the seventeen WASPs assigned to the program, thirteen completed the course. No WASP was involved in any aircraft accident while at Lockborne.

Over time, Lockbourne Army Air Field

AAF 42-29577, a Boeing-built B-17G, lands at Lockbourne AAF, Ohio. Harold Weekley instructed in B-17s at Lockbourne AAF when this particular B-17 was based there and very possibly flew it.   (James B. Zazas)

became Rickenbacker Air Force Base, home to many active duty Air Force Reserve and Ohio Air National Guard units. Today, the Rickenbacker Port Authority controls most of the land with only a small part occupied by the Ohio Air National Guard.

Lockbourne Army Air Field during the war was a busy base and many different types of aircraft shared the ramp space and runways. Quite often, these differences caused problems. Two incidents aptly describe the difficult conditions I routinely faced.

One day, as I taxied my B-17 onto the active runway, a Piper L-4 liaison airplane taxied behind me. Unfortunately, the L-4 pilot got too close and when I added power with the four engines to pull onto the runway, he became airborne from my propeller blast. Then, as I got on the runway and reduced my power, he crashed onto the taxiway on his nose, ruining the prop and the engine. Parts of his damaged airplane scattered all over the place mixing with the snow and ice that covered the taxiways and nearby open spaces.

The other incident occurred on another cold, winter morning while I was doing the engine checks prior to takeoff. During the runup, I tried to maintain a high RPM to get the engine oil and the superchargers warm enough so that they could be activated, but I couldn't maintain our position on the taxiway's slippery surface. Even with the brakes applied, the big Boeing bomber slid on the ice.

Even though the superchargers were barely warm enough for takeoff, I decided to make a takeoff anyway. I pulled onto the active runway and added power. About the same time, one of the superchargers ran away and I pulled it back. Almost immediately, another supercharger ran away and I pulled that one back. Then, a third one ran away and I shutdown that engine and taxied back to parking.

I was frustrated! I went to Personnel and told them that I thought that I should be stationed someplace where I could be a little more productive. Using my evader status, I asked for reassignment in the southern

Harold Weekley flew North American AT-6 airplanes while attending the Instrument Instructor School at Bryan Army Air Field, Texas. He continued to fly and instruct in this type of pilot trainer at Gunter Field in Montgomery, Alabama. Here, co-author James Zazas flies a restored T-6G over the Moore County Airport in 2004 near his Carthage, North Carolina home.   (James B. Zazas)

United States.

I reviewed the available options and noted instructors were needed to train French students in North American AT-6s at Gunter Field outside of Montgomery, Alabama. I had a very warm feeling for the French because they had been so gracious and helpful to me in the last few months. I told the Assignments Personnel that I was more than happy to go to Alabama and work with the French students. Billie, in turn, stayed in Steubenville, Ohio during this assignment.

Within a week, I was transferred down to Gunter Field to train the French pilots in the AT-6, undoubtedly one of the best trainers ever designed to convert fuel to noise! This plane was renowned for its "growling" as the propeller tips went supersonic at takeoff power. Though I had flown the BT-13 and the BT-15 during my initial Army Air Forces

training, I never had the opportunity fly the AT-6. Consequently, I went through a short aircraft familiarization and training course to get me up-to-speed on the aircraft. With a 600-hp engine mounted on its nose, the AT-6 was a delightful and responsive aircraft to fly.

Shortly after I became AT-6 qualified, some people came through the base's Ready Room and asked if there was anyone in there that would like to go to Bryan Army Airfield at Bryan, Texas, to attend the Instrument Instructor School. Bryan was home to one of the finest instrument schools in the Army Air Forces and anyone who wished to make a career in the military certainly wanted to go through that program.

In fact, while I was training at Lockbourne, a couple of slots became available for crewmembers to go to Bryan. I requested the opportunity to go and, in considering my re-

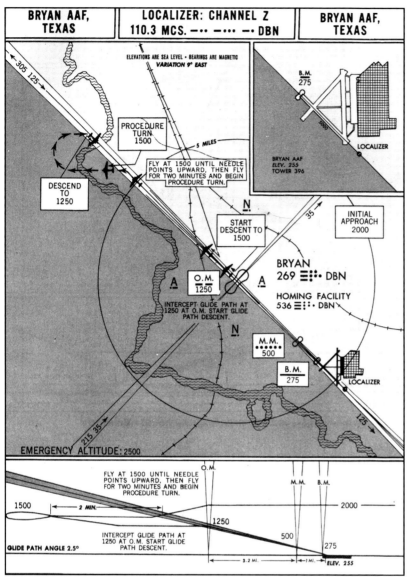

BRYAN AAF, TEXAS — **LOCALIZER: CHANNEL Z 110.3 MCS. —·· —·· ·· —· DBN** — **BRYAN AAF, TEXAS**

ELEVATIONS ARE SEA LEVEL · BEARINGS ARE MAGNETIC
VARIATION 9° EAST

305 125

PROCEDURE TURN 1500

5 MILES

FLY AT 1500 UNTIL NEEDLE POINTS UPWARD, THEN FLY FOR TWO MINUTES AND BEGIN PROCEDURE TURN.

DESCEND TO 1250

START DESCENT TO 1500

35

INITIAL APPROACH 2000

N

B.M. 275

LOCALIZER

BRYAN AAF ELEV. 255 TOWER 396

BRYAN 269 ≡¦·· DBN

HOMING FACILITY 536 ≡¦·· DBN

O.M. 1250

INTERCEPT GLIDE PATH AT 1250 AT O.M. START GLIDE PATH DESCENT.

N

M.M. 500

B.M. 275

LOCALIZER

215 35

125

EMERGENCY ALTITUDE: 2500

FLY AT 1500 UNTIL NEEDLE POINTS UPWARD, THEN FLY FOR TWO MINUTES AND BEGIN PROCEDURE TURN.

O.M.   M.M.   B.M.

1500   2 MIN.   2000

1250

INTERCEPT GLIDE PATH AT 1250 AT O.M. START GLIDE PATH DESCENT.

500

275

GLIDE PATH ANGLE 2.5°   3.2 MI.   1 MI.   ELEV. 255

(USAAF T.O. No. 30-100F-1, 15 January 1945)

quest, I was given an instrument check ride to see if my instrument flying was good enough for me to attend the course at Bryan.

I had planned to go out and do a less than average job of flying instruments in the B-17 as a ploy to attend the instrument school, but try as I could, my instrument flying was good. I guess experience is hard to hide. Certainly, no pilot that I've ever known would like to be considered less than one of the best pilots available. The powers-that-be determined I didn't need the additional training so I did not go to Bryan.

It was ironic that as hard as I tried to get to the Instrument Instructor School while I

was stationed at Lockbourne, my opportunity to attend this prestigious school came from a couple of pilots walking through the Ready Room at Gunter and asking if anybody wanted to go.

Another young officer and myself decided that was the place for us, so we volunteered and off we went to Bryan. I picked up a used Oldsmobile Coupe, a 1937 Olds with a '36 engine in it, a vehicle labeled as a 1936 Oldsmobile. We loaded our gear and drove to Bryan, Texas. The Instrument Instructor School at Bryan was every bit as good as we had heard.

I flew the AT-6 at Bryan Army Air Field. Many years later, lasting well into the 1950s, most of the AT 6 series airplanes were re-manufactured through an IRAN (Inspection and Repair As Necessary) process. When they returned to duty, the AT-6 was identified simply as the T-6.

The AT-6 was an excellent instrument trainer but, ironically, the prevailing weather at Bryan was ideal for visual flying. Those of us attending the school had to chuckle to ourselves at times because here we were, attending an Instrument Instructor School, and the predominant weather was usually very clear and very warm. The only time I lost any "instrument" flight training time was due to inclement weather. It was raining so hard that I couldn't get the engine started.

While attending the Instrument Instructor School at Bryan, I checked out on the ILS (Instrument Landing System) and the GCA (radar/controller-guided Ground Control Approach system). I flew the latter approaches at College Station, Texas, an auxiliary field not far from Bryan. This field was adjacent to Texas A&M University, the home of the Texas Aggies.

I was able to spend some time at College Station. While there, I learned of a fine leather and boot making shop named Horlicks. I went to Horlicks and had a custom pair of brown leather boots designed and made for me. They were very well done, beautifully handcrafted and were shipped to my home in Ohio at a total cost of $23.23. I wore those Jodhpurs for at least ten years.

After completing the course at Bryan, I returned to Gunter Field in Montgomery, Alabama to resume my flight instructor duties.

Driving back to Gunter Field, I worked a little angle to procure additional gasoline. I don't know how many other folks ever did something similar or not, but my little ploy worked well for me. Cigarettes were a rationed item. Though I did not smoke, I still went to the PX to get my normal ration for the week, which I saved.

On the way home from Bryan, Texas to Gunter Field, I was given enough gas rationing stamps to assure I could get to Montgomery. While driving to Gunter Field, I would stop at a service station and see if the owner and I could arrive at some kind of arrangement to trade one pack of cigarettes for one gallon of gasoline. In lieu of using my gas rationing stamps, I would trade some of the packs of cigarettes that I had saved up from my weekly allotments. I worked my way all across the southern tier of the United States like that, from Texas to Alabama.

Upon arriving in Alabama, I found a friendly service station and traded the balance of my cigarettes for gas. In addition, I gave them all of my gas rationing stamps and formed a sort of an account. I maintained a reasonable amount of gasoline available, which allowed me some limited mobility in the area.

Upon returning to Gunter Field, it was quite evident that there was a reduction in the number of French pilots being trained. This reduction was a direct result of the decrease of wartime activities in France and the overall military successes the Allies were enjoying in Europe.

Concurrently, other, more historic changes had taken place. While I was in training at Byran Army Air Field, President Roosevelt passed away from a cerebral hemorrhage at his Warm Springs, Georgia home and President Harry S. Truman took over as Commander In Chief. A stunned nation grieved Roosevelt's death.

Shortly afterwards, on May 9, 1945, the war in Europe ended and V-E Day - Victory in Europe - was declared. Virtually everyone in the United States and most of the world rejoiced this momentous event.

Meanwhile, the powers-that-be at Gunter Field took no chances that a spirited pilot celebrating might cause a potentially embarrassing accident or crash. Though I can't vouch for the rest of the Army Air Forces, at least as far as V-E Day was concerned, I do know that all pilots in the Montgomery area were restricted from flying for the next two days. The general fear was that one of us might be foolish enough to go up in a party mood and, thus, jeopardize his life, the lives of the civilians on the ground, and of course, the equipment he was flying.

Shortly after V-E Day, most of the pilots in our group were given leave. I had not been home in some time, so I drove back to Steubenville.

I had been home for a week or ten days when I received a call from the Army Air Forces personnel office at Gunter Field advising me that I had sufficient points and/or credits and could be released from active duty if I so desired. I wasn't particularly anxious to leave active duty, my military career was going well, but Billie seemed to be thrilled I had the opportunity to come back home and stay full time. I advised Personnel that I would return to Gunter Field to pick up my personal effects and proceed with my out processing.

I was at Gunter Field when I received

A proud Harold Weekley stands in front of his first car, a 1946 Ford Business Coupe, which he bought new for $1336.33.   Harold D. Weekley)

orders to proceed to Camp Atterbury near Columbus, Indiana. At Camp Atterbury, I was given a complete physical and my records were reviewed. I received part of my salary and the medals that I had been awarded but had not received, including the Purple Heart. When all the paperwork and out-processing was completed, I returned to Steubenville.

By this time, information was filtering back to me regarding the status of the rest of my crew. Of course, Ben Clark was back, as I had met him in the free territories in France, so I knew already Ben's condition and post-bailout experiences. After the war, Ben continued his legal schooling and eventually became a federal judge in Pineville, Louisiana. Sadly, he is now deceased.

While he was alive, Ben shared some other amusing information. During his time in France, he became close to the family and apparently, out of the goodness of his heart, he had invited this family to come over to the

United States and visit him any time they were able to get out of France.

As I was told later by Ben, he got a call at work from his wife, Barbara. She asked him to come home if he could possibly break away, which he did. Upon arriving at home, he was met at the front door by the daughter of the family that he stayed with in France, who had really taken him seriously and came to the United States to visit with him. That's all that Ben told me of that situation, so I can't elaborate any further.

I learned later that Ray Delbart, my bombardier, had made a miraculous escape from the burning aircraft. Crewmen in several nearby B-17s reported in the post-mission debrief of seeing only eight parachutes before the *Bronx Bomber II* blew up. They never saw Ray bailout. Likewise, none of my own crew saw Ray bailout either and many believed he perished. Many years later, Joe Skarda asked his friend, "How did you get out?"

Ray's extraordinary bailout and subsequent survival on the ground was quite the saga.

As Ray moved towards the back of the mortally wounded B-17, he had to use the control cables that were routed through the bomb-bay to guide him through as the bomb-bay catwalk was damaged and severely warped. Along the way, he kept getting snagged by jagged metal pieces, which hindered his escape.

Upon reaching the waist gunner position, one of his legs fell through a gaping hole in the aircraft's belly, its jagged metal edges tearing at his flight suit and flesh. His leg was pinned on the outside of the airplane by the violent slipstream rushing past the bomber.

Fighting a rising fear, Ray managed to extricate his leg, struggled to the bomber's rear side hatch and bailed-out. Just as he cleared the *Bronx Bomber II*, Ray saw that the entire airplane was engulfed in fire. In the next instant, he saw the left wing fold up and over the tail, tearing it from the fuselage. Then, in the next briefest of seconds, the

Bronx Bomber II blew up! Pieces flew in all directions with one or more striking Ray in the head and left ankle, knocking him unconsciousness.

When Ray regained consciousness, incredibly under a full canopy, he saw the *Bronx Bomber II*'s severed tail section falling to earth somewhat flat, gently rocking back and forth as it fell. It landed near the spot where he was going to land.

Approaching the ground, Ray could tell by his descent that he was going to land near a haystack and he hoped to land upon it, but this was not to be. Instead, he landed on its side, slid down and was knocked unconscious once again when he hit the ground hard.

His first recollection when he regained consciousness was being carried on a litter by two Frenchmen, both running to get him out of sight. Then, hearing an approaching German mechanized unit, a half-track, the Frenchmen dropped him and ran for their own protection. Ray was captured shortly thereafter. The German sergeant commanding the half-track took great pride showing off his prize catch to all who would listen.

Ray was made to stand at attention, even in his injured state, while being taunted by the German troops. Eventually, he was taken to Paris, Munich and Dachau. At Dachau, he was deprived of food and water, then interrogated before he received any medical attention. Also, he was made to stand at attention at the German officers' mess during each meal, but was not allowed to eat. Ray was housed with a severely beaten American OSS (Office of Special Services) Major, who eventually died from the injuries sustained in these beatings. Ray feared he would meet a similar fate.

During one of his many moves as a prisoner of war, Ray saw firsthand the horrors of war. He witnessed Allied fighters strafing the unmarked German troop trains that carried Allied prisoners. He was stunned beyond words by the utter destruction of Berlin and surrounding areas caused by the relentless Allied bombing campaign. Years later, Ray shared his deeply buried feelings with Joe Skarda and commented that these wrenching sights changed him forever.

Following normal procedure, the Germans interrogated Ray as to his unit, his base and his crew. When Ray refused to provide any information, the interrogator, a Luftwaffe Lieutenant who had gone to school in Boston, Mass., commented in perfect English, "You are just a Second Lieutenant and don't know anything anyway and I don't know why I am fooling with you." He then proceeded to divulge the entire mission information, including a substantial amount of data about the 398th Bomb Group. Ray Delbart was stunned and his morale badly shaken!

The German officer then produced a large loose-leaf notebook that contained all the names of the crew, where they were from and the names of Ray's family, even clippings from his hometown newspapers. Ray was dumbfounded by what this German-American was telling him. Obviously, the Germans had an extensive intelligence gathering system.

Ray was taken to Stalag Luft I near Barth, Germany in Upper Silesia. He was near Peenemunde which we had bombed on two previous occasions. Ray later related that the Germans had an anti-aircraft school near the POW camp.

Looking back on our missions to Peenemunde, I later related, "Most likely, the Germans had their graduate students firing at us on our second mission to Peenemunde."

Ray was a gifted self-taught artist and he put his talents to good use in the camp. He made many pencil and ink drawings, cartoons and pinups showing the very Spartan conditions of his captivity. Unfortunately, none of these drawings were ever published and they remain closely held by his family to this day.

At the end of the war, Ray was airlifted from the camp to a recovery and processing camp called Camp Lucky Strike by aircraft of the 398th Bomb Group. Camp Lucky Strike was a sprawling tent city located in Northern France and was where most former prisoners of war were taken to be given food, proper medical attention and clothing before being returned to England, then to their units or back to the United States.

As an interesting sidelight, all of the POWs at Stalag Luft I were evacuated to Allied facilities during May 1945. The senior ranking officer at Stalag Luft I was Col. H. Zemke, who at the time he was shot down was leading a famed P-47 Fighter Group nicknamed the "Wolfpack."

As a First Lieutenant, Ray was called to active duty for the expanding Korean War and stayed in the Air Force Reserve until he took a medical retirement in 1950. Afterwards, he worked at the Union Carbide Technical Center in South Charleston, West Virginia as an industrial equipment designer. After graduating from Morris Harvey College, he moonlighted designing homes for folks in and around St. Albans and nearby Charleston.

Sadly, Ray died on February 1, 1968 from a heart attack while getting in a car with his wife in St. Albans. The Veterans Administration ruled that the injuries he sustained on his bailout, subsequent malnutrition and stresses related to his captivity contributed to his early and most unfortunate death.

Paul James, my navigator, survived his bailout, but not without some embarrassment.

The day of our bailout was quite warm and the mission was planned to be short, so Paul decided he would not wear the heavy restricting leather sheepskin trousers we normally wore. The rest of the crew followed Paul's lead. I reminded them to readjust their parachute harnesses to compensate for the loose leg straps.

Apparently, Paul failed to heed my advice. On bailout, one of the loose straps looped over his private parts. When the parachute opened, the strap stretched taut and hurt Paul dearly.

Paul opened his chute fairly early, but he nevertheless ended up with about a dozen holes in his parachute during his descent. He hit the ground about six miles south of Dieppe. James landed hard, spraining his left ankle and hurting his left wrist. Almost immediately, a French family picked him up and harbored him in the woods for five days. This French family's patriarch was a kindly gentleman named Paul Grenet, a woodchopper. He had seven children, including four very attractive, teenage daughters.

After Paul's time in the woods, he was moved into a barn near the family's house in Brachy (Seine-Inferieure), then into the family's home shortly thereafter. He stayed there until he was repatriated by Canadian troops on September 1, 1944.

Paul James poses with two of the Paul Grenet's daughters near Brachy, France in late August 1944. The Grenet family aided with Paul James evading enemy forces after his successful bailout from the *Bronx Bomber II* on August 13, 1944. (Harold D. Weekley)

Shortly after Paul returned to England, he visited a local hospital where a friendly and understanding doctor completed the job the parachute had started.

After the war, I lost complete contact with Paul James and had no idea what happened to him, until I returned to France for a special monument dedication in 1999. Since then, we have remained in contact. I learned that he stayed in the United States Air Force Reserve and served in some capacity working with strategic missiles. He retired in the mid-1970s as a Colonel. He and his wife make their home near Detroit.

Though I was never able to directly contact Louis Buchsbaum, our radio operator, I learned he had sustained some of the worst injuries and broke his leg when he landed. Though he was given shelter initially by a French family, they were German collaborators and, so he was turned over to German troops.

With Louis being Jewish, our crew feared for his safety, as we knew how the Germans felt about his people. In fact, Louis feared for his own safety every time we flew a mission. He had heard rumors of the unspeakable atrocities committed against the Jewish people and feared he would meet a similar fate if he was ever shot down and captured.

Most fortunately, Louis was able to hide his religion from his captors and, in time, was made an interpreter due to his ability to speak German fluently. He soon joined six other prisoners of war and made a daring escape. Being imprisoned in Germany, the POWs found it very difficult to evade recapture and had to rely on their own skills to steal food, sleep in barns and travel at night. During their escape attempt, three of the six were caught and their fate remains unknown.

Louis eventually made contact with Allied forces. At the time he was repatriated, he weighed 98 pounds. He returned to the United States, married and had one daughter named Claudia. He prospered in the clothing business in upstate New York. Sadly, he died in 1999.

I found out that Gene Leonard and Joe Fabian ended up together and both were able to evade capture through the good graces of some French families and the French Underground. Over time, I lost complete contact with them.

Bob Stickel, my waist gunner, had his own close brush with death as he escaped the *Bronx Bomber II*. As Bob was exiting the fiercely burning aircraft, his parachute opened inside the airplane. Remembering that a spare chute was nearby, he grabbed it and made a successful bailout.

The fact Bob Stickel had that extra parachute began with a tradition Ven Unger started when he was with my crew. On all training flights and combat mission, the resourceful Ven Unger and Joe Skarda tossed an extra pair of boots, gloves, oxygen mask, oxygen bottle and parachute into an A-3 bag. After Ven was wounded, Joe carried this tradition forward, and his foresight saved Bob Stickel's life.

Bob landed in a grain field near Doudeville, France, about twenty-five miles southeast of Dieppe, where he hid until a French family came to his rescue. During his evasion, several French families in and near the French village of La Crique gave him food and shelter, and kept him from the Germans. He returned to England on September 5, 1944 with another group of evaders.

I lost contact with Bob Stickel after the war. Unfortunately, I learned in 1991 that he had passed away.

After the war, Joe Skarda, my flight engineer and top turret gunner, returned to rice farming in Hazen, Arkansas. He leased his first couple of farms south of town, eventually buying one. He and his younger son, Randy, worked this farm together until Joe retired from farming in the early 1980s. His older son, Gary, pursued aviation as a crop duster/sprayer and developed a successful agricultural application business near Hazen.

During one of our conversations about

Joe Skarda, second from left, poses with the other Allied crewmembers and his French hosts shortly after he was liberated by Canadian forces in early September 1944.   (Harold D. Weekley)

Joe Skarda's escape and evasion photograph. This photograph was taken in England and became an important part of the Skarda's escape kit.   (Harold D. Weekley)

our bailout, I learned that Joe had landed hard near Vestonville and bruised his pelvis and tailbone. The French Marquis got to him before the Germans, gave him medical attention and took him to the home of Mr. and Mrs. Robert Beaudoin of La Fontelye, Bourdainville par Yerville (Seine Inferieure). He was one of four Allied airmen, including a Royal Canadian Air Force sergeant and a Royal Australian Air Force officer, harbored

by this courageous family. The Beaudin's secured the services of a friendly doctor who treated Joe's minor injury.

During his Intelligence debriefing in England, Joe wrote in his Escape & Evasion Report, "The Beaudoin's help was the finest kind, and they refused to accept money, though I had 20,000 Francs which I was anxious to give them. They treated me like a son."

During his tenure with this gracious French family, Joe learned through some manner that I was safe, but that the Germans had captured Ray Delbart and Louis Buchsbaum.

Joe remained very active in community affairs and formed a little league baseball team. After his death in late December 1992, the local little league tournament was named the Joe W. Skarda Tournament in his honor.

Joe Skarda remained one of my best friends throughout my life and I continued to see and talk to Joe frequently until his death.

Some time later, I learned that Charlie "Pop" Stombaugh recovered from his wounds, but with a permanent disability, and became a security officer near Washington, D.C., eventually retiring as a senior member of its force. After retirement, Charlie lived in New Market, Maryland where he made and repaired cane rocking chairs and enjoyed a brisk business until his eyesight failed. He sold antiques as a side business.

Charlie Stombaugh became very active in veterans' affairs after the war and joined the Disabled American Veterans (AMVETS), eventually becoming the chapter's commander. He later joined Post 2 of AMVETS and volunteered countless hours for this organization as well as for the local Boy Scouts of America.

Charles "Pop" Stombaugh died on May 11, 1989 at 79 years of age. Friends and family members remembered Charlie as a quiet and caring worker who sought neither publicity nor fanfare.

Gene Leonard, my left waist gunner, returned to Emporia, Kansas where he attended college for one year, but never finished the requirements for a degree. Shortly afterwards, he moved to Kansas City and attended a heating and air conditioning school. He returned to Emporia and stayed in this business for thirty-six years, twenty of which he and a partner owned and operated a prosperous business. He retired in late 1984 and died from cancer in May 1987.

Shortly after our last mission together, I learned later Ven "Bob" Unger had a difficult time trying to explain to others why he wasn't wearing his flak jacket at the time he was wounded. Upon hearing of Ven's story, Chaplain James Ziegler, the Base Chaplain, thought Ven deserved to receive the well known morale booster, the bright red "Tough Shit" ticket. The chaplain gave this flashy "T S" card to any crewmember wounded in combat. Ven's card was signed by James Duvall, the 398th's Protestant Chaplain.

Ven recovered with a 30% disability and was grounded from further flight duties. He returned to Nuthampstead seven months later where he was assigned to work in the personal equipment section. There, he issued the flight equipment to aircrews departing on missions. Ven Unger remained with the 398th at Nuthampstead until the end of the war, whereupon he returned to the United States aboard an LST troop ship.

After the war, Ven went to Stockton, California, where he managed a movie theater. A year later, he moved to Winnemucca, Nevada where he managed the Sage Theatre for thirty-five years and did some cattle ranching. He married Iola in 1949 and has two sons. Ven and I still keep in contact.

I wasn't fortunate enough to see all our crew when they got back from England, but I did try to maintain contact with as many as possible. Though I lost contact with Joe Fabian, I am still in touch with Paul James, Ven Unger and the Skarda, Buchsbaum, Leonard, Stickel, Clark and Stombaugh families. It has been a real thrill for Billie and me to grow up with these fellows and to know their children and their

"TS" TICKET

ISSUED BY

Chaplain James N. Zeigler

J. T. Duvall

Intended to be a morale booster for a wounded crewmember, the "TS" or "Tough Shit" ticket was bright red and was usually issued by the Base Chaplain. Ven Unger's "TS" ticket was issued and punched by Chaplain James N. Zeigler, Nuthampstead's Base Chaplain and was signed on the back by James Duvall, the 398th Bomb Group's Protestant Chaplain. Unger received this card as a result of the wounds he received on July 6, 1944.   (Ven B. Unger)

grandchildren. Unger now has five grand-children and five great-grandchildren.

Additional facts about my old bomb group and my fateful mission of August 13, 1944 came to light. I learned that of the thirty-six bombers from the 398th that took-off from Nuthampstead on August 13th, my airplane was the only one lost. Thirty-six bombers went out and thirty-four returned to England. One airplane landed at another base in England and a second made an emergency landing on the European Continent.

The latter B-17, flown by Capt. Willis Frazier, took a hit on the propeller dome of his number three engine, which resulted in a runaway propeller and a rapidly disintegrating engine. He was able to land in France on a P-47 fighter strip, an American-controlled airfield near Bayeux, Normandy.

The crew abandoned this airplane and, in turn, found another B-17 at the airfield, whereupon they repaired it and flew it back to England several days later. In the interim, many of Frazier's crew took the opportunity to explore the local territory and battle-ground on the Allied side of the line with an Infantry Captain in his jeep. The wonderful sights mixed with the incredible devastation left all of them dumbfounded.

"The desolation and devastation in those towns…it was unbelievable!" Frazier later re-called. Relating a humorous moment, he added, "Capt. Griffin, my pilot on this mission, tried to assemble a captured German tank as a souvenir, but couldn't find any way to get it back across the English Channel."

All but two of my crew, including myself, were wounded in action and received the Purple Heart. Considering the sobering per-centages of bomber crewmembers killed in action, we were very lucky as a whole.

Life moved quickly for me after my combat flying days. The next five years found me building a general aviation airport. Concurrently, I was involved heavily in training students enrolled in the GI Bill. I owned and operated a trucking company hauling steel to automotive manufacturers in the Detroit area. Later, I became involved in operating heavy equipment in the coal fields and in general construction.

While all of these pursuits were well paying and had a reasonably good future, they did not provide me with the challenges and future that were available in the military.

In the early 1950s, the Korean War was building-up and flight instructors were needed. I rejoined the service as a civilian flight instructor in 1952 and went to the 3300th Training Squadron in Greenville, Mississippi, which was a military contract school, using rebuilt North American AT-6s as the primary trainer.

I was transferred to Graham Air Base at Marianna, Florida on January 21, 1953 and remained there until July 17, 1959. I was the first pilot on this base and my initial assign-ment as Housing Officer responsible for pro-viding housing for the large number of instructor pilots coming to this base. Shortly thereafter, I was the President of Standardiza-tion Board and Supervisor of the Pilot In-structor School (PIS). In the former role, I lectured each and every incoming class of Aviation Cadets and Student Officers on their duties and responsibilities and included an in-depth discussion of all the aerial maneu-vers, flight checks and evaluation standards expected of them. In the latter role, I was re-sponsible for the training of all newly as-signed instructor pilots and the upgrading all pilot instructors, some 135 total, in the newly acquired aircraft, which included the Piper PA-18, the North American T-6G, the Beech T-34, the North American T-28, and the Cessna T-37. The T-37 was the only jet trainer we had on the base at the time. Since I was in charge of the PIS, my call sign was "Pistol One."

During my assignment as President of the Standardization Board, the Air Force evalu-ated our training program and we always re-ceived the highest rating, which showed less than one error per mission.

In addition, I wore several other hats

during this time. I was responsible for all the training of Foreign Pilot Instructor trainees with most coming from the Republic of Vietnam. I was also responsible for the schooling of all Training School Base Commanders, other than the ones assigned to Graham Air Base.

Moreover, I was an advisor to the Air Force Academy during its first year at Lowry Air Force Base, Colorado and assisted Brigadier General "Moose" Stillman in establishing some of the Academy's flight training requirements and assisted in the physical layout of the students' quarters. I trained the first class of Academy Cadets in the Cessna T-37 and continued as director of this program until its completion.

Overall, I trained jet fighter pilots for the Korean War and, later, jet instructor fighter pilots for the Vietnam War.

One hat I wore did not protect me from a "battle scar" I still wear to this day. I gave flying checkrides to many Aviation Cadets and their spirited approach to their flying created many memorable moments. One such moment involved a Cadet Richard Ervin and a Piper PA-18 in October 1953.

Cadet Ervin was a good student and he flew very well. When he came to me for his Contact Flying Phase Checkride, his flying instructor told him that I preferred an aggressive recovery from spins. True to his instructor's comments, Cadet Ervin made a very aggressive spin recovery in the PA-18. I was not prepared for it and hit my head on the Cub's tubular structure above my seat. The hit was hard enough to cut my head. I thought twice about passing Cadet Ervin on his checkride, and had a rather frank discussion with him after the flight regarding spin recoveries, but the crease in my head remains.

That, however, is not the end of this little story. In 1982, while I was attending the EAA Convention in Oshkosh, Wisconsin, one of the T-28 warbird pilots approached me and bellowed, "Weekley, you son-of-a-bitch!"

Surprised, I looked at him with a puzzled

Lt. Col. Harold Weekley's official U.S. Air Force photograph taken in 1967 when he served as the Project Officer on the development of the AC-119G *Shadow* gunship. (Harold D. Weekley)

look and asked, "Do I know you?"

"Yes! You busted me on my very first check ride in the Air Force!"

"When was that?" I asked.

The gentleman standing in front of me started to tell me his story when it all flashed back in an instant. "Oh," I responded. "That was in October of 1953 when you put this crease in my head."

We both had a hearty laugh remembering this mutual experience and since that meeting, Dick Ervin and his wife, Joan, have become two of my dearest and closest friends. Sadly, Dick passed away in 2004. Until his death, Dick was a respected member of the warbird community, and has restored several T-28 airplanes and has served as president of the EAA Warbirds of America.

The most memorable event during my time at Marianna was the birth of our second son, Harold Gary Weekley. He was born on

March 21, 1955. Billie and I couldn't be happier with a new son joining us and William, our older son.

At the conclusion of the Marianna assignment, my family and I moved to Mobile, Alabama. We spent nine years in Mobile where I was assigned originally as an Air Reserve Technician to fly North American F-86s as an instructor. The aircraft assigned to Mobile changed before I arrived and the unit became a transport squadron, which had a group of sixteen Fairchild C-119 "Boxcars." Regardless, my new assignment proved very rewarding and I commanded several emergency rescue operations during this period, and advanced quickly in rank.

My most rewarding position was serving as Project Officer on the development of the Fairchild AC-119G gun ship called *Shadow.* Loaded with three sideways firing 7.62mm, multiple-barrel machine guns (later upgraded to 20mm machine guns), this formi-dable aerial weapon was used successfully in Vietnam and was the forerunner to even more formidable airborne gunships such as the Lockheed AC-130 *Specter.*

I was particularly proud that William, my oldest son, served under my command as a Technical Sergeant, were he did a fine job. Though both he and Gary, my younger son, had aspirations to fly, vision difficulties kept William from flying in the service. Gary, on the other hand, attended the Citadel in South Carolina and wanted to fly fighters, but no pilot training vacancies were available at the time, so he returned to civilian life and raised a fine family.

At the conclusion of this tour, which was in 1968, I moved to Atlanta to become a Federal Aviation Administration inspector in both Air Carrier and General Aviation while maintaining my Air Force Reserve status. At the conclusion of my tenure with the FAA in early 1982, I went to work with an air travel

The Fairchild AC-119G *Shadow* spearheaded a second a second generation of aerial gunships between the AC-47 *Spooky* and the AC-130 *Spectre.* Derived from the USAF's twin-boom "Dollar Nineteen" transport, this stable gunship proved to be a very potent foe in battle with its four GAU-2B/A 7.62mm machine guns. The *Shadow* began operational sorties in South Vietnam in January 1969 with the USAF's 71st Special Operations Squadron. A jet-boosted version, the AC-119K, was called the *Stinger.* (Harold D. Weekley)

club, the Atlanta Skylarks, and worked for them for another three years as a pilot and Director of Flight Operations.

In July 1979, I had the chance to fly a B-17 for the first time since World War II. At the time, this former bomber was owned by Dr. Bill Harrison and several other associates from Tulsa, Oklahoma. I was genuinely thrilled by this opportunity!

Shortly thereafter, I joined Bill and his team as a volunteer pilot, a position I maintained for twenty-three years. Today, this gleaming bomber is the Experimental Aircraft Association's flagship, the *Aluminum Overcast*. Resplendent in 398th Bomb Group markings, this wonderfully restored airplane undertakes a nationwide tour every year and makes dozens of stops before enthralled veterans and visitors alike.

A very happy Hal Weekley flying the Experimental Aircraft Association's B-17G *Aluminum Overcast* in May 1988. (Harold D. Weekley)

"What through youth gave love and roses,
Age still leaves us friends and wine."
Thomas Moore (1779–1852), *National Airs [1815],*
Spring and Autumn, st., I

CHAPTER 13

A Welcome Return

On a beautiful, warm, summer Sunday afternoon on August 13, 1944, a small boy of seven was standing in his father's farm field in the Normandy region of Northern France watching American B-17 bombers fly back to their air base in England. They had just dropped their bombs on military targets in occupied France.

As he watched the spectacle above him, he noticed one of the bombers began to fly in a wide circle trailing a long stream of smoke. After about two circles, the bomber blew up scattering pieces over a wide area. Parts of the aircraft landed not too far from the boy's location, which was near a small village of Lammerville. The bomber a young

Harold and Billie Weekley pose in front of the polished granite monument erected in Lammerville, France honoring Hal's crew and a British Halifax bomber crew, both shot down very near this town in 1944.

(Harold D. Weekley)

Bernard Noel observed that fateful day was the *Bronx Bomber II*.

Fifty-five years later, Bernard Noel would become this village's mayor. In his official capacity, Noel knew he could honor the men who contributed so much to free his countrymen from German control in World War II.

This chapter describes a grateful French people who take great pride remembering and honoring the sacrifices other people from many nations made to return their freedom. This heartfelt narrative ties together a remarkable story that began fifty-five years earlier.

It begins in early 1998 when Randy Skarda received a phone call from France. A Laurent Viton was asking about his father,

237

Joe Skarda, my wartime flight engineer. Monsieur Viton indicated he was interested in the aircrew of the *Bronx Bomber II* and wanted as much information as was available. He told Randy that he was working on the histories of the aircraft that were shot down in his area of France during World War II.

Randy advised Monsieur Viton to contact me. In turn, I provided as much information as I had available, including dates, crew names, addresses and any other appropriate specifics. Initially, our communications were by phone and letter until I got a computer. Thereafter, we corresponded almost exclusively by e-mail, which proved to be very fast and efficient.

In August 1998, I learned the French people of Normandy had erected a monument to honor our crew along with the crew of a British Halifax that had crashed nearby a couple months earlier. The monument was dedicated on September 27, 1998, in the French hamlet of Flamanville, near Lammerville.

Billie and I were invited to attend, but we had to decline due to the short notice and commitments I had flying the B-17G *Aluminum Overcast* on tour for the Experimental Aircraft Association based in Oshkosh, Wisconsin. I conveyed my profound appreciation and honor and expressed a desire to visit in the near future to thank the people for their commemoration.

After considerable planning, Billie and I decided that we would fly to Paris in 1999, departing on May 18th and arriving on May 19th. Monsieur Viton agreed to meet us and he became our contact for our trip to France.

Monsieur Laurent Viton is a postal worker in the village of Goderville, which is some distance from the crash site. He is married to a beautiful young lady named Anne-Laure and they have two young children and live in a quaint cottage in the country.

Laurent drove for two hours to arrive at the Paris airport one hour ahead of our scheduled arrival. However, the airline really fouled up and we arrived ten hours late. This meant our friend had to wait at least eleven hours before we got there. Understandably, we were profoundly grateful for his patience.

After we packed his small car with our luggage and ourselves, Laurent drove us through Paris on our way northward to where we would be spending our nights in France, a Bed and Breakfast that was near the actual crash site.

Billie and I always thought the traffic jams in Atlanta were quite extensive, that is until we saw the ones in Paris. Cars were everywhere! I think everyone in town was trying to get out of town and everyone out of town was trying to get back in.

Our ride to the B&B took us two hours, plenty of time to get acquainted and to get accustomed to hearing the French language. Though our friend had studied English in school and did reasonably well, Billie and I often had a difficult time understanding him.

The natural beauty of the French countryside left us stunned. It was pristine!

We arrived late in the evening and were greeted by Monsieur and Madame Ropars, owners of the Bed and Breakfast. We learned that Madame Ropars was the daughter of Bernard Noel, the gentleman who orchestrated the reunion. The Ropars treated us to a fine dinner, something we did not expect from a Bed and Breakfast.

The Ropars' home was very beautiful. Built originally as a horse barn, they had restored it as a lovely home and Bed and Breakfast in 1992. Located a short distance from a country road, their home overlooked a beautifully landscaped garden beyond which lay a small lake. Beyond the lake there was a pasture occupied by several fine horses. Their most picturesque home and its location were hard to beat. I soon learned that Monsieur Ropars was a landscaper and this lovely home and its surrounding was the result of his hard work.

Two swans guarded the area near the lake and they had no love for me. Several

On their return to France in 1999, Hal and Billie Weekley stand in front of the house where Hal was housed for the first couple days of his escape and evasion in France. The small, white square on the roof at the far right marks the small room where Hal stayed during this brief period.   (Harold D. Weekley)

thoughts came to mind as to what to do to these ill-tempered swans, but I refrained from acting as I was only a guest.

After we had a good night's rest and enjoyed a great breakfast the next morning, a lady in her early fifties arrived wearing work clothes and fairly large rubber boots. She came to the B& B to greet us. She spoke beautiful English and, as a result, she and Billie got on famously and chatted for some time. Up to this point in our journey, Billie had a difficult time with the French language and our hosts' attempts at English.

We learned that our newest friend, Mary, had lived in the United States with her family for several years. When she returned to France, she became a veterinarian and raised race horses. She stayed only for a short time, but told Billie she would visit frequently and would be available whenever needed.

Shortly after Mary's departure, Mayor Noel, accompanied by another gentleman, drove into the driveway. He was Monsieur Bernard Langlois, a cattle dealer who frequently bought cattle from the mayor and ran a slaughterhouse. This man was the answer to my prayers. While Laurent Viton spoke good English, this man spoke excellent English. He had been an exchange student and had spent quite some time in the U.S. Needless-to-say, he and I became very close.

Laurent soon arrived and joined the four of us for lunch. When Madame Ropars started to serve, I had to convey my surprise that I thought we were there for Bed and Breakfast, but were served a delicious dinner last night, and now were being served lunch. We had not expected that.

With our newest friend interpreting, the mayor waved his hand and explained that we should not give it another thought. We were his guests. Then he commented that Billie and I were to be sure to attend dinner the next night in Lammerville's new community center. I asked the mayor what was the occasion of the dinner. Both the mayor and our friend smiled and replied, "You are the occasion."

After lunch, we took two cars to Brametot, the village nearest where I landed after I bailed-out of my B-17 in 1944. Monsieur Langlois, the Deputy Mayor of Brametot, lived nearby and was anxious to show our party the house I had hidden in during my first stay in Brametot. In 1944, it was the home of Mayor Dubuc and his wife, now both deceased. Today, another family occupies the residence.

The current occupants allowed us to visit the gardens and for me to take Billie upstairs to the attic room where I spent my first two nights in France. My mind filled with memories. I felt I was stepping back in time.

Before we left Brametot, the mayor invited us to his home for refreshments which included wine, cheese and cookies. If it hadn't been for the cookies, Billie wouldn't have had anything to eat as she did not favor the wine and cheese.

During our visit with the mayor in Brametot, an elderly lady came from across the street to see us and presented me with a photo. It was one of the escape photos I had on me when I arrived in 1944. On the back of the photo, written in pencil, was a simple, "Parachutist 1944." Her mother, father and sister were the first people I met when I walked into Brametot so many years earlier.

After my parachute jump and landing, I had little time to enjoy the idyllic scenery that surrounded me, as a successful escape was my primary concern. Now, I could enjoy the inherent beauty of the French countryside.

That night, we all had dinner at Monsieur Langlois' home. Later in the evening, Mayor Noel returned us to his daughter's home. Billie and I had quite a day! So much for Thursday.

Friday began with Laurent arriving before Billie and I had awakened. Thank goodness we slept well because the day before had been an emotional and event-filled day, especially for me. We needed our rest to recharge our bodies for another exciting day, and to get accustomed to the six-hour time zone change from Atlanta to France.

After breakfast, the three of us went to the town of Yvetot and Monsieur Durmaney's farm where I had spent some of my earlier time in France evading capture. We learned Monsieur Durmaney and his wife had passed away and that his children had left the area.

We walked the grounds briefly before heading into town. I shared with Billie and Laurent stories of what I saw and did on the farm to pass the time. I described, also, the night I had to leave the farmhouse quickly before I had anything to eat and, instead, ate only raw beans I found in the fields for supper.

I described my transfer into town to stay with Monsieur Rault, an ex-fighter pilot from World War II and the area's district attorney. I learned Monsieur Fern Raoult had become a high level judge in War Crimes after the war. He was very well-respected by his community and was given the #1 Ham Radio license. He, too, passed away well before my return to France.

I told Billie and Laurent how I departed on a bicycle to the town of Caudbec on the Seine River in an effort to contact Allied Forces.

When I came to the same spot fifty-five years later, it certainly did not look the same.

A beautiful bridge stands today at the location where I crossed the river in 1944.

After reminiscing some more, we all returned to the Bed and Breakfast so Billie could get some rest before getting ready for the evening's activities. Meanwhile, Laurent and I went into Bacqueville to visit a florist where I purchased a wreath to place at the monument prior to the evening's ceremony. We went to the monument where I placed the wreath and took some photographs. Afterwards, Laurent took me to the B&B where Billie and I got ready for the evening ceremony and dinner.

The ceremonies began late in the afternoon. Everyone met at the new community house before departing for the monument.

The monument is shared with the men from a Halifax bomber that was shot down on April 19, 1944. Five of the crew were Royal Air Force; three of which were captured and two were killed. Two other crewmen, both Royal Canadian Air Force, also lost their lives. The wreckage of the Halifax bomber landed approximately 200 yards from the monument's present day location. Likewise, the largest portion of my B-17's wreckage landed approximately fifty yards from where the Halifax landed. Therein lies the reason for the location of the monument.

Mayor Noel gave a fine speech, which lasted ten minutes followed by Monsieur Andre Gross. Though Mayor Noel initiated the reunion and collected the funds to build the monument, it was Monsieur Gross who really initiated everything. Though he was 91 years old at the time of ceremony, everybody present listened intently to all he had to say. Most fortunately, Billie and I each had our own interpreter, so we didn't miss a word of what was said by either gentleman.

Monsieur Andre Gross was known as the "Leopard" during the war. He was very active in saving Allied crewmen from capture. His record was impressive! He saved 17 airmen, including four from my own crew - Skarda, Leonard, Fabian and Stickel. Then as

now, he commands tremendous respect and influence in the area.

People from many miles around came to the ceremony that afternoon. The weather required a light jacket but fortunately, there was no rain even though there was a low overcast. When the ceremony began, the clouds parted and a bright sun shined through. When the ceremony concluded, the clouds returned and the sun was not seen again during the rest of our stay in France.

I often reflect upon the events of that afternoon and believe that some higher authority approved of what we were doing, honoring some fine men and real heroes!

Lammerville's community center is on a small knoll overlooking the village. On this evening, it was a beehive of activity. All the lights were on, French and American flags flew outside and a large crowd gathered, all awaiting our arrival. They had to wait as we were the last folks to leave the monument. It appeared as if everyone had a camera and all wanted to take photographs at the same time.

When we arrived at the community center, we were met immediately by Monsieur Daniel Renault, the Commissioner General of the area. He presented us with a gift, a very large book that contained copies of paintings of the most prominent French artists with a considerable text describing each painting. This book was the largest I have ever seen! It was fifteen inches high, twelve inches wide and two inches thick. It had to weigh at least ten pounds!

We were then introduced to a Monsieur J. Noel Lefebevre. He had been in contact with the Air Force's Historical Research Center in Maxwell AFB, Alabama, and had researched my aircraft, my crew and the circumstances regarding our shootdown on August 13, 1944. He presented Billie and me with a folder containing his correspondence with the Air Force, photographs of various pieces of our aircraft, a photograph of the target we hit, copies of the Missing Air Crew Report, a crew list with all the serial numbers, and a

Hal and Billie Weekley's participated in many activities during their visit to France in 1999, all honoring Hal, his crew and the many courageous French citizens who helped Hal and most of his crewmembers evade capture from enemy forces. (Harold D. Weekley)

parts list of primary items on the aircraft. Finally, he gave us a detailed drawing showing the route of flight that fateful day.

In addition, he had prepared a fairly large display, which contained parts of our aircraft, including the fluxgate compass, some ammunition and the A-3 bag that once belonged to Louis Buchsbaum, our radio operator. The bag looked as good as new! While I stood there totally awed and practically speechless, Monsieur Lefebevre presented me three small, broken pieces from my airplane.

And more surprises came. The war veterans of Lammerville produce a calendar each year that shows a significant wartime or war-related photograph. In 1998, the photograph displayed my aircrew. In 1999, it showed the dedication of the monument. In 2000, it showed one of the many dozens of photographs they took of Billie and me posing with these veterans at the community center. We have copies of each calendar.

We walked into the new community center and were awestruck. The center's interior was just as beautiful. It could seat at least 100 people and was well organized and beautifully decorated. Each place setting contained a small display of American and French flags as well as multicolored menus, all showing a photograph of my crew and a color photograph of the B-17 I now fly for the EAA. I think I autographed every menu in the center that night and I loved every minute of it.

The dinner, like everything else, was outstanding! The main course consisted of several seafood items, no doubt caught from the English Channel or the Atlantic Ocean, each not that far away. When it came time for dessert, the lights were turned off and a cart was rolled out, the flaming dessert creating a most impressive display.

During the course of the evening, we were introduced to two ladies who, along with their father, had harbored Paul James, my navigator, from the Germans until the Allies liberated the area. Through them, I learned James was still living and got his address. We have maintained close contact since then.

Many other special events occurred that memorable evening, all taking me back to events that occurred fifty-five years earlier. During the dinner, a Madame Sylviane Basire came forward and presented us a beautifully gold-framed certificate, signed by General Eisenhower, given to her father acknowledging his help in aiding an American airman escape capture. Her father was Pierre Basire, the same gentleman who accompanied me on my bicycle ride from Mayor Dubuc's home in Brametot to the farm in nearby Yvetot on August 15, 1944. After the war, Monsieur Basire sent me several letters, all of which I saved.

Sylviane told me that her father had died a year earlier and that he had spoken of me often. I then told her of the letters I had received from her father after my escape. She asked if I would be good enough to make copies and send them to her. I replied I would be more than happy to do so.

The activities continued well into the evening. Whether it was due to the day's activities or still trying to adjust to the time change from the U.S. to France, Billie and I became exhausted. Around 11 o'clock in the evening, we excused ourselves whereupon the mayor returned us to his daughter's home, the Bed and Breakfast.

The following day, after breakfast, our good friend and driver, Monsieur Laurent Viton, came to take us to his home to meet his family. Their cottage was exactly what one would expect to see in the French countryside. We stayed all morning and had lunch with them. Their two children, in addition to a family friend, named Henri, and his lady friend, who joined us for lunch.

Henri brought a strawberry pie for Madame Viton and a bouquet of roses for Billie, which was very thoughtful and deeply appreciated. Later, Billie presented the roses to Madame Ropars in appreciation for her hospitality.

That night, we shared dinner with another family. Since the gentleman of the house spoke English and could translate for us, everyone had a most enjoyable time.

The following day, Monsieur Viton took us to Paris, but only after Mayor Bernard Noel had presented us with a folder containing enlarged photographs of my downed airplane and the bridge at Le Manior. All of these items are sealed in plastic, which should last for a very long time.

Looking back, I always feel particularly proud that the monument was erected fifty-five years after our shootdown and the Halifax crash, as opposed to a monument erected immediately after the war. The engraving on the base of the monument says it all, "Lest We Forget," in both French and English. I won't forget either!

When I returned to the United States, I sent Madame Sylviane Basire three of the original letters I received from her father after my escape. In reply, I received the following letter dated July 16, 1999:

> Dear Mr. and Mrs. Weekley
> There is no word to explain my emotion when receiving my father's letters - as well as no word strong enough to say thank you to you. I hope they will stay in the family for long because we must always think of that period.
> After talking with my family, I found out that my brother PATRICE was born in 1947 had something you gave my father and we are very happy to give it back to you and we hope you will be happy as much as when I received my father's letters.
> Hoping to see you and your wife again and many thanks for the letters.
> Yours sincerely,
> Sylviane

What Sylviane returned to me was my wartime USAAF identification bracelet. I gave this bracelet to Pierre as a gesture of thanks for what he was doing to help me escape. I understand he wore it for many years.

To receive this bracelet after so many years was an unbelievable, indescribable emotional experience for me. I took the bracelet to a jeweler and had some of the worn links and catch replaced. On August 13, 1999, fifty-five years to the day I was shot down, I put the bracelet back on my wrist.

Barely days later, I received the following letter dated July 10, 1999:

Dear Sir,

We have learned by the local newspaper your visit and the commemoration made in your honor by the villages of Lammerville and Brametot.

My father and my uncle - Mr. Dubuc, Mayor of Brametot - both passed away now, would have been very happy to see you again. My mother - sister of Mr. Dubuc - now 97, is still witness of this part of your life, as well as my brother and myself.

In fact, your parachute has been taken off by my father and two young boys, and hidden by my parents in a hay barn. The tissue has been used later on to make blouses and shirts, and the strings, braided, used to make a cradle which received in 1955 my father's first grandson! I am very glad to enclose here - with some pieces, which are still left, as precious memories of the past emotional days.

I now live in the center of France, near the Futurscope. If you foresee another trip to France, we would be very happy to meet you.

My mother and I wish you all the best, with our best wishes.

This letter was signed by Michael Auvray.

There is no way Billie or I can express our gratitude to the French people and all of the gracious hospitality they showered upon us. The many gifts, especially the bracelet and the pieces of my parachute, leave us filled with warm and most wonderful memories.

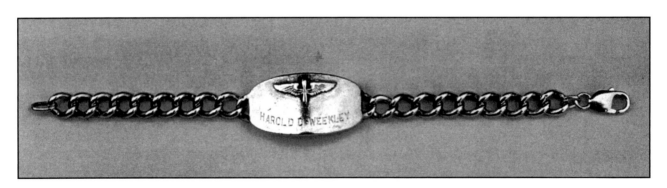

This photograph shows the USAAF bracelet Hal Weekley gave to Pierre Basire in appreciation for the efforts Pierre and his family made to protect Hal from capture in mid-August 1944. Sylviane Basire, Pierre's daughter, returned this same bracelet to a stunned Hal Weekley fifty-five years later!

(James B. Zazas)

"Of a good beginning cometh a good end."
John Heywood (c.1497–c.1580),
Proverbs [1546], pt. I, ch. 2

EPILOGUE

Remembrances: The Aluminum Overcast and the End of an Era

The Boeing B-17 Flying Fortress that eventually became the *Aluminum Overcast*, the Experimental Aircraft Association's (EAA) flagship, was built by the Lockheed Aircraft Company's Vega Division at Burbank, California. It was delivered to the USAAF on May 17 1945 as B-17G-105-VE, AAF 44-85740, whereupon it was assigned to the Air Transport Command and sent to the Modification Center in Louisville, Kentucky.

The Second World War was almost over and there was little need for this Flying Fortress in combat. Thus, this virtually new aircraft was flown to a storage depot near Syracuse, New York on June 24, 1945 to join at least 228 new and 33 war-weary B-17s already in storage. At the war's end, this particu-

Until his retirement flying the B-17 in 2001, Col. Harold D. Weekley, USAF (Ret) was the last "First Pilot" rated World War II B-17 pilot still flying a Boeing B-17 as Pilot-in-Command into the 21st Century! *(Harold D. Weekley)*

lar bomber was declared surplus on October 12, 1945 and on November 7th, it was flown to Altus, Oklahoma by a ferry crew, where buyers could inspect former military aircraft and offer bids for purchase through the War Assets Administration's Aircraft Disposal Division. There were at least twenty-seven such sites around the country after the end of the war.

This particular airplane remained in storage at Altus for eighteen months, having accumulated only ferry time, before being purchased by the Metal Products Company of Amarillo, Texas for $750.00 and was issued the civilian registration of NC5017N. The company did not take delivery of the B-17 and, instead, let

245

it sit for a month before selling it to Universal Aviation Company of Tulsa, Oklahoma, a high altitude aerial mapping company, for $1500. Universal Aviation registered the aircraft with the Federal Aviation Administration as NL5017N. (See Endnotes, Epilogue, Number 1)

Universal Aviation sold this Flying Fortress to Charles T. Winters of Miami, Florida on August 2, 1947. Winters held this airplane briefly before he sold it to Joe A. Lopez, a native of Puerto Rico and founder of the Vero Beach Export and Import Company in Vero Beach, Florida for $3500. A ferry crew flew the airplane from Oklahoma to Florida, whereupon Thomas W. Cobb, Lopez's personal pilot and instructor, flew it to Hendricks Field in Sebring, Florida, to be configured to haul cattle and other livestock. The Eighth Air Depot, a post-war modification and service center located on Hendricks Field, accomplished this work.

According to Robin Mitchell, a B-17 historian, the "cargo conversions included the addition of a 3/8" thick Micarta cargo floor extending from the rear bomb-bay bulkhead to the tail, removal of the radio room bulkhead and the addition of tie-down straps at a cost of some $11,000.00. The total cost of this new bomber-turned-cargo plane, equipped with Tokyo tanks for extended range, now stood at $14,500.00. The total operational time on the airplane stood at just 37 hours!"

Lopez began his Flying Fortress beef-hauling operations from his cattle ranch west of Melbourne, Florida in December 1947 when Cobb hauled 16,000 pounds of dressed beef from the slaughter house in Malabar, Florida and flew either to San Juan or Ponce, Puerto Rico. On the return flight, the cargo consisted of a load of green, undressed cowhides. During its tenure with Joe Lopez, Jr., NL5017N performed extremely well and needed only routine maintenance. The livestock hauling operations ceased in early 1949 with a last shipment of baby chickens transported from Miami to San Juan.

(See Endnotes, Epilogue, Number 2)

On June 27, the Aero Service Corporation of Philadelphia, Pennsylvania purchased the Flying Fortress for $28,000. Aero Service Corp. converted the airplane into a high-altitude camera platform and survey aircraft and operated it from their facility at the Mercer County Airport in West Trenton, New Jersey, one of three B-17s the company used for the role. The company believed the B-17 to be an excellent camera platform due to its range, reliability, inflight stability and high altitude capability.

Following conversions during June and July of 1949, NL5017N was flown to Saudi Arabia where it flew in the photo-mapping role until May 1953. In June 1953, the airplane returned to the Mercer County Airport for extensive overhaul and maintenance. Over the next five weeks, the wings were removed, the control surfaces were replaced and four new wing tanks were installed. The airplane was completely rewired and a new Bendix Pioneer PB-10 auto-pilot was installed. In addition, the landing gear, instruments and hydraulic systems were either overhauled or rebuilt. An improved oxygen system and updated radios were installed, including a SHORAN (SHOrt RAnge Navigation) system and a magnetometer, the latter to determine underground metallic deposits using magnetic force measurements. Finally, NL5017N received four new engines and propellers. In September 1953, this better-than-new bomber returned to active-foreign service in the Middle East.

In 1954, this airplane completed aerial mapping, SHORAN and magnetometer surveys of Libya before flying to Thailand to undertake similar duties for the next few months. The airplane returned to Libya briefly before embarking on duties in Italy and, later, Egypt.

During the next three years, this very active B-17 flew extensively in Libya, Saudi Arabia and Lebanon. While in Saudi Arabia, it flew forty-four consecutive days during

NL5017N as it appeared in January 23, 1970 at Dothan, Alabama, when owned and operated by Hugh Wheelless, Sr. as a govenrment contracted sprayer.

(Ben Marion)

September and October 1956 photo-mapping more than 150,000 square miles. In 1957, adding to an already impressive record, the airplane photo-mapped 64,000 square miles before being sent to Lebanon for a month-long overhaul and maintenance.

Before it was sold, this B-17 flew almost one million air miles, much of it above 30,000 feet, during its career with Aero Service Corporation. The airplane photo-mapped most of Saudi Arabia as well as Iran, Egypt, Jordan, Libya, Thailand, Vietnam, Cambodia and Laos.

Citing economic cutbacks, Aero Service Corporation sold this well-used B-17 on August 10, 1962 to Chris D. Stoltfus and Associates of Coatsville, Pennsylvania. Stoltfus planned to use the airplane as an aerial sprayer but, instead, it sat inactive at the Coatsville Airport. When the airport expanded and became the Chester County Airport, Stolzfus moved the airplane to his private, 3,000-foot airstrip across the road. Stolzfus flew his B-17 without any formal instruction and later commented that the airplane flew better than a Douglas DC-3.

Hugh Wheelless, Sr. of Dothan, Alabama purchased the B-17 on December 16, 1966.

Wheelless operated Dothan Rental and Leasing Company, Inc. (later the Dothan Aviation Corporation) and he added this B-17 to his fleet of B-17's to be modified as sprayers in the government's fire ant eradication program taking place in the Southern United States. By 1969, this aircraft had accumulated over 6,000 hours, which was more than any military B-17 had ever flown.

The B-17 proved to be a reliable and hard-working sprayer and aerial fire bomber for many operators around the country during the 1970s and early 1980s. However, the harsh reality economics and the need for airplanes forced many operators to seek larger capacity aircraft. Thus, several civilian-owned B-17s came up for sale including the Wheelless' B-17.

Wheelless' spraying contracts concluded at the end of 1976 and Dothan Aviation Corporation went out of business in 1978. Wheelless placed this B-17 for sale.

On February 20, 1978, Dr. William E. Harrison, Jr. of Tulsa, Oklahoma purchased the tired bomber for $75,000.00 and began a lengthy ongoing restoration to return this historic bomber, now called the *Aluminum Overcast,* to its former glory, one that contin-

The future *Aluminum Overcast* makes its first flight from Dothan, Alabama to Griffin, Georgia in December 1978, where it underwent an extensive restoration effort.

(Dr. William E. Harrison)

NL5017N receives a new nose in Dothan, Alabama in 1978.

(Dr. William E. Harrison)

ues to this day. He and five friends formed a group known as "B-17s Around the World, Inc." Their plan was to take this B-17 around the world with an emphasis on landing at places where B-17's had served with the military.

After some maintenance work, the plane was flown from Dothan, Alabama to the Griffin, Georgia airport, where the initial restoration efforts were undertaken. It was there I met Tony Gurerro, a maintenance supervisor for United Airlines at the Atlanta-Hartsfield International Airport. He volunteered many long hours and did an outstanding job of bringing the aircraft up to acceptable civilian safety standards. Within a few months, the *Aluminum Overcast* was ready to fly with its new owners and purpose.

Concurrently, I became associated with Dr. Harrison during this period. I was an Air Carrier Operations Inspector with the FAA in the Atlanta office and soon learned Bill was interested in getting a type rating on the B-17. I entertained thoughts of getting my rating, also. On February 9, 1979, I made my first B-17 flight in almost 34 years and received my B-17 type rating. Bill received his as well. Very shortly after this flight, Bill invited me to join his elite group of pilots. I did not know it at the time, but I would fly N5017N for the next 23 years as pilot!

Flying a B-17 once more was special for me. My participation was my effort to keep alive the memory of all the young men who had crewed and flown in the war. I wanted to try to meet the families, talk to them and express what a wonderful job they and their loved ones had done in the war and how much I appreciated flying and fighting alongside them. If they had lost a loved one in combat, I shared their grief and told them how much I felt their loss.

Since that check ride, Bill and I have enjoyed a close friendship that has grown stronger through the years and one that has contributed immeasurably to both my family and myself, and for which I shall be forever grateful. Bill's recognition of this historic aircraft's significant role in aviation history and his untiring efforts to maintain it as a flying museum have been of great service to hundreds of thousands of Americans both young and old alike. His efforts will long be remembered!

vention and Fly-in at Oshkosh, Wisconsin, it was obvious *Aluminum Overcast*'s future was in doubt unless changes were made flying and presenting the airplane.

Bill and his partners were very active pilots in the growing, restored warbird movement and they worked closely with the EAA staff and membership. They believed their B-17 would receive the recognition it deserved if it was a part of the EAA. Thus, Bill and his partners decided to donate the *Aluminum Overcast* to the EAA Aviation

Dedicated pilots and mechanics keep the *Aluminum Overcast* flying. Here, several of the early volunteers pose for a group photograph. Left to right are George Enhorning, Max Hoffman, Bill Harrison, Hal Weekley, Paul Poberezny, Tony Gurerro and Tom Camp. (Dr. William E. Harrison)

The obstacles that confronted Bill and his "B-17s Around the World" partners were many. Plans to fly this airplane on a world tour were cancelled when diplomatic problems in certain countries and the shortage of aviation fuel in others proved insurmountable. Although we had a great time visiting air shows over the following years, primarily in the southeast, but also the 1979 EAA Con-

Foundation. Bill and his partners made this donation with the provision the restoration program would continue as long as parts availability and money allowed, and the airplane would be maintained in an airworthy condition.

Immediately prior to this acceptance, the *Aluminum Overcast* was at a maintenance facility at the airport near Ft. Collins, Colorado

and at the completion of the required annual inspection, Bill Harrison, George Enhorning and I flew the airplane to Burlington, Wisconsin, the EAA's large maintenance facility at that time. On March 31, 1981, the EAA Aviation Foundation acquired the *Aluminum Overcast*.

Upon our arrival, we were met by Paul Poberezny, the founder and then President of the EAA. Paul told me he wanted me to fly the aircraft as long as I desired. Later in the year, I gave Paul his type-rating ride and he

shows across the United States, mostly on a limited and by invitation only basis. This Flying Fortress was always the highlight of every EAA Fly-in and Convention at this organization's home field in Oshkosh, Wisconsin. Unfortunately, the harsh Wisconsin weather affected the bomber's exterior appearance.

In August 1988, the *Aluminum Overcast* participated in one of its last significant public displays prior to another major restoration effort when she joined five other flying B-17s

The *Aluminum Overcast* is always met with enthusiastic crowds wherever it is flown and displayed. Here, the crew poses in front of the airplane at a tour stop in the early 1980s. Left to right, front row are Tom Camp, Max Hoffman and Bill Harrison. Left to right, back row are Scott Smith, George Enhorning, Hal Weekley, Tony Gurerro and Al Shirkley. (Dr. William E. Harrison)

did an outstanding job, which was no surprise since he is one of the most accomplished and respected pilots in the aviation community. Paul and I became good friends. In fact, the many personal friendships I gained through my association with this aircraft have been one of its premier benefits.

During its early tenure with the EAA, the *Aluminum Overcast* visited numerous air

in a dazzling formation display before 100,000 spectators at Geneseo, New York.

In October 1988, the EAA Aviation Foundation's Board of Directors voted to retire the *Aluminum Overcast* from active service. They cited many reasons for this difficult decision, including operational and insurance costs, parts availability, and the desire to restore and maintain this airplane in an original

The *Aluminum Overcast* makes a stop at the Fond du Lac County Airport in Fond du Lac, Wisconsin after the 1979 EAA Fly-in and Convention. Note the small homebuilt aircraft positioned underneath the fuselage.

(Dr. William E. Harrison)

wartime configuration. Moreover, the *Aluminum Overcast* was slated to be the main attraction in the EAA Air Museum's Eagle Hanger that was nearing completion.

Obviously, many of us were disappointed by this decision, but we understood fully the reasons to "park" the *Aluminum Overcast*. Meanwhile, a search was soon started to find a suitable wartime paint scheme for this airplane.

In 1989, while I was attending an Eighth Air Force Reunion in Pittsburgh, I was reunited with my old WWII bomber group, the 398th. Members of my former bomb group decided they would like to participate in the restoration of their favorite aircraft, the B-17. The 398th Bomb Group had flown 195 missions into enemy territory and these individuals had great respect for the strength of the B-17. The group lobbied the EAA Aviation Foundation to have the *Aluminum Overcast* painted in a 398th color scheme.

The EAA and Bill Harrison agreed to have the aircraft repainted with the group's markings and they had six possible paint schemes to choose from. Each of the four squadrons wanted it painted with their identifying numbers. Many within the 398th wanted the plane painted in honor of the Group Com-

mander, Col. Frank Hunter. The 398th Bomb Group Memorial Association's Board of Directors presented six possible paint scheme options, each with its own unique historical perspective. In the end, the EAA and Dr. Harrison selected the markings of the airplane in which I was shot down in France. Obviously, I was very honored and pleased by their selection.

In the spring of 1989, the *Aluminum Overcast* was flown to the Hayes Aircraft facility near Dothan Alabama, to be repainted. The 398th donated approximately $25,000 to paint this airplane in our group's colors. The work was done in March of 2000 at a much greater cost and with much better results. Many people have asked me why we did not leave the exterior in its original, bare aluminum finish. When I asked them when they would be available to assist in the polishing the metal, they immediately understood our decision to paint the airplane.

On its return from Alabama to Wisconsin in 1989, the *Aluminum Overcast* was placed in the EAA Eagle Hanger where it resided for the next five years, rarely flying at all and then only on special occasions. During this time, a dedicated group of volunteers undertook the airplane's interior restoration. The

A very proud Hal Weekley stands near his beloved B-17G while an admiring crowd wait to tour this historic aircraft.   (Harold D. Weekley)

bomb bay was restored to original configuration with original bomb racks. The radio room was restored to original specifications with original radios, as was the cockpit and the bombardier and navigator stations. A complete ball turret was installed, as was a tail turret assembly.

In addition, the aircraft's structure was inspected thoroughly and parts were replaced as necessary. All engines, propellers, electrical components and hydraulic systems were overhauled or replaced. All work was done to maintain this Flying Fortress in an airworthy status. In sum, the *Aluminum Overcast*, resplendent in its new paint scheme, was ready to fly when called upon to do so.

In 1993, the EAA Aviation Foundation Board of Directors voted to undertake a concentrated and well-organized tour of selected areas of the US during 1994. Moreover, with the concurrence of the Federal Aviation Administration, we were permitted to carry passengers on revenue flights to demonstrate the capabilities of the aircraft. This activity was Dr. Bill Harrison's original idea when he and his group donated the aircraft to the EAA and they never lost sight of this goal. Now, our fondest hopes were realized. Soon, the public would be able to see and fly on the *Aluminum Overcast*. As a result, this B-17 became a major fundraiser for the EAA and a focal point for its many volunteers.

In the fall of 1993, Greg Anderson, Executive Vice-President of the EAA, called me and asked if the 398th could donate approximately $12,000 to combat the internal corrosion on the *Aluminum Overcast* in preparation for its forthcoming national tour. When I presented this request to the president and Board of Directors of the 398th Bomb Group, the president presented me with the task of heading up the fund drive. I wrote a letter to the entire group membership advising them of the opportunity to preserve the very aircraft the EAA had dedicated to our bomb group and the positive publicity our bomb group would receive on future tours. As an added advantage, we could locate former bomb group members during the tour and, concurrently, gain the pleasure of renewed friendships.

I requested that all donations be sent to Ralph Hall, our bomb group's treasurer. In turn, I asked Ralph to forward the donation results to me. Additionally, I sent a letter of acknowledgement and thanks to each donor and included a B-17 crewmember patch for each person that had donated at least $17.00. As a result of our efforts, the 398th's membership collected $21,000, all of which was donated to the EAA for the restoration of the *Aluminum Overcast*.

Summary of the *Aluminum Overcast*'s **Flight Activities: 1979 through 1993**

The *Aluminum Overcast*'s limited flight activities during this period averaged approximately sixty flights per year, conducted in twenty-eight states including the District of Columbia and several provinces of Canada. I had the opportunity of flying with fourteen different pilots. All of these flights were performed in conjunction with air shows on an invitational basis and with one exception no passengers were carried on any flight.

On May 17, 1987 Dr. Harrison and I participated in a seven ship B-17 formation, the largest since World War II, flying from West Memphis, Arkansas for the rededication of the famous *Memphis Belle*, the first B-17 to complete twenty-five combat missions over wartime Europe. The *Memphis Belle* had been restored, for the second time, after having lost a battle with local vandals. She was placed in a new, enclosed facility on Mud Island and the event was cause for great celebration and our flyby. We flew the right wing on the lead aircraft; a B-17G called *Chuckie*, AAF 44-8543, flown by Dr. Wm. Hospers of Fort Worth, Texas. Dr. Hospers did an outstanding job leading the formation. His bomb load that day was rose petals, most which fell into the laps of the attending VIP's, including Col. Robert Morgan who was the original wartime pilot of the *Memphis Belle*.

At the 1987 EAA Convention and Fly-in at Oshkosh, Wisconsin, Bill Harrison and I flew

Resplendent in the markings of the 398th Bomb Group, 601st Bomb Squadron, the EAA's *Aluminum Overcast* as it appears today.

(Experimental Aircraft Association)

Bill Harrison, flying a North American P-51D Mustang, joins up on the *Aluminum Overcast*'s left wing during a flight over New York City. Both aircraft were returning from a tour in Canada in 1979. Hal Weekley was flying the B-17 when this photograph was taken.

(Dr. William E. Harrison)

Aluminum Overcast in a five-ship "missing man" formation to honor all service members who had paid the ultimate sacrifice to defend their country. We were selected to make the "pull" and create the missing space in this formation. This bomber formation, consisting of three B-25s, the *Aluminum Overcast* and one privately-owned Lockheed P2V-7 Neptune, was the first of its kind ever held at this venue and was received very well. Co-author Jim Zazas piloted the Neptune in the far right wing position and undoubtedly had the best view of the *Aluminum Overcast* making its upward climb over the crowd.

Aluminum Overcast saw very little further flying in 1987, but returned to limited tour flying in 1988. It returned to West Memphis, Arkansas in 1988 for the West Memphis Air Show. The late Capt. Sam Huntington accompanied me on this flight. Sam was a United Airlines captain at the time and had been one the original owners of the bomber when it was purchased by Universal Aviation in 1947. On this flight, we made two ILS approaches to Blytheville Air Force Base, Arkansas, where I had graduated from USAAF Advanced Flying Training 45 years earlier! Everyone at the air show was thrilled to see us.

On September 20, 1992, the 398th Bomb Group held its annual reunion in Nashville, Tennessee and I pre-positioned the *Aluminum Overcast* at the old Stewart Air Force Base near Smyrna, Tennessee, not far from Nashville. This was the first time 398th Bomb Group members were able to see the *Aluminum Overcast* in their unit's colors. Additionally, we flew ten members, five people on each of two flights, for a nominal donation.

The primary reason for the limited activity during period from 1989 to 1994 was that the aircraft spent a considerable amount of time in the EAA Museum at Oshkosh, which was not in keeping with Dr. Bill Harrison's original plan to use the aircraft as a flying museum. Fortunately, this was to change in 1994.

Heritage Tour: 1994

The tour success of the *Aluminum Overcast* began when Dr. Bill Harrison convinced the EAA Aviation Foundation Board of Directors that the aircraft could be better utilized as a flying museum and fundraiser when properly coordinated with the many EAA chapters across the country. The board weighed

Dr. Harrison's arguments and agreed there was a great opportunity to raise the funds necessary to keep the *Aluminum Overcast* flying. Most importantly, these flight operations would be self-sustaining and would require little or no financial commitment from the EAA itself. The EAA and Bill Harrison recognized the value of good publicity and planned to give names to each tour year starting with the "Heritage Tour" in 1999.

At the start of the year, the Federal Aviation Administration issued a Letter of Exemption for two B-17 operators, including the EAA, exempting certain portions of the Federal Aviation Regulations. This much-sought letter allowed an "experimental-exhibition" or "limited category" registered aircraft, such as the EAA's B-17, to carry passengers on a "flight experience mission" for a nominal charge. This exemption allowed seven passengers and a crew of three, and was very specific in the crewmember training and maintenance requirements. Dr. Bill Harrison and I made the first flight under this exemption on March 19th to the Mt. Comfort Airport, a very nice airfield on the far eastside of Indianapolis, Indiana. We carried a doctor and his entire family as our passengers.

One of the many joys flying the EAA B-17 was the opportunity to fly with some truly talented individuals. One such flight was with Capt. Connie Bowlin, a Delta Airlines Boeing 767 pilot. Connie was the second female to attain an FAA type rating in the B-17,

This photo of Hal Weekley and Sam Huntington in front of the *Aluminum Overcast* was taken at Oshkosh, Wisconsin on May 3, 1988. Sam gave Hal four landings and an hour and fifteen minutes ¡of dual instruction, then put Hal up for a type rating, which he passed the next day while having an electrical emergency. Isn't life fun? Sam Huntington was a significant part of the EAA B-17 pilot cadre. He died in 1990 and he is deeply missed by all who knew him. (Harold D. Weekley)

Bill Harrison and Hal Weekley pose with the Honorable David Hinson, FAA Administrator, at the 1994 EAA Fly-in and Convention in front of the *Aluminum Overcast*. The Administrator made a flight with Harrison and Weekley in this aircraft during the Convention.

(Experimental Aircraft Association)

and she is a very gracious and lovely lady, besides being a very talented and accomplished aviator. It was a genuine pleasure to fly with her. We made our flight from Peachtree-DeKalb Airport, north of Atlanta, to Cartersville, Georgia.

On May 18th, EAA pilot Larry New and I took the aircraft to the airport near Collegedale, Tennessee. Unfortunately, we were unable to conduct any flights due to the airport's narrow runway width and the excessive crosswinds; however, we had an excellent turnout for the ground tours.

While conducting the ground tours, we had the good fortune of meeting Mr. & Mrs. O.D. McKee, founder of the Mckee Baking Company in Collegedale and the originator of the Little Debbie cakes and snacks. He kindly took our crew on a tour of his baking facility and offices. We were quite amazed at the quantity of cakes and snacks produced each day and the overall quality of the baking operation. Upon leaving, Mr. McKee presented us with a number of cases of their products, which were enough for the crew to feast on for several weeks. In fact, there were enough extra cases that I was able to donate a case to each of my two grandchildren's classrooms for their pleasure.

Dr. Harrison and I took the *Aluminum*

Overcast from Collegedale to Gallatin, Tennessee a few days later, where we were met by an American color guard and the Mayor of the city who presented us with the key to the city. At the conclusion of the festivities we were invited to beautiful luncheon buffet held inside the hangar owned by Reba McIntyre, a very popular country-western singer. The hangar floor was spotless! Unfortunately, Mrs. McIntyre was not able to attend due to business commitments, but she sent her good wishes along with two chefs and three assistants to insure we had a meal to remember.

I left the tour during the summer months to be home with my family, but rejoined my team at the annual EAA Convention in Oshkosh, Wisconsin. Two months later, Dr. Harrison and I flew the *Aluminum Overcast* to Tucson, Arizona, arriving on September 21st to attend the 398th Bomb Group's annual reunion. We made three flights on each of the next two days before departing for Tulsa, Oklahoma to participate in the Bartlesville Fly-in and Air Show.

During 1994, I had the opportunity to fly with five different pilots at twenty-nine locations in thirteen states. The EAA's new approach to displaying the *Aluminum Overcast* proved wildly successful. Moreover, the passengers we carried were permitted to fly from the left seat, handle the controls and have their photos taken in that position. Then, as now, we never had a passenger depart the aircraft that didn't have a smile on their face.

Victory Tour: 1995

The Victory Tour began for me on May 5, 1995 in Kansas City, Kansas at a large air show, where I was interviewed for the CBS Evening News. During the following three months, we traveled through Tennessee, Georgia, New York and Ohio. In Farmingdale, New York, on Long Island, I reunited with Jim Brostman, a former flying student of mine in Weirton, West Virginia in 1946. Jim had made aviation his career and was quite successful, which made me very proud.

I left Long Island and flew to the Beaver County Airport west of Pittsburgh, Pennsylvania. Our stop lasted only a few hours. Several years earlier, this airfield proved disastrous for another B-17, the *909* (AAF 44-83575) owned by the Collings Foundation of Stow, Massachusetts, when it was damaged seriously in a landing accident. It has since been repaired and flies actively.

Flying to Youngstown, Ohio, I enjoyed a very successful tour stop where I was met by my only sister, Maxine, and her husband, George, a World War II Navy veteran.

The next stop on the Victory Tour was at the EAA Convention at Oshkosh, Wisconsin in late July. This fly-in was as great as ever and EAA had several air show surprises planned for the attending crowds. As 1995 was the 50th anniversary of the end of World War II, the EAA planned to make this celebration one to remember. The EAA invited my family and I to attend the entire fly-in. Everyone but Loretta, my older son's wife, was able to attend.

To capture this special family occasion, *Life* magazine sent an editor and a photographer to do an eight-page feature on our two grandchildren. My entire family and the EAA

spent a great amount of time working with the *Life* magazine folks, including taking the children on two flights in the B-17. The magazine staff was thrilled to work with my grandchildren, my family and the EAA. However, recent and very tragic events half a continent away spoiled our fun.

When the interviews and the photograph sessions were completed, the magazine's senior editors felt it was a bad time to publish the story because Brandi, our granddaughter, looked too much like a young girl who was killed in a light plane accident a short time earlier. We learned this young lady was making a flight in a small single-engine aircraft with her father and a flight instructor in an attempt to break a record for the youngest pilot to fly cross-country in the shortest time and her exploits were covered daily by the media. Tragically, the trio crashed shortly after taking off in a thunderstorm and all three perished. The aviation community was stunned by this unfortunate accident.

We learned later that this accident was preventable, but the damage had been done. Public opinion swayed against having youngsters flying airplanes, even going so far as having Congress intervene and pass some unneeded regulatory legislation. Brandi's photograph was never published in *Life*, and the story was cancelled.

On Friday night of the EAA Convention, David Hartman, a well-known and respected television personality, hosted a program in the Theater in the Woods called "Tribute to Valor." Mr. Hartman introduced nine decorated aviators from World War II and described some of their accomplishments.

In alphabetical order, they were as follows:

1. Col. Andy "Bud" Anderson, USAF (Ret.), a triple ace and test pilot;

2. Don Downie, C-46 Hump pilot and author;

3. Brigadier General Joe Foss, USMC (Ret.), Marine Ace with twenty-six kills, twenty-three of which he shot down in

ten days, two-term Governor of South Dakota and awarded the Medal Of Honor;

4. Brigadier General "Tex" Hill, USAF (Ret.), of the American Volunteer Group (better known as the Flying Tigers) with twelve kills;

5. Col. Travis Hoover, USAF (Ret.), pilot of the second crew flying off the USS Hornet after Lt. Col. James Doolittle on the raid to Japan;

6. Major General Charles Sweeny, USAF (Ret.), the only pilot to fly on both missions dropping atomic bombs on Japan. He piloted the plane that dropped the bomb on Nagasaki;

7. Commander Alex Vachu, USN (Ret.), Navy pilot who shot down six Japanese aircraft in eight minutes and shot down a career total of nineteen airplanes;

8. Brigadier General Charles "Chuck" Yeager, USAF (Ret.), fighter pilot and ace, and the first pilot to break the sound barrier.

9. And last but not least, me.

It was an honor for me to meet David Hartman and some of the most distinguished wartime pilots in the world. I never believed I would enjoy the same stage with all of these renowned individuals. I shall never forget the experience. A short time later, I was amazed when Col. Travis Hoover asked for my autograph.

Other Oshkosh events kept me very busy and the most notable was the EAA's very popular warbird air show. On July 29th, Dr. Bill Harrison and I flew in the longest warbird air show we had ever flown together where we spent almost two hours in the air. This show had been two years in the planning and involved 172 aircraft. Dr. Harrison was in command of the whole formation and he occupied the left seat while I flew from the right seat.

We flew the lead airplane in this show, the venerable *Aluminum Overcast*, with approximately sixty aircraft flying immediately behind us as two other similar sized warbird

formations converged towards us at different altitudes. In order for the crowd to appreciate fully this part of the warbird air show, proper timing was imperative and essential as all 172 aircraft were choreographed to cross a specific mark on the ground at the same time!

We approached the crowd on an east-to-west direction at 1,700 feet above the ground. Our flight path took us directly over nearby Lake Winnebago as we headed towards our briefed mark. Another group of about sixty restored World War II airplanes approached from the southeast at 1,200 feet. A third group of about sixty restored warbirds approached from the northeast at 2,200 feet. On the ground, Dave Schlingman, the EAA Warbirds of America air boss, coordinated our every move and Walt Troyer, the EAA Warbirds of America narrator, described our every move to an enthralled crowd.

As busy as we were, Bill and I were awestruck by the sight of so many airplanes converging towards one spot on the ground, but we had absolutely no fear of any mishap in this meticulously planned aerial event. Everyone involved in this show was professional and all performed their flight and ground duties exactly as briefed. Their hard work and dedicated efforts paid tremendous dividends that afternoon, both in good will and proper recognition of our fallen wartime comrades.

For the many thousands of spectators who looked up towards a beautiful Wisconsin blue sky, they witnessed an aerial event that was totally unique, if not incredibly wonderful: all airplanes arrived over the show center at virtually the same time while a solo bugler played "Taps."

The crowd was awestruck and fell silent. Only the muffled, throaty roar from several hundred warbird engines could be heard. This portion of the warbird show was a very emotional experience for everyone that day. Several people taping the show later told me they could not continue because they were crying too hard to operate their cameras.

At the pilots' debriefing held later that afternoon, the smiles on everybody's faces said it all: the show was a success.

Dr. Harrison and I made our next flight together when we picked up the *Aluminum Overcast* at Altus, Oklahoma on September 28th to ferry it to Midland, Texas for the annual three day Confederate Air Show. Unfortunately, we arrived to a somber mood; the CAF's B-26 had crashed only a few hours earlier killing all five on board. This plane was on its second flight after years of restoration.

Shortly after we arrived, a young man of approximately 50 years old - when you are 74, almost everyone in the aviation community seems to be young - advised us he would be on our only revenue flight the following day. Furthermore, he wanted to assist us with any preparation for that flight. We saw no problem with his request as we can always use a few extra hands to assist us in various preflight duties, mostly rotating the propellers prior to engine start. He arrived promptly the next day in time to provide us the muscle we needed and accompanied us on our flight.

We were flying our first year under the new FAA Letter of Exemption and we were allowed to let the passengers fly the aircraft from the left seat. This young man was the last of the passengers to occupy the left seat during this flight. Dr. Harrison vacated his seat soon after take off and I was in control of the airplane from the right seat. When it came time for our young volunteer to get into the left seat, I questioned him, as I did everyone, about his connection with the B-17. His story left us stunned.

His father was a B-17 bombardier and had entered combat prior to his birth. On one of his father's missions, his aircraft was shot down with all the crew bailing out. His father and a few of the others landed in a German SS training camp. To demonstrate how tough these feared German soldiers were, they murdered all the aircrew. Our guest said he had never known his dad and his dad had never seen him. He just wanted to fly in a B-17 to see what his father was flying when he lost his life so as to feel a little closer to him.

Bill Harrison and I were deeply touched. Those of us on the tour like to think we can handle the many heartfelt stories we hear along the way, but I am sure not all of us are as emotionally tough as we think we are.

Throughout our organized tours, we began to notice varying numbers of ladies that observed the *Aluminum Overcast* from a respectful distance. We soon learned that many of them were widows of bomber crewmembers who had perished during war or had passed away after their return. These gracious ladies had heard about the B-17 all their lives and most of them had never seen one up close. When they heard one was to be in the local area, they had to see the object of so much conversation and adulation. There were many occasions when another EAA crewmember or I would escort one or more or these ladies to the aircraft and show them the positions their husbands occupied. There were several instances when the individual we escorted never had the chance to marry her loved one before he was killed in the war. These experiences were very emotional for all of us. Always gracious, all of these wonderful women expressed their gratitude for our meager efforts.

On October 22nd, while flying with Bob Davis at an air show at Daniel Field near Augusta, Georgia, I had the honor of having Col. Robert Morgan, the aircraft commander of the Memphis Belle, fly in the left seat on a particularly memorable flight. He beamed with joy as he deftly manipulated the *Aluminum Overcast*'s flight controls and throttles. His flying skills were smooth and flawless, and he flew the airplane as if he had stepped from it only yesterday.

Reviewing 1995, I had the good fortune to be able to fly with seven different pilots at fifteen locations in twelve states for a total of sixty-three flights. All my flying was enjoyable, memorable and rewarding.

Aluminum Overcast pilots Bill Harrison, Hal Weekley and Larry New enjoy a few moments together during a tour stop in Lebanon, Tennessee during the 1996 tour. Hal Weekley is shown here wearing his leather A-2 jacket resplendent with a 601st Bomb Squadron patch.

(Dr. William E. Harrison)

Coming Home Tour: 1996

My participation with the 1996 tour year began on March 8th at Smyrna, Tennessee. I joined Danny Bowlin to move the *Aluminum Overcast* to the Millington Naval Air Station at Memphis. Danny, now retired, was a Northwest Airlines captain flying Boeing 747's to Europe. He is also Connie Bowlin's brother-in-law. When I arrived, Tennessee was enduring its coldest weather since in the 1880's. We had to be in Memphis in a few hours and the cold weather made starting engines a challenging proposition. Even though the B-17 had been in a somewhat heated hanger during the night, we still had a terrible time starting the engines. As soon as we got one started, another would quit. After several aborted attempts and lots of individual head scratching, we got all four engines started, running smoothly and warmed to proper operating temperatures. Anyone involved with radial engines know they have "personality" and this day, the engines on the *Aluminum Overcast* showed they had lots of "personality."

While we flew above a frozen Tennessee landscape towards NAS Millington, I was interviewed by a local Memphis television station reporter. Later, several people who saw the interview said they could see my breath. It was so cold in the airplane that Danny had to get out of his seat a couple times and stomp his feet on the flight deck to get the circulation restarted before he could feel his feet again. We arrived safely, but chilled to the bone. We were supposed to be met by the Lt. Governor, but other commitments kept him from appearing.

We stayed in Memphis only a couple days before flying to Muscle Shoals, Alabama. The cold weather sapped my strength completely and I was so sick at this stop that I couldn't even leave my room for meals. I had to leave the tour shortly afterwards to return home where Billie nursed me back to health.

I rejoined the B-17 tour in May with Don Taylor, another accomplished EAA B-17 pilot. During a stop in Ft. Wayne, Indiana, a production crew from the Discovery Channel's "Wings" television program interviewed Don and me. The concept of the program was to determine the best bomber in the history of aerial warfare. The B-17 took top honors.

On a visit to the Barnum Festival, at Bridgeport, Connecticut, a family approached me and said they had some photos that had been taken by one of the family member's brother, who had been a waist gunner on a B-17 operating out of England with the Eighth Air Force. They wanted to know if I was interested in looking at them. I told them I would be delighted to do so.

I was glad I looked at these photographs because I saw my wartime B-17, the *Bronx Bomber II,* at the top of one of the 8 X 10, black and white photographs. I had absolutely no doubt about this photograph's identification as I recognized my group and squadron markings, and the nose of the aircraft was painted black back to the windshield. As far as I know, no other wartime B-17 carried these markings. I think the gentleman was as surprised as I was by the discovery and he promised to send me a copy of the photo but, unfortunately, I never received it.

A few years later, I did receive a copy of another incredible photograph, but from a different source. Purportedly, Clark Gable of Hollywood fame had taken this photograph when he flew with various B-17 groups as an Army Air Forces combat photographer, but I learned later this was not accurate, as Gable flew in combat year earlier than I had.

During the course of the Coming Home Tour, I flew with eight different pilots at sixteen locations in ten states. I made a total of forty-nine flights in 1996 in the EAA B-17.

Honor Tour: 1997

I began my participation with the EAA Honor Tour on April 4, 1997 at an airport near Aurora, Illinois. The EAA chapter at this location has a fine facility, including a hanger and offices, with a very active membership. They were very pleased to host the *Aluminum Overcast*. This stop was particularly gratifying for me, as there were several 398th Bomb Group veterans who lived in the local area. All were good enough to come visit us at the aircraft. I always enjoy the opportunity to visit with old comrades.

Additionally, this chapter was very active in the EAA Young Eagles Program. The Young Eagles Program was initiated in 1993 with the goal to take one million youngsters, between the ages of eight and eighteen, on a free airplane ride before December 2003, the one-hundredth anniversary of powered-flight. This lofty goal was achieved in mid-2003.

As of this writing, more than 1,300,000 kids have enjoyed a free airplane flight in this worthy program. EAA chapters, pilots and other interested individuals continue to volunteer their airplanes and their time to make the EAA Young Eagles a wonderful flying opportunity for today's youth.

During our visit in Aurora, I had an unusual in-flight experience. A young man approached us in the cockpit and asked us to fly over his family farm. I told him we could oblige his wishes as long as we were not in violation of any airspace or FAA regulation. About the time we turned to return to the Aurora Airport to land, this same young fellow approached us once more and said, "Colonel I know I should have asked you for permission before I did it, but my father was a ball turret gunner on a B-17 during the war and he just recently passed away. His body was cremated in accordance with his wishes and when we passed over our farm, I poured his ashes out through the crack that surrounds the ball turret. I hope you don't mind."

I was surprised by his comments, but there was no point in discussing the point after the fact. I am glad he did it before he asked me, as I understand each state has their own laws about the disposal of human remains.

A couple years later, I was speaking to a group of adult B-17 enthusiasts at the EAA Air Academy Lodge adjacent the EAA AirVenture Museum in Oshkosh. I related this story, whereupon one of the attendees commented that he had done the same thing while we were flying on an orientation flight out of Pellston, Michigan. I was somewhat stunned and have no idea if these were just isolated instances.

In May, I joined Capt. Al Malecha and spent four wonderful days at the airport near

Winchester, Virginia in the Shenandoah Valley. This was the first time the *Aluminum Overcast* had been there. We received a fine reception and made a lot of local B-17 flights. Without a doubt, the Shenandoah Valley is one of the most beautiful areas we have ever flown over in the B-17.

In addition, I had the pleasure of seeing Wally Blackwell, the president of the 398th Bomb Group Memorial Association. Wally had been in my squadron in England and flew my replacement aircraft after my crew was shot down. We had a lot to talk about that afternoon.

On July 30th, I flew the *Aluminum Overcast* into Oshkosh for the annual EAA Convention. Much to my surprise, Dr. Bill Harrison was waiting for me with a Cable News Network (CNN) crew and we did a flight and an interview for their live program. Obviously, I was thrilled and honored by this opportunity.

I left the tour for a couple months before returning on September 9th. This day proved to be interesting and unforgettable, and involved a flight I shall always remember, even

though I had no knowledge of the circumstances during the flight. We stayed in Cheboygan, Michigan, but flew the *Aluminum Overcast* from the nearby Pellston Airport, as it was the only airport in the area capable of handling an aircraft the weight and size of a B-17.

Sometime that afternoon, after we completed our one and only flight for the day, a lady approached us and identified herself as the secretary of the superintendent of Fort Mackinaw, which was near the Mackinac Island Resort in northern Michigan. She told us that the superintendent had asked her to locate us and relate the following incident. The superintendent's father had been a member of the Eighth Air Force during World War II and he had passed away only recently. He was being lowered into his grave at the burial site inside the fort when we passed over in the *Aluminum Overcast*, as if in final tribute to one of its own. The superintendent wanted to convey his appreciation for our timely flight.

In retrospect, the timing of our flight over the fort was purely coincidental. While I remember one of our passengers asked us to fly

EAA pilots
Al Malecha,
Hal Weekley
and Bill Harrison
pose in front of the
Aluminum Overcast
during one of the
many 1997 tour
stops.
(Dr. William E. Harrison)

The *Aluminum Overcast*'s pilots gather for a group photograph during one of the annual EAA B-17 Recurrent Ground School. From left to right are Paul Pobrezny, Bill Harrison, Larry New, Randy Sohn, Ed Bowlin, Connie Bowlin, Linc Dexter, Dan Bowlin, Don Taylor, Sam Bass, Bob Davis, Bill Dodds, Chuck Parnell, Vern Jobst and Hal Weekley.
(Dr. William E. Harrison)

over the fort so he could take some photos, I did not see the cemetery or the activity involved with the burial and we continued to our destination. The probability of this happening is almost impossible to calculate, as this was the only time a B-17 had been the area in many years and this was our only flight for the day. The timing could not have been better if in fact it had been scheduled. The crew and I were very proud to participate in the last rites of this veteran, especially one of our own.

Nineteen ninety-seven was one of my most active years flying the *Aluminum Overcast* for the EAA. I flew with four different pilots at fifteen locations in eleven states and made a total of eighty flights. With only minor exceptions, I made all of my flights with Al Malecha, a United Airlines captain, an outstanding pilot and true gentleman.

Wild West Tour: 1998

In 1998, the EAA decided to take the *Aluminum Overcast* on tour in the western United States. Up to that time, the bomber had never been further west than the Rocky Mountains. A great deal of planning and effort went into this tour, and everyone looked forward to spending time in Arizona, California, Oregon, Washington and other western states. The EAA called this tour the Wild West Tour.

The tour started in Tucson, Arizona in grand style with Peggy Malecha, Al's wife, volunteering as the tour stop coordinator. Through her almost Herculean efforts, with Al assisting, the Tucson stop was probably the most productive of any of our stops for the entire year as the gross revenue came to almost $70,000. On the last day of this stop, Al and Bob Davis flew a total of eleven, forty-five minute flights in the *Aluminum Overcast*, with only one rest break during the entire day.

We left Tucson for California thrilled the tour was off to a very good start. The balance of the Wild West Tour proved very rewarding, both in numbers of folks who flew and toured the *Aluminum Overcast*, and in the revenue these tours and flights generated.

In October of this year, the EAA attempted to pair its Douglas DC-3 with us on tour; however, it did not prove to be as financially productive, even though we tried several approaches at various air shows. Any further plans to add the DC-3 on tour were abandoned shortly thereafter. Other types of aircraft were considered as a replacement, including a North American B-25, but nothing further came from discussions at EAA Headquarters.

Looking back, 1998 was not a productive tour year for me as I was hampered by a major operation that kept me from being as active as I normally am during a tour. Regardless, I managed to fly with six other pilots at eight locations in five states. I made a total of twenty-two flights.

1999

Nineteen ninety-nine was the first year we did not have a year appropriately identified. Even without a name, this year proved very productive and we visited several new locations in Florida, Georgia, the Carolinas and Virginia. As always, the tour participants made new contacts and friends. For me, I had the chance to renew friendships with many 398th Bomb Group members, some I had not seen or heard from in as many as 55 years.

The *Aluminum Overcast* started its tour schedule in Florida that spring and continued north through the Eastern United States, before returning to Oshkosh, Wisconsin for the start of the annual EAA Convention. During its five tour stops in North Carolina in May, the airplane grossed more than $95,000 for the EAA Aviation Foundation. My co-author, Jim Zazas, served as the tour coordinator during these stops, but it was the EAA chapters that sponsored the airplane that made this portion of the tour and all stops on the tour a resounding financial success.

In late October and early November, I joined EAA pilots Don Taylor and Larry New at the EAA Air Academy Lodge in Oshkosh, Wisconsin where we conducted two EAA B-17 Ground Schools, with twenty people attending each session. Afterwards, we gave these students a familiarization ride in the *Aluminum Overcast*.

I felt this year was a much better year for me as I was back to my old self. I flew with eight different pilots at thirteen locations in eight states and made a total of sixty-five flights in the *Aluminum Overcast*.

2000

Once more, the EAA B-17 embarked on another profitable tour year in 2000 and, once again, the tour had no particular name assigned to it. As always, the airplane was well received and all activities continued to bring the EAA closer to its chapters and growing membership. As in previous years, local EAA chapters hosted our tour stops, which often added many new EAA members. Moreover, the *Aluminum Overcast*'s expanding tour schedule allowed many 398th Bomb Group veterans the opportunity to see "their" bomber in or near their hometown.

The B-17 tour program has always been, and will continue to be one of the major, positive contributions EAA makes to the aviation community, veterans and all citizens alike.

During the fall, the tour schedule had the *Aluminum Overcast* flying in the Northeast United States. The B-17 traveled to New Hampshire, Maine and upstate New York. The tour stops were productive and we left everyone with a promise we would return soon.

I was able to contribute approximately five weeks to the B-17 tour during 2000. I flew to twelve locations with nine other pilots in eight states for a total of sixty-one flights.

2001

As my life moved into the twenty-first century, I took stock of my many wonderful experiences in the B-17 and decided it was time to hang-up my flying goggles, boots and scarf. I turned 80 years old that year and I believed the time was right for me to retire from active flying. I thought of no better way than to make my last B-17 flight, and my last flight as pilot-in-command in any airplane for that matter, at the 2001 EAA AirVenture (formally called the EAA Convention) in Oshkosh, Wisconsin.

EAA and I set July 27, 2001, as the day the last of the World War II combat B-17 drivers would make his last B-17 flight.

In anticipation of my retirement, the EAA invited my entire family to attend this year's EAA AirVenture celebration. Billie, our two sons, Bill and Gary, Gary's wife Jan and their two children Timothy and Taylor, accompanied me to Wisconsin. This was Billie's third time, Jan's second time, and Taylor's first time to attend the fly-in. The rest of us had been there numerous times, me especially, since I had missed this convention only once since 1979 and that was in 1993, for our golden wedding anniversary.

Many folks came forward to make my retirement flight special. I delighted in all of the activities and attention. Over the course of several days, I made two flights in the *Aluminum Overcast* before I made my last and final flight.

My first flight at Oshkosh was with Dr. Bill Harrison and Verne Jobst, a good friend, a fellow EAA pilot and a retired United Airlines Boeing 747 captain. We took-off on a sunrise photo shoot with Mr. Paul Bowen as the primary photographer. Mr. Bowden sat in the tail of a B-25 while we flew the *Aluminum Overcast* in close formation. After Mr. Bowden took all the photographs, we returned to Oshkosh to make a few landings. I had not flown the B-17 for a few months and I wanted to make a few landings before I made my re-

tirement flight. More importantly, I did not want to make a fool of myself with a poor landing in front of 80,000 spectators. Bill, Verne and I played musical seats as I made two landings from the left seat. My landings were satisfactory so it was on to the festivities.

It was on this flight we had Mr. Don Gaddo on board. Don is an author, a good friend of the 398th and the cousin of a navigator who had been in my bomb squadron in the 398th Bomb Group at Nuthampstead. Tragically, Don's cousin was killed on the July 19, 1944 mission to Lechfeld, Germany, in which I had participated. I was honored to have Don on board.

On the evening of the July 26th, the EAA sponsored a fine dinner for all the people who had been involved in the B-17 tour operation since its inception. The evening's theme was "OH TO B-17 AGAIN." Invited guests included David Hartman, a noted TV personality, Andy "Bud" Anderson, a triple ace, and test pilot and Gen. Chuck Yeager of 'Speed of Sound' fame, actor Cliff Robertson and a great number of B-17 pilots and support personnel. Dr. Bill Harrison was in charge of the program in which I was afforded much recognition from Bill, Tom Poberezny, current EAA President, and Paul Poberezny, former EAA president and a close friend. Bill read a letter from Senator Inhofe to President George H. W. Bush that had gone in the Federal Register recognizing this special occasion. The many generous gifts included a photo of the *Bronx Bomber II* dropping bombs, the letter from the Senator, a beautiful set of miniature gold EAA wings and a large, in-flight photograph poster of the *Aluminum Overcast* covered with well-wishes, comments and signatures from all in attendance that evening.

The following day, July 27th, was my retirement day. I was keenly disappointed to learn FAA regulations in force at the time precluded my family from flying with me on my final flight. Recognizing my frustration and my families' disappointment, Jim Zazas, my

Hal Weekley shares several of his fondest memories flying the B-17 with his family and many friends at a special retirement party hosted by the EAA.

(James B. Zazas)

only two, low passes down the flight line. While we were airborne, Bud Anderson and Chuck Yeager flew above us in a pair of restored P-51s, resplendent in their individual wartime markings. They flew combat patrol like they had in World War II.

Walt Troyer, my good friend and the EAA warbird announcer for many years, and Roscoe Morton announced our little program. Walt was thrilled to have my family nearby on the announcer's stand. I learned later Walt fought hard choking back tears as he announced the program. I learned, also, that the crowd became very quiet as I made my two passes down the runway and the only sound heard was the soft, throaty growl of the *Aluminum Overcast*'s four, Wright R-1820 engines.

I returned to Oshkosh's Runway 18 and made a very respectable landing. After taxiing to a designated spot in front of the EAA crowd, I shutdown this Flying Fortresses' four engines for my last time and sat in the left seat for a few brief minutes of quiet reflection. Then, I climbed from the seat and exited the *Aluminum Overcast* through the forward hatch. When my feet hit the ground, a thun-

good friend and co-author of this book, took my family in hand and led them to the announcer's stand located in front of the thousands of attending spectators where they could have an unobstructed view of my last flight as "First Pilot" in the B-17 Flying Fortress.

My slotted time to fly was at the beginning of the warbird air show. Dr. Bill Harrison, Al Malecha and I took to the air for my final flight, with Don Coester performing the crew chief duties. We were given twenty minutes in the air, which allowed enough time to make

A very happy Hal Weekley poses with actor Cliff Robertson on the left and EAA president Tom Poberezny on the right. (James B. Zazas)

derous applause erupted from the crowd and my family rushed over to greet me. All had tears of joy in their eyes. I felt tears welling up in my eyes, as well.

I walked over to Bill where he made a short speech for the spectators and presented me with a beautiful plaque. I responded with a few words of thanks to Bill, the EAA staff, the EAA members and the fine group of people I had worked with on all the tours. There is no doubt in anyone's mind, especially mine, that the people we had in our operation were the finest anywhere. Without a doubt, the pilots and crew associated with the EAA's *Aluminum Overcast* are unquestionably the finest group anywhere in the world.

After all the presentations, congratulatory handshakes and photographs, we gathered at the B-17 mobile trailer and office to enjoy champagne provided by my very good friends Dick and Joan Ervin (the same Dick Ervin I busted on his first Air Force checkride forty-eight years earlier) to celebrate my retirement. A most wonderful and memorable

Walt Troyer narrated Hal Weekley's final flight before the EAA AirVenture 2001 crowd. He later commented he "choked-up with emotion" during his narration.

(James B. Zazas)

Hal Weekley, flying the EAA's B-17 *Aluminum Overcast*, makes a final pass before an admiring crowd prior to landing.

(James B. Zazas)

Hal Weekley brings the EAA B-17 to a complete stop, then shutsdown the engines for the last time as First Pilot.
(James B. Zazas)

Stepping from the *Aluminum Overcast* Hal Weekley is greeted by a thunderous applause from the EAA AirVenture 2001 crowd and from close friends nearby.
(James B. Zazas)

career involving one airplane type and lasting fifty-eight years had ended and is now history.

The last of the combat B-17 drivers had retired.

Billie, my wife, my keenest supporter and my best friend was with me every step and every flight of the way.

Bill Harrison presents Hal Weekley with a heartfelt plaque acknowledging his and EAA's appreciation for all of Hal's many contributions to the EAA B-17 program.

(James B. Zazas)

Jim Zazas offers his heartfelt congratulations to Hal Weekley for his many contributions to the EAA B-17 program and to aviation history.

(James B. Zazas)

Hal Weekley with his family, Jan, Gary, Billie, Taylor, Bill and Timothy, pose in front of the *Aluminum Overcast*. (James B. Zazas)

Endnotes

Chapter 1: From Boy to man to Future Combat Pilot

Later in life, Maxine Weekley married George Hreha, a World War II U.S. Navy veteran now deceased. Today, Maxine lives in Titusville, Florida. We maintain a close and constant contact.

Chapter 2: The Pace to Combat Flying Quickens

According to Wesley Frank Craven and James Lea Cate, authors of the definitive Army Air Forces history book series, *The United States Army Air Forces in World War II,* they describe the AAF classification system in *Volume Six, Men and Planes,* as follows:

> The establishment of separate classification centers for aircrew candidates was recommended by a training conference convened at Randolph Field on 12-13 January 1942. Such installations were to be essentially pooling places where thousands of civilians coming into the Army for aviation cadet training would receive a physical examinations and inoculations and be quarantined for several weeks. During this period cadets would receive uniforms and equipment, be indoctrinated in the ways of military life, and be classified for aircrew training in one of three specialties, or, if elimi-

nated from aircrew training, be assigned to one of the enlisted combat-crew training programs or ground duty.

> The Flying Training Command desired to locate these "pooling" installations near its training schools which, with few exceptions, were strung out across the nation in an area south of the 37th parallel where weather conditions were most conductive to year round flying. Moreover, the distribution of population in the United States had to be considered. Training officials therefore wanted one classification center in the vicinity of Nashville, Tennessee, another in Texas, and a third at Santa Ana, California. This division took into account of the fact that four-ninths of the total population of the nation would be served by the Tennessee location, three-ninths by the Texas site, and two-ninths by a California site.

Chapter 3: Earning the Silver Wings

In April 2000, co-author Jim Zazas flew to Decatur, Alabama to research the Southern Aviation Training School, the Stearman PT-17 and the facilities available during the World War II period. As a result of his efforts, in addition to the many documents and photographs he was able to obtain, Jim was able to locate Mr. Owens.

Mr. James Owens resides currently in the Gulf Shores, Alabama area, still owns and flies an aircraft, and is active in the aviation insurance business as he has been since his release from the military in the late 1940s.

Incidentally, when Jim related to me his research efforts, I learned that Mr. Owens first name was James. During my training at the Decatur Primary School, there was no need to know the instructors' first names, only their last names.

I contacted Mr. Owens in early May 2000 and learned, much to my surprise, that when I was his student, James Owens was the youngest civilian instructor in the Southeastern Training Command and that he is only eight days older than I am!

Mr. Owens remained in Decatur as a flight instructor for a month shy of two years whereupon he became a member of the USAAF Ferry Command. Ironically, Mr. Owens' first assignment was ferrying B-17s. He remained in the Ferry Command until the end of the war and had the opportunity to fly most of the aircraft in the military inventory.

Upon his release from his military commitments, Mr. Owens moved to Birmingham, Alabama and entered the aviation insurance industry.

Chapter 4: Meeting and Mastering the B-17

On our 50th anniversary, we went back to Sebring and the Sebring Hotel is now a parking lot. I bet that place could tell some stories!

Billie and I found out later that the hotel clerk on duty the two nights we were in residence would ten years later become one of our best friends and fly with me for at least twenty years before he died in his mid-fifties of a massive heart attack. His passing was a tremendous loss to our family!

Chapter 5: Getting Closer to Combat Flying

I contacted Paul James after my trip to France, the first time we had communicated since our bailout. During our conversation, Paul commented that he and the crew did not like me much for all the extra training and duty I required we do in England but, in retrospect, he believed this extra training saved his life and the lives of our crew.

Chapter 6: Nuthampstead, the 398th Bomb Group and My Baptism by Fire

1. High Wycombe, or Pinetree, was actually a girl's boarding school called Wycombe Abbey Girls' School at the time it was obtained by the RAF, then quickly transferred to the USAAF in early 1942 to become Eighth Bomber Command Headquarters. This abbey's large, white stone, castle-like structure was situated on an immaculately landscaped lawn about a mile and half south of the town of High Wycombe and featured tree-lined roads and walkways, and a large pond where swans and ducks made their home. The British Bomber Command's headquarters was only a few miles away, which facilitated liaison between the two commands.

2. The USAAF's "Maximum Effort" mission of June 21, 1944 integrated the second *Operation Frantic* mission of the war, which involved the staging of heavy bombers to the Soviet Union and, later, flying missions from there. An earlier *Operation Frantic* mission had heavy bombers flying from Italy and North Africa to the Soviet Union, but the June 21st raid was the first time the heavy bomber missions had originated from United Kingdom bases. One hundred and fourteen B-17s of the Third Air Division flying from English bases, escorted by seventy Allied fighters, attacked targets south of Berlin before proceeding to bases in the Soviet Union.

Operation Frantic allowed Allied strategic air forces the opportunity to attack targets they could not reach normally. Bombers flew from their bases, bombed the objectives, then landed in Russia. Returning to their home base a few days later, the bombers could make another raid on selected targets.

3. The Army Air Forces used two types of assembly radio beacons known as Splasher Beacons and Buncher Beacons to assemble their aircraft formations before proceeding towards their assigned targets. Developed by the British, Splasher Beacons, or simply Splashers, employed a series of three, later four transmitters that operated on different frequencies, but broadcast the same identifying code. The date and time these signals were broadcast was varied so as to minimize any attempts by the enemy to override or jam these frequencies and, thus, confuse the assembling bombers. The beacon's range was about thirty miles. In early April 1943, the Eighth Air Force secured an agreement with the Royal Air Force to use these powerful, medium frequency radio beacons for their own missions from takeoff to landing.

Splashers were used initially to assemble small groups of aircraft at a stated time. By the middle of July 1943, the Splashers proved to be invaluable and they were used to assemble entire bomb groups, wings and divisions of bomber and fighter aircraft.

The Eighth Air Force was so pleased with the Splasher beacon system that they developed the Buncher beacon system, which consisted of low frequency transmitters developed specifically to assemble the U.S. heavy bombers. The Buncher beacons were placed near operational AAF airfields. The Buncher beacons played an important role in Eighth Air Force operations, regardless of weather conditions.

Forming thirty, forty or more fully-loaded heavy bombers in combat formation, in all kinds of weather, day or night, required good flying skill, careful timing and a small amount of luck. The Combat Bomb Wing Leader and the high and low box leaders, and their deputies, would takeoff about ten minutes ahead of the main force. They would fly to the assigned beacon - the 398th used the Debden Beacon for most missions - and would assume their proper position upon reaching this beacon. With wheels down, they would entering a left hand turn at a prescribed rate, usually a constant-rate turn requiring four minutes to make a full 360 degree turn. In turn, the pilots in the other bombers in the formation would fly a briefed heading for a prescribed number of minutes, usually five minutes or so then make a constant-rate turn towards the beacon.

After assembly was complete, the pilots in the assembled combat box would fly on briefed bearings to and from the beacon, at a briefed speed and rate-of-climb, usually 150 miles-per-hour indicated airspeed and 250 to 350 feet-per-minute, respectively. Most timed patterns took six to ten minutes. If a climb was briefed or needed, the Combat Bomb Wing leader in the Lead Group would climb to this assigned altitude with the other groups assembling on this Lead Group as briefed.

4. PFF, derived from the British term Path Finding Force, was a means to bomb a target electronically through an overcast. The official Eighth Air Force term was BTO, or Bombing Through Overcast, however the PFF term was used more commonly.

Chapter 7: Adding to the Mission Count

1. GEE-H was a British developed blind bombing system. The system used an airborne transmitter/receiver that interrogated two ground-based beacons to obtain a position fix. GEE-H was used by the First and Second Air Divisions during 1944. The system had a good range, roughly 300 miles at 20,000 feet, but was susceptible to enemy jamming.

2. Strategic bombing accuracy was gauged as excellent if any bombs fell within 1,000 feet of the Main Point of Impact. Other results were judged accordingly if any bombs fell beyond this 1,000-foot radius.

Bomber crews often knew they would return to a particular target if the bombing results were poor or if the bombs were not released. Hence, several lead aircrews opted to make a 360 degree turns to find and bomb the target rather than return to the same target on another mission at a later date.

Chapter 8: Hell From Heaven: The War Continues

1. According to Martin Blumenson, author of the definitive United States Army history book series, *United States in World War II, The European Theater of Operations, Breakout and Pursuit*:

> General Bradley presented the Cobra idea at a conference with his staff and his corps commanders on 12 July. He characterized the battle of the hedgerows as "tough and costly...a slugger's match...too slow a process," and spoke of his hope for a swift advance made possible by "three or four thousand tons of bombs" from the air. He stated that aggressive action and a readiness to take stiff losses if necessary. "If they [the Germans] get set [again]," he warned, "we go right back to this hedge fighting and you can't make any speed. He insisted, "This thing [Cobra] must be bold."

2. Historian Martin Blumenson describes the miscommunication between General Bradley and the Air Chiefs quite well. He writes:

> At the conference between General Bradley and air representatives on 19 July, when the Cobra air arrangements were being worked out, the direction of the bombing approach had "evoked considerable discussion." General Bradley had insisted on his parallel plan, while all the Air Forces representatives had argued that perpendicular runs

were more suitable. At the end of the conference the question had not been settled formally, though General Bradley must have assumed that his recommendations for lateral bomb runs would be accepted. The Air Forces representatives had understood that General Bradley "was aware of the possibility of gross [bombing] errors causing casualties" among his troops, and they thought he had said "that he was prepared to accept such casualties no matter which way the planes approached." Unaware of this conception, General Bradley had considered the conference "very satisfactory."... The result of what in reality had been an unsatisfactory conference was an absence of firm understanding and mutual agreement.

3. History of the St. Lo carpet bombing reveals some very interesting facts. Overall enemy casualties amounted to less than ten percent, sometimes approaching only five percent within some companies. Those troops not killed outright by the bombing were concealed in one-man fox holes. More often than not, only a direct hit kill them. Those troops located in the open, including armored and support vehicles such as tanks and trucks, suffered tremendous losses.

The greatest military advantage gained was the psychological effect on the enemy. The seemingly endless stream of Allied aircraft overhead without any opposition destroyed the moral of many enemy units. Many captured soldiers later reported, after regaining their hearing, that the mere presence of so many unopposed aircraft "was sufficient to produce a mental state bordering on panic."

With respect to the Allies losses, military planners understood the dangers of placing so many Allied troops close to the area to be bombed. Their forces had to rush in quickly to take advantage of enemy's mental paralysis and shock before they could recover. This calculated risk succeeded, and the Allies were able to achieve the "breakthrough" sought by General Omar Bradley.

Chapter 11: Freedom's Cry

According to archived World War II Allied Escape and Evasion Reports, crewmembers Hal Weekley, Paul James and Joe Skarda were debriefed by the Military Intelligence Service in England on September 6, 1944. Bob Stickel was debriefed a day earlier.

Epilogue: Remembrances: The Aluminum Overcast and the End of an Era

1. The Civil Aeronautics Administration, forerunner to the Federal Aviation Administration, awarded the NC5017N registration to this B-17 in error. As issued, this registration number meant that the airplane carried no operating restrictions when, in fact, it should have been placed under a "Limited" use classification. This error was corrected when the airplane was re-issued a NL5017N registration on September 23, 1947 denoting that the airplane could be operated in a "Limited" use only, in this case, for cargo transport. In 1949, the CAA deleted the need to include the airplane's classification its registration number. Thus, this B-17 received the civil registration of N5017N on June 29, 1949, the same number the airplane carries to this day.

2. According to B-17 historian Robin Mitchell:

> ...the first flight to San Juan left Vero Beach about midnight. On the way, all four (4) voltage regulators went out, apparently due to the Fortresses' time of inactivity, causing the batteries to boil and spill acid into the belly of the plane. With the electrical systems almost out, Cobb made an uneventful landing in San Juan. After the cargo of meat was removed, the floor was lifted and baking soda was spread liberally inside the hull. Following a thorough flushing with water, a close inspection revealed no structural damage to the frame or skin. New regulators were obtained in San Juan and after installation, the Fortress returned to Florida without further incident.

Aircraft Data Plates representing the three aircraft companies that built the B-17 are shown here in original size.

(Curtiss Aldrich)

Combat Missions and Training Flights Listing

GRP MSN NUMBER	MY MSN NUMBER	DATE (1944)	PRIMARY TARGET	ACTUAL TARGET BOMBED	FLIGHT TIME	FLOWN	AIRCRAFT
		6-17	Local Area Familiarization and Training		3:00		
		6-18	Formation Training		4:10		
36	1	6-21	Berlin	Berlin	9:10	42-102516 (3O-H)	
37	2	6-22	La Vaupaliere	Le Houline	5:20	42-97338 (3O-C)	
39	3	6-24	Belloy-sur-Somme	RTB w/bombs	4:45	42-102469 (N7-Q)	
41	4	6-27	Biennais	Biennais	5:25	42-102607 (3O-F)	
	5	6-29	Wing assembled, but aborted		4:15	42-102445 (3O-R)	
		7-1	Copilot Training		2:00		
42	6	7-4	Tours	RTB w/bombs	8:00	42-102445 (3O-R)	
		7-5	Copilot Training		3:15		
43	7	7-6	Cauchi D'Ecques	Ostend	4:00	42-102516 (3O-H)	
44	8	7-7	Leipzig	Leipzig	8:30	42-107080 (3O-S)	
48		7-12	Munich (Aborted due to weather)		2:15	42-102516 (3O-H)	
		7-15	Copilot Training		2:00	42-102516 (3O-H)	
50	9	7-16	Munich	Munich	10:00	42-97401 (3O-T)	
		7-17	Navigation, Formation Lead Crew Training		2:00		
51	10	7-18	Peenemunde	Peenemunde	9:30	42-102516 (3O-H)	
52	11	7-19	Lechfeld	Lechfeld	8:20	42-102516 (3O-H)	
53	12	7-20	Dessau	Dessau	9:00	42-102516 (3O-H)	
		7-23	Navigation, Formation Lead Crew Training		5:15		
54	13	7-24	St. Lo	St. Lo	6:10	42-102516 (3O-H)	
55	14	7-25	St. Lo	St. Lo	6:30	42-102516 (3O-H)	
58	15	7-31	Munich	Munich	8:30	42-102516 (3O-H)	
60	16	8-3	Saarbrucken	Saarbrucken	7:10	42-97394 (3O-P)	
61	17	8-4	Peenemunde	Peenemunde	9:30	42-102596 3O-N)	
62	18	8-5	Dollberg	Dollberg	8:00	43-37874 (3O-W)	
63		8-6	Brandenburg (Aborted. See Note #4)		4:15	42-102516 (3O-H)	
		8-8	Engine time and test work				
		8-10	Ferry damaged a/c to Alconbury Depot		2:15		
67	19	8-12	Buc/Versailles	Buc/Versailles	8:00	42-102565 (3O-M)	
68	20	8-13	Le Manoir	Le Manoir	4:00	42-102516 (3O-H)	

NOTES:

1. Lt. Harold Weekley flew the above missions from Army Air Forces Station 131, Nuthampstead, England, from June 21, 1944 to August 13, 1944.

2. T/Sgt. Ven B. Unger, the Radio Operator, was wounded on Group Mission #43, July 6, 1944. T/Sgt. Louis Buchsbaum replaced T/Sgt. Unger prior to the next mission.

3. Lt. Weekley and crew returned to base on three engines on Group Mission #58, July 31, 1944.

4. Lt. Weekley's tail gunner, S/Sgt. Charles E. "Pop" Stombaugh, was wounded on Group Mission #63, August 6, 1944, on a mission to Munich. Two hours into the flight, the navigator in the airplane on Weekley's right wing cleared his guns without looking and shot off "Pop's" left knee. Weekley returned to base to save his life. The navigator was not seen again after the mission.

5. Lt. Weekley and crew were shot down on their twentieth mission, Group Mission #68, on August 13, 1944.

6. The following airplanes carried these names:

42-102516 (3O-H)	*Bronx Bomber II*
42-97338 (3O-C)	*Ugly Duckling*
42-102607 (3O-F)	*Lodian*
42-107080 (3O-S)	*OXO*
42-97401 (3O-T)	*Stinker, Jr.*
42-97394 (3O-P)	*Kentucky Colonel*
42-102596 (30-N)	*Doodit*
42-102565 (3O-M)	*The Ugly Duckling*
43-37874 (3O-W)	*Georgia Peach*

What Became of the B-17G's Flown in Combat by Harold Weekley

42-102516 (3O-H) *Bronx Bomber II*—Reported MIA (Missing In Action) after mission to Le Manoir, France on August 13, 1944. Aircraft hit by flak and set on fire. Lt. Weekley and crew bailed out successfully. Crashed near Bosville, France; 7 EVD (Evaded), 2 POW (Prisoner of War), MCAR (Missing Air Crew Report) 7910

42-97338 (3O-C) *Ugly Duckling*—Landed on Continent near ten kilometers southwest of Abbeville, France during mission of January 8, 1945. Salvaged by 5 SAD (Strategic Air Depot) on March 12, 1945.

42-102469 (N7-Q) Landed on Continent following mission of January 8, 1945 to attack the marshalling yards at Speyer, Germany. Salvaged by the 5 SAD on January 11, 1945.

42-102607 (3O-F) *Lodian* - Reported MIA on mission to Magdeburg, Germany on September 28, 1944. Aircraft hit by flak; crashed near Schorstedt, Germany; 10 POW; MACR 9382

42-102445 (3O-R) Reported MIA on July 8, 1944 while attacking V-1 *Noball* sites. Hit by flak and crashed near Money Cayeux, France; 1 KIA (Killed in Action), 2 EVD, 7 POW; MACR 7217

42-107080 (3O-S)   *OXO* - Reported MIA on mission to Soest Marshalling Yards, Germany on December 4, 1944; later discovered to have crash-landed on Continent near Ursal, Belgium. Repaired by the Service Command on Continent, but set on fire and destroyed by German air attacks on January 1, 1945.

42-97401 (3O-T)   *Stinker, Jr* - Reported MIA on October 17, 1944 on mission to Cologne, Germany. The aircraft was subsequently salvaged by the Service Command on the Continent on November 29, 1944.

42-97394 (3O-P)   *Kentucky Colonel* - Hit by flak in tail on August 8, 1944 on mission to Bretteville Le Rabet, France; Tail gunner was blown out and killed, rest of crew bailed-out. Plane crashed near Falaise, France. 2 MIA, 7 RTD (Returned to Duty), MCAR 8065

42-102596 (3O-N)   *Doodit* - Landed on Continent following mission to Liepzig, Germany on February 23, 1945. Reassigned to the 398th by the 2SAD on April 4, 1945. Returned to the United States on June 1, 1945, only to be broken-up for scrap in Kingman, Arizona in late 1945.

42-102565 (3O-M)   *The Ugly Duckling* - Damaged by flak on mission of August 30, 1944, one crewman bailed-out over enemy territory. Aircraft brought back to England and landed at RAF Langham. *The Ugly Duckling* was reported MIA on November 26, 1944 on a mission to Misburg, Germany. Aircraft was hit by flak and crashed near Zwolle, Holland. 9 KIA; MCAR 11147.

43-37874 W (30-W)   *Georgia Peach* - Assigned as 398th B.G. replacement aircraft on July 15, 1944. Landed on Continent four times, repaired and returned to Group each time. The aircraft survived the war only to be broken-up for scrap in Kingman, Arizona in late 1945.

Col. Harold Weekley's logbook and wartime records do not reflect the aircraft tail numbers he flew on June 17, June 18, July 1, July 5, July 17, July 23, and August 10, 1944.

After their service in WWII, thousands of B-17's were cut into scrap at the Reconstruction Finance Corporation's facility in Kingman, Arizona.   (William T. Larkins)

The Department of the Army commissioned Lt. Col. Tom B. Woodburn to create a series of six posters between 1939 and 1941. This poster was printed in 1940 to encourage enlistment.

(National Archives)

Missing Air Crew Report (MACR) 7910

Missing Air Crew Reports (MACR) provided invaluable information as to the status of wartime crews and individual crewmembers lost in combat operations during World War II. Eyewitness accounts and whatever other information was available at the time were were added to these report.

Missing Air Crew Report 7910, which describes the loss of Lt. Harold Weekley and his crew in the *Bronx Bomber II*, is reproduced from microfilm stored at the National Archives and Records Administration, Archives II, College Park, Maryland.

CONFIDENTIAL

7310

WAR DEPARTMENT
HEADQUARTERS ARMY AIR FORCES
WASHINGTON

Classification changed
RESTRICTED
E. A. BRAUNAS, Lt. Col., AC
M. KLENSH, Capt., AC
Date ___ 15 1946

MISSING AIR CREW REPORT

IMPORTANT: This report will be compiled in triplicate by each Army Air Forces organization within 48 hours of the time an aircraft is officially reported missing.

1. ORGANIZATION: Location __AAF Station 131__ ; Command or Air Force __8th Air Force__
   Group __398th Bomb Gv__ ; Squadron __601st Bomb Sv__ ; Detachment __None__

2. SPECIFY: Point of Departure __AAF Station 131__ Course __per atchd track chart__
   Intended Destination __Le Manoir, France & Return__ Type of Mission __Operational__
   WEATHER CONDITIONS AND VISIBILITY AT TIME OF CRASH OR WHEN LAST REPORTED: _____
   1/10 cumulus cloud. Visibility 20-30 Mi. No Contrails.

4. GIVE: (a) Date __13 Aug 1944__ ; Time __Approx 1322__ ; and Location __Approx 4942N-0040E__
   of last known whereabouts of missing aircraft.
   (b) Specify whether (x) Last Sighted, ( ) Last Contacted by Radio,
   ( ) Forced Down, ( ) Seen to crash, or ( ) Information not Available.

5. AIRCRAFT WAS LOST, OR IS BELIEVED TO HAVE BEEN LOST, AS A RESULT OF: (Check only one ( ) Enemy Aircraft, (X) Enemy Anti-Aircraft, ( ) Other Circumstances as Follows _____

6. AIRCRAFT: Type, Model and Series __B-17G__ ; A.A.F. Serial Number __42-102516__

7. ENGINES: Type, Model and Series __R-1820-97__; A.A.F. Serial Number _____
   (a) __SW-014433__ ; (b) __45-61923__ ; (c) __SW-014611__ ; (d) __SW-014247__

8. INSTALLED WEAPONS (Furnish below Make, Type and Serial Number)

	MAKE	TYPE	SERIAL NUMBER
(a)	Frig. Div. General Motors	.50 Cal A/C Mach Gun	226351
(b)	Frig. Div. General Motors	.50 Cal A/C Mach Gun	226180
(c)	General Motors	.50 Cal A/C Mach Gun	646972
(d)	Frig. Div. General Motors	.50 Cal A/C Mach Gun	651737
(e)	Frig. Div. General Motors	.50 Cal A/C Mach Gun	969161
(f)	Frig. Divl General Motors	.50 Cal A/C Mach Gun	648788
(g)	Frig. Div. General Motors	.50 Cal A/C Mach Gun	77287
(h)	Frig. Div. General Motors	.50 Cal A/C Mach Gun	971922
(i)	Frig. Div. General Motors	.50 Cal A/C Mach Gun	971981
(j)	Frig. Div. General Motors	.50 Cal A/C Mach Gun	77340
(k)	Frig. Div. General Motors	.50 Cal A/C Mach Gun	649296
(l)	Frig. Div. General Motors	.50 Cal A/C Mach Gun	652287
(m)	Frig. Div. General Motors	.50 Cal A/C Mach Gun	89363
(n)			
(o)			
(p)			
(q)			
(r)			
(s)			
(t)			

9. THE PERSONS LISTED BELOW WERE REPORTED AS: (a) Battle Casualty __MIA__
   or (b) Non-Battle Casualty _____

CONFIDENTIAL

CONFIDENTIAL

10. NUMBER OF PERSONS ABOARD AIRCRAFT: Crew __9__; Passenger _____; Total ____

CREW POSITION		NAME IF FULL (Last Name First)	RANK	SERIAL NUMBER	
1.	Pilot	WEEKLEY, HAROLD D	1st Lt	O-8?? 02	RTD
2.	Co-Pilot	CLARK, BENJAMIN L., JR	2nd Lt	O-705?23	RTD
3.	Navigator	JAMES, PAUL M	2nd Lt	O-716657	RTD
4.	Bombardier	DELBART, RAYMOND S	2nd Lt	O-1995744	RTD
5.	Top Turret Gunner	SKARDA, JOSEPH W	T Sgt	38445382	RTD
6.	Radio Gunner	BUCHSBAUM, LOUIS	T Sgt	12144624	RTD
7.	Waist Gunner	LEONARD, GENE F	S Sgt	37513937	RTD
8.	Tail Gunner	STICHEL, ROBERT F	S Sgt	11067379	RTD
9.	Ball Turret Gunner	FABIAN, JOE R	S Sgt	38529720	RTD
10.					
11.					
12.					

11. IDENTIFY BELOW THOSE PERSONS WHO ARE BELIEVED TO HAVE LAST KNOWLEDGE OF AIRCRAFT AND CHECK APPROPRIATE COLUMN TO INDICATE BASIS FOR SAME: (Check Only One)

	Name in Full (Last Name First)	Rank	Serial Number	Contacted By Radio	Last Sighted	Saw Crash	Saw Forced Landing
1.	JESSOP, RICHARD B	S Sgt	33563973		X		
2.	MORRIS, STACEY JR	S Sgt	35632394		X		
3.	KOLB, KENNETH E	Cpl	38370891		X		

12. IF PERSONNEL ARE BELIEVED TO HAVE SURVIVED, ANSWER YES TO ONE OF THE FOLLOWING STATEMENTS: (a) Parachutes were used __Yes__; (b) Persons were seen walking away from scene of crash _____; or (c) Any other reason (Specify) _____

13. ATTACH AERIAL PHOTOGRAPH, MAP, CHART, OR SKETCH SHOWING APPROXIMATE LOCATION WHERE AIRCRAFT WAS LAST SEEN.

14. EYEWITNESS DESCRIPTION OF CRASH, FORCED LANDING, OR OTHER CIRCUMSTANCES PERTAINING TO MISSING AIRCRAFT:

    (Descriptions Attached)

15. ATTACH A DESCRIPTION OF THE EXTENT OF SEARCH, IF ANY, AND GIVE NAME, RANK AND SERIAL NUMBER OF OFFICER IN CHARGE HERE No knowledge of search being made.

Date of Report __15 August 1944__

RECEIVED SEP 23 1944

(Signature of Preparing Officer)
WALLIS L CAMPBELL
1st Lt, Air Corps

CONFIDENTIAL

CONFIDENTIAL

398th Bombardment Group Hv
Le Manoir, France Mission 13 August 44

Lead Group 1st "K" CBW Formation Over Target Area

B
Col Hunter-Latson
8075-A

B   B
Meyran   Davidson-Durtschi
2469-Q   8086-C

B   B   B
Kaufman   Novak   Lee
2570-F   6083-V   7825-J

B   B   B
Sleaman   Moore   Lehner
2562-G   2568-N   7892-K

C
Ford
8126-J

C
Reed
7214-V

B
Johnson, J
2507-F

- -

High Group 1st "A" CBW Formation Over Target

D
Frazier-Miller
8121-Q

B   L
Stallcup   Dalton
8091-L   7874-W

D   D
Weekley   Wierney
2516-H   2596-N

D   D   D   D
Taylor   Falkenbach   Cucco   Brown
7885-X   7203-Z   2565-M   7190-L

C
Slavin
8147-L

C   C
Mann   Armor
6157-W   2592-G

- -

Low Group 1st "A" CBW Formation Over Target

F
Scott-Rudrud
7374-X

F   F
Doerr   Cobb
094-M   7337-H

F   F
Brown   Boehme
7387-H   2610-Y

F   F   F   F
Richardson   Evans   Leukhardt   Link
7510-S   2593-C   2543-B   2597-V

C
Fritog
7294-P

C   C
Rogers   Atkinson
2519-A   2418-M

CONFIDENTIAL

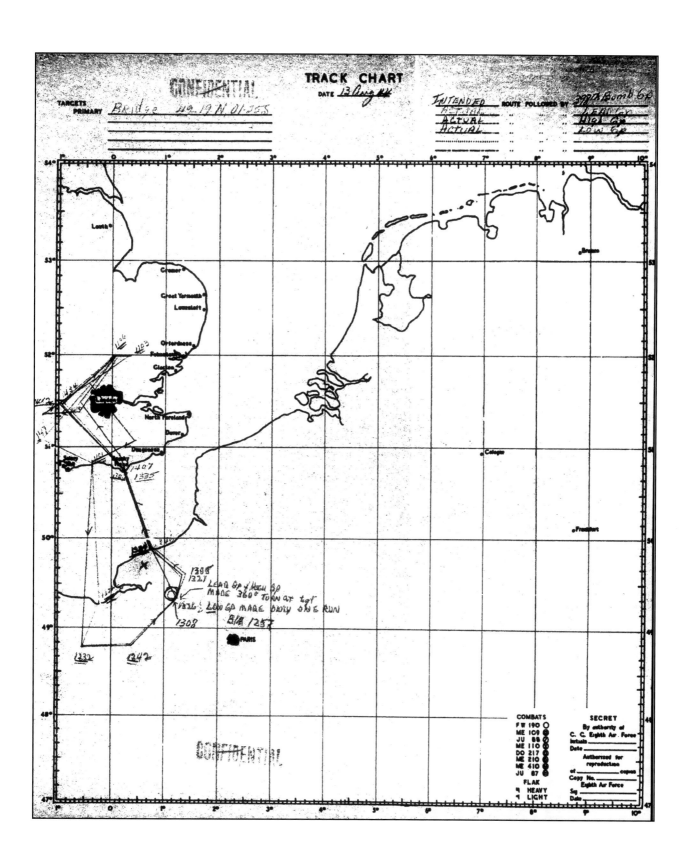

~~CONFIDENTIAL~~

Eye Witness Description of Missing Aircraft B17G 42-102516, Pilot, 1st Lt Harold D Weekley, O-807802, 601st Bomb Squadron, 398th Bomb Group missing from Combat Mission to Le Manoir, France 13 August 1944.

We were flying the high squadron of the high group and Lt Weekley was flying the low squadron of the high group. After we left the target Lt Weekley flew along and looked all right. There was no sign of a fire that I could see but the men started bailing out about two minutes before we hit the coast. I saw all nine men come out--eight opening their chutes shortly and evidently one pulled a delayed jump. I didn't see him open his chute. Probably because of the heavy Maze down towards the ground and my attention was occupied otherwise just about this time.

Richard B Jessop

RICHARD B JESSOP, 33563973
S Sgt
Tail Gunner, B17G 42-102596

CONFIDENTIAL

Eye Witness Description of Missing Aircraft B17G 42-102516, Pilot, 1st Lt
Harold D Weekley, O-807802, 601st Bomb Squadron, 398th Bomb Group missing
from Combat mission to Le Manoir, France 13 August 1944

On the recent raid near Rouen, France, 13 August 1944 we were flying
high squadron high group and Lt Weekley was flying lead of the low squadron
of the high group. We had left the target when I first observed that
Lt Weekley's ship had the number three prop feathered and I saw his men
start bailing out but his plane seemed to be under control. Seven of the
men came out while Lt Weekley's ship was on our left and then his ship
came under us, going to our right side and I saw two more come out. Eight
of the men opened their chutes almost immediately and the other evidently
pulled a delayed jump. I didn't see his chute open before he dissappeared
into the haze.

STACEY MORRIS JR, 3563239
S Sgt
Ball Turret Gunner, B17G 42-102596

CONFIDENTIAL

~~CONFIDENTIAL~~

Eye Witness Description of Missing Aircraft B17G 42-102516, Pilot, 1st Lt Harold D Weekley, O-807802, 601st Bomb Squadron, 398th Bomb Group missing from Combat Mission to Le Manoir, France 13 August 1944.

I saw Lt Weekley's ship with a feathered propellor on number three engine. I saw eight fellows bail out and all their chutes opened. They jumped about three minutes inland from the channel. The plane then made three or four complete circles in the far distance and then went out of sight.

It is possible that a ninth chute came out later since the ship was still under control, but I never saw the ninth chute.

KENNETH E KOLB, 38370891
Cpl, 601st Bomb Sq
Ball Turret Gunner, B17G 42-102565

~~CONFIDENTIAL~~

abs/12/7/44.

1st Lt Harold C. Weekley   Mrs. Wilma J. Weekley, (Wife)
2204 Sunset Boulevard,
Steubenville, Ohio.

2nd Lt Benjamin L. Clark, Jr.   Mrs. Nancy J. Clark, (Mother)
16 Crosby Avenue,
Lockport, New York.

2nd Lt Paul M. James   Mrs. Ivan D. James, (Wife)
800 West 7th Street,
Wilmington, Delaware.

2nd Lt Raymond S. Dolhert   Mrs. Kathryn M. Dolhert, (Wife)
Box 441,
Saint Albans, West Virginia.

T/Sgt Joseph W. Edwards   Mr. Albert E. Edwards, (Father)
Route Two,
Magnet, Arkansas.

T/Sgt Louis Buchsbaum   Mrs. Frieda Buchsbaum, (Mother)
2121 Barnes Avenue,
New York, New York.

S/Sgt Gene F. Leonard   Mr. Frank A. Leonard, (Father)
826 South East,
Emporia, Kansas.

S/Sgt Robert V. Stichel   Mrs. Helen Stichel, (Wife)
57 Lincoln Avenue,
Saint Albans, Vermont.

S/Sgt Joe R. Fahlen   Mrs. Hattie Fahlen, (Mother)
Penelope, Texas.

REPORT ON SHOT-DOWN AIRCRAFT

ASUALTY NO

DATE AND TIME AIRCRAFT
WAS SHOT DOWN: 9 Aug, 1944

PLACE OF CRASH: Kandile, near Phonp

TYPE OF AIRCRAFT: Fortress

REPORTING OFFICE: Limburg

CREW

SURNAME, AND
FIRST NAME: DELMAR, Raymond Sylvain

DATE OF BIRTH: 10 June 1923

RANK: 2nd Lt.

SERIAL NUMBER: O-1999744

CAPTURED: yes   WOUNDED: DEAD:

DISTRIBUTION: WHICH CAMP: Dulag-Luft   TYPE OF INJURY:

GRAVE LOCATION:

REMARKS:

Dulag-Luft, 5 Oct. 1944 . No.

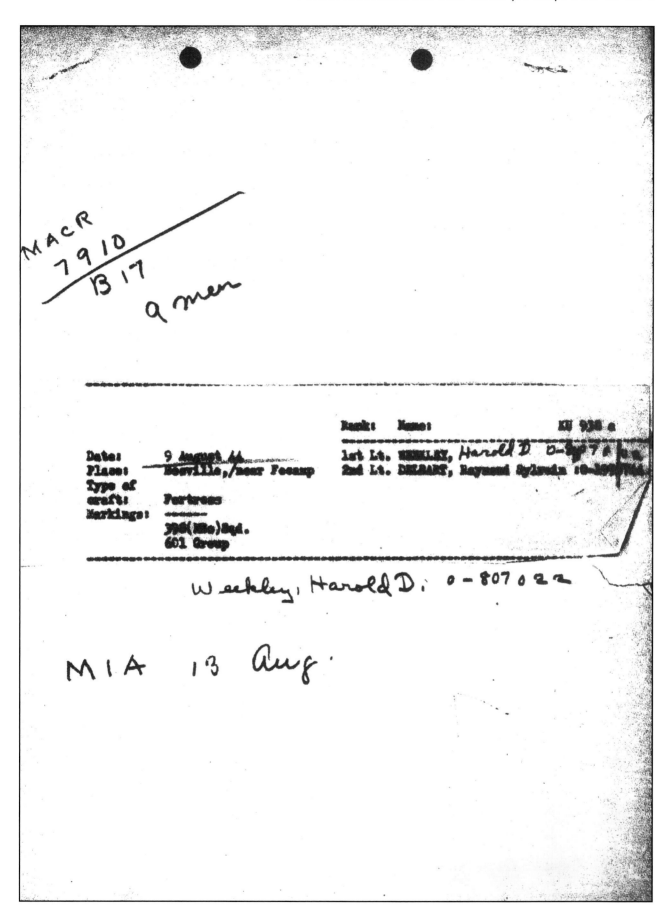

MACR
7910
B 17
9 men

Weekley, Harold D. 0 - 807022

MIA 13 Aug.

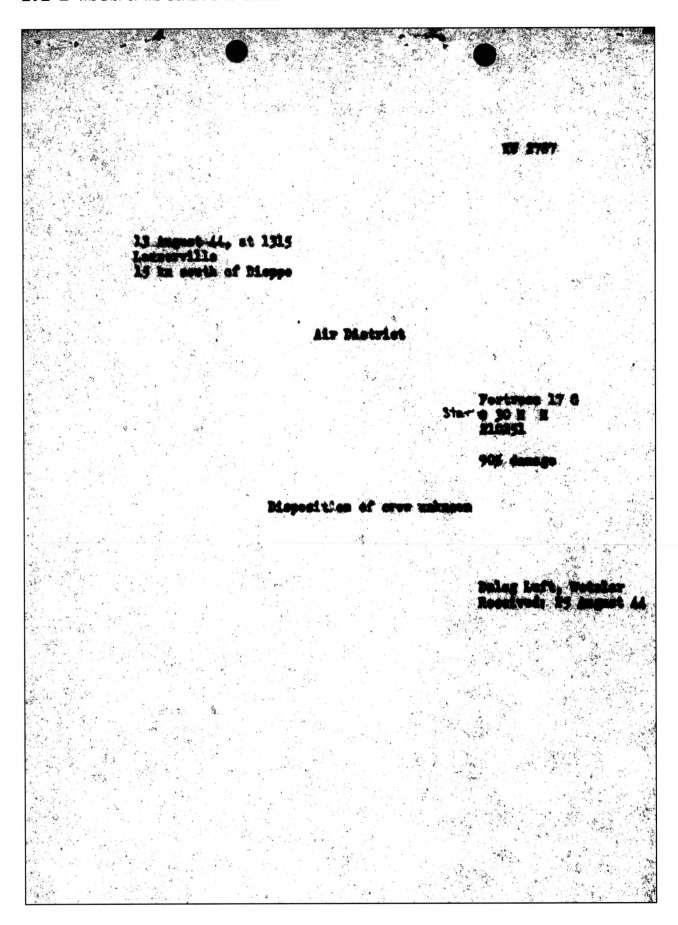

The B-17 Flying Fortress: A Brief History

The B-17 Flying Fortress began its life in 1934 as a Wright Field, Ohio issued specification for a multi-engine, four-to-six place bomber to replace the Martin B-10. The requirements were simple: carry a 2,000 lb. bomb load over a distance of 1,020 to 2,000 miles at a speed of 200 to 250 mph. In addition, this new bomber had to be capable of maintaining level flight with the design useful load at a minimum of 7,000 feet with any one engine inoperative. Not long afterwards, all competing manufacturers - including Boeing - learned the prototype had to be built at their own expense.

The Boeing Aircraft Company responded to the challenge and created the Model 299 which rolled-out on July 17, 1935 and first flew on July 28, 1935. Sadly, this prototype was lost in a fatal crash at Wright Field, Ohio on October 30, 1935. Subsequent investigation revealed that the pilots had not unlocked the mechanical control locks prior to take-off, though controversy still surrounds this original finding.

Despite this setback, Boeing received contracts from the Army Air Corps to pursue further development of what became known as the YB-17. Despite several initial flight-testing problems, the Army Air Corps awarded Boeing contracts for B-17 production. While Boeing touted its new "Flying Fortress," the world at large found itself facing the clouds of war. When the war started, the B-17 proved to be an excellent choice. Aircrews praised the airplane's inherent ruggedness and survivability, even in the worst of wartime conditions.

B-17 Flying Fortresses were built by the renamed Boeing Aircraft Company in Seattle, Washington; Douglas Aircraft in Long Beach, California; and by Lockheed-Vega in Burbank, California.

B-17s were manufactured by the following companies, and in the models and numbers indicated:

Model 299	1
Boeing YB-17	13
Boeing YB-17A	1
Boeing B-17B	39
Boeing B-17C	38
Boeing B-17D	42
Boeing B-17E	512
Boeing B-17F-BO	2,300
Boeing B-17G-BO	4,035
Douglas B-17F-DL	605
Douglas B-17G-DL	2,395
Vega B-17F-VE	500
Vega B-17G-VE	2,250

• The total B-17 production run was 12,731 airplanes. The Boeing Aircraft Company manufactured 6,981 aircraft, or 54.83% of all B-17s built. The Douglas Aircraft Company manufactured 3,000 aircraft, or 23.56%. The Lockheed-Vega Aircraft Company manufactured 2,750 aircraft, or 21.60%.

• The average cost for each B-17, from prototype to 1943 production model, was $357,655.

• Some 4,750 B-17s were lost in combat, more than any other type during the war.

• B-17s dropped a total of 640,036 tons of bombs on European targets. All other types of aircraft dropped a total of 889,052 tons of bombs.

• On average, B-17s shot down 23 enemy fighters per 1,000 plane raids as opposed to 11 enemy fighters shot down by Allied fighters during these massive raids.

• B-17 Flying Fortresses in the Eighth Air Force outnumbered B-24 Liberators by about four-to-one.

• Today, less than fifty intact B-17 airframes exist. Incredibly, only a scant dozen remain airworthy worldwide.

(U.S. Air Corps Series, AC-10)

The Eighth Air Force:
A Brief Historical Overview

The Eighth Air Force was activated on January 28, 1942 at Hunter Field in Savannah, Georgia. Its first commander was Major General Carl "Tooey" Spaatz. In mid-February 1942, he sent Brig. General Ira C. Eaker to England to closely study British bombing techniques and procedures, make recommendations to incoming American units, and command the newly-formed Army Air Forces in Britain (AAFIB) Bomber Command with the headquarters set up initially at Bushy Park near London.

With British help, new facilities were soon located and amidst much public fanfare, Eaker opened his new headquarters at High Wycombe, Buckinghamshire, England on February 23, 1942 in the Daws Hill Lodge, once the seat of nobility and later the evacuated Wycombe Abbey Girls' School. Eaker's AAFIB Bomber Command was re-designated VIII Bomber Command on April 12, 1942. Eaker had the responsibility of organizing the VIII Bomber Command to become the backbone of U.S. strategic bombing airpower in the European Theatre of Operations.

Concurrently, Brigadier General Frank "O.D. "Monk" Hunter arrived at High Wycombe, to establish the VIII Fighter Command, another component of the Eighth Air Force. Fighter units assigned to the Eighth

Air Force served initially in an escorting role. VIII Fighter Command later moved to Bushy Hall near London.

On June 15, 1942, Major General Spaatz arrived at High Wycombe to establish a Headquarters for his newly formed Eighth Air Force. The Eighth Air Force had the primary responsibility for the strategic, long-range bomber offensive against German-occupied Europe and operated primarily from bases in England.

Major General Frederick Anderson succeeded Major Gen. Eaker on July 1, 1943. Eaker, in turn, took command of the Eighth Air Force when Spaatz was re-assigned to North Africa and held this post until December 18, 1943 when he was ordered to assume command of the Mediterranean Allied Air Forces as soon as his relief - the Fifteenth Air Force's Major General James Doolittle - could get to England.

On January 1, 1944, the U.S. Strategic Air Forces in Europe (USSAFE) was created to coordinate the strategic bombing efforts of the British-based Eighth Air Force and the Italian-based Fifteenth Air Force against Germany. Lt. General Carl "Tooey" Spaatz became its commander. Within days, the Eighth Air Force was reorganized with the Headquarters Eighth Air Force becoming the

U.S. Strategic Air Forces (USSTAF) with the former Headquarters, VIII Bomber Command becoming the Headquarters, Eighth Air Force. As of January 6, 1944, VIII Bomber Command no longer existed, per se, and its functions were folded into the 1st, 2nd and 3rd Bomb Divisions with the various Bomb Wings and Bomb Groups reporting to these Divisions. Other commands that reported directly to Headquarters, Eighth Air Force included the VIII Fighter Command, the VIII Service Command and the VIII Composite Command. The 8th Recon Wing, 9th Photo Group and the 802 Recon Group also reported directly to Headquarters, Eighth Air Force.

The Eighth Air Force's first combat mission was on July 4, 1942 using borrowed British DB-7s (Douglas A-20 Havocs). Their first B-17 Flying Fortress combat mission was flown on August 17, 1942 to Rouen, France. This raid, an afternoon attack against a railroad marshalling yard, consisted of twelve aircraft, all which returned safely. This mission established the pattern for the strategic bombing of Nazi Germany - the Eighth Force by day and the Royal Air Force (RAF) by night.

The Eighth Air Force completed 444,000 aircrew bombing missions - over 330,000 heavy bomber missions alone - delivered almost 700,000 tons of bombs and destroyed over 15,000 German aircraft. During one mission on December 24, 1944, the Eighth Air Force sent over 2,000 B-17s and B-24s and 1,000 fighters into the skies over Germany.

The Eighth Air Force compiled an enviable record and *was never turned back from a mission by enemy forces.*

During World War II, the Eighth Air Force's strength comprised of 43 heavy bomber groups, 4 medium bomber groups, 20 fighter groups and 50 support groups. Forty-two B-17 and B-24 Bomb Groups (H) were based in England during the war, 63% comprised of B-17s and 37% being B-24s. B-17s and B-24s flew a total of 294,879 sorties,

with B-17s accounting for 68% of the bombing sorties and B-24s accounting for 32%. Finally, B-17s and B-24s dropped 688,440 tons of bombs, with the same ratios as expressed previously. Thus, the ratios of B-17 aircraft versus B-24 aircraft based in England during the war with respect to Bomb Groups, Sorties and Payload were approximately 2 to 1.

Between August 1942 and May 1945, the Eighth Air Force lost 4,754 B-17 Flying Fortresses and 2,112 B-24 Liberators and another 3,357 fighters. While in service, the typical B-17 lasted only 147 days.

The Eighth Air Force had a total of 350,000 personnel, of which 120,000 were combat crewmembers during World War II. Some 26,000 men were killed in action, 28,000 were prisoners of war and 1,500 were internees. In other words, approximately 21.5% of its personnel were lost to combat deaths in action (KIA), 23.1% as prisoner of war (POW), and about 6% as wounded and unable to return to flight status, and evadees of 1%. Thus, the overall loss rate was approximately 52%. Looking at these sobering numbers another way, a crewmember had a 1 in 2 chance of completing his tour. The possibility of being killed on each mission was approximately 0.88% and the chance of becoming a POW on each mission was approximately 0.95%. After ten missions, a crewmember was considered to be operating on "borrowed time."

Thirty-five percent of the initial Eighth Air Force crewmembers who flew the original twenty-five bomber mission tour from 1942 through 1943 survived. In 1944, this number increased to 66% for those who flew the twenty-five to thirty-five mission tours. In 1945, 81% of the crewmembers survived their thirty-five mission tours.

A Royal Air Force Commander suggested the initial 25-mission requirement, later changed to 30 and then 35 missions by the Eighth Air Force Commander Major General James Doolittle.

The 303rd Bomb Group's *Hell's Angels*, a well-worn B-17F (AAF 41-24577, VK-D), and crew were the first crew to complete 25 missions, but public and political acclaim was bestowed upon the 91st Bomb Group's Capt. Robert Morgan and his crew flying the *Memphis Belle*, another B-17F (AAF 41-24485, DF-A), that completed 25 missions at about the same time. Though they were, in fact, the second crew to complete 25 missions, they and their historic airplane returned to the United States for public relations and bond drive duties. *Hell's Angels* remained in the European Theater of Operations with another crew where it added many more missions to an already impressive tally, all without a mechanical abort.

Many of these earlier losses can be attributed to the fact that early Eighth Air Force missions were conducted without the benefit of long-range fighter escort. Thus, the bomber crews had to face the "cream" of the Luftwaffe fighter pilot cadre. In the waning months of the war, as more and more of the experienced enemy fighter pilots were killed in action and Allied forces gained air superiority, the predominant threat facing the bomber crews became the increasing numbers of destructive anti-aircraft weapons deployed throughout the European Theatre of Operations.

Eighth Air Force personnel in the air and on the ground fought and served with valor. Seventeen individuals received the Medal of Honor. Moreover, 226 Distinguished Service Crosses were awarded, as were 864 Silver Stars, 45,977 Distinguished Flying Crosses, 442,300 Air Medals, 2,984 Bronze Stars, 12 Distinguished Service Medals, 209 Legion of Merit Medals, 480 Soldiers Medals, 27 Presidential Unit Citations, and 19 Meritorious Service Plaques.

To date, over one million men and women have served in the Eighth Air Force since its inception.

The 398th Bomb Group (H): A Brief Historical Overview

The 398th Bombardment Group (H), consisting of Group Headquarters and the 600th, 601st, 602nd and 603rd Bombardment Squadrons (H), was formed on February 15, 1943 and activated on March 1, 1943. The 34th Bombardment Group, based at Blythe Army Air Base at Blythe, California, furnished the initial cadre. Lt. Col. Frank P. Hunter was assigned as Group Commander.

The permanent station for the 398th Bomb Group was supposed to be Ephrata Army Air Base in Ephrata, Washington, but the Group was never physically stationed there. A cadre of eighty-five officers and enlisted men attended the Army Air Forces School of Applied Tactics in Orlando, Florida from April 3 - 24, 1943. Upon completion of this course and acting upon a series of Special Orders, this cadre left Orlando on April 24th and arrived at Geiger Field, Washington on April 29th. The remaining cadre of 398th personnel stationed at Blythe Field arrived at Geiger Field, Spokane, Washington on May 1, 1943. On June 20th, the entire 398th moved to Rapid City Army Air Base, Rapid City, South Dakota with the Ground Echelon arriving two days later.

The 398th B.G. prepared for combat with B-17s as an Operational Training Unit as per orders issued July 8, 1943, but these activities were interrupted between July and De-cember 1943 to train replacement crews for other organizations. Thus, the 398th B.G. was re-designated as a Replacement Training Unit, much to the keen disappointment of the crews that worked hard with the promise of an early overseas assignment. Any hard feelings were quickly forgotten as the Group immersed itself in training the new crews that arrived by the dozens. On January 1, 1944, while stationed at Rapid City, the 398th regained its status as an Operational Training Unit and prepared to go to combat.

On March 24, 1944, the first contingent of officers and enlisted men, the Ground Echelon, were ordered to England, embarking from Camp Myles Standish, Massachusetts on former luxury liners converted to combat troop ships. A Special Order, dated March 31, 1944, directed the Air Echelon of the 398th Bomb Group to proceed in their B-17 aircraft to Grand Island, Nebraska, enroute to an overseas assignment.

On April 22, 1944, the Air Echelon of the 398th B.G. deployed to England and was transferred to the Eighth Air Force. This deployment began on April 7th with ten aircraft departing each day until a total of 72 aircraft and crews were in place.

The group, commanded by Colonel Frank P. Hunter, was stationed at Nuthampstead,

England, as part of the 1st Combat Bomb Wing of the 1st Bomb Division of the Eighth Air Force.

While at Nuthampstead, Station 131, the 398th Bombardment Group (Heavy) included the following units:

Headquarters, 398th Bombardment Group (H)
600th Bombardment Squadron
601st Bombardment Squadron
602nd Bombardment Squadron
603rd Bombardment Squadron
226th Quartermaster Company (attached)
206th Finance Detachment (attached)
478th Sub Depot (attached)
449th Ordinance Company (attached)
18th Weather Squadron (attached)
344th Medical Squadron (attached)
1142th Military Police Company (attached)
860th Chemical Company (attached)
325th Station Complement Squadron (attached)
426 Air Service Group.

The 398th Bomb Group entered combat on May 6, 1944, bombing the target at Sottevast, France. Operational missions continued until April 25, 1945 and concluded with the bombing of the Skoda Munitions Works at Pilsen, Czechoslovakia. During this period, the 398th Bomb Group flew a total of 195 combat missions and 6,419 sorties.

Shortly after the war in Europe, the 398th participated in a series of missions to pick-up prisoners of war at Barth, Germany. These missions were flown in mid-May 1945 with most flights originating from airfields in France.

In retrospect, the 398th Bomb Group dropped 15,781 tons of bombs on German and enemy targets. The Group lost 70 aircraft to hostile action, with another 50 that were abandoned after forced landings. In addition, 33 more aircraft were damaged so severely in England that they were reduced to salvage.

The human cost for the 398th Bomb Group is chilling. According to the late Lt. Col. Wills Frazier, USAF, the former 398th Bomb Group, 601st Bomb Squadron Operations Officer, the total number of flight personnel in the 398th

Bomb Group numbered approximately 2,200 personnel (Group and Squadron leaders plus aircrews). Their overall combat losses were 292 (13.3%) killed in action, 298 (13.6%) became POWs, 83 (3.8%) were wounded (excluding the wounded who became POWs) and 25 (1.1%) evaded capture. Furthermore, eight were rescued at sea and 44 were liberated by Allied troops.

The losses for the original group who flew to England in April 1944 were 11% KIA and 9% POW in operations in Europe in World War II. These losses were slightly lower than the Group's overall losses probably due to better flying conditions during the summer months and tactical operations in France following D-Day with mission flights of shorter duration than the deeper penetration missions into Germany.

The 398th Bomb Group received orders on May 13, 1945 to return to the United States, when its wartime mission was complete. On May 26th, ten B-17s, with a crew of ten plus ten passengers, were the first to leave. Subsequent departures of airplanes and men occurred every few days, depending upon the weather. The last contingent of the Air Echelon departed Nuthampstead on June 2, 1945. The last elements of the Ground Echelon left on June 22nd.

After processing at individual reception centers in the United States, all members of the 398th were granted a 30-day leave. At the completion of this leave, they gathered at Drew Field, Florida for redeployment, reassignment or separation.

Pursuant to General Order No. 12, Headquarters Third Air Force, Central Assembly and Processing Station, Drew Field, Florida, the 398th Bombardment Group (H) was deactivated effective on September 1, 1945.

398th Bomb Group Statistics— June through August 1944

	JUNE	JULY	AUGUST
Total number of operational missions assigned	24	21	19
Total number of operational missions flown	17	17	17
Total number of sorties flown	583	572	574
Total number of operational hours flown	3726	3984	4226
Total number of mechanical aborts	6	9	5
Total number of personal aborts	1	0	3
Total number of combat crews missing in action	4	9	7
Percent of crews missing in action to number of sorties flown	0.69%	1.57%	1.22%
Average number of crews assigned per mission	35	34	34
Percent of crews attacking per mission assigned	98.80%	98.45%	98.61%
Average number of crews assigned per day	73	80	86
Average number of crews available per day	58	53	54
Average number of aircraft available per day	54	46	45
Average number of aircraft assigned per day	68	60	57
Average number of missions per crew	14	17	16
Average percent of aircraft operational per day	79%	77%	79%
Total aircraft lost	2	14	9
Total aircraft salvaged	1	4	0
Total number of aircraft accidents (Non-Operational)	0	2	0
Percent of aborts to total number of sorties flown	1.2%	1.6%	1.3%
Total number of major battle damaged aircraft	46	45	49
Total number of minor battle damaged aircraft	93	96	78
Average number of hours per engine change	162.81	211.48	289.91
Total operational mission fuel consumption (gals.)	902,265	1,042,556	1,034,579
Total training hours flown	266	956	627

Types and Number of Bombs Expended

100 lb. AN-M30 (GP)	5113	3452	1239
250 lb. AN-M57 (GP)	2543	1764	736
260 lb. AN-M81 (Fragmentation)	1091		
500 lb. AN-M64 (GP)	2237	2232	1385
1000 lb. AN-M65 (GP)	642		
2000 lb. AN-M34 (GP)	52	4	0
Fragmentation Clusters M1A 1	456	0	0
100 lb. M-47A2 (Incendiary)	0	2194	1504
500 lb. M-17 (Incendiary)	74	610	1373
Total number of all types of bombs dropped	10,475	10,256	7,970
Total pounds of bombs dropped	2,461,270	2,434,600	2,762,960
Total tons of bombs dropped	1230.6	1217.3	1381.8
Total amount of ammunition (rounds) expended	63,309	64,470	66,600

The AN-M64 was a 500 lb General Purpose, high explosive bomb suitable against ammunition dumps, railway engines and cars, airplanes on the ground, light surface vehicles and all types of construction. This type of bomb was usually equipped with a 1/10 second fuse in the nose of a 1/40 second fuse in the tail.

(National Archives, 342-FH-3A6434-C-57898 A.C.)

The AN-M17A1 was an aimable, 500 lb cluster bomb. (National Archives, 342-FH-3A6431-A-57898 A.C)

The AN-M41 fragmentation cluster bomb was highly effective against personnel targets. Here, the 20 lb bombs are clustered on an eight-unit frame. (National Archives, 342-FH-3A6430-57898 A.C.)

The AN-M47A2 was a 100 lb napalm-filled incendiary bomb. (National Archives, 342-FH-3A6432-B-57898 A.C.)

The AN-M81 was a 250 lb fragmentation bomb. The scored casing was designed to explode into multiple fragments. (National Archives, 342-FH-A6433-C-57898 A.C.)

398th Bomb Group Formations—1944

Tight bomber formations were used for high altitude, daylight missions. The formation structure evolved during the war years to improve bombing effectiveness, defensive firepower and address new situations, all without impacting any aircraft positioned underneath.

The use of the word formation, as used by the Eighth Air Force in World War II, referred to the orderly assembly of airplanes, lead by one of the airplanes, arranged together for their mutual protection that could bomb the target in a coordinated and efficient manner. The group bombing formation used by the 398th Bomb Group when it arrived at Nuthampstead (Station 131) in April 1944 was called the Combat Box Formation, and usually consisted of thirty-six airplanes, though some Combat Box Formations employed upwards of fifty-four airplanes. The Combat Box Formation was developed by General Curtis LeMay, learned from his experiences as an 8th Air Force strategic bomb group commander.

The Eighth Air Force bomb groups had used various formation schemes with some degree of success beginning in 1942, but the Combat Box Formation eventually became the standard for all Eighth Air Force group formations. This type of formation was accepted at the time as the best arrangement of airplanes for maximum defensive firepower from all guns of all the planes, while providing a bombing pattern with maximum effect.

The Combat Box Formation was made up of a number of basic airplane relationships. From the smallest to the largest, these formations were:

1. Element Formation: three airplanes
2. Squadron Formation: four Elements twelve airplanes
3. Group Formation: three Squadrons thirty-six airplanes
4. Wing Formation: three Groups - one hundred and eight airplanes

Element Formation

An Element of three airplanes was the basic unit in all formations. The Element lead was responsible for maintaining his Element's position relative to the Squadron lead at all times. One plane flew off his left wing and one off his right wing, the Element wing positions. Those pilots flying in the left and right wing positions were responsible for staying in "tight formation" with the Element lead at all times, especially on the bombing run to the target. Pilots of the Element wing positions tried to maintain their positions about the same altitude, one wing length horizontally from and one wing length behind the Element lead.

This Basic Element Formation was the most tedious and most dangerous position to fly, be it the Element in the Squadron or Group formation because of the close operating distances and total reliance the "other guy" would do his job well. Usually, the pilots and copilots took turns, fifteen minutes or so at a time, maintaining their airplane's position in reference to the Element lead. In a tight formation, the vertical and horizontal distance between the Element leads might be only a few hundred feet.

Squadron Formation

A number of Squadron formations were tried and used in combat by the Eighth Air Force with varying degrees of success. During many missions, the 398th used a squadron box formation that was comprised of four Element formations, each as described previously. The four Elements of the Squadron formation were arranged as follows:

1. The Lead Element became the Squadron lead with the other three Elements flying positions oriented on his lead position.

2. The High Element flew above, to the right and behind the Squadron lead.

3. The Low Element flew below, to the left and behind the Squadron lead.

4. If used, the Low Low Element flew directly below and behind the Squadron lead.

Group Formation

A three-squadron formation formed the Group formation, such as the 398th Bomb Group. The basic Squadron formation described above became one of the three-squadron formations that comprised the Group formation. The Group formation was identified with that group's insignia, such as the Triangle W of the 398th. The three-squadron formation that formed the Group formation was arranged as follows:

1. The Lead Squadron formation of twelve airplanes was in front.

2. The High Squadron formation flew above, behind and to the right of the lead.

3. The Low Squadron formation flew below, behind and to the left of the lead.

Wing Formation

The same Group Formation relationship was applied to the Wing Formation. The terms Lead, High and Low also referred to the positioning of individual group formations in relation to each other in the wing formation. There was a Group Lead, Group High and Group Low in the Wing formation as was arranged as follows:

1. The Lead Bomb Group formation of thirty-six airplanes was the front of the Wing formation.

2. The High Bomb Group formation flew above, behind and to the right of the lead.

3. The Low Bomb Group formation flew below, behind and to the left of the lead.

Division Formation

A Division formation, or simply called a Division, consisted of two or more wings assigned to fly together.

Distances between the Squadron Formations were measured in hundreds of feet. Distances between Group Formations were measured in thousands of feet. Wing and Division Formations could stretch for many miles. The actual distance between all types of formations varied due to weather, combat conditions and flying skill.

Composite Formation

Composite formations happened infrequently when, out of necessity, a formation was made up of crews and planes from more than one organization. Examples included filling out the necessary number of crews to complete a Squadron/Group formation from another Squadron or Group due to combat losses or personnel availability. Additionally, composite formations were used in maximum effort missions, often comprised of crews from different bomb squadrons.

Combat Bomb Wing Postions and Field Order Identification

The 1st Bomb Division was one of three Bomb Divisions within the command structure of the Eighth Air Force, the other two being the 2nd and the 3rd Bomb Divisions. Each Bomb Division was comprised of four or five Combat Bomb Wings.

For example, the 1st Bomb Division was comprised of the 1st, the 40th, the 41st and the 94th Combat Bomb Wings. Each of these Combat Bomb Wings had two or more individual Bomb Groups assigned to it. For example, the 1st Combat Bomb Wing of the 1st Bomb Division of the Eight Air Force in World War II was comprissed of the 91st, 381st and 398th Bomb Groups. When any of the Bomb Groups flew on a combat mission, their position within the overall formation was annotated according to the identifying Combat Bomb Wing or CBW. For example, whenever the 1st Combat Bomb Wing flew on a combat mission, their position was noted on the Field Order as the 1st "A" CBW, or 1st "B" CBW, 1st "C" CBW, etc., the individual letter representing the positions of the Bomb Groups assigned within that CBW. If the 40th CBW flew, then it was identified within the Field order as the 40th "A" CBW, 40th "B" CBW and so forth. The same identifying method was applied to all other Combat Bomb Wings involved in a bombing mission.

This excellent photograph shows 398th heavy bombers flying in close formation as they head towards Neumunster, Germany on April 13, 1945.

(Peter M. Bowers)

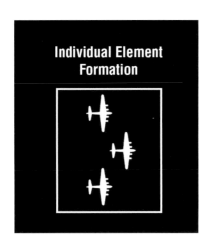

**Individual Element
Formation**

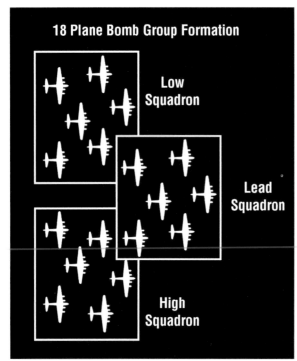

18 Plane Bomb Group Formation

**Low
Squadron**

**Lead
Squadron**

**High
Squadron**

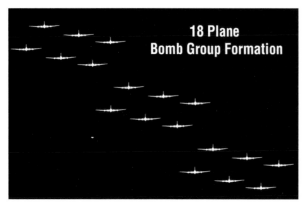

**18 Plane
Bomb Group Formation**

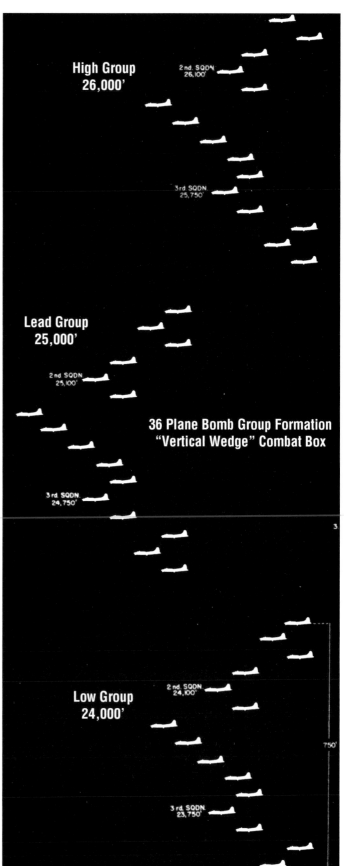

**High Group
26,000'**

2nd. SQDN.
26,100'

3rd. SQDN.
25,750'

**Lead Group
25,000'**

2nd SQDN.
25,100'

**36 Plane Bomb Group Formation
"Vertical Wedge" Combat Box**

3rd. SQDN.
24,750'

**Low Group
24,000'**

2nd. SQDN.
24,100'

750'

3rd. SQDN.
23,750'

World War II Statistics (12/7/41 through 9/2/45)

U.S. bombers dropped approximately 1,500,000 tons or more of bombs during World War II.

In 1944, U.S. and Allied bombers dropped 1,200,000 tons of explosives.

The Eighth and Fifteenth Air Forces had 3,600 bombers in action in mid-1944.

A total of 350,000 personnel served with the Eighth Air Force in Europe of which 120,000 were combat crewmembers, 26,000, were killed and another 28,000 airmen became prisoners of war.

The United States Marine Corps lost 2.94% of its personnel to combat deaths.

The United States Army lost 2.08% of its personnel to combat deaths.

The United States Navy lost .88% of its personnel to combat deaths.

Allied and Enemy Totals:	Military casualties—24 million plus killed	
	Civilian casualties—40 million plus killed	
United States Totals:	Involved in combat	16,112,566
	KIA	292,131
	Other	113,842
	Wounded	671,278
	POWs	130,201
	MIAs	78,773
	COST	$288,000,000,000

B-17s leaving Bremen, Germany in formation. (National Archives, 342-FH-A20967-D-26958 A.C.)

Bibliography

Books, Manuals, and Periodicals

Andrews, Paul M. and Adams, William H. *Heavy Bombers of the Mighty Eighth.* Warrenton: Eighth Air Force Memorial Museum Foundation, 1995.

_____. *The Mighty Eighth Combat Chronology.* Warrenton: Eighth Air Force Memorial Museum Foundation, 1997.

_____. *The Mighty Eighth Combat Chronology Supplement.* Warrenton: Eighth Air Force Memorial Museum Foundation, 1997.

_____. *The Mighty Eighth Roll of Honor.* Warrenton: Eighth Air Force Memorial Museum Foundation, 1997.

Angle, Glenn D., ed. *Aerosphere 1942.* New York: Aircraft Publications, 1942.

_____. *Aerosphere 1943.* New York: Aircraft Publications, 1943.

_____. *Aerosphere 1944.* New York: Aircraft Publications, 1944.

Army Air Forces Aid Society. *The Official Guide to the Army Air Forces.* New York: Simon and Schuster, 1944.

Assistant Chief of Air Staff, Intelligence. "England Suffers a New Blitz as the Germans Strike with the V-1 Robot Flying Bomb." *Impact: The Army Air Forces' Confidential Picture History of World War II,* August 1944, pp. 43-51.

_____. "8th AF Blasts Peenemunde." *Impact: The Army Air Forces' Confidential Picture History of World War II,* November 1944, pp. 44-43.

_____. "U.S. Tactical Air Power in Europe." *Impact: The Army Air Forces' Confidential Picture History of World War II,* May 1945, pp. 27-32.

Astor, Gerald. *The Mighty Eighth: the air battle in Europe as told by the men who fought it.* New York: Dust Fine Books, 1997

Bell, Dana. *Air Force Colors, Vol. II, ETO & MTO 1942-45.* Carrollton: Squadron/Signal Publications, 1980.

Birdsall, Steve. *Fighting Colors: B-17 Flying Fortress in Color.* Carrollton: Squadron/Signal Publications, 1986.

_____. *Hell's Angels.* Canoga Park: Grenadier Books, 1969.

_____. *The B-17 Flying Fortress.* Dallas: Morgan Aviation Books, 1965.

Birdsall, Steve and Freeman, Roger A. *Claims to Fame: The B-17 Flying Fortress.* London: Arms and Armor Press, 1994.

Bishop, Cliff T. *Fortresses Over Nuthampstead: The 398th Bombardment Group (H) 1943 - 1945.* Bishop's Stortford: East Anglia Books, 2004.

Blumenson, Martin. *United States Army in World War II, The European Theater of Operations, Breakout and Pursuit.* Washington, D.C.: Department of the Army, 1961.

Boeing Aircraft Company. *Boeing Model B-17G Field Service Manual.* Seattle: Craftsman Press, 1945.

Bowden, Ray. *Tales to Noses Over Berlin, The 8th Air Force Missions.* London: Design Oracle Partnership, 1996.

Bowers, Peter M. *50th Anniversary Boeing B-17 Flying Fortress, 1935 - 1985.* Seattle: Museum of Flight, 1985.

_____. *Fortress in the Sky: The Story of the Boeing's B-17.* Granada Hills: Sentry Books, 1976.

Bowman, Martin W. *Boeing B-17 Flying Fortress.* Ramsbury: Crowood Press, 1998.

_____. *Flying to Glory: The B-17 Flying Fortress in War and Peace.* Somerset: Patrick Stephens Limited, 1992.

Cass, William F. *The Last Flight of Liberator 41-1133.* Asheland: The Winds Aloft Press, 1996.

Chamberlin, Peter and Gander, Terry. *Anti-Aircraft Guns.* New York: Arco Publishing, 1975.

Coffey, Thomas M. *Decision over Schweinfurt: The U.S. 8th Air Force Battle for Daylight Bombing.* New York: David McKay Company, 1977.

Cohen, Stan. *V for Victory: America's Home Front During World War II.* Missoula: Pictorial Histories Publishing, 1991.

Collison, Thomas. *Flying Fortress: The Story of the Boeing Bomber.* New York: Charles Scribner's Sons, 1943.

Connor, John. *Combat Crew.* Waco: Texan Press, 1986.

Crafano, James J. LTC. "The Ethics of Operation Cobra and the Normandy Breakout," Paper presented to Joint Services Conference on Professional Ethics, Washington, D.C., 27-28 January 2000.

Craven, Wesley Frank and Cate, James Lea. *The Army Air Forces in World War II, Volume III, Europe: Argument to V-E Day, January 1944 to May 1945.* Chicago: The University of Chicago Press, 1951.

_____. *The Army Air Forces in World War II, Volume III, Men and Planes.* Chicago: The University of Chicago Press, 1951.

Davis, Kenneth S. *Dwight D. Eisenhower: Soldier of Democracy.* Konecky & Konecky: New York, 1945.

Davis, Larry. *B-17 in Action.* Carrollton: Squadron/Signal Publications, 1984.

Dillon, Neal B. *A Dying Breed: The True Story of A World War II Air Combat Crew's Courage, Camaraderie, Faith and Spirit.* Grants Pass: Hellgate Press, 2000.

Durr, Charles F. *All Present and Accounted For.* Fredricksburg: Bookcrafters, 1994.

Fletcher, Eugene. *The Lucky Bastard Club: A B-17 Pilot in Training and in Combat 1943 - 1945.* Seattle: University of Washington Press, 1993.

Foreman, Wallace R. *B-17 Nose Art Name Directory.* North Branch: Phalanx Publishing, 1996.

Freeman, Roger A. *Airfields of the Eighth: Then and Now.* London: Battle of Britain Prints International, 1978.

_____. *B-17 Fortress at War.* New York: Charles Scribner's Sons, 1977.

_____. *Combat Profile: B-17G Flying Fortress in World War II.* London: Ian Allen, 1990.

_____. *Mighty Eighth War Diary.* London: Jane's Publishing Company Limited, 1981.

_____. *Mighty Eighth War Manual.* London: Jane's Publishing Company Limited, 1987.

_____. *The Mighty Eighth.* London: Jane's Publishing Company Limited, 1970.

_____. *The Mighty Eighth Warpaint & Heraldry.* London: Arms & Armour Press, 1997.

Freeman, Roger A. and Osborne, David. *The B-17 Flying Fortress Story, Design - Production - History.* London: Arms & Armour Press, 1998.

Fox, George H. *8th Air Force Remembered.* London: ISO Publications, 1991.

Freitus, Joseph and Anne. *Florida: The War Years 1938 - 1945.* Niceville: Wind Canyon Publishing, 1998.

Frisbee, John L. "Double Feature." *Air Force Magazine,* August 1996.

Gaddo, Don and Barnett, Leslie. *Angel: A Mighty Fortress, The Fortress, The Crew, The Mystery.* Chapel Hill: Palmaya Publishing, 1999.

Hammel, Eric. *Air War Europa: America's Air War Against Germany in Europe and North Africa, 1942 - 1945: Chronology.* Pacifica: Pacifica Press, 1994.

Harris, Steven K. ed. *The B-17 Remembered.* Seattle: Museum of Flight, 1998.

Hawkins, Ian L. ed. *B-17s Over Berlin: Personal Stories from the 95th Bomb Group.* Winston-Salem: Hunter Publishing Company, 1987.

Havelar, Marion H. and Hess, William N. *The Rugged Irregulars at Bassingbourn: The 91st Bombardment Group in World War II.* Atglen: Schiffer Military, 1995.

Heitman, Jan. "The Peenemunde Rocket Centre." *After the Battle* 74 (1981): 1 - 26.

Hess, William N. *B-17 Flying Fortress: Combat and Development History of the Flying Fortress.* Osceola:Motorbook International, 1994.

Isby, David C. *B-17 Flying Fortress.* London: Harper Collins Publishers, 1999.

Jablonski, Edward. *Airwar: Terror from the Sky/Tragic Victories.* Garden City: Doubleday, 1971.

_____. *Airwar: Outraged Skies/Wings of Fire.* Garden City: Doubleday, 1971.

_____. *Flying Fortress.* Garden City: Double-day, 1965.

Johnson, Frederick A., ed. *Winged Majesty: The Boeing B-17 Flying Fortress in War and Peace.* Tacoma: Bomber Books, 1980.

Le Strange, Richard and Brown, James R. *Century Bombers: The Story of the Bloody Hundredth.* Thorpe Abbott: 100th Bomb Group Memorial Association, 1997.

Lay, Beirne, Jr. and Bartlett, Sy. *12 O'Clock High.* Reynoldsburg: Buckeye Aviation Book Company, 1948.

Lloyd, Alwyn T. and Moore, Terry D. *B-17 Flying Fortress in detail and scale, Part 1 - Production Versions.* Fallbrook: Aero Publishers, 1981.

Lloyd, Alwyn T. *B-17 Flying Fortress in detail and scale, Part 2 - Derivatives.* Fallbrook: Aero Publishers, 1983.

MacKay, Ron. *381st Bomb Group.* Carrollton: Squadron/Signal Publications, 1994.

Maurer, Maurer, ed. *Air Force Combat Units of World War II: History and Insignia.* Washington, D.C.: Zenger Publishing Co., 1961

_____. *Combat Squadrons of the Air Force in World War II: History and Insignia.* Zenger Publishing Co., 1969.

McLachlan, Ian and Zorn, Russell J. *Eighth Air Force Bomber Stories.* Sparkford: Patrick Stephens Ltd., 1991.

Mizrahi, Joeseph V. "Fortress in the Sky." *Wings,* August 1971, pp 16 - 35.

Monday, David. *The Hamlyn Concise Guide to Axis Aircraft of World War II.* London: Temple Press, 1984.

Morrison, Wilbur H. *Fortress Without a Roof: The Allied Bombing of the Third Reich.* New York: St. Martin's Press, 1982.

Neillands, Robin. *The Bomber War: The Allied Air Offensive Against Nazi Germany.* Woodstock: The Overlook Press, 2001

Nichols, Mark. ed. *8th Air Force.* (Classic Aircraft Series No. 10). Stamford: Key Publishing, 2005.

_____. *B-17 Tribute.* (Classic Aircraft Series No. 22). Stamford: Key Publishing, 2005.

Ogley, Bob. *Doodlebugs and Rockets: The Battle of the Flying Bombs.* Kent: Froglets Publications, 1992.

O'Leary, Michael, "Last Warrior." *Air Classics,* September 2001, pp. 34-44.

O'Mahony, Charles. *Blue Battlefields.* Usk: Aviation Usk, 1994.

Osborne, Richard E. *World War II Sites in the United States: A Tour Guide & Directory.* Indianapolis: Rebel-Rogue Publishing Co., 1996.

Ostrom, Allen. *398th Bomb Group Remembrances.* Seattle: The 398th Bomb Group Memorial Association, Inc., 1994.

Perrett, Geoffry. *Winged Victory: The Army Air Forces in World War II.* New York: Random House, 1993

Pollard, A.W. *Hendricks Field...a look back.* Sebring, Fla.: By the Author, 1439 Colmar Ave., 1994.

_____. *Sebring Men Who Gave All.* Sebring, Fla.: By the Author, 1439 Colmar Ave., 1997.

Pyle, Ernie, "Straight From the Front." *Stars and Stripes,* 11 August 1944, p. 2.

_____. "Straight From the Front." *Stars and Stripes,* 14 August 1944, p. 2

Rust, Ken C. *Eighth Air Force Story...in World War II.* Terre Haute: Sunshine House, 1978.

Scutts, Jerry. *B-17 Flying Fortress.* Cambridge: Patrick Stephens Limited, 1982.

Stapfer, Hans-Henri. *Strangers in a Strange Land.* Carrollton: Squadron/Signal Publications, 1988.

Stapfer, Hans-Henri and Kunzle, Gino. *Strangers in a Strange Land, Vol. II: Escape to Neutrality.* Carrollton: Squadron/Signal Publications, 1992.

Streitfield, Leonard. *Heaven from Hell: Memories of a B-17 Bombardier.* Egg Harbor City: Laureate Press, 1994.

Taylor, Charles. *Iowans of the Mighty Eighth.* Paducah: Turner Publishing Co., 2005.

Thomas, Geoffrey J. and Ketley, Barry. *KG 200 - The Luftwaffe's Most Secret Unit.* Friars Gate Farm: Hikoki Publications, 2003.

Towers, Frank W. "The Battle of St. Lo and the Normandy Breakout." 30th Infantry Division Veterans of WWII, Brooker, Fla.: By the Author, 2915W. SR #235, 2006.

Thole, Lou. *Forgotten Fields of America: World War II Bases and Training Then and Now.* Missoula: Pictorial Histories Publishing Company, 1996.

_____. *Forgotten Fields of America: World War II Bases and Training Then and Now, Volume III.* Missoula: Pictorial Histories Publishing Company, 2003.

Thompson, Scott. *Final Cut: the Post-War B-17 Flying Fortress: The Survivors.* Missoula: Pictorial Histories Publishing Company, 1990.

United States Air Force, *USAF Manual AN 01-20EG-1, Handbook Flight Operating Instructions, USAF Series B-17G.* Nashville: Collom & Ghertner Co., 1949.

United States Air Force Historical Research Agency, *Mar 1943 - Aug 1944 History, 398th BG.* Southern Pines, N.C.: Sandhills Community College, B0476, GP-398-HI, 2004.

_____. *Sep 1944 - Sep 1945 History, 398th BG.* Southern Pines, N.C.: Sandhills Community College, B0477, GP-398-HI, 2004.

_____. *Jun 1944 Mission Reports, 398th BG.* Southern Pines, N.C.: Sandhills Community College, B0480, GP-398-SU-OP, 2004.

_____. *July 1944 Mission Reports, 398th BG.* Southern Pines, N.C.: Sandhills Community College, B0481, GP-398-SU-OP, 2004.

_____. *July 1944 Mission Reports, 398th BG.* Southern Pines, N.C.: Sandhills Community College, B0481A, GP-398-SU-OP, 2004.

_____. *Aug 1944 Mission Reports, 398th BG.* Southern Pines, N.C.: Sandhills Community College, B0482, GP-398-SU-OP, 2004.

_____. *Aug - Sep 1944 Mission Reports, 398th BG.* Southern Pines, N.C.: Sandhills Community College, B0483, GP-398-SU-OP, 2004.

U.S. Army Air Forces. *Four Years of Progress: Hendricks Field, Sebring, Florida.* Sebring: 1945.

U.S. Army Air Forces. *AAF Manual AN 01-20EF-1, Pilot's Flight Operating Instructions for Army Models B-17F and G, British Model Fortress II.* New York: Ardlee, 1943.

U.S. Army Air Forces. *AAF Manual AN 01-20EG-1, Pilot's Flight Operating Instructions for Army Model B-17G, British Model Fortress II.* Patterson Field: ASCMT4A, 1944.

U.S. Army Air Forces. *AAF Manual 50-15, Pilot Training Manual for the B-17 Flying Fortress.* St. Louis: Con. P. Curran Printing Company, 1945.

U.S. Army Air Forces. *The Official Pictorial History of the Army Air Forces.* New York: Arno, 1979.

Wiener, Willard. *Two Hundred Thousand Flyers: The Story of the Civilian-AAF Pilot Training Program.* Washington: The Infantry Journal, 1945.

Willis, Steve and Holliss, Barry. *Military Airfields in the British Isles 1939 - 1945 (Omnibus Edition).* Sherington: Enthusiasts Publishing, 1987.

Willmott, H.P. *B-17 Flying Fortress.* Secaucus: Chartwell Books, 1980.

Wise, James E. Jr. and Wilderson, Paul W. III. *Stars in Khaki: Movie Actors in the Army and the Air Services.* Naval Institute Press: Annapolis, 2000.

Woolnough, John H. *The 8th Air Force Album.* San Angelo: Newsphoto Yearbooks, 1978.

_____. *The 8th Air Force Yearbook.* San Angelo: Newsphoto Yearbooks, 1981.

398th Bomb Group Memorial Association Photographs and Records on the Internet and on CD-ROM

The 398th Bomb Group Memorial Association's web site (http://www.398th.org) provided invaluable photographs and information. In particular, much of the information describing bombing formations was gleaned from this Internet web site.

Additionally, a two-set CD-ROM, created by the 398th Bomb Group Memorial Association, contains the Group's wartime records, the original records which are stored on microfilm and held by the United States Air Force Historical Research Agency, Maxwell AFB, Alabama.

Archived Records and Photographs - National Archives and Records Administration, College Park, Maryland (Archives II)

Many of the original textural 398th Bomb Group Mission Reports, 398th Bomb Group, Statistical Reports, and 398th Bomb Group Mission Statistical Summaries are stored at the National Archives and Records Administration II at College Park, Maryland (Archives II). The original textural documents are found in Records Group 18.

Declassified Missing Air Crew Reports (MACR) are stored at Archives II. These reports are stored on microfilm and are held in the Microfilm Reading Room.

Declassified Escape and Evasion Reports are also held at Archives II. The original textural Escape and Evasion Reports are found in Records Group 498.

Many of the photographs used in this book are copies made from the original U.S. Army Air Force and U.S. Army Signal Corps photographs held at Archives II. The original photographs may be viewed and copied in the Still Pictures Research Room.

Archived Records - United States Air Force Historical Research Agency, Maxwell AFB, Alabama

The USAF Historical Research Agency, Maxwell AFB, Alabama, has the 398th Bomb Group Mission Reports, 398th Bomb Group Statistical Reports, 398th Bomb Group Mission Statistical Summaries Records and other 398th Bomb Group records stored on microfilm.

Private Collections and Military, Public and University Libraries

Antique Airplane Association Airpower Museum and Library, Ottumwa, Iowa.

Boyd Library, Sandhills Community College, Southern Pines, North Carolina.

Dolph Overton Aviation Library, Carolinas Aviation Museum, Charlotte, North Carolina.

Duke University Library, Durham, North Carolina.

Experimental Aircraft Association Library, Oshkosh, Wisconsin.

Jefferson County Historical Association, Steubenville, Ohio.

Mighty Eighth Air Force Heritage Museum Library and Archives, Savannah, Georgia.

National Air and Space Museum Library and Archives, Washington, D.C.

National Museum of the United States Air Force, Research Department, Dayton, Ohio.

San Diego Aerospace Museum Library and Archives, San Diego, California.

United States Air Force Academy Library, Colorado Springs, Colorado.

United States Air Force Historical Research Agency, Maxwell AFB, Alabama.

United States Library of Congress, Washington, D.C.

XIT Museum, Dalhart, Texas.

Personal Correspondence Relating to Harold Weekley's Crew

Delbart, Tony, personal letters and telephone conversations.

Frazier, Willis, personal letters and telephone conversations.

Freeman, Roger A., personal letters.

Leonard, Norma, personal letters.

Mitchell, Robin A., personal letters and telephone conversations.

Skarda, Gary, personal letters and telephone conversations.

Skarda, Randy, personal letters and telephone conversations.

Stombaugh, Pearl, personal letters.

Unger, Ven "Bob", personal letters.

Weekley, Harold D, personal letters and telephone conversations.

AAF 42-97401 (3O-T), *Stinker, Jr.* was reported Missing In Action after a mission to Cologne, Germany on October 17, 1944. This aircraft was subsequently salvaged on the Continent by the Service Command. An unknown group of three civilians pose atop the wrecked heavy bomber.

(James B. Zazas)

Index

Keep 'em flying!

Dear friends,
 I hope you enjoyed reading *The Last of the Combat B-17
Drivers* as much as Jim Zazas and I had writing it.
Sincerely,

Hal Weckley

*"The best damn B-17 Driver
that ever flew the Flying Fortress!"*

About the Authors

Harold D. Weekley, Colonel USAF Retired

Harold D. Weekley, the first child of Clara Johnson Weekley and Okey Weekley was born on July 17, 1921 in Carrollton, Ohio. Harold saw his first flying machine in this mid-western town and has been hooked on aviation ever since, a career that has spanned almost six decades. He began flying lessons in 1936 and paid for this training by selling newspapers. Progress was very slow until Word War II, during which time everything was accelerated, including Harold's education.

Prior to becoming an Aviation Cadet, Harold was a member of the 305th Combat Engineers, attached to the 80th Division, located near Tullahoma, Tennessee. In the fall of 1942, he was assigned to the U. S. Army Air Forces and completed his training in the Southeastern part of the United States. During this period he flew the Stearman PT-17, the Vultee BT-13A, BT-15 and the Curtiss-Wright AT-9 and Beech AT-10. On July 28, 1943, he graduated from flight school at Blytheville, Arkansas as an U.S. Army Air Forces pilot and, concurrently, was commissioned as a Second Lieutenant.

At the completion of flight school, Harold was sent to Sebring, Florida for B-17 Transition Training. On August 4, 1943, he married his high school sweetheart, Miss Wilma (Billie) J. Wigginton of Steubenville, Ohio. In November 1943, Harold reported to Dalhart Army Air Field for Combat Crew Training.

Harold went to England on May 6, 1944, where he was assigned to the 601st Bomb Squadron of the 398th Bomb Group (Heavy) at Nuthampstead. He flew 20 combat missions, the first being to Berlin and the last to Le Manoir, France, which was the mission on which he was shot down by flak. After bailing out at 20,000 ft., Harold successfully evaded capture for three weeks hidden by the local French people until he escaped to friendly lines and was returned to the United States.

331

After the war, Harold Weekley served as commanding officer and/or operations officer of various training, bomber and transport units. During the Korean conflict, he trained jet fighter pilots. During the Vietnam War, he trained jet instructor pilots and commanded development of the Fairchild C-119G gunship, called the *Shadow*, which was used in Vietnam. Additionally, he was an advisor to the Air Force Academy and served as Supervisor of Pilot Instructor Schools and Standardization Board President.

After retirement from the U.S. Air Force as a Colonel, Harold worked with the Federal Aviation Administration for 14 years in the Atlanta, Georgia area. He was qualified in both General Aviation and Air Carrier functions. He was a Principal Operations Inspector responsible for the certification of new airlines, flight engineer schools and commercial operators and responsible was for the surveillance of all air carrier operations within the FAA Southern Region. He was also an accident investigator and incident and violation coordinator.

Weekley's impressive aeronautical licenses include Airline Transport Pilot, Airplane Multi-engine Land with type ratings in DC-9, B-727, CV-240/340/440. Commercial privileges include Airplane Single-engine Land and Sea plus B-17 and B-25 type ratings, Airplane and Instrument Instructor, Flight Engineer and Advanced Ground Instructor. He has amassed over 20,000 hours in 97 different types of aircraft.

Since his retirement from the FAA, Weekley has acted as Captain on worldwide air carrier operations, worked for several years as an aviation consultant and volunteered as a pilot on the Experimental Aircraft Association's restored B-17G Flying Fortress, *Aluminum Overcast*.

He has been a member of the Free and Accepted Masons, Harmony Lodge #3 in Marianna, Florida for over fifty-two years. His son, William, has been a Mason for over forty years. Both father and son have been Shriners for over thirty-five years.

Today, Harold Weekley enjoys his retirement with his wife, Billie.

James B. Zazas

Jim Zazas was born in Tampa, Florida, yet grew up in aviation-rich Indianapolis, Indiana. The model airplanes of his youth quickly gave way to flying real Cessnas, Pipers and Stearmans. Active in many civic and outdoor activities including the Boy Scouts of America, he earned the Eagle Scout rank during his teens. Following four years at DePauw University where he graduated in 1977 with a B.A. degree in Political Science, Jim was commissioned through the AFROTC program at Indiana University and started Undergraduate Pilot Training at Columbus Air Force Base, Mississippi in February 1978.

Twin-engine Cessna T-37B and Northrop T-38A jet trainers soon led to four-engine airplanes, most notably Lockheed C-130E/H Hercules transports. A five-year tour followed at Pope Air Force Base, North Carolina, where he flew Lockheed's rugged and reliable "Herky Bird" with the 39th and 41st Tactical Airlift Squadrons, 317th Tactical Airlift Wing.

Though exciting, including four deployments to Europe and as an Aircraft Commander in Operation Urgent Fury (the Grenada Invasion), Jim separated from the U.S. Air Force and joined Piedmont Airlines as a pilot in early 1984. He flew as a Line Check Flight Engineer on the Boeing 727 in 1985 and 1986. In 1988, he began flying the Boeing 767ER for Piedmont Airlines, later US Airways, a position he occupies today.

During the mid-1980s, Jim served as a volunteer Chief Pilot for the Indiana Museum of Military History based in Indianapolis, Indiana, where he flew a civilian-owned Lockheed P2V-7 (SP-2H) Neptune. He was also an FAA pilot examiner in this former U.S. Navy anti-submarine aircraft.

In 1989, he started flying the restored Piedmont Airlines-marked DC-3 as a volunteer pilot. At the time, this historic airplane was owned and operated as a popular show plane by Piedmont Airlines, later USAirways, until sold to the Carolinas Aviation Museum in Charlotte, North Carolina in 1995, where it is based and flown regularly today.

In the mid-1990s, Jim joined the Collings Foundation as a volunteer B-17 and B-24 pilot, a position he occupied for five years.

Jim calls Carthage, North Carolina his home and he devotes his much of his free time flying a wide variety of World War II and vintage aircraft, including a restored Boeing B-17G, the Piedmont Airlines DC-3, and his own 1946 Luscombe 8A and 1940 Piper J-3 Cub. He has flown his 65 hp

Luscombe from Kitty Hawk, North Carolina to Pt. Barrow, Alaska twice, once around North America and five times from Kitty Hawk to San Francisco, California and return. He also instructs in various World War II aircraft, including the Stearman PT-17, the North American T-6/SNJ and P-51D Mustang, and the Douglas DC-3. He has flown over 140 different aircraft and has logged over 24,000 hours.

Jim is an active member of the Experimental Aircraft Association (EAA), EAA Warbirds of America, EAA Vintage Aircraft Association, Antique Airplane Association, Soaring Society of America, National Association of Flight Instructors, Commemorative Air Force, Air Force Museum Foundation, Naval Institute, The Nature Conservancy as well as other aviation and service organizations. He is a member of the American Legion, a life member of the VFW and the Air Force Association.

Hobbies include writing, researching aviation history, canoeing, kayaking, hiking, and collecting, restoring and displaying vintage aircraft engines and World War II-era flight clothing and equipment. His close friendship with Hal Weekley, coupled with his keen interest and knowledge of World War II aircraft and Eighth Air Force combat flight operations, led him to write this book.

Previous books he has written include *Visions of Luscombe – The Early Years* and a glider aerobatic training manual.

The Last of the Combat B-17 Drivers is his first collaborative effort.